Through Switzerland with Turner

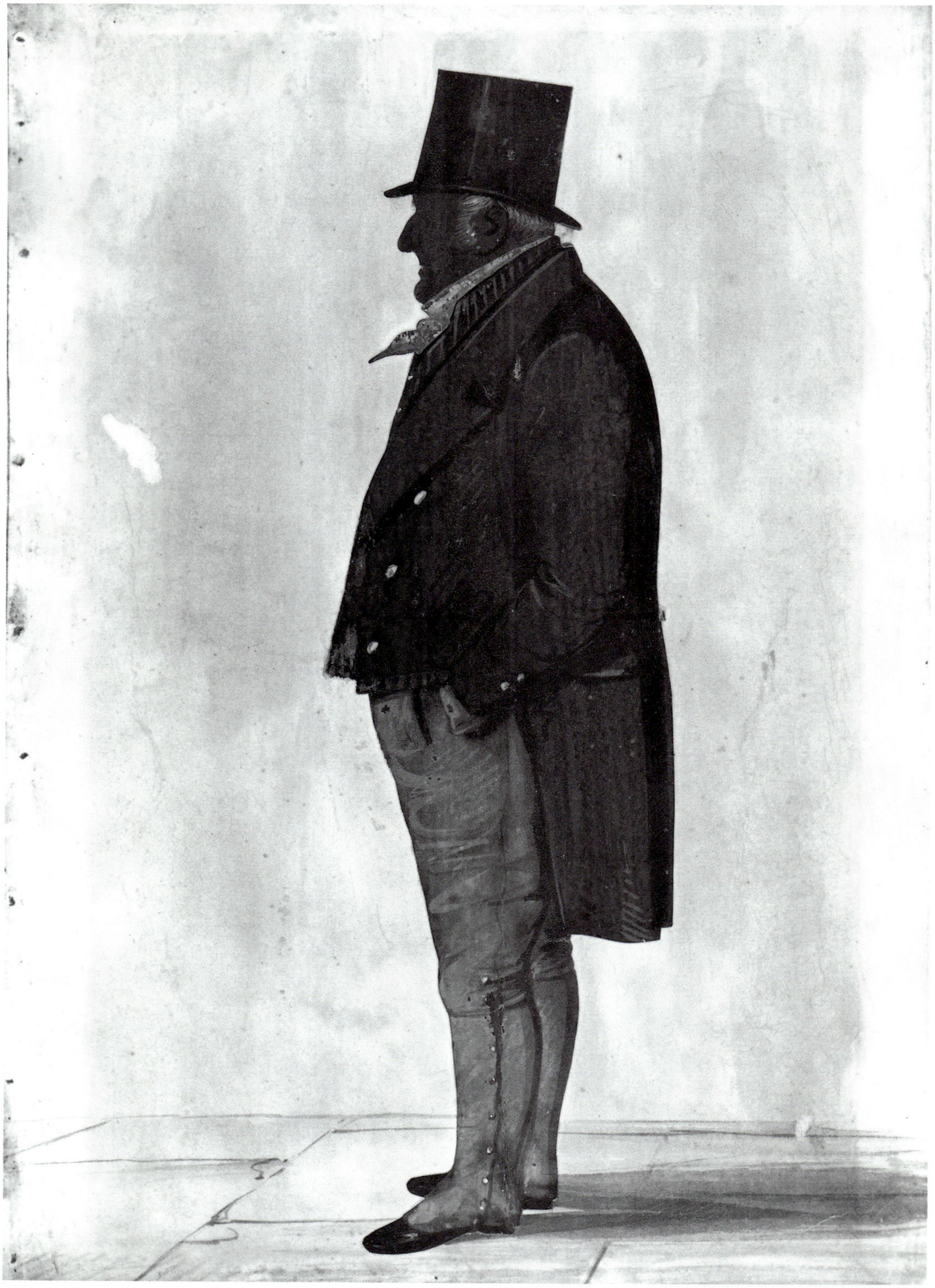

IAN WARRELL

Through Switzerland with Turner

Ruskin's First Selection from the Turner Bequest

TATE GALLERY PUBLICATIONS

Sponsored by Switzerland Live – the promotion for
Swiss business, industry, tourism and culture – and Pro Helvetia Arts
Council of Switzerland and the Swiss National Tourist Office

front cover:
J.M.W. Turner, 'Brunnen from the Lake of Lucerne:
Sample Study' ?1843–5 (cat.no.32), detail

back cover:
J.M.W. Turner, 'The Lake Lucerne from Fluelen'
?1843–5 (cat.no.38)

frontispiece:
John Ruskin, 'J.M.W. Turner, R.A. as he Was
Dressed for a Visit to the Royal Academy' *c.*1840,
silhouette. *Royal Academy of Arts, London*

ISBN 1 85437 151 7

A catalogue record for this publication is available from the British Library

Published by order of the Trustees 1995
on the occasion of the exhibition at the Tate Gallery
8 February – 7 May 1995
Designed and typeset by Caroline Johnston
Map on p.12 by John Flower
Published by Tate Gallery Publications, Millbank, London SW1P 4RG

Printed and bound in Great Britain by Balding + Mansell,
Peterborough, Cambridgeshire

Contents

Sponsors' Foreword

It is flattering for a nation to receive favourable attention from foreign artists. During the eighteenth and nineteenth centuries, Italy was pre-eminent for the many artists who enriched their education by undertaking the classic Grand Tour of Europe. Switzerland, however, grew in importance by being at the crossroads of Europe.

A number of artists became fascinated by the drama and versatility of the Swiss landscape and Joseph Mallord William Turner was one of the most prominent painters to fall in love with the stunning Alpine scenery. His watercolours are modern and novel in their appreciation, with an appeal that transcends time.

This timeless quality is always a sure sign of excellence, raising great works to the ranks of the select few that can claim almost universal appeal. Turner's ageless masterpieces evoke a sense of *déjà vu* that instills in the viewer a desire to retrace the steps of the artist and experience at first hand the landscapes he saw and captured one hundred and fifty years ago.

Pro Helvetia, Arts Council of Switzerland and the Swiss National Tourist Office are delighted to collaborate with the Tate Gallery in presenting this outstanding, even surprising, exhibition to the public.

Urs Frauchiger
Director, Pro Helvetia
Arts Council of Switzerland

Marco Hartmann
President
Swiss National Tourist Office

Foreword

In looking at the paintings and watercolours of the last decade of Turner's life, there has always been an overwhelming temptation to seek guidance from the published works of John Ruskin (1819–1900). After all, during this period, Ruskin not only published the first volumes of his protracted defence of Turner's work, but was also a valued client and friend of the artist.

Ruskin wrote about Turner's art so acutely, so extensively and with such passion that the authority of his writings, as a vital starting point for all students of the artist's pictures, has remained largely unchallenged. In *Modern Painters*, for example, Ruskin set down evocative and thought-provoking descriptions of paintings such as 'Slavers Throwing Overboard the Dead and Dying – Typhon Coming On', which have been endlessly quoted, and which continue to stimulate strong reactions in new readers (see, for example, David Dabydeen's recent poem, 'Turner', 1994).

Although selections from his writings were published in his lifetime, Ruskin disliked his work being presented in that form, and it is to this end that we have chosen to republish in its entirety the earliest, and one of the most interesting, of his catalogues of the watercolours in the Turner Bequest.

His commentary on a group of one hundred (and one) late works, arranged as a tour from Normandy to Venice, by way of a large selection of the evanescent views of the lakes and mountains of Switzerland, has long been acknowledged as a source of valuable information. Many of the details were clearly recorded from Ruskin's first-hand knowledge of Turner at the end of his life. But he was also not averse to the imaginative recreations of events. So vividly does Ruskin suggest his understanding of Turner's working practice during the course of his travels across Europe that at least one scholar has been deceived into believing that the catalogue describes an actual, rather than an imagined, journey.

But Ruskin is not always completely dependable. Apart from the fallibility of his memory, he was also prone to a tendency which sought to minimise the significance of other Turner collectors in order to exaggerate his own importance. Thus the particulars he presents as absolutes occasionally need to be treated with some caution.

The two halves of the title of the present publication perhaps suggest something resembling a set of interlocking Chinese boxes: should it not be 'Through Switzerland with Ruskin'? The second half of the title reflects the significance of Ruskin's catalogue, which was without precedent as an attempt to make Turner's preparatory sketches available to the British public. Although his apparent objective was to elucidate Turner, Ruskin inevitably also revealed much about himself and his other preoccupations while he was writing his notes on this collection of watercolours. In short, we hope that admirers of Ruskin and Turner will each find much that is of interest.

When Ruskin first began to envisage a Turner museum, he started by thinking in terms of a labyrinth, with each finished work given a kind of devotional space of its own. His ideal, with its anticipation of the spare installations of more modern aesthetics, was, however, quickly abandoned when Ruskin was confronted with the practicalities of acting as an advisor to the National Gallery. An outline of this change of heart is given in the Introduction.

My colleague, Ian Warrell, who has written this catalogue to accompany the first complete exhibition of the watercolours that Ruskin selected in 1857, sets out the connections between Ruskin and Turner in his introductory essay. The nature of their relationship as artist and client is further documented in the second appendix, which brings together information from Ruskin's letters and diaries, thereby shedding light on the evolution of the justly admired final groups of Swiss watercolours.

It is the Swiss watercolours that Ruskin most longed to own himself which form the heart of his selection. So it is particularly appropriate that both the exhibition and its catalogue have received the enthusiastic support of Pro Helvetia, Arts Council of Switzerland and the Swiss National Tourist Office. Their considerable generosity has enabled us to reproduce all the watercolours in colour, as well as comparative illustrations of most of the finished works discussed by Ruskin, many of which were once in his own collection.

Nicholas Serota
Director

Acknowledgments

In the course of preparing this catalogue I have called on the expertise and good will of many people. These include colleagues at the Tate Gallery and in other institutions, scholars of Ruskin or Turner, enthusiasts and friends, who have all exceeded the calls of duty to give generously of their time and knowledge: Clive and Jill Adams; David Beevers; Peter Bower; Ann Chumbley; Andrew Clayton Payne; Phillip Dalziel; Harriet Drummond; Judy Egerton; John England; Jacqueline Ford; Gillian Forrester; Ann Forsdyke; Antony Griffiths; John Hayman; Robert Hewison; Evelyn Joll; Celia Jones; Emma Jones; Virginia Murray; Suzie O'Hare; Ronald Parkinson; Guy Peppiatt; Jan Piggott; Nicholas Serota; Stephen Tate; Rosalind Tennant; Giles Waterfield; Henry Wemyss; Michael Wheeler; Scott Wilcox; Stephen Wildman; Reginald Williams; and Andrew Wyld.

The project has benefited greatly from the help of Jackie McComish and the other staff of the National Gallery Library. I have also been able to consult the important collection of Ruskin-related manuscripts and drawings, which, for the moment, is still housed at Bembridge School on the Isle of Wight. My guide through this material has been James Dearden, who has readily solved many of my niggling questions and offered much useful advice. I am grateful to the Trustees both of the National Gallery and of the Education Trust Ltd at the Ruskin Galleries, Bembridge School, for permission to quote from the documents in their collections.

Among other Ruskin scholars, I should like to thank Pia Haertinger, whose new research into Ruskin's involvement with museums during the course of his life has fed and stimulated my own work.

As usual, Andrew Wilton has kept a watchful eye on the growth of this project, offering valuable advice when it was most needed.

I must also single out Dr Cecilia Powell for special thanks, since she has selflessly shared her new identifications of seven of the German subjects in Ruskin's selection (cat.nos.9–11, 17, 79, 81–2). The identity of these towns resisted Ruskin's best efforts to identify them and the interested reader is encouraged to seek further information about these watercolours in the forthcoming exhibition *Turner in Germany* (Tate Gallery, 23 May – 10 September 1995).

I owe a debt of thanks to Heidi Reisz, of the Swiss National Tourist Office, who has frequently answered my enquiries about various topographical details. It is especially pleasing, therefore, that this contact has also resulted in the support of the Swiss National Tourist Office for the exhibition and its catalogue. This happy solution is also due to the imaginative enthusiasm of Eva Brechtbühl.

Finally, the exhibition of the Turner watercolours selected by Ruskin, and the publication of this accompanying catalogue, could not have taken place without the dedicated work of my colleagues in the Conservation, Development, Photographic and Exhibition departments at the Tate Gallery and in Tate Gallery Publications.

Ian Warrell

Introduction

When J.M.W. Turner died in 1851, the news of his death was quick to reach John Ruskin, then in Italy engaged in writing *The Stones of Venice*. This was not just a personal loss; the sun and sky, as Ruskin lamented, had also lost their 'Great witness'.[1]

When he came to respond to the letter from his father, which had carried the news, Ruskin admitted that he had been expecting the event to occur for some time. His thoughts then turned rapidly to the collection of watercolours awaiting discovery at Turner's Gallery in Queen Anne Street. The extent of this collection was still unknown to him; however, his highest priority, in anticipating a great studio sale, was to buy '*all his Swiss sketches since 1841*' (fig.6).[2] These highly prized sketches lie at the heart of this catalogue, and were the basis for the now celebrated finished watercolours of Switzerland that Ruskin and a small group of other collectors commissioned from Turner between 1842 and 1851. What is important to note is the value Ruskin placed on these colour memoranda above any conventionally finished watercolours (then often referred to as 'drawings'). He wrote, 'I understand the meaning of these sketches – and I can work them up into pictures in my head – and reason out a great deal of the man from them which I cannot from the drawings'.[3]

As is well known, the sale of Turner's sketches and drawings never took place and, instead, the whole collection eventually became the property of the nation. This, however, did not mark the end of Ruskin's involvement with Turner's late Swiss watercolours. In fact, it was simply the beginning of his connection with the much larger group of over twenty thousand works on paper found in Turner's studio, from all periods of his career, which was to continue to the end of Ruskin's life.

In the middle of the nineteenth century the prevailing aesthetic favoured paintings that demonstrated the laborious efforts of the artist to capture precise details. Consequently the notion of exhibiting 'unfinished' drawings and watercolour sketches was still unusual. But this was what Ruskin sought to achieve when, from 1856, he championed the idea of making selections of Turner's sketches available, not solely for the benefit of students and artists, but also to the general public. Ultimately, he arranged a considerable part of the Turner Bequest at the National Gallery in an educational series, complete with catalogue, that was not dismantled until the beginning of this century.[4]

Since the connections between Turner and Ruskin are well documented elsewhere, the first half of the following essay provides only an outline of the last decade of the artist's life, drawing together the areas where the two men's lives overlapped, especially where relevant to the watercolours later selected by Ruskin. The second part of the essay charts the history of Ruskin's eventually successful campaign to ensure that the Turner Bequest was made available to the public. At the centre of this enterprise was a group of one hundred watercolour sketches, which Ruskin arranged as an imaginary tour from Normandy, up the Rhine to Switzerland and Venice. These works were described in a catalogue published in 1857, which was his first attempt to document Turner's watercolours, and it is this important volume that is reprinted here in its entirety (pp.33–147). As suggested above, a particular interest of

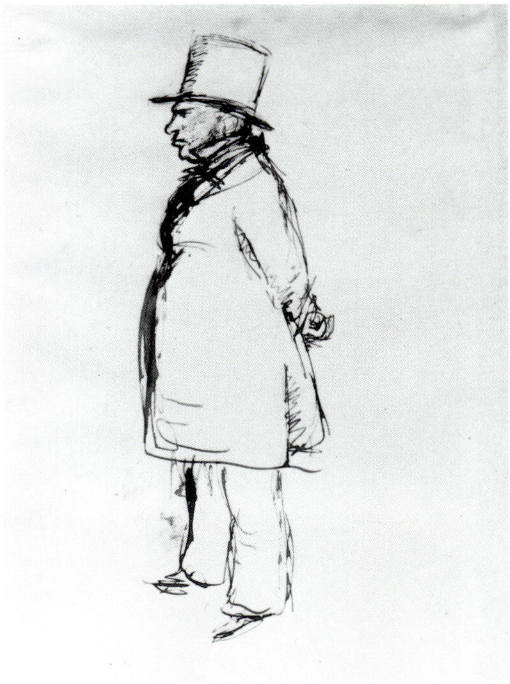

fig.1 J.E. Millais, 'Turner at the Royal Academy' 1851, brown ink on paper. *Whereabouts unknown*

the catalogue lies in the fact that it represents a very subjective selection; these are watercolours which Ruskin coveted for his own collection. Although the group was never presented to the public in the form described by Ruskin, the catalogue acted as a kind of quarry from which comments on individual works were integrated into other catalogues, as well as later reappearing in *Ruskin on Pictures: Volume 1*, the miscellany of Ruskin's writings on Turner, which Edward Cook published two years after his death in 1900.

As one of the editors of Ruskin's complete works, Cook was a strong advocate of the 1857 catalogue, stressing the range of 'topographical, biographical, and technical' information it contains. He was firmly of the opinion that 'The whole of Ruskin's catalogue ... will be found of peculiar interest to students of Turner'.[5] But, of course, it is not only Turner's life and works which are illuminated by the catalogue; as always, Ruskin reveals just as much about himself and his own aesthetics in writing about the artist he admired most highly.

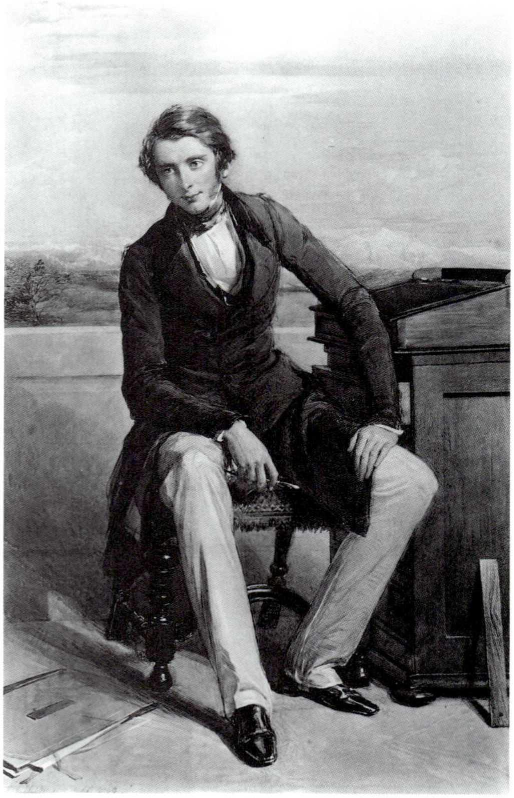

fig.2 G. Richmond, 'The Author of *Modern Painters*' 1843, engraving. *The Education Trust Ltd, Ruskin Galleries, Bembridge School, Isle of Wight*

Turner and Ruskin: 1840–51

On 22 June 1840, J.M.W. Turner was introduced to John Ruskin in the garden of Thomas Griffith's house at Herne Hill. Ruskin was then twenty-one and still a student at Oxford, while Turner, at sixty-five, was one of the grand old men of the Royal Academy, even if the critics and the public did not always see him in quite such an uncontroversial light. This crucial meeting initiated an association lasting until Turner's death in 1851, in which the pleasures of friendship were mingled with the anxieties of patronage and perhaps a slight unease about the zeal with which Ruskin set out to propagate the artist's achievements.[6]

During the decade, Turner gradually became more aware of his advancing years. Yet this did not prevent him from making a number of significant tours to Switzerland and other parts of the Continent, in which he continued to seek out unfamiliar terrain. The watercolours which resulted from these final travels have long been held in high esteem as the climax of a lifetime devoted to the expression of light and colour in landscape subjects. Again and again in his studies, Turner simply amazes the viewer by his ability to distil the sublimities of Alpine scenery into perfectly balanced compositions, condensing his visions on to small sheets of paper, which were originally bound as the leaves of sketchbooks.

Ruskin had been aware of Turner's work even before his thirteenth birthday in 1832 when he received a copy of Samuel Rogers's poem *Italy* in the edition illustrated with vignettes by Turner.[7] His first direct contact with the artist occurred four years before they actually met. This was in 1836, when Ruskin sent a letter to Turner, in the guise of 'J.R. Esq.', via Messrs Smith, Elder & Co. In his letter he offered to defend the group of Turner's paintings then on display at the Royal Academy; the pictures had recently been the subject of criticism by the Revd John Eagles.[8] Nothing came of this, because Turner graciously declined the offer, stating that his policy was never to react to criticism, and his reply apparently brought the correspondence to a close. Since Ruskin's proposal was made anonymously, there is no reason to suppose that Turner would have recalled the incident when he eventually met the young Ruskin. But there is in this event the germ of Ruskin's characteristically combative stance on behalf of the artist.

When they did meet in 1840, Ruskin was introduced primarily as a potential collector of Turner's work. He had recently bought the watercolour of 'Harlech Castle' (W 867), and at the end of June the total number of watercolours by Turner in the family collection amounted to five.[9] Even though the dealer Thomas Griffith undoubtedly had his own motives for introducing a new client to his famous artist, it is not readily apparent from the existing correspondence that the introduction that followed was the explicit purpose of the gathering in south London. Indeed, Turner had actually revised the date of his visit twice to suit his own arrangements.[10] This impression is further supported by E.T. Cook, who knew Ruskin at the end of his life. Apparently, although 'Turner spoke kindly to Ruskin, he took no particular notice of him on this occasion'.[11]

However, the meeting was clearly of great significance to the young Ruskin, even if his later recollections, eloquently evoked in *Praeterita*, do not quite tally with what he actually recorded in his Diary at the time.[12] Shortly afterwards Ruskin and his parents set out for an extended tour of Italy and Switzerland, from which they did not return until the following summer. During this journey Ruskin fed his hunger for Turner's works by consulting, as his first and last sight each day, the popular line engravings after Turner's designs. By the end of 1840 he was convinced that Turner was 'the epitome of all art, the concentration of all power; there is nothing that ever artist was celebrated for, that he cannot do better than the most celebrated. He seems to have seen everything, remembered everything, spiritualised everything in the visible world; there is nothing he has not done, nothing that he dares not do.'[13]

During 1840, Turner was also away travelling. His goal that year was Venice, which he had already visited twice before, but this was his longest stay and he recorded his impressions in some of his most atmospheric watercolours (cat.nos.51–70). He left London early in August, and, unusually for him, seems to have been accompanied for much of the way by a married couple, from whom he parted company at Bregenz.[14] After two weeks in Venice, he began the return journey on 3 September, travelling back across Germany.[15]

The surviving sketchbooks and watercolours that document this tour are typical of Turner's method of responding to new (as well as already familiar) sights, and preserve forcibly a sense of his omnivorous curiosity for visual information. On page after page of his small notebooks, Turner made hasty scribbles of the passing scenery. He was especially interested in architectural features, but he also recorded people and their occupations. As well as these rapid impressions, he would 'compose' his views onto the larger sheets of soft-covered sketchbooks, which could be rolled and stored in the pockets of his coat. The huge collection of this reference material that now forms the Turner Bequest testifies better than any anecdote the centrality of travel in his life.

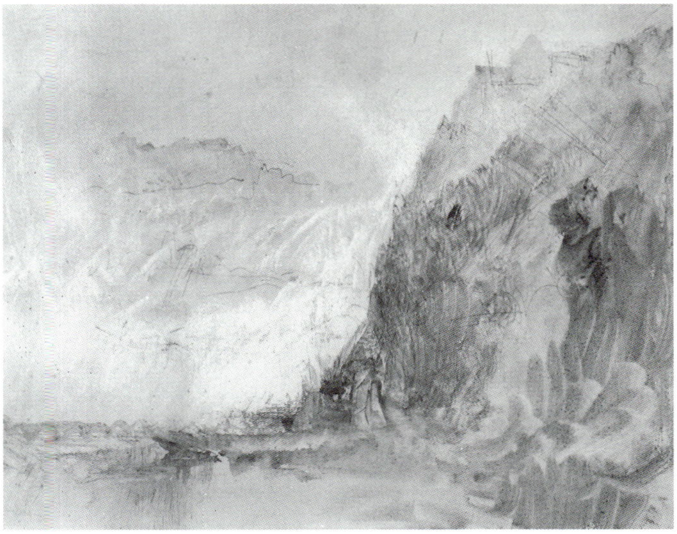

fig.3 J.M.W. Turner, 'Falls of the Rhine at Schaffhausen' 1841, watercolour (W 1469). *Museum zu Allerheiligen, Schaffhausen*

He was abroad again at the end of August 1841. This time he travelled up the Rhine as far as Coblenz (cat.nos.6–8) before going on to Switzerland. His interest in Switzerland may have been reawakened by a slightly earlier tour, made in 1836 with his friend Hugh Andrew Johnstone Munro of Novar (1797–1864), a Scottish laird and amateur artist.[16] On their way to the Val d'Aosta they had stopped at Lausanne and Geneva. So deep was the impression made on Turner by the Alps that this was one of the first subjects he discussed with Ruskin in 1840, apparently 'talking with great rapture of Aosta and Courmayeur'.[17]

In 1841, after making an extended study of the Rhine Falls at Schaffhausen (cat.no.19), Turner progressed east to Constance (cat.no.20). His journey then took him down towards the Splügen Pass (cat.no.75), before he headed back across country towards Zurich (cat.no.22). A large group of watercolours of Lucerne and the mountains above its lake suggest that he spent at least a few days there, while also making visits to some of the villages on the edge of the lake (cat.nos.23, 25, 26, 30, 31, 33, 35). The tour continued, via Thun, to Vevey on Lake Geneva (cat.no.99), from where he returned once more to Lausanne and Geneva (cat.nos.91–6, 100). In heading north for the Rhine route to the sea, he stopped at Fribourg (cat.no.77), Berne and Olten. By 22 October, he was back in England, the tour having taken around seven weeks.[18]

Before setting out, Turner had encountered Ruskin a second time, and had been introduced to Ruskin's father, John James Ruskin (1785–1864). Of his meeting with Turner on 5 July, the younger Ruskin noted, 'Turner there is no mistaking for a moment – his keen eye and dry sen-

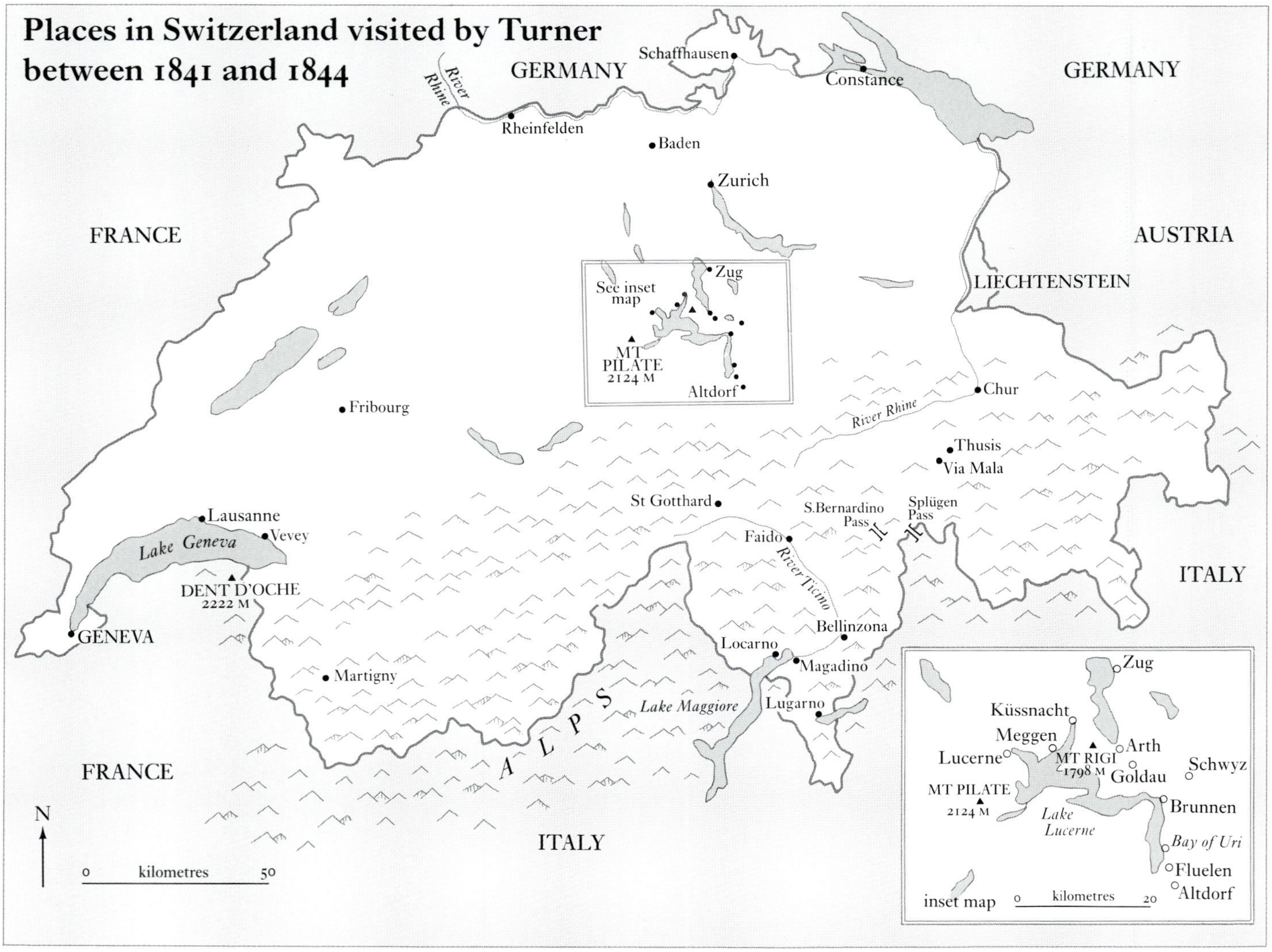

tences can be the signs only of high intellect'.[19] In contrast with his son's enthusiasm, Ruskin's father was more cautious in his response to members of the 'art world' and was initially temperate in his admiration for Turner's work. He recorded his first impression of the artist in a letter of 27 August: 'I saw Turner at Griffiths but greatly prefer his pictures'.[20] There was in these meetings the tentative beginning of a friendship, which intensified during the last months of 1841. From the existing evidence, it is impossible to build up a complete picture of this period, but it is clear that Ruskin began to visit Turner's Gallery regularly, an opportunity not readily granted to everyone.

With regard to the works in this catalogue, an important event involving the Ruskins took place at the beginning of the following year. This was the production by Turner of his first set of ten Swiss watercolours. The details concerning this project were first outlined by Ruskin in the 1857 catalogue (cat.no.8) and later elaborated in the Epilogue notes he supplied for an exhibition of his own Turner watercolours in 1878.[21] Briefly, what happened was that Turner set out to make a group of finished watercolours based on the colour sketches he had produced during his tour in the September and October of the previous year. A recently discovered letter from Turner to Benjamin Godfrey Windus (1790–1867), another important collector of his work, suggests that he initially hoped to produce twenty subjects. These were clearly intended to be seen as a group, but as the sketches were not all of the same size, or brought to the same degree of finish, Turner decided to 'take fresh pieces of paper of a uniform size and follow the same idea and keep the original sketch in the primitive state'.[22] This process, however, took longer than he had anticipated, so that the original group of twenty was reduced to ten. It was at this stage that Turner asked Griffith to attempt to seek commissions from a small group of his regular clients. Fifteen sketches, or 'samples', and four 'specimens' of what the finished works would look like, were presented at Griffith's showroom in Waterloo Place, off Pall Mall, priced at eighty guineas each.

According to Ruskin, Windus was the first to see the collection, but did not like the style of the new works, which was indeed a dramatic departure from the delicate sets of vignette book illustrations that he had acquired during the last few years.[23] The Swiss subjects were also considerably more expansive than the last of the *Picturesque Views in England and Wales*, published in 1838.[24] However, this may not have been the only reason why Windus declined to commission any Swiss views in 1842, for another letter from Turner attempts to reassure him that the 'Sketches and Drawings therefrom are not at Mr Griffiths "for sale to anyone"', implying that Windus had perhaps felt slighted by Turner's new business arrangements.[25]

Ruskin later claimed that 'Nobody, in all England, at that time … cared, in the true sense of the word, for Turner, but [Windus] the retired coachmaker of Tottenham, and I'.[26] It is ironic, then, that the chief purchasers of Turner's Swiss drawings at this date, apart from Ruskin himself, should be Munro of Novar and Elhanan Bicknell (1788–1861), a whaling entrepreneur.[27] That Ruskin should seek retrospectively to minimise the significance of Turner's other patrons in his autobiography confirms John Dixon Hunt's suspicion that *Praeterita* reveals Ruskin's 'instinct for myth, for re-ordering the world of experience into sustaining wholes and healing visions'.[28] The reality, at least in 1842, was that Munro bought five, in other words half, of the set of ten finished drawings, while Ruskin and Bicknell each bought two; the tenth subject, 'Constance' (see cat.no.20), was made for Griffith as remuneration for his role as Turner's agent.

Throughout his life, Ruskin felt that these watercolours were the pinnacle of Turner's achievement. He referred to them generically as the 'Sunset Drawings'[29] and related them to Turner's sense of his own mortality. In his *Notes on the Turner Gallery at Marlborough House* (1857), he stated his belief

> that in powerful minds there is generally, towards age, a return to the superstitious love of Nature which they felt in their youth: and assuredly, as Turner drew towards old age, the aspects of mechanical effort and ambitious accumulation fade from his work, and a deep imaginative delight, and tender rest in the loveliness of what he had learnt to see in Nature, take their place.[30]

Inevitably, the focus of attention in 1842 fell on the finished drawings, but Ruskin was not completely immune to the 'mighty power' of the preparatory sketches, although he certainly found them strange at first. He confessed to his father shortly after Turner's death that he had not initially really appreciated their quality: 'I thought them beautiful – but sketchy and imperfect compared with his former works.'[31]

In subsequent years Turner sought to make further sets of Swiss watercolours on a similar pattern. Altogether Ruskin estimated that Turner produced a total of twenty-seven late Swiss subjects, but it seems that the actual number the artist hoped to complete may have exceeded thirty. The subjects of these works are suggested in many of Ruskin's notes in the 1857 catalogue, but this information is supplemented here by the lists in Appendix II (pp.149–55).

During the summer after the first set of Swiss subjects was produced, both Turner and Ruskin set out independently for Switzerland, the latter travelling with his parents. The example of Turner's 1841 sketches seems to have been effortlessly absorbed by Ruskin, who on this journey produced a breathtaking drawing of 'The Falls at Schaffhausen' (fig.4). Earlier, in 1840, he had reported Turner's advice to deploy 'everything' that was relevant to the subject when sketching from nature.[32] This was advice he surely followed in his vivid impression of the falls, with its sophisticated use of pencil, watercolour and brown ink, animated by restless swirls of gouache; the watercolour was apparently the only work by Ruskin in which Turner ever expressed an interest.[33]

On his journey in August 1842, Turner again went to Lucerne, from where he travelled to Küssnacht (cat.no.29), Arth (cat.no.28) and Goldau (cat.no.27). Although he was already familiar with this area, the route he took southwards incorporated spectacular 'new' subjects in the St Gotthard Pass (cat.no.40), before he reached more conventionally picturesque sights at Bellinzona (cat.nos.41, 45, 48) and the Italian Lakes (cat.nos.49–50).

It was also during 1842 that the critics renewed their attacks on Turner's paintings at the Royal Academy, causing Ruskin to plan a more ambitious form of defence. He referred to this project privately as 'Turner's work',[34] and was preoccupied with it throughout the winter and early spring of 1843. His connection with Turner had by this time strengthened, so that the artist made his first appearance at Ruskin's birthday party on 8 February, an event that became something of a fixture in the following years.[35] However, Ruskin remained anxious that Turner 'may not be mortally offended with the work'.[36]

The 'work', or, as it is better known, volume one of *Modern Painters*, was published anonymously as the work of 'a

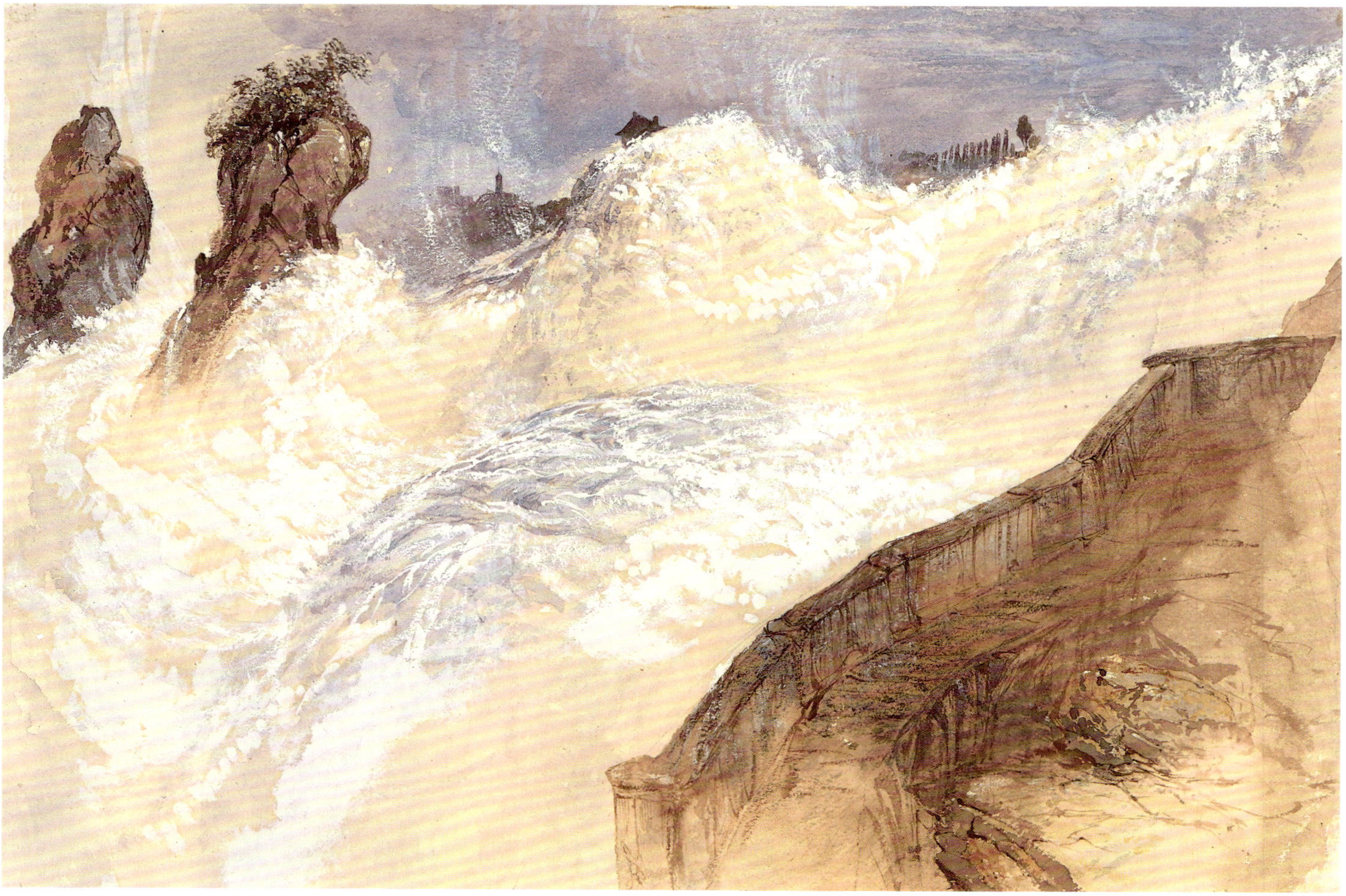

fig.4 John Ruskin, 'Falls of Schaffhausen' 1842, gouache, watercolour, brown ink over graphite on cream paper. *Courtesy of The Fogg Art Museum, Harvard University Art Museums. Gift of Samuel Sachs*

Graduate of Oxford' in May 1843. But despite Ruskin's fears, there are no indications that Turner was affronted. Indeed, although Ruskin found Turner 'particularly gracious' when he visited him on 15 May, and suspected that this was due to his book, it is impossible to know what the artist thought, or if he had even read Ruskin's volume.[37]

It is worth pausing here to consider the significance of *Modern Painters*. Although Ruskin himself extensively revised the first volume, and later considered it a work flawed by his partial knowledge of his subject, it is, in fact, one of the indisputable landmarks in art history. If the book was not an overnight success, it began to attract a steady stream of admirers, including several notable literary personalities, such as William Wordsworth, George Eliot and Charlotte Brontë. A letter to the collector Francis McCracken from H. Hewitt, a minor landscape painter, expresses one reason why the book was cherished by many of Ruskin's first readers: 'It is almost as though Turner had written an important & mysterious Letter & sealed it, and the Graduate has broken the seal, & laid open the Epistle to be seen by all, such is the simplicity, clearness, & truth of his work. Thanks to him!'[38] However, Ruskin's belief that Turner was greater than all other artists was an idea that was bound to provoke controversy, especially at a time when the artist's works were considered incomprehensible.

Ignoring the public debate that followed the book's publication, Turner again travelled to Switzerland in the summer of 1843. He had already explored much of the route, and even revisited the St Gotthard Pass and Bellinzona (cat.nos.42–4, 46), which had been the principal discoveries of the previous summer. The Swiss part of the tour was concluded by his passage through the vertiginous ravine of the Via Mala (cat.nos.71, 74, 80). A letter from Turner written in London on 23 November 1843 records that he also visited 'the Tyrol and parts of Northern Italy',[39] and it was presumably on this trip that he was seen sketching on Lake Como by William Lake Price (1810–1891).[40]

The autumn was dominated for Ruskin by his hopes of acquiring one of the oil paintings Turner had exhibited in 1840. This was 'Slavers Throwing Overboard the Dead and Dying – Typhon Coming On' (Museum of Fine Arts, Boston; B&J 385), a picture he had especially recommended to the readers of *Modern Painters*. But he need not have worried, for on 1 January 1844 he awoke to find the painting at the foot of his bed, a New Year present from his father.

There was no set of finished Swiss subjects in the spring of 1844, and Ruskin had to content himself with visits to Turner's gallery. It was on one of these visits that he managed to elicit from Turner a rare and revealing comment about his own work. As related in Ruskin's Diary, the exchange was as follows: 'I alluded to the peculiar atmosphere of his recent drawings. "Yes", he said "atmosphere is my style".'[41] As is evident from any of the watercolours included in this catalogue, there is a truth to this statement, which was apparently thrown off casually without a great deal of forethought. Here indeed is the artist's own perception of the ever more visionary quality of his late style.

Again, in 1844, Turner sought new stimulus in a further tour to Switzerland. He complained later in the year that 'The rains came on early so I could not cross the Alps, twice I tried, was set back with a wet jacket and worn-out boots and after getting them heel-tapped I marched up some of the small valleys of the Rhine and found them more interesting than I expected'.[42] This impression is somewhat qualified by a note in the *Grindelwald* sketchbook, used on the journey, which asserts that 'No matter what bef[ell?] Hannibel – W.B. and J.M.W.T. passed the Alps from Fombey Sep 3, 1844'.[43] It also reveals that Turner was accompanied on this part of his tour of Switzerland, probably by William Brockedon (1787–1854), who had published guidebooks to the Alps. But as the quotation from Turner's letter suggests, the tour fulfilled its purpose by providing him with attractive subjects at Baden (cat.nos.83–5), Rheinfelden (cat.nos.86–90) and along the northernmost part of the River Neckar, a tributary of the Rhine (cat.nos.9–18, 82).

On 17 October, shortly after his return to London, Turner attended a dinner at Windus's home. This appears to have been organised by Griffith and Ruskin in order to effect a reconciliation between Turner and Windus, who had yet to commission any Swiss subjects. The evening was clearly successful in other respects, for it was on this occasion that Turner thanked Ruskin for *Modern Painters* for the first time, a somewhat overdue expression of his appreciation, which may have partly rewarded Ruskin for his recent work on a revised edition.

The possibility of another set of Swiss subjects was surely one of the topics discussed at the gathering. The collectors may even have weighed the relative merits of the watercolours resulting from the tours of 1841 and 1842 against Turner's earlier work. Certainly, within a few days of the meeting, Ruskin sent Windus a letter explaining his reluctance to part with any of his own collection: 'I so love *Switzerland* that Turner's Swiss drawings are to *me* – worth two of the English subjects and if I parted with any of the England series it would be in a way either to enable me to give Turner a commission – [or] in direct exchange for one of his recent works.'[44] In the same letter, Ruskin urged Windus to complete his collection by joining him in commissioning a couple of finished drawings, referred to here as 'peculiar & vigorous conceptions'.

Although his appeal to Windus succeeded, the Swiss subjects of 1845 were judged by Ruskin to be less successful than those of earlier years. Another problem seems to have been that they took much longer to produce, for Turner worked well into the summer in order to complete the set (see p.153). His health during the last two years had begun to deteriorate and during May he was forced to retire to Margate, from where he made a brief trip to the French coast.

At the same time, the twenty-six-year-old Ruskin was making his first tour to Switzerland without his parents. He had faced some opposition to the tour from Turner, who was concerned that he would get caught up in the political unrest currently gripping that country. One of the principal reasons for undertaking the journey was to seek out the actual location of Turner's 1843 view of the St Gotthard Pass (see cat.no.40). He was resolutely single-minded in his research, noting to his father as he passed through

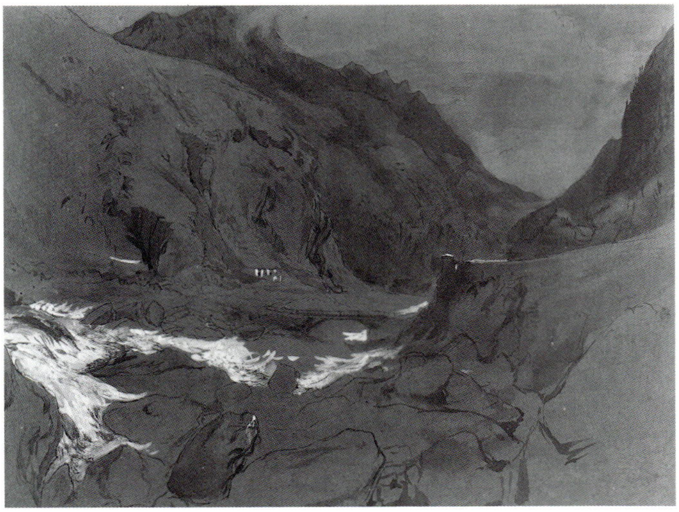

fig.5 John Ruskin, 'Pass of Faido on the St Gothard' 1845, pen and brown ink, watercolour, graphite heightened with white gouache on brown paper. *Courtesy of The Fogg Art Museum, Harvard University Art Museums. Gift of the Friends and Former Pupils of Prof. C.H. Moore*

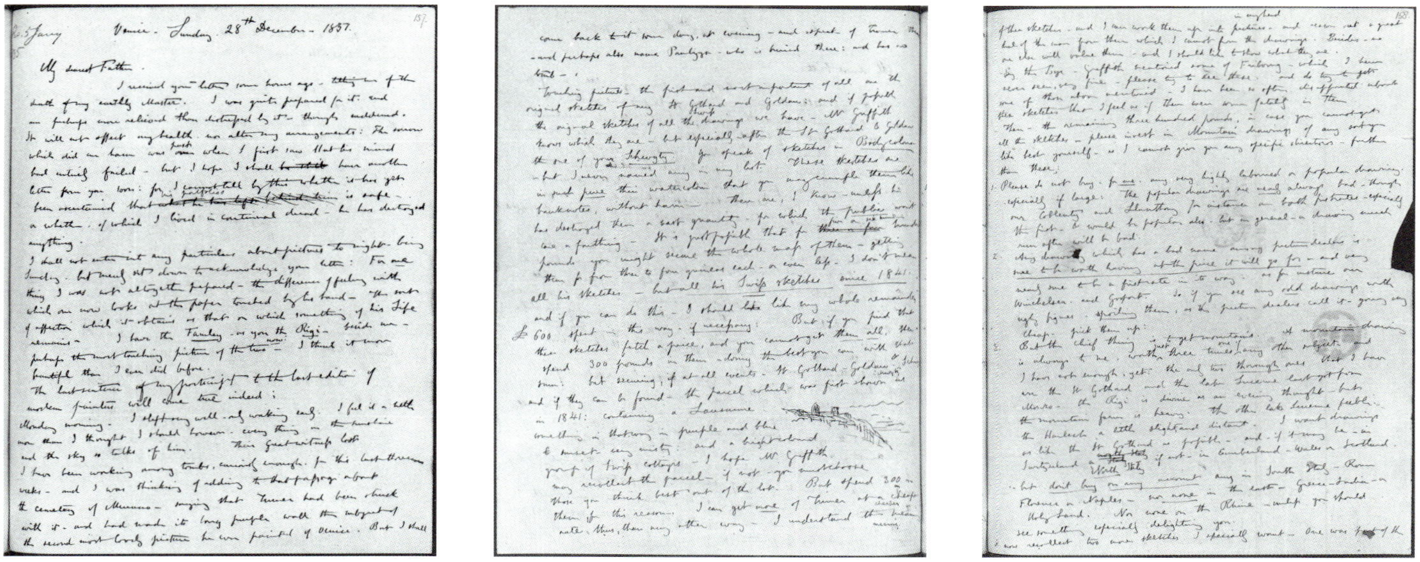
Venice. Sunday 28th December. 1851.

My dearest Father

fig.6 John Ruskin, letter to his father from Venice, 28 December 1851, including three sketches of drawings he hoped to buy: 'Lausanne' (cat.no.94), 'Dazio Grande' (fig.7) and 'The Devil's Bridge, St Gotthard' (TB LXXV 34). *Beinecke Rare Book and Manuscript Library, Yale University*

the mountains, 'Titian's all very well, but I don't see anything like him here. It is all Turner, and Turner *only*, nobody else'.[45] When he finally reached the Pass of Faido, on 15 August 1845, he studied in great detail how Turner had adapted the actual facts visible to produce his sublime and expressive vision of the great Swiss pass (fig.5). His resulting conclusion that the purpose of landscape painting was not so much to produce an 'image of the place itself, as the spirit of the place', was later expressed in the fourth volume of *Modern Painters*, published in 1856.[46]

In September, while Ruskin was still abroad, Turner made what appears to have been his last journey to the Continent. On this short trip, he remained close to the coast of Normandy, returning to the ports of Dieppe and Le Tréport, as well as to the town of Eu, where King Louis-Philippe had a small château (cat.nos.1–5). Turner was already acquainted with the French king, who had spent some of his years in exile at Twickenham, along the river from Turner's home. An early memoir contains the oft-quoted story that while Turner was at Le Tréport in 1845, he received an ad hoc invitation to join his former neighbour for dinner.[47] But the tale had perhaps been gilded a little to impress Turner's fellow artists, for it appears that there had already been a communication from the French king much earlier in the summer. News of this was sent to Ruskin in Switzerland, who asked defiantly 'What do the infernal french princes – with their beaux arts & libertas over church doors, & pulling down St Mark's Convent – say to him?'[48] Unfortunately, John James Ruskin's reply can no longer be traced.

The years following 1845 Ruskin later described as the period of Turner's decline. He was referring specifically to Turner's art, but, inevitably, he could not fail to notice the increasing signs of frailty in the man himself. Several entries in Ruskin's Diary give the impression that Turner's behaviour was occasionally a little too animated, something he implicitly relates to a fondness for wine. But in these contemporary documents, there is no suggestion of the madness that Ruskin subsequently detected in the artist's final years, which may reflect the critic's own later predicament rather than the artist's. They continued to remain in contact, both professionally and socially, but it appears they may have fallen out when Turner attempted to raise the price of the 1845 watercolours.[49] However, this disagreement was not of lasting significance, for in 1848 Turner revised his will to make Ruskin one of his executors. But in any case, during this period Ruskin became increasingly preoccupied with his own work, firstly on *The Seven Lamps of Architecture* (1849)[50] and, after his marriage to Euphemia Gray in 1848, on *The Stones of Venice* (1851–3).[51] The first volume of the latter work was published in March 1851, a copy of which was sent to Turner inscribed 'with the author's affectionate & respectful regards' (private collection).

This was to be the final year of Turner's life. It is not known when Ruskin and Turner last met, but by September 1851 Ruskin and his wife were established in Venice, where they remained until late in the following spring. Turner had retreated into his own private world more and more during his later years, apparently living obscurely

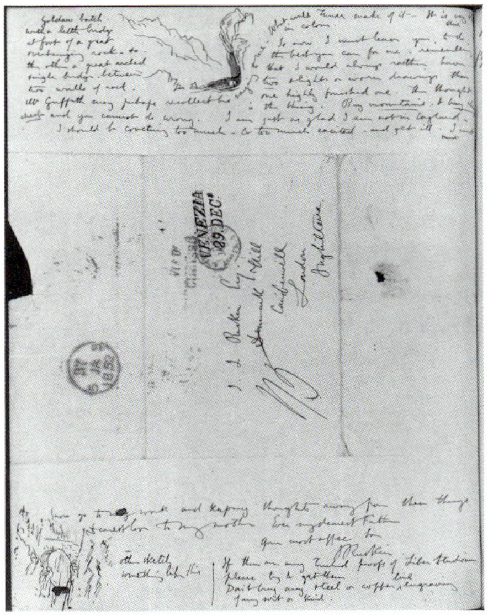

under the name of Captain Booth at Chelsea. At the time of his death on 19 December very few people were aware of this second home, including Ruskin, who learnt from his father the rumour that Turner had 'died in a Hovel at Chelsea where he has a Woman'.[52] It is clear that by this stage Ruskin had erected his own neat division between Turner's art and life. His closer acquaintance with the artist seems to have revealed Turner's human failings, and he possibly felt a need to protect from contamination the excellence he discerned in Turner's work.

The news at the end of the year of the death of his 'earthly Master' did, however, upset him much more than he had at first anticipated.[53] With incredible foresight, he had managed to express perfectly its significance a decade before, during the year he first met Turner: 'when he dies, there will be more of nature and her mysteries forgotten in one sob, than will be learnt again by the eyes of a generation'.[54] His first reaction on the day he received his father's letter bearing the fatal news was to note the difference of feeling he had towards 'the paper touched by his [Turner's] hand'; he had two of his Turner watercolours with him in Venice.[55] This was, in part, an echo of the consolation John James Ruskin had already sought in the 'Red Rigi' (p.76, fig.31), which he claimed 'fed and soothed me like a Dead March all this Evening'.[56]

But, while Ruskin remained outwardly calm and objective, the impact of Turner's death quickly expanded to encircle him. He noted in a letter to H.F. Fawkes, the son of Turner's greatest patron, 'For myself, I had been expecting it, and yet it has cast more shadow than I thought over these lagoons which he painted so often – what must it over your secret walks and glens?'[57] The sense of profound loss grew upon him over the years, so that in 1856 he protested to Pauline, Lady Trevelyan that 'every day of my life I regret Turner's death more'.[58]

As was suggested at the beginning of this essay, Ruskin was initially hopeful of acquiring many of the late Swiss watercolour sketches left in Turner's portfolios, specifying a number of works included in this catalogue as his 'first and most important' priorities (figs.6 and 7; see also cat.nos.27, 32, 40, 94). However, this urge was soon tempered by his excitement at the prospect of the much bigger entity of Turner's complete collection becoming national property. He immediately saw the implications of this for his own work, and outlined to his father his desire to be the person who supervised the construction of a gallery to house the works where, through his arrangements and explanations, he would 'take the position of [Turner's] Interpreter to future generations'.[59] If, at the beginning of January 1852, he was perhaps not altogether certain whether 'this was what I was meant to do', he was absolutely convinced by the end of February that 'my great mission is to interpret him'.[60] He declared to his father, 'Either I know this man Turner to be *the* man of his generation – or I know *nothing*'.[61]

Of course, as we now know, Turner's confused will, with its various codicils, was challenged by his relatives, making it impossible for anyone to begin the work of organising the huge collection. This was to continue until the lengthy hiatus, caused by legal wrangling, was resolved in the Chancery Decree of 1856. The difficulties surrounding the will were readily perceived by Ruskin, who resigned from his role as one of Turner's executors while still away in Italy.

During this period, however, he remained committed to his professed goal of acting as a mouthpiece for Turner, his enthusiasm for his cause spilling over into other areas of his work. Two projects that are particularly noteworthy in this respect were initiated before his immersion in the Turner Bequest in 1857, and have a direct bearing on his involvement with the collection.

First, he was commissioned by the dealer Gambart to write a text which was eventually published as *The Harbours of England* (1856).[62] Ruskin provided a richly discursive introduction for this, in which he established for Turner an exalted place in the tradition of marine painting. This was accompanied by individual notes on each of the twelve mezzotints after Turner's designs that made up the set. The project had originated in 1825 under the name *The Ports of England*, but only six subjects were published dur-

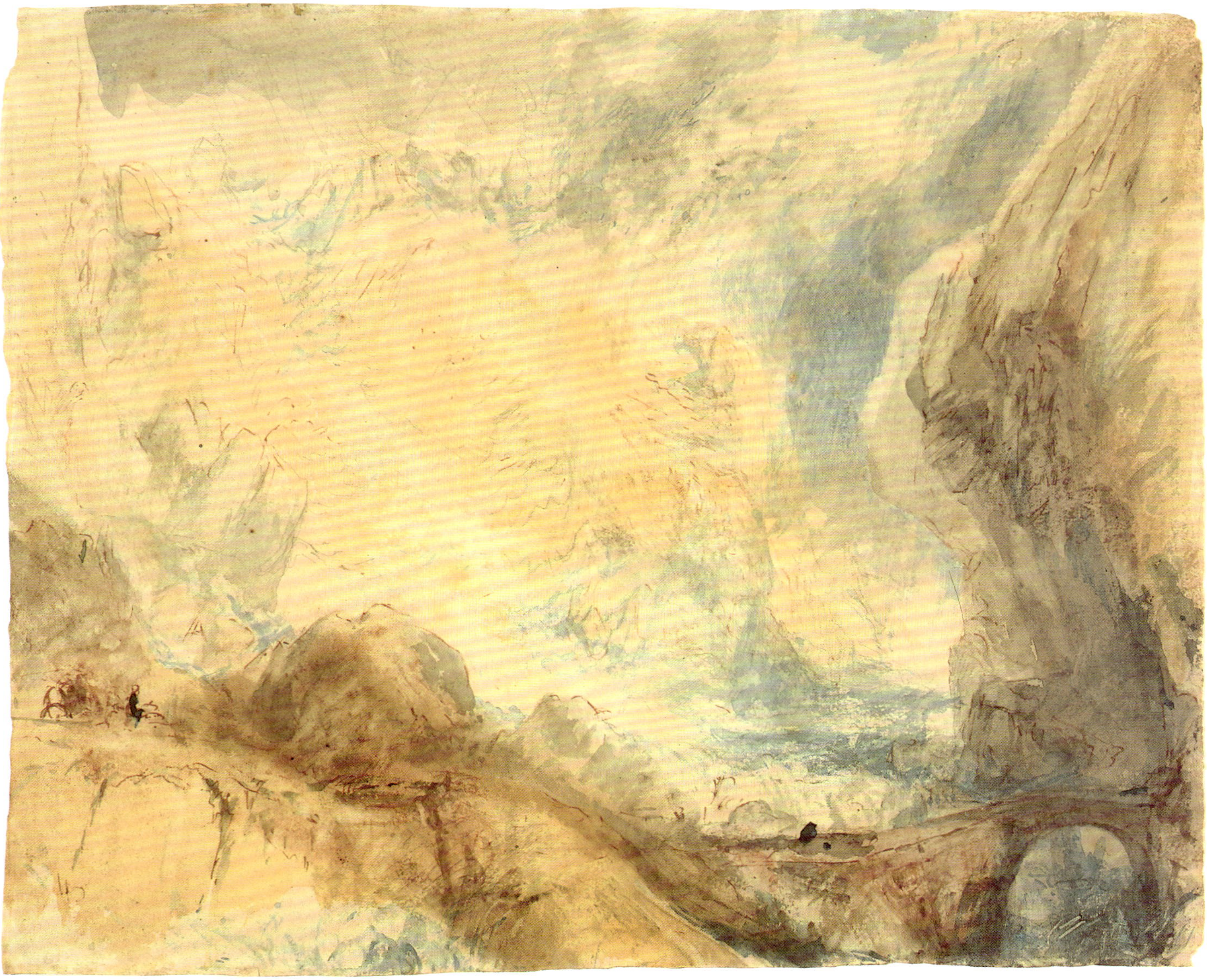

fig.7 J.M.W. Turner, 'Dazio Grande' 1843, watercolour. *Museum of Art, Rhode Island School of Design. Gift of Richard Brown Baker in memory of Harvey and Marion Baker*

ing the artist's lifetime. The watercolours on which these first mezzotints were based remained in Turner's collection, and were, even as Ruskin was writing, the subject of the protracted Chancery case.

His second project has a more direct connection with the Swiss watercolours that figure so prominently in this catalogue. Although he seems to have conceived this second scheme in 1854, he did not set out its aims explicitly until 1856, when he explained to Lady Trevelyan the reason for his recent tour to Switzerland:

> I have a plan for etching views of seven Swiss towns, and bequeathing them to foolish posterity, that it may mourn and gnash its teeth in its Hotels. I mean to draw, if I can, Basle, (1) Schaffhausen, (2) Lucerne,

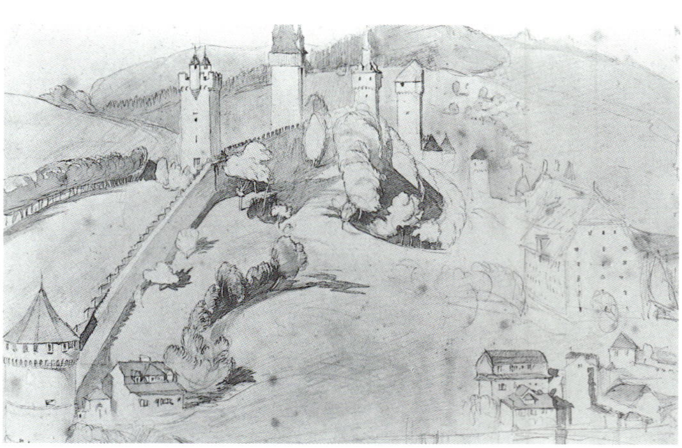

fig.8 John Ruskin, 'Lucerne: Walls and Towers' *c.*1854, watercolour. *The Education Trust, Ruskin Galleries, Bembridge School, Isle of Wight*

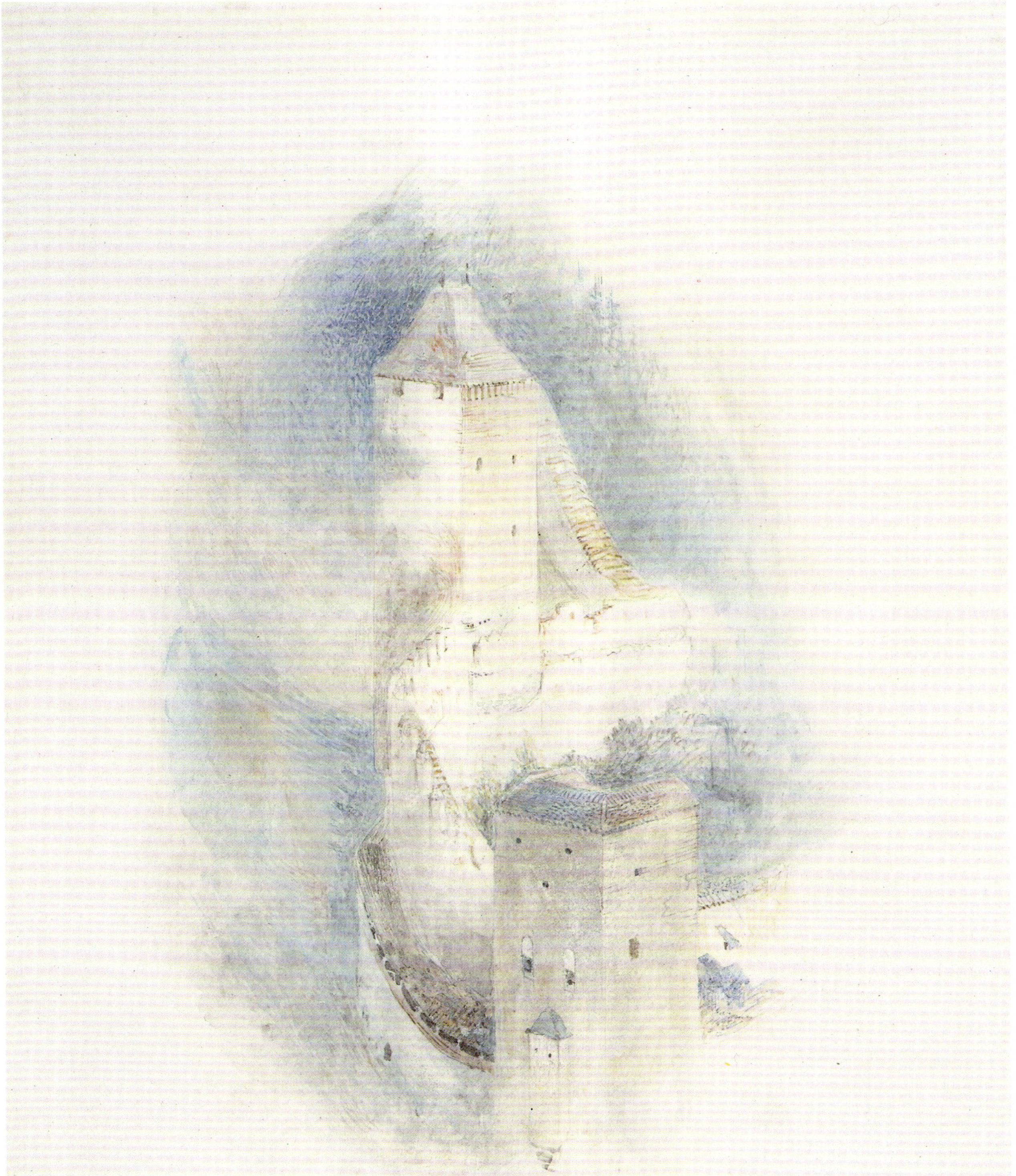

fig.9 John Ruskin, 'Towers of Fribourg' 1854, watercolour. *British Museum*

Thun, (3) Fribourg, Sion, and (4) Bellinzona; the 1, 2, 3, 4, elaborately to illustrate Turner's multitudinous sketches of them. There are at least sixteen of Fribourg, seven or eight of Lucerne, thirty of Bellinzona, and four or five of Schaffhausen among the sketches left to the nation, and I can realise these a little with detail, so as to explain them ... and I hope that Berne and Geneva will be properly humiliated at being left out of the list, as too much spoiled to be worth notice.[63]

During his tours to Switzerland in both 1854 and 1856, Ruskin consciously set out to make sketches that would help to elucidate Turner's Swiss subjects. It was probably while at Lucerne in 1854 that he made the outline sketch of the town's walls, the Museggmauer (fig.8), as a means of illustrating both the finished drawing in his own collection (p.60, fig.22) and the sample study of the same view in the Turner Bequest (cat.no.23).

As is so often the case in Ruskin's work, any stated objective can be reached by a number of different routes, and this Swiss project was no exception. During the mid-1850s particularly, he was preoccupied with many overlapping ideas, so it was inevitable that his Swiss Turner research fed other publications. For example, the work he did at Fribourg served as a means of explaining in the fourth volume of *Modern Painters* how Turner used topography for his own ends, while remaining true to the places themselves. To prove this, Ruskin produced an exquisitely subtle view of the Tour des Chats and the Porte de Berne, adopting in his watercolour the vignette form which had been his chief introduction to Turner's work (fig.9). In his text he compared the vignette with a daguerreotype of the same view. He commissioned other photographic reproductions of the actual subjects of Turner's watercolours (fig.10). But generally, he preferred to make his own detailed sketches, such as those he completed at Rheinfelden in 1858 after discovering it was the subject of a group of the Turner watercolours he had attempted to catalogue the previous year (fig.11; see cat.nos.86–90). These sketches were included in his first catalogue of the Turner Bequest, and it is to the origins of this publication that we must now turn.

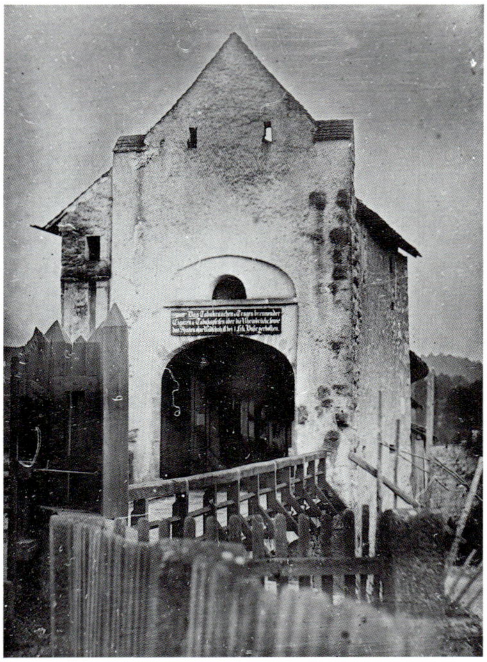

fig.10 Frederick Crawley, 'The Covered Bridge, Rheinfelden' 1858, daguerreotype. *The Education Trust Ltd, Ruskin Galleries, Bembridge School, Isle of Wight*

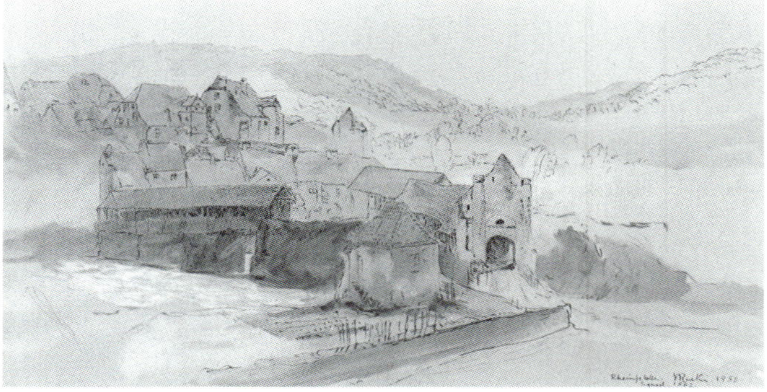

fig.11 John Ruskin, 'Rheinfelden Bridge' 1858, pen and watercolour. *Whereabouts unknown*. From *Modern Painters*, V, *Works*, VII, p.xxx, plate B, chromolithograph

Ruskin's First Catalogue of the Turner Bequest, 1857

The other projects undertaken by Ruskin during the 1850s demonstrate his continuing allegiance to Turner's art. But they were all subsequently overwhelmed (or actually subsumed) by his attempts to organise the artist's bequest. In this, Ruskin was to realise the wish he had expressed early in 1852, when he wrote to his father: 'If the rest of the executors would only make me a curator of the gallery I should be perfectly happy.'[64] As the following history relates, this was only achieved through a combination of obstinate perseverance, subterfuge and, ultimately, sheer hard work, which occupied him solidly for more than eighteen months.

Although the Court of Chancery passed its decree on the fate of the Turner Bequest in March 1856, it was not until September that Ruskin began to address the problem of what he felt ought to be done. Upon his arrival back in Britain after a journey to Switzerland, he wrote to Lady Trevelyan on 26 September, indicating that his future plans were inextricably bound up with the Turner Bequest, 'which I mean now to make as much noise about as I have voice for'.[65]

He may have been aware that the remaining contents of Turner's Gallery were just then being transferred to the National Gallery. At this date the building constituted little more than the line of galleries parallel with the Trafalgar Square façade, the eastern half of which was occupied by the Royal Academy. The arrival of almost three hundred paintings by Turner immediately provoked a crisis, highlighting the want of space for the national collection (an all-too familiar problem in the history of British art galleries). As an interim measure, a proposal was made to hang some of the oil paintings in Marlborough House, then owned by the Government. News of this idea came to the attention of the *Times*, who transformed what was merely a possibility into something much more concrete, announcing on Friday 24 October that the pictures would be available to the public from the following Monday.[66] While this impression was hastily corrected by a letter from Ralph Wornum (1812–77), the Keeper at the National Gallery, the incident seems to have spurred Ruskin to enter the fray.

In trying to intervene, Ruskin was in an extraordinary dilemma. Firstly, he had no official status with regard to the Turner Bequest, having renounced his executorship, on his father's advice, soon after the will was first examined. Moreover, his frequent criticisms of the National Gallery had created a palpable friction between him and Sir Charles Lock Eastlake (1793–1865), its Director, making it unlikely that Eastlake would openly seek Ruskin's advice about how the Bequest could best be managed. It is also of some significance that, during the spring of 1856, Ruskin's authority as a writer on art had been questioned in such publications as the *Edinburgh Review* and the *Quarterly*, causing Frederick Pollock to reflect, 'It is a pity that persons competent to the task have not before now interfered to prevent so seductive a writer from obtaining any authority in matters of art. He is unprincipled in art, but has been allowed to acquire an influence which has been chiefly for mischief, and it is probably now too late to undo it.'[67] In this comment it is possible to gauge something of the reservations felt by many in the art establishment towards Ruskin.

It is worth stressing the kind of opposition Ruskin faced at this time, for, in retrospect, we tend to forget that his was often a lone voice, time having engendered a security to his position as a Victorian prophet. However, Ruskin was not one to avoid controversy, and like a fish swimming against the current, to use his own metaphor, he set out his views on the Turner Bequest in a letter to the *Times*, which was published on 28 October 1856.[68] Subsequently, even Ruskin had to admit that this was a somewhat 'irregular' (if not foolhardy) way of proceeding. His motives were obviously altruistic, but he was also driven by an overriding belief in his superior knowledge of Turner, a quality that underlies a great deal of his work on the artist.[69] His principal concern was not so much for the oil paintings, as for the huge collection of watercolours and sketches, an area in which he felt his own knowledge as a collector gave him better experience than the institution's officials. In this respect he certainly had a point, for unlike other London collections the National Gallery owned no works on paper until the arrival of the Turner Bequest, since the British Museum had always been the national repository for this sort of material.

Ruskin's letter conveys a first-hand awareness of the particular problems associated with the Turner Bequest. In it he reported that he had already seen, and made notes on, the collection, which he divided into three distinct types of material (finished watercolours, studies from nature, and sketches in pencil, or in pen and ink). He then explained the potential of the Bequest as a reference collection, which contained, 'if rightly arranged, a perfect record of the movement of the master's mind during the whole of his life'.[70] However, since the majority of the sketches were then unidentified, and often very slight in execution, Ruskin advised that an 'extended acquaintance with Turner's works' was necessary 'to ascertain their intention'.[71] It was in this that he felt most able to offer assistance, proposing himself as the person best able to perform the task: 'I believe none would treat these drawings with more scrupulous care, or arrange them with greater patience, than I should myself.'[72]

Although Ruskin emphasised the importance of achieving public access to the collection, he stressed that before this could be achieved there was a need for careful preservation of the fragile sketches. He offered in his plan to provide, at his own cost, for one hundred of the watercolours to be 'enclosed each in a light wooden frame, under a glass, the surface of which a raised mount should prevent them from touching. These frames should slide into cases, containing about twelve frames each, which would be portable to any part of the room where they were to be seen.'[73] If granted permission to undertake this work, Ruskin promised to finish it, complete with an explanatory catalogue, within six weeks. As a final thought, he noted that other drawings might subsequently be added to this group, but that the less interesting works would only be available by special application, as at the British Museum. In other words, he felt that the National Gallery needed to establish its own print room for the Turner collection.

Ruskin closed his appeal by stating that he had elected to adopt the unconventional approach of the 'Letters' page of the *Times* as a means of saving time and avoiding the drawn-out formalities associated (then as now) with great British institutions. But he was possibly also anticipating public support for his idea from the readers of *Modern Painters*, who knew him to be an ardent champion of Turner's art.

There was no immediate response to his offer by the National Gallery, where the staff were busy making arrangements for the display of a first group of twenty Turner paintings at Marlborough House. But it was, in any case, surely a foregone conclusion that, despite the strength of Ruskin's arguments, the public nature of his offer would go against him.

Two days after the *Times* published his letter its columns carried a criticism of his plan signed by 'A TURNERITE', the vehemence of which reveals that not all admirers of Turner accepted Ruskin's position as 'the great exponent of his genius'.[74] The letter questioned whether Ruskin was any better able to supervise the mounting of the delicate Turner watercolours than the professionals he had derided in his letter: 'Mr Ruskin's knowledge of Turner came by inspiration, and verily his power to preserve his works is to come in the same manner.' The anonymous writer went on to express a hope that 'no single person will be intrusted with the important task of preserving and arranging Turner's drawings and sketches', suggesting instead a committee of artists. As a final insult, the letter ended by stating that 'Mr Ruskin's remarks on the subject of these drawings prove him to be only an experimentalist in the matter, and therefore the last person to be intrusted with such an important charge'.[75]

A more official response to Ruskin's proposal took the form of a letter from William Russell (1800–84), one of the National Gallery Trustees, to Eastlake on 7 November. Russell had re-examined the Chancery Decree in order to establish that Turner's drawings were also understood to be part of the Bequest, and therefore had to be made accessible. Russell was firmly opposed to the idea of transferring the watercolours to the British Museum, an idea that seems to have occurred to the National Gallery as a means of overcoming the lack of space. He rightly noted that if the British Museum was not able to accommodate the 'treasures' already in its charge, it could hardly be expected to take on even more. And further, he felt that once Turner's collection had been divided between different institutions, it would prove impossible to attempt to reunite them if sufficient space was provided. It was quite obvious to him that 'so complete a collection ought not to be broken up or impaired'.[76] In consequence, he believed it was the duty of the Trustees to impress on the Government the need for adequate accommodation.

In the public sphere, momentum was gathering for action. An editorial in the *Times*, which appeared on Thursday 13 November 1856, drew the public's attention to the fact that there had been no indication of what the National Gallery thought about Ruskin's offer, which it outlined once again. The paper seemed to lend its weight to Ruskin's campaign by stating that 'Turner cannot be fairly judged unless his drawings are studied at least as much as his oil pictures. On the whole, few artists, we believe, will dissent from the opinion that his drawings are the more important of the two.'[77] It should be pointed out that the 'drawings' referred to were the masterly watercolours that Turner had produced for his various engraving projects, or which he had exhibited in his lifetime, and not the hundreds of sketches in which Ruskin had expressed his special interest. This was in accordance with contemporary taste, which placed its highest value on 'finish' and 'detail'. Indeed, it was not until 1862 that the Society of Painters in Water-Colours inaugurated displays of sketches at its annual winter exhibitions, while the British Museum only began to exhibit the less finished drawings in its collections from 1858.[78]

At the beginning of the week after the *Times* published its editorial, the Trustees met to consider the issues arising from the arrival of the Bequest, in effect endorsing Russell's viewpoint. As a first step, it was decided that a 'portion' of the collection of finished watercolours should be exhibited at Marlborough House, a suggestion refined by Eastlake, who insisted this should be a changing series to prevent any work suffering damage from being exposed to too much light. To deal with further issues relating to the Turner collection, it was proposed that a small committee be established including three of Turner's executors – Munro of Novar, William Clarkson Stanfield (1793–1867) and David Roberts (1796–1864). The Minutes of the meeting do not refer to the letter Ruskin had sent to the *Times*, but as a final point, the Trustees agreed formally to approach him for his suggestions as to 'the mode of exhibiting the drawings'.[79]

Even before 4 December 1856, when Wornum wrote to Ruskin with news of this decision[80], it had been agreed to position screens in the rooms containing Turner's paintings at Marlborough House. By this means it was thought that at least eighty drawings could be shown. A meeting took place on the following day, where Eastlake, Wornum and the three executors selected one hundred and two of the more finished subjects, at the same time drawing up a report dealing with the practical considerations of how to avoid exposing the works to any sort of damage (see Appendix 1).

From this series of events, one is inclined to suspect that the National Gallery (as personified by Eastlake) felt it could get along without Ruskin's intervention. This was an impression that must have been given greater substance by a letter from Ruskin of 8 December, which merely echoed the concern for the preservation of the sketches that the gallery's committee had already expressed in the report of their meeting three days earlier.

In this letter, however, Ruskin, revised his opinion as to which works should be exhibited. Envisaging a permanent display, he suggested that 'the works selected for exhibition should not be the *very* finest in the collection; but specimens of average excellence, while the *best* drawings might be framed in the same manner, and placed in cases in the British Museum, visible on application'.[81] Those included in the display could be arranged 'in two rows along a well lighted wall not exposed to sunshine'. He again offered to pay for one hundred of the drawings to be mounted, framed and accommodated in mahogany cases designed on his own model.

The final point to come out of Ruskin's letter of 8 December is his sense of a mission to interpret Turner's sketches. Once again, he emphasised the need for an explanatory catalogue stating the subject of each work. Here he stressed the meaning given to Turner's watercolours once their correct subject and date of execution are understood, a knowledge only possible through extensive fieldwork at the sites of the subjects depicted, what a more recent Turner scholar has described as 'the iconography of landscape'.[82] With reference to the one hundred watercolours Ruskin eventually selected, it is important to note that already at this stage it was the Swiss (and 'especially *mountain*') subjects that he singled out as the area of his particular interest.

Ruskin was, of course, attempting to do the right thing. But he was an outsider, and there is a real sense of him punching air beyond the arena of the official fight. The response he received from the Trustees, as conveyed by Wornum, was that their staff had very largely anticipated his ideas. However, Wornum assured Ruskin that they would, of course, contact him if the need arose.[83]

By this stage Ruskin sensed that the public announcement of his proposal would now prejudice his offer and result in its opposition. Consequently, on 13 December, two days before the Trustees' meeting, he sought a higher authority by writing to Lord Palmerston, the Prime Minister. In briefly setting out his scheme, Ruskin admitted that he had been at fault in the way he had tried to secure the task through an 'irregular channel'. But in explaining his generous offer to work for nothing, *and* to pay the costs of his proposal, he made an impassioned case which Lord Palmerston must have felt at least curious to examine. Throughout his letter, Ruskin reiterates the special skills he would be able to bring to the task, noting at first that 'there are a large number of [Turner's sketches] whose subjects are at present unknown, but which, having devoted a great part of my life to inquiries into the mode of Turner's studying from nature, I believe myself to be able, more or less, to elucidate'. He continues, persuasively,

> my motives for making this offer are, first, that I heartily desire the sketches may be taken care of, and believe I should take more loving care of them than any one else; secondly, that I desire they should be useful to the public, and believe I could make them *more* useful by the way I would arrange them; and lastly, that I should have pleasure in the work itself. On this last ground I have good hope that the results I should obtain in a given period would not be less satisfactory than if the work were entrusted to a salaried officer.[84]

This stirring address seems to have provoked no immediate results. Privately, Ruskin was still optimistic. He wrote to his friend Charles Eliot Norton early in 1857 expressing his belief that whatever the Trustees 'may determine upon just now, I shall have to do it for them, for the simple reason that they *cannot* do it themselves; nor get it done, there being literally nobody, except myself, who knows where Turner's subjects were taken, or their sequence, chronologically'.[85]

However, Ruskin was not the only one seeking to be appointed curator of the Turner Bequest. A rival petition had been made by Joseph Dupuis, Turner's son-in-law, which was considered, and declined, at the National Gallery on 19 January 1857.[86]

Meanwhile, the Turner display at Marlborough House was proving more popular than had perhaps been anticipated. So much so that by the beginning of February 1857 it was necessary to extend the number of days it was open to the public from four to six days a week.[87] In December the *Times* had congratulated Eastlake and Wornum for the means by which they had brought about the display of Turner's paintings, noting that it was

> a way not ill-calculated to whet the public interest, and provoke a public sense of the want of house-room for the nation's art treasures. 'Look how rich you are in pictures!' each installment of Turner's seems to say to John Bull; 'But look how miserably off you are for a place to hang them in' say, in the same breath, the curators of the National Gallery.[88]

Ruskin anticipated that he would be able to marshal the heightened interest of the public to achieve his purpose. In his letter to Norton of 11 January 1857, he spoke of the catalogue he had just written of the thirty-four oil paintings by Turner, then accessible to the public: *Notes on the Turner Gallery at Marlborough House*.[89] This he saw as a 'specimen of what may be done in this way, and if the public likes it, they will perhaps want the drawings catalogued too'.[90]

If Ruskin had simply been over-zealous in presenting his theories for the display of the Bequest in the pages of the *Times*, he was in the publication of this catalogue actually 'trespassing' on official ground, for the gallery had already listed the pictures in its own published catalogue. It is not surprising, therefore, to find that only four days after Ruskin's *Notes on the Turner Gallery at Marlborough House* was issued on 12 January, he was forced to write to Wornum at the National Gallery to explain why his publication had assumed the appearance of an official catalogue, sold with the Trustees' permission.[91] Although some of his ideas about this group of pictures are already familiar from *Modern Painters*, the catalogue remains a valuable and original study, discussing each painting in some detail within a chronological structure. In his recent biography of Ruskin, Tim Hilton has noted that, although this is Ruskin's shortest volume on Turner, it 'contains a wonderful amount of his understanding of the artist', displaying judgements which are 'less wayward, more considered' than elsewhere.[92]

As Ruskin had hoped, it did indeed prove popular with the public, who genuinely needed assistance in their efforts to understand Turner's later work. The American novelist Nathaniel Hawthorne (1804–64), for example, planned to look at the paintings a second time using Ruskin's book as his guide, but doubted whether the catalogue could change his opinion that 'a picture ought to have something in common with what the spectator sees in Nature'.[93] So successful was this guidebook that it had reached a fifth edition by July 1857, a fact that is not solely due to the great attention focused on the Turner Bequest at that time. However, even in its content, Ruskin could not resist controversy; he concluded the catalogue with a criticism of the way the pictures were displayed and a further plea for the finished drawings to be made available, which can hardly have won him support within the National Gallery.

By the end of January 1857, the group of one hundred and two finished watercolours, selected by the committee, was being hung in Marlborough House. Ruskin expressed his fears for the drawings to Ellen Heaton, saying 'too probably those in the national collection will be spoiled', meaning they would be badly mounted and framed.[94] However, when he visited Marlborough House for himself on 31 January, he was pleasantly surprised by what the mounters at Colnaghi's had achieved, and wrote to Wornum a few days later to express his approval.[95]

The same letter reveals that Wornum had encouraged him to state, yet again, his proposal to make a further one hundred drawings available in frames stored in cases, accompanied by a printed catalogue. Once again, Ruskin's plans were forestalled by action at a higher level of the bureaucratic hierarchy. On the very same day Eastlake expounded his thoughts on the unexhibited material to William Russell. The tenor of his letter was that the Gallery should 'frame not one hundred only but all the remaining *coloured* and *finished* drawings of Turner', estimating a total of about three hundred works. This plan would, of course, make Ruskin's long-standing proposal 'unnecessary'.[96]

As Director, Eastlake's recommendations would inevitably have great weight with his Trustees. However, at the meeting which followed on 9 February, he allowed them to consider Ruskin's plan yet again before setting out the modifications he had already suggested to Russell. Whatever the politics behind the order of the agenda, the Trustees on this occasion at last agreed to allow Ruskin to go ahead with his plan. They were perhaps swayed by the provision his scheme made for ensuring that the drawings were protected from strong light – a problem that was also of great concern to them. Accordingly, Ruskin was at last invited to make a prototype to illustrate his idea.

On 10 February, Wornum wrote to congratulate Ruskin, assuring him at the same time that 'as regards the cost the Trustees desire me to say that if they should ultimately have the benefit of your aid, they would not consider it just to recommend that the expense should fall upon you'.[97] This letter from Wornum is one of several documents which contradict the oft-stated assumption that the costs of mounting and framing the Bequest drawings were met entirely from Ruskin's own pocket. As is shown below, the fact that his actions were dependent on the National Gallery's budget caused him to be more cautious and thorough in his planning than he might have been otherwise.

The go-ahead from the Trustees marks the beginning of a period of intense activity for Ruskin. Having campaigned for the job so fiercely under the glare of public scrutiny, he was suddenly aware of the pressure he was under to deliver an exemplary working model of his proposal, which could be applied to other drawings in the collection. His anxiety can be discerned in the draft of a letter to Thomas Griffith, written on 16 February 1857: 'I have many enemies and I know already there is no falsehood too gross for some of them to venture upon, if they had the slightest hope of injuring me in public opinion or report.'[98] If the task itself provoked a sense of his exposure to criticism, he must have found some consolation in his renewed involvement with Turner's works and the proximity it gave him to the essence of the artist. Indeed, on the same day that he expressed his fears to Griffith, his Diary suggests that he had experienced a kind of visitation from the 'Imaginary spirit of Turner'.[99]

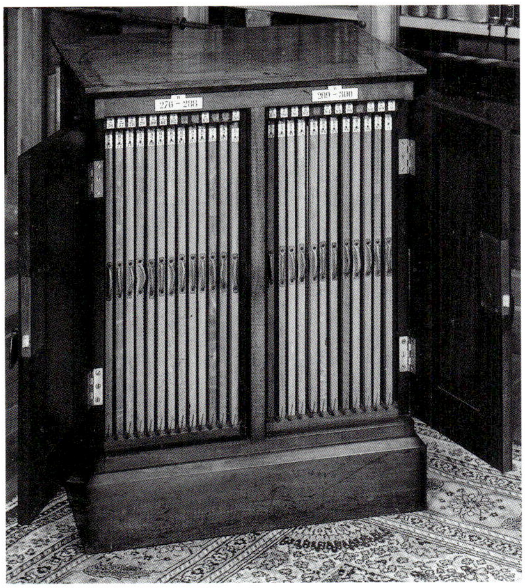

fig.12 One of the cases designed by Ruskin for the Oxford Drawing School collection. *The Education Trust Ltd, Ruskin Galleries, Bembridge School, Isle of Wight*

It seems he had not yet received a complete sanction to embark on his project, for on 2 March he was using examples from his own collection of Turner drawings in a prototype frame to help the Trustees visualise how the finished scheme would work. At this progress meeting he also submitted a more detailed outline of his specifications for frames and storage cabinets. The frames were to be of white pine, 'because the whiter the wood, the less it hurts the colour of the sketch', while also making the frames physically lighter and less prone to damage. The backs of the frames were to slide exactly into place and then to be given an official seal. Ivory tablets with the number of the frame were to be inserted into the wood, as well as a leather handle with which to draw the frame from the case. The mahogany cases were based on those he had designed to hold his own Turner watercolours (fig.12). Inside the cases, the frames were to be separated by grooves, for which Ruskin provided a design (fig.13), that he explained as follows: 'In the drawing annexed, the purple represents the case with its fillets, the frames are yellow, the dark space represents the space when a frame is taken out; the most careless or hasty person could not *miss* the place in re-inserting it, and it must slide on its fillet, of necessity.'[100] Sadly, none of the cases eventually constructed seems to have survived.

As to the content of his selection, Ruskin here suggested that the protected group should ultimately include pencil drawings and some of the smaller coloured works as well as more obviously appealing watercolours. His first concern, however, was for the group of one hundred colour sketches he had been planning for so long, and which constitute the catalogue republished here. At this stage he had not arrived at the final form of the circular tour he eventually published, and instead proposed that the series would illustrate 'the journey from Venice, over the St Gothard, by Lucerne and the Rhine, to Eu on the coast of France'.[101]

In agreeing to allow him to continue with his project Eastlake and his Trustees believed that the proposal could have wider implications for the 'conservation and convenient inspection' of collections of drawings in other museums.[102] Indeed, as Ruskin noted in the Preface to his 1857 *Catalogue of the Turner Sketches in the National Gallery*, neither the Louvre nor the Uffizi allowed visitors to see their best drawings in a way that was conducive to proper study.

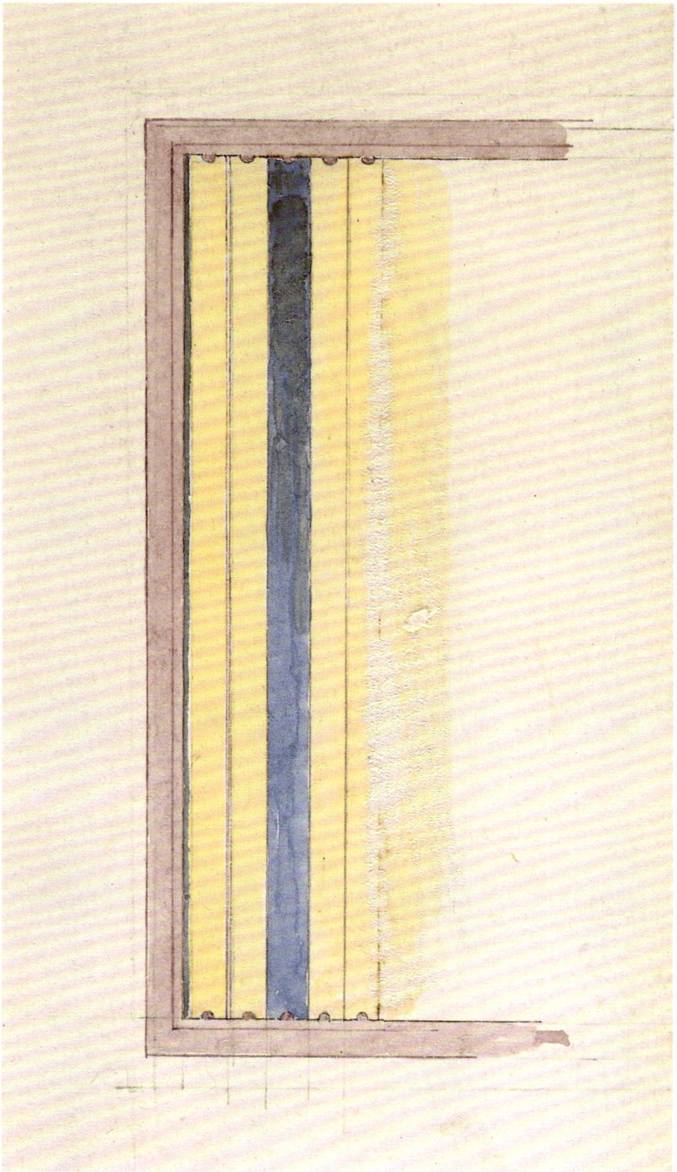

fig.13 John Ruskin, design for the interior of the Turner cabinets, 1857. *The Trustees of The National Gallery, London*

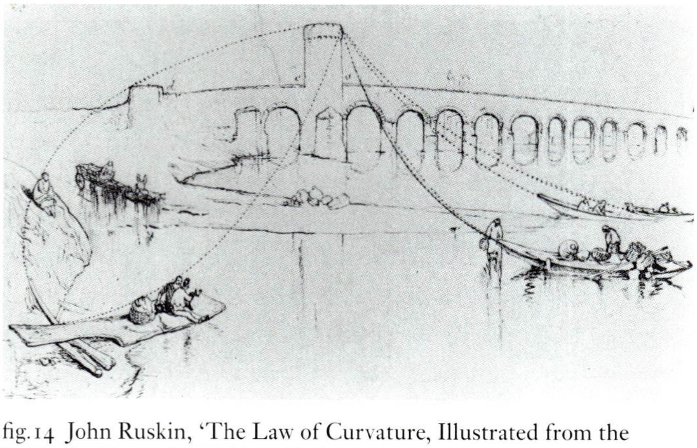

fig.14 John Ruskin, 'The Law of Curvature, Illustrated from the Bridge in Turner's "Coblenz"' 1857, pen and brown ink, fig.34 in *The Elements of Drawing*. *Private Collection*

By May 1857 Ruskin was again protesting to Norton of the onerous reponsibilities he faced in his task, although characteristically he had further complicated matters by working simultaneously on *The Elements of Drawing*, his 'nice little book for beginners in drawing' (fig.14).[103] Although none of the letters from the National Gallery stipulated that Ruskin had to complete his job within the six weeks stated in his letter to the *Times* the previous autumn, Ruskin seems to have convinced himself that this was a binding obligation. He suggested to Norton that the preparation of the one hundred sketches 'has cost me much thought, for had I done the thing at my own cost, I would have mended it afterward if it had gone wrong in any way; but now I must, if possible, get it all perfect at first, or the Trustees wont [*sic*] be pleased'.[104]

He apologised for the delay to Wornum in a letter of 30 May, stressing his disinclination to waste public funds by making mistakes, but also blamed the huge exhibition of 'Art Treasures' in Manchester for taking up all the best cabinet- and frame-makers.[105] He had, however, written a catalogue of the first twenty-five of his selection, which was presented to the Trustees, with the works themselves, on the following Monday. Copies of the first edition of the catalogue are now a rarity among 'Ruskiniana', but, despite a shuffling around of some of the catalogue entries, the text differs very little from that he expanded in the full second edition later that spring. The sketches appear in largely the same order in both editions; the one work that was dropped between the two publications is included here, as in Cook and Wedderburn's edition of *The Works of John Ruskin*, as cat.no.11A, bringing the total number of works catalogued by Ruskin at this time to one hundred and one.

When the Trustees of the National Gallery next met on 22 June, Ruskin had finished his work on the first hundred watercolours and the enlarged catalogue. It was published by Spottiswoode and Co., who printed a limited edition of only a hundred copies, with a title-page bearing the notice 'for private circulation' (fig.15). Ruskin also included the words 'Part I' in his title, indicating that his work remained unfinished and that he assumed he would be allowed to produce additional volumes.

One would expect the catalogue to read like a sustained manifesto for Ruskin's arguments, but it is only in his Preface that he provided a résumé of the points he had been making for the past eight months. At the end of these introductory comments he outlined Turner's method in making the sketches selected, stressing their appeal as impressions recorded directly from nature.

As discussed earlier, Ruskin arranged the sketches as an imaginary tour, ignoring a sense of their actual chronology.

This was, of course, a means of demonstrating his own knowledge of the scenery depicted in Turner's sketches, but his decision perhaps also reflects a characteristically English preoccupation with topography above aesthetic considerations of technique or effect; another very English obsession lies behind Ruskin's comments on the weather, which form a link throughout the notes. The topographical method of classifying his material seems to have particularly suited Ruskin's purpose, for he subsequently also adopted the outline of a tour for his 1879 catalogue of the works of Samuel Prout.[106]

On reading the catalogue, it becomes quickly apparent that the tone of Ruskin's comments can be divided into two distinct styles. The first is almost that of a fireside narrative, founded on biographical information, and is a style Tim Hilton has described in his biography of Ruskin as best suited for addressing children.[107] Of more enduring interest are Ruskin's acute remarks about exactly how Turner has achieved some of his effects. Since these notes were being written while Ruskin was at work on *The Elements of Drawing*, it is not surprising that there should be an overlap between the projects. Through these comments, Ruskin drew his reader's attention not only to the assured use of varied techniques that underlies Turner's sketches, but also to the compositional balance that was always an instinctive strength of Turner's art.

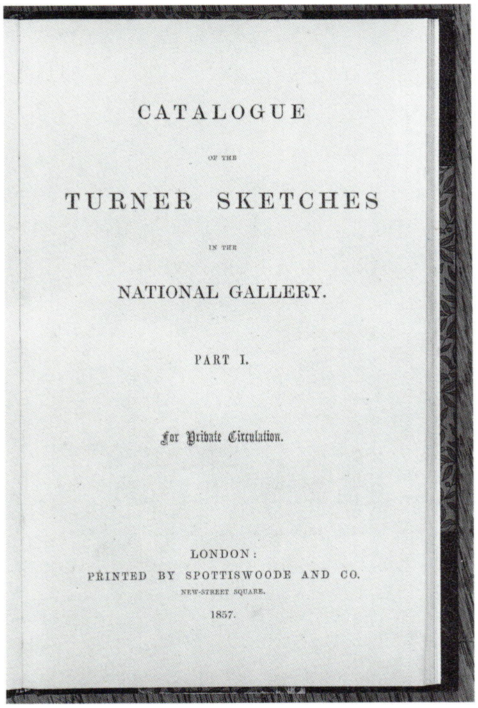

fig.15 Title-page of *Catalogue of the Turner Sketches in the National Gallery, Part 1*, 1857. *The Education Trust Ltd, Ruskin Galleries, Bembridge School, Isle of Wight*

One of the chief delights of the catalogue is the idiosyncrasy of Ruskin's opinions. We might well agree with him that cat.nos.72 and 74 are indeed among the most spectacular of the group. But how many readers will agree with his opinion that cat.no.95 is 'the worst'? Even here, however, he is refreshing in his observations on what Turner has achieved.

All the sketches that Ruskin selected date from the final decade of Turner's working life, the time of the commissioned views of Switzerland. By selecting almost the whole series of sample studies for this group, including the majority of those relating to works in his own collection, Ruskin was able to suggest (possibly subconsciously) his special connection with the artist, as well as his suitability as Turner's interpreter.

The minutes for the meeting on 22 June 1857 do not detail the Trustees' response to Ruskin's catalogue. However, Eastlake recommended that the plan be approved, but (as he had suggested in February) that similar provision should also be made for all the coloured drawings 'deemed sufficiently finished', while the gilt frames provided for the one hundred and two finished watercolours selected by the Committee were to be redeployed for pencil drawings and other works less likely to be injured by exposure to light.[108]

As a result, Ruskin continued to work for the Gallery, expanding his original group of one hundred sketches into a larger series representative of the whole of Turner's career. It is important to note, therefore, that despite his diligent work, and the publication of his notes, the first hundred watercolours were never exhibited to the public in exactly the form described in the catalogue. About three-quarters of them remained in the specially designed mahogany cabinets as part of a core group, which also included the finished watercolours for *The Rivers of France*, *The Rivers* and *Ports of England*, and the vignettes for Rogers's *Italy* and *Poems*.[109] But as E.T. Cook noted in 1905, many of Ruskin's first selection 'have from that day to this remained hidden in the tin boxes' in the National Gallery basement.[110]

Ruskin's later work on the Turner Bequest lies outside the scope of this essay. However, it was inevitably to be of great importance to his understanding of the artist, since it introduced him to vast areas of Turner's work with which he had not been familiar. In December 1857, he confessed to Norton that he had never seen 15,000 of the 19,000 studies he was then cataloguing, and early the next year he attempted to give some idea of the incredibly diverse material he had discovered (fig.16).[111] By May 1858, he had prepared several hundred sketches and watercolours for display at the National Gallery, a series that was revised and added to over the years. This was a more representative selection of works from all periods of Turner's career, redressing the imbalance towards the later watercolours of his 1857 catalogue (fig.17).[112]

For the public, who for many years had heard so much and seen so little of the collection, the eventual display of Turner's sketches must have come as a revelation. Samuel Palmer was one of many who waited in keen anticipation for the new Turner rooms to open.[113] It is also clear that Ruskin's work was appreciated by the young students who came to copy Turner's watercolours. A letter from an unnamed artist to his friend, dating from shortly after the sketches were first put on display, was quoted by E.T. Cook in support of Ruskin's endeavours:

> I wish you were near enough to go with me to see them. They are very interesting and profitable ... The leaves from his sketchbooks reveal to me how he lived, pencil in hand: every variation of coastline, every heave of the vessels he saw; every pulley, and block, and tackling; every utensil and costume; every fact of growth, time, place and size. To me this is wonderfully fascinating.[114]

As a final thought, it should again be stressed that if Ruskin ultimately won the fight to interpret Turner's works, a vital part in his victory was played by this first catalogue. It vividly demonstrated that there could be an intrinsic interest to the watercolour studies of a great artist such as Turner. In the light of his advocacy for Turner's sketches, Ruskin's opposition to the nocturnal impressions that Whistler exhibited at the Grosvenor Gallery in 1877 may at first appear inconsistent. However, an explanation lies in the fact that Ruskin always considered the sketches in the Turner Bequest to be essentially preliminary studies, which were of interest in as much as they showed what Turner might have done, rather than being exhibitable works in their own right. Although he prized them very highly himself, he believed their value was always secondary to conventionally 'finished' works. Yet what Ruskin was attempting to do in 1857 was part of a wider trend and one of a number of ways in which the traditional hierarchies of painting were gradually broken down as the century marched irresistibly towards an acceptance of the looser handling achieved by the Impressionists. Although Ruskin himself retained his independence from the institution, his work for the National Gallery, as embodied in the catalogue of 1857, can perhaps be seen as evidence of the academic tradition recognising and absorbing the romantic impulse of an earlier age.

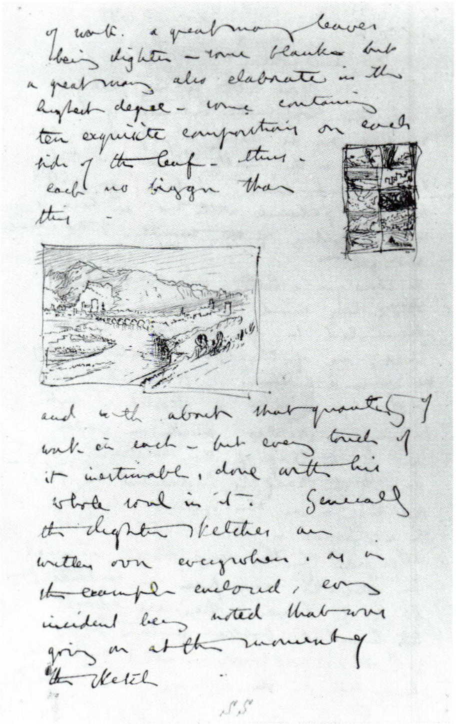
of work. a great many leaves being slighter – some blanks but a great many also elaborate in the highest degree – some containing ten exquisite compositions on each side of the leaf – thus – each no bigger than this –

and with about that quantity of work in each – but every touch of it inestimable, done with his whole soul in it. Generally the slighter sketches are written over everywhere, as in the example enclosed, every incident being noted that was going on at the moment of the sketch

fig.16 John Ruskin, letter to C.E. Norton, 28 February 1858. *By permission of the Houghton Library, Harvard University*

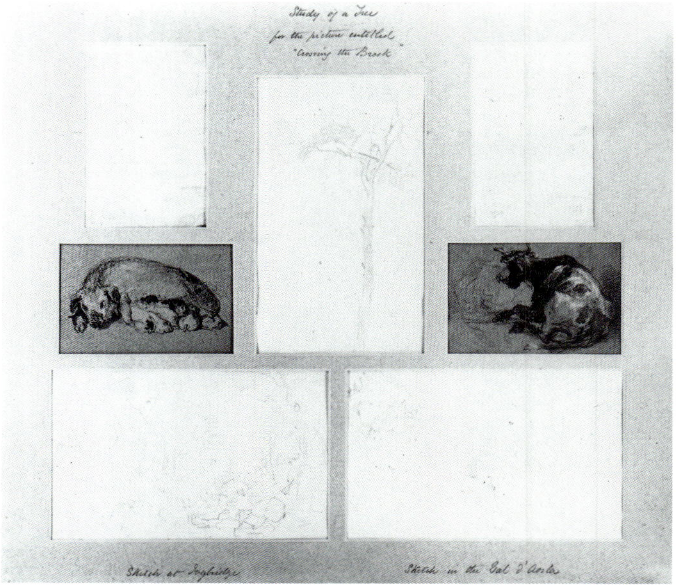

fig.17 Drawings from the Turner Bequest: Frame 16, in the *Catalogue of the Sketches and Drawings by J.M.W. Turner, R.A. Exhibited in Marlborough House in the Year 1857–8* (NG 407; see n.112)

Notes

(for abbreviated references, see Bibliography)

1 Bradley1955, p.112, letter to John James Ruskin (JJR) of 28 Dec. 1851.
2 Ibid.
3 Ibid., pp.112–13.
4 *Works*, xiii, pp.350–88.
5 Cook 1905, p.9.
6 After Turner's death, it was reported that he had said that Ruskin saw 'much more' in his pictures than he had himself intended. Although the accuracy of this story has been questioned, it perhaps suggests that Turner felt he could not wholly endorse Ruskin's view of him or his interpretation of his work (see *Works*, vi, pp.274–5, n.2).
7 See *Works*, xxxv, pp.28–9, 79, 216, 254.
8 Turner exhibited three paintings at the Royal Academy in 1836, but the focus of attention was 'Juliet and her Nurse' (B&J 365, private collection, Argentina). Ruskin later related the incident in *Praeterita*; see *Works*, xxxv, pp.217–8.
9 These were all subjects from the *Picturesque Views in England and Wales* series, were acquired in the following order: 'Richmond Hill and Bridge, Surrey' (w 833, British Museum), 'Gosport' (w 828, c/o Agnew's, London); 'Winchelsea' (w 821, British Museum), 'Harlech' (w 867, untraced) and 'Nottingham' (w 850, City Museum and Art Gallery, Nottingham). Although Luke Herrmann's catalogue of the Turner watercolours in the Ashmolean Museum established how Ruskin came to own that group of works, there is still a need for a thorough study of the history of Ruskin's entire collection of Turner sketches and drawings. The compulsion to acquire new examples of Turner's work was, after all, a central obsession in Ruskin's life, often to the extent that it obliterated his many other interests.
10 Gage 1980, p.177, no.234, letter to Thomas Griffith of 31 May 1840, and p.178, no.235, letter to Thomas Griffith of 4 June 1840.
11 E.T. Cook, *Life of John Ruskin*, 1911, i, p.108.
12 There is an interesting discrepancy between the account of the meeting preserved in Ruskin's Diary and that he later published in *Praeterita*, although the fuller account may have occured on some of the pages which haven since been removed from Ruskin's Diary. On 23 June 1840 he recorded 'Yesterday at Griffith's at dinner: J.M.W. Turner, Jones, Dr Fitton of the Geological, Augustus Liddell. All worked well together, Jones laughing at Cambridge and some others of the Royal Dukes, for passing over one of his largest pictures, because there was a Chalon on each side of it. They know no more of painting than so many infants. Turner talking with great rapture of Aosta and Courmayeur' (*Diaries*, i, pp.82–3). Much later, in *Praeterita*, written in the mid-1880s, Ruskin claimed he had recorded the meeting in his diary as follows: '"Introduced to-day to the man who beyond all doubt is the greatest of the age; greatest in every faculty of the imagination, in every branch of scenic knowledge; at once the painter and poet of the day, J.M.W. Turner. Everybody had described him to me as coarse, boorish, unintellectual, vulgar. This I knew to be impossible. I found in him a somewhat eccentric, keen-mannered, matter-of-fact, English-minded-gentleman; good-natured evidently, bad tempered evidently, hating humbug of all sorts, shrewd, perhaps a little selfish, highly intellectual, the powers of the mind not brought out with any delight in their manifestation, or intention of display, but flashing out occasionally in a word or a look". Pretty close, that, and full, to be seen at a first glimpse, and set down the same evening' (*Works*, xxxv, p.305). Parts of this account resemble the entry in Ruskin's Diary for 5 July 1841 (*Diaries*, i, p.209, quoted here p.12), which leads one to deduce that he may have conflated the two events and embellished them in his autobiography.
13 *Works*, i, pp.428–9, letter to Edward Clayton of 3 Dec. 1840.
14 Gage 1980, pp.178–9, no.236, letter to Turner from E.H.
15 During the three years since the exhibition *Turner's Rivers of Europe: The Rhine, Meuse, and Mosel* (1991), Dr Cecilia Powell has been continuing her research into Turner's tours through Germany. Her findings, which provide much new information about the later journeys Turner made across Europe, will be incorporated in the exhibition *Turner in Germany*; this will be shown first at the Tate Gallery in 1995, before travelling on to Mannheim and Hamburg.
16 Munro of Novar owned one of the largest collections of paintings and watercolours by Turner; it was gradually dispersed through a number of sales at Christie's (26 March 1860; 11 May 1867; 2 June 1877; 6 April 1878). According to Thornbury, he paid for Turner to travel to Venice (Thornbury 1877, p.105). John Gage provides a useful biographical outline (Gage 1980, pp.272–3), while new information about Turner's visit to Munro's home in Scotland has recently been published by David Wallace-Hadrill and Janet Carolan; 'Turner at Novar House, Evanton, 1831', *Turner Society News*, no.68, 1994, pp.14–15.
17 *Diaries*, i, pp.82–3, entry for 23 June 1840.
18 Gage 1980, pp.184–5 no.246, letter to William Miller of 22 Oct. 1841.
19 *Works*, iii, p.617; *Diaries*, i, p.209, entry for 5 July 1841.
20 Van Akin Burd 1973, ii, p.684.
21 *Works*, xiii, pp.475–85.
22 Whittingham1993, p.97; letter from Turner to Windus, 18 March 1842.
23 For further information about Windus and his extensive collection of Turner watercolours, see Gage1980, pp.299–300, and S. Whittingham, 'The Turner Collector: Benjamin Godfrey Windus 1790–1867', *Turner Studies*, vol.7, no.2, 1987, pp.29–35.
24 See w 877–80.
25 Whittingham 1993, pp.96–7; letter from Turner to Windus, 14 March 1842.
26 *Works*, xxxv, p.253.
27 The range of Bicknell's interests is set out in Gage 1980, p.240. See also the article by P. Bicknell and H. Guiterman, 'The Turner Collector: Elhanan Bicknell', *Turner Studies*, vol.7, no.1, 1987, pp.34–44.
28 Hunt 1982, p.2.
29 Hayman 1982, p.52, letter of 20 June 1858.
30 *Works*, xiii, p.146.
31 *Works*, xxxvi, pp.125–6 and Bradley 1955, p.129, letter of 9 Jan. 1852. In *Praeterita*, Ruskin later suggested that he immediately understood the purpose of the new sketches (*Works*, xxxv, p.310).
32 *Works*, xxxvi, p.23, letter to Henry Acland, 1 Sept. 1840.
33 Bradley and Ousby 1987, pp.313–14, letter of 11 April 1874.
34 *Works*, xxxv, p.298; see also *Diaries*, i, p.242, entries for 5 and 6 Feb. 1843.
35 *Diaries*, i, p.242, entry for 8 Feb. 1843 – 'the happiest birthday evening (save one) I ever spent in my life. Turner happy and kind'. Turner was also present at Ruskin's birthday parties in 1847 and 1848.
36 *Diaries*, i, p.245, entry for 24 Feb. 1843.
37 Ibid., i, p.247, entry for 15 May 1843.
38 Transcribed in a letter to Ruskin (JR) from John James Ruskin (JJR), dated 4 Jan. 1850, Bembridge.
39 Gage 1980, pp.192–3, no.261, letter of 23 Nov. 1843 to an unknown correspondent.
40 Wilton 1987, pp.226–7.
41 *Diaries*, i, pp.273–4, entry for 29 April 1844; *Works*, iii, p.251.
42 Gage 1980, pp.202–3 no.275, letter to F.H. Fawkes of 28 Dec. 1844.
43 TB CCCXLVIII f.17 verso.
44 Whittingham 1993, p.103, letter from Ruskin to Windus of 21 Oct. 1844.
45 Shapiro 1972, p.164.
46 *Works*, vi, p.36.
47 Richard and Samuel Redgrave, *A Century of Painters of the English School*, 1866, ii, p.86.
48 Shapiro 1972, p.133, letter from JR to JJR, 29 June 1845.
49 See Shapiro 1972, p.230, letter from JR to JJR, 23 Oct. 1845. The cause of the temporary rift between Turner and Ruskin is the subject of speculation by a number of scholars: Gage 1980, p.281; Whittingham 1993, p.104; and Hilton 1985, pp.101–2.
50 *Works*, viii.
51 *Works*, ix–xi.
52 Bembridge MS, letter from JJR to JR, 30/31 Dec. 1851.
53 Bradley 1955, p.111, letter from JR to JJR, 28 Dec. 1851.
54 *Works*, i, pp.428–9, letter from Ruskin to Edward Clayton, 3 Dec. 1840.
55 Bradley 1955, p.111, letter from JR to JJR, 28 Dec. 1851. One of the watercolours was a view of Farnley Hall (?w 613, Rijksmuseum, Amsterdam).
56 Bembridge MS, letter from JJR to JR, 21 Dec. 1851.
57 Fawkes 1900, p.617, letter of 8 Feb. 1852.
58 *Works*, xxxvi, p.244, letter from JR to Lady Trevelyan, 26 Sept. 1856.

59 Bradley 1955, pp.124, letter from JR to JJR, 5 Jan. 1852.
60 Ibid., p.199, letter from JR to JJR, 26 Feb. 1852.
61 Ibid., pp.202–5, letter from JR to JJR, 28 Feb. 1852.
62 *Works*, XIII, pp.1–76.
63 *Works*, XXXVI, p.244, letter from JR to Lady Trevelyan, 26 Sept. 1856.
64 Bradley 1955, p.120, letter from JR to JJR, 1 Jan. 1852.
65 *Works*, XXXVI, p.245, letter from JR to Lady Trevelyan, 26 Sept. 1856.
66 The *Times*, Friday 24 October 1856, p.8. Wornum's reply appeared the following day, p.6.
67 Quoted in Robertson 1978, p.383.
68 The *Times*, Tuesday 28 October 1856, p.10; reprinted in *Works*, XIII, pp.81–5. Ruskin had previously aired his views in the *Times* with regard to the conservation of paintings in the National Gallery collection (7 Jan. 1847, p.5).
69 Long after he had won his fight to be allowed to catalogue the Turner sketches, Ruskin remained defiant that he was the only person able to complete the task. Some idea of his self-confidence can be gained from the 'First Draft of a Catalogue of Drawings Recommended for Oxford, 31 July 1878', in which he wrote of the *Small Roman C. Studies* sketchbook (TB CXC), 'I can make sense of it all and nobody else can' (National Gallery Archives).
70 *Works*, XIII, p.82.
71 *Works*, XIII, p.83.
72 *Works*, XIII, p.84.
73 *Works*, XIII, pp.83–4.
74 Thornbury 1862, I, p.X.
75 The *Times*, Thursday 30 Oct. 1856, p.4.
76 National Gallery Archives: NG5/130/1856 – letter from Russell to Eastlake, 7 Nov. 1856.
77 The *Times*, Thursday 13 Nov. 1856, p.7.
78 See the essays by Scott Wilcox in *Victorian Landscape Watercolors*, exh. cat., New Haven 1992, p.23 and pp.43–4; and A. Griffiths and R. Williams, *The Department of Prints and Drawings in the British Museum: User's Guide*, 1987, pp.14–15.
79 Report of a Meeting of the Trustees of the National Gallery, 17 Nov. 1856, p.60.
80 National Gallery Archives; NG 6 1 – Letters from the Gallery 1851–61, letter from Wornum to JR, 4 Dec. 1856.
81 National Gallery Archives; NG5/131/1856, letter from JR to Wornum, 8 Dec. 1856.
82 A. Wilton, 'Turner and the Iconography of Landscape', a transcript of the Ninth Kurt Pantzer Memorial Lecture, *Turner Society News*, no.49, Aug. 1988, pp.5–10.
83 National Gallery Archives; NG 6 1 – Letters from the Gallery 1851–61, letter from Wornum to JR, 16 Dec. 1856.
84 *Works*, XIII, pp.85–6, n.2, letter from Ruskin to Lord Palmerston, 13 Dec. 1856.
85 *Works*, XXXVI, p.255, letter from Ruskin to Charles Eliot Norton, 11 Jan. 1857.
86 This is revealed in the following documents in the National Gallery Archives; NG5/131/1856, letter dated 18 Dec. 1856, and in the Minutes of a Meeting of the Trustees, 19 Jan. 1857.
87 National Gallery Archives; NG 6 1 – Letters from the Gallery 1851–61, letter from Wornum to Sir Richard Mayre, 7 Feb. 1857.
88 The *Times*, Tuesday 2 Dec. 1856, p.4.
89 *Works*, XIII, pp.89–181.
90 *Works*, XXXVI, p.255.
91 National Gallery Archives; NG5/216/1857, letter from JR to Wornum, 16 Jan. 1857.
92 Hilton 1985, p.243.
93 N. Hawthorne, *The English Notebooks*, ed. R. Stewart, 1941, p.614.
94 V. Surtees (ed.), *Sublime and Instructive: Letters from John Ruskin to Louisa Machioness of Waterford, Anna Blunden and Ellen Heaton*, 1972, p.202, letter from Ruskin to Ellen Heaton, 24 Jan. 1857.
95 National Gallery Archives; NG5/216/1857, letter from JR to Wornum, 2 Feb. 1857.
96 National Gallery Archives; NG5/216/1857, letter from Eastlake to Russell, 2 Feb. 1857.
97 National Gallery Archives; NG 6 1 – Letters from the Gallery 1851–61, letter from Wornum to JR, 10 Feb. 1857. This contradicts the view that Ruskin did actually pay for the cabinets himself, as suggested by Cook and Wedderburn (*Works*, XIII, p.xxxiv).
98 Bembridge MS, *Diaries*, X, opp. p.65.
99 *Diaries*, II, p.527, entry for 16 Jan. 1857.
100 National Gallery Archives; NG5/220/1857 and NG/5/134/1857. A much fuller analysis of the designs of the cabinets used by Ruskin can be found in Pia Haertinger's dissertation, 'John Ruskin und das Museum: Porträt eines Pioniers und einer Museumsepoche', Augsburg 1994.
101 Ibid.
102 *Report of the Director of the National Gallery*, 1857, pp.38–9.
103 *Works*, XXXVI, pp.261–2, letter from JR to C.E. Norton, May 1857.
104 Ibid.
105 National Gallery Archives; NG5/226/1857, letter from Ruskin to Wornum, 30 May 1857. In Dec. 1856 the Trustees had declined Thomas Fairburn's request to borrow fifty watercolours from the Turner Bequest for the Manchester exhibition (Report of a Meeting of the Trustees of the National Gallery, 15 Dec. 1856).
106 *Notes by Mr Ruskin on Samuel Prout and William Hunt*, catalogue of the exhibition at the Fine Art Society, 1879–80 (*Works*, XIV, pp.367–454). Elizabeth Helsinger has identified Horace-Bénédict de Saussure's *Voyages dans les Alpes* as the model for Ruskin's travel narratives (E.K. Helsinger, *Ruskin and the Art of the Beholder*, Harvard 1982, p.148).
107 Hilton 1985, p.243.
108 National Gallery Archives; NG5/230/1857, letter from C.L. Eastlake to the Trustees of the National Gallery, 22 June 1857.
109 *Works*, XIII, pp.319–21 and pp.609–22.
110 Cook 1905, p.8.
111 Bradley and Ousby 1987, p.42, letter from Ruskin to Norton, 28 Feb. 1858. The watercolour copied by Ruskin in his letter was not actually one of the Turner Bequest works; it is the view of Huy on the Meuse (W 1024, Fitzwilliam Museum, Cambridge), which he had only recently acquired.
112 This illustration shows how Ruskin would sometimes juxtapose different types of sketches within the same frame. This group of seven subjects was placed as Frame 16 in the *Catalogue of the Sketches and Drawings by J.M.W. Turner, R.A. exhibited in Marlborough House in the Year 1857–8* (*Works*, XIII, pp.257, 276–8). The sketches are as follows (clockwise, from top right): Six sketches on the Mosel near Burgen and Burg Bischofstein (from the *Rivers Meuse and Moselle* sketchbook, TB CCXVI f.126); Study of a cow lying down (from the *Wilson* sketchbook, TB XXXVII f.128); Fort Bard, in the Val d'Aosta (from the *Val d'Aosta* sketchbook, TB CCXCIII f.92); Ivy Bridge, Devon (from the *Devon Rivers, No.2* sketchbook, TB CXXXIII f.45); A sow feeding her piglets (from the *Studies near Brighton* sketchbook, TB XXX f.94); Seven sketches of the Meuse at and near Samson (from the *Rivers Meuse and Moselle* sketchbook, TB CCXVI f.259); Study of a Tree for 'Crossing the Brook' (from the *Devon Rivers, No.2* sketchbook, TB CXXXIII f.37).
113 R. Lister (ed.), *The Letters of Samuel Palmer*, 1974, I, p.556, letter from Palmer to his wife, ?June 1859.
114 Cook 1905, p.6.

Catalogue

Explanations

The text of the following catalogue is based on that in the Library Edition of *The Works of John Ruskin* (*Works*, XIII, pp.183–226). Many of the notes and corrections, which are there appended to the commentaries on each watercolour, have been absorbed into this publication.

At the top of each entry is Ruskin's title. This is followed by more recent topographical identifications, the likely date at which the work was executed, together with measurements and other factual information, as well as the Tate Gallery accession number.

Measurements are given in millimetres, followed by inches in brackets; height before width. All items included in the catalogue are on white wove paper, unless otherwise specified. Any watermarks or inscriptions have been transcribed where legible.

Ruskin's text appears in italics, with annotations in square brackets. It should be noted that Ruskin uses the term 'drawing' only to refer to a completed watercolour. All the works catalogued here are what he would have considered preliminary 'sketches'.

Abbreviations

For the sake of brevity, the following abbreviations have been used:

Bembridge	This indicates that the work referred to can currently be found in the collection of the Education Trust Ltd at the Ruskin Galleries, Bembridge School, Isle of Wight
B&J	Martin Butlin and Evelyn Joll, *The Paintings of J.M.W. Turner*, revised edition, 2 vols., 1984
D	This is the Tate Gallery accession number for works on paper in the Turner Bequest. The letter is followed by a five digit number (e.g. 'D36139')
Diaries	Joan Evans and John Howard Whitehouse, *The Diaries of John Ruskin*, 3 vols., 1956, 1958, 1959
TB	A.J. Finberg, *A Complete Inventory of the Drawings of the Turner Bequest*, 2 vols., 1909
R	W.G. Rawlinson, *The Engraved Work of J.M.W. Turner, R.A.*, 2 vols., 1908 and 1913
R on P	E.T. Cook, *Ruskin on Pictures: A Collection of Criticisms by John Ruskin not heretofore Re-printed and now Re-edited and Re-arranged. Vol.1, Turner at the National Gallery and in Mr Ruskin's Collection*, 1902
W	Andrew Wilton, *The Life and Work of J.M.W. Turner* [with a catalogue of watercolours outside the Turner Bequest], 1979
Works	*The Works of John Ruskin*, ed. E.T. Cook and Alexander Wedderburn, 39 vols., 1903–12

The entries now also make reference to exhibitions in which the watercolours have featured since the static arrangement of the Bequest at the National Gallery (i.e. 'NG') came to an end at the beginning of this century. Full details of these shows and temporary displays, together with a short bibliography, will be found at the end of the catalogue (pp.156–9). Where reference is made to an exhibition shown at more than one venue, only the first institution is named.

Ruskin's Preface to his *Catalogue of the Turner Sketches in the National Gallery*

PREFATORY

The principal object I have had in view in the arrangement of these sketches has been to exemplify a method by which the collections of drawings existing in European galleries might be rendered completely serviceable to the public, without compromising their safety. As matters stand at present, the studies by the great masters, which exist in the museums of Florence, Paris, and London, cannot be seen by the public, either with ease to themselves or with security to the drawings. If the curators rightly estimate the value of the works intrusted to them, they avoid, as far as possible, bringing out the best, except to specially worthy and favoured visitors; to the young student and the general public such drawings are, and ought to be, on the present system inaccessible, since they must not be exposed to the handling of the ignorant or inadvertent. Not only so, but both in Paris and Florence it frequently happens that the first-class drawings cannot be seen at all, owing to the absence of the curators or other accidental hindrances; and those which may be seen cannot be studied at leisure, bound as they are in volumes which must continually be required by other visitors, or, if separately mounted, exposed to dust and accidental injury all the while they are being examined. In the Louvre, it is true that a certain number – a very small proportion of the whole collection – are placed on tables under glass; but in such circumstances the light is only good or sufficient for the one or two that happen to be near the windows; the rest are seen imperfectly and with difficulty, and some of their most delicate execution is lost sight of altogether.

I believe the method in which the first hundred of the Turner sketches are now arranged will be found to do away with all these inconveniences. The visitor has five or ten drawings at once put at his disposal, which he can take one by one in his hand into the best light and place as he chooses, and which he can copy or describe at his ease, without interfering with any one else's examination of other portions of the series, and with no fear of injury to the drawing, protected as it is completely from dust, and from all accident except that of a heavy fall, which might indeed break the glass or strain the frame, but could not injure the sketch, which does not touch the glass anywhere. And while there are these advantages in this method considered with reference only to the safe exhibition of drawings in general, there is a farther one in it considered as a means of preserving those of Turner. It is a fact, already well known to the curators of museums, that works in water-colour lose vigour and value if they are exposed to light; and Turner's are, of all drawings, those in which such loss must be at once most extensive and fatal, owing to the excessive thinness and tenderness of the tints on which their chief effects depend. There is of course no objection to a drawing being placed in a strong light (not, of course, the direct rays of the sun) while it is actually under examination; but it is quite unnecessary that it should continually be exposed to the glow of summer heat while no one is looking at it; and I am perfectly certain that the precious vignettes to the Italy and the drawings for the Rivers of France and Rivers of England, now exhibiting in Marlborough House [see Appendix I, p.148], *will suffer seriously even from their exposure during the present year.*

It would be quite easy to arrange a most precious and interesting series of sketches for the general public, consisting chiefly of pencil and chalk drawings, which would not suffer from the light, together with a certain number of the less important water-colour drawings, while the more valuable works in colour might be arranged with perfect safety in this manner, and seen on proper application, as the prints are at the British Museum.

The series of sketches which I have chosen to illustrate the possible arrangement are precisely those which presented the greatest difficulties; for they are among the largest and the brightest in colour, requiring therefore a broad white margin to give them sufficient relief. This necessitates a stronger and heavier frame than will usually be required; in general, frames about two-thirds of this size will be quite large enough, and the cases will therefore be far less cumbrous and more conveniently portable.

The sketches themselves require some slight explanation of their character, before their value will be completely felt. They are not, strictly speaking, sketches from nature, but plans or designs of the pictures which Turner, if he had had time, would have made of each place. They indicate, therefore, a perfectly formed conception of the finished picture; and they are of exactly the same value as memoranda would be, if made by Turner's own hand, of pictures of his not in our possession. They are just to be regarded as quick descriptions or reminiscences of noble pictures; every touch in them represents something complete and definite; and, for the most part, as much is done with the given number of touches and quantity of colour as is possible to be done by human hand. They are all of the period in which Turner's work is full of the most characteristic excellencies, and they are all interesting in subject, being of well-known and beautiful scenes. I look upon them as in some respects more valuable than his finished drawings, or his oil pictures; because they are the simple records of his first impressions and first purposes, and in most instances as true to the character of the places they represent as they are admirable in composition; while in his elaborate drawings and paintings, he too frequently suffered his mind to be warped from its first impression by attempts at idealism.

I believe, however, that nothing but the pencilling in them was done on the spot, and not always that. Turner used to walk about a town with a roll of thin paper in his pocket, and make a few scratches upon a sheet or two of it, which were so much shorthand indication of all he wished to remember. When he got to his inn in the evening, he completed the pencilling rapidly, and added as much colour as was needed to record his plan of the picture.

These rolled sheets of paper (some of them actually the covers of the cheap stitched sketch-books) were always, necessarily, warped and bent by the colouring, But Turner did not in the least care for this, and I think, therefore, that we should not. They are, as I have mounted them, flatter than he ever cared to see them, and they are perfectly safe; while any process of mounting which at once secures flatness, necessitates some degree of injury to the colour. I may be able to get them to lie much flatter, but my present object is only to get them securely protected, and allow them to be quickly visible.

I have arranged these hundred so as to form a connected series, illustrative of a supposed tour up the Rhine, and through Switzerland, to Venice and back. The suggestions offered in the text, of the probable circumstances under which Turner might have made the drawings, give the reader a just idea of the painter's general manner of setting about his work, though the conjecture may of course be wrong or right, with respect to any given sketch.

John Ruskin, 1857

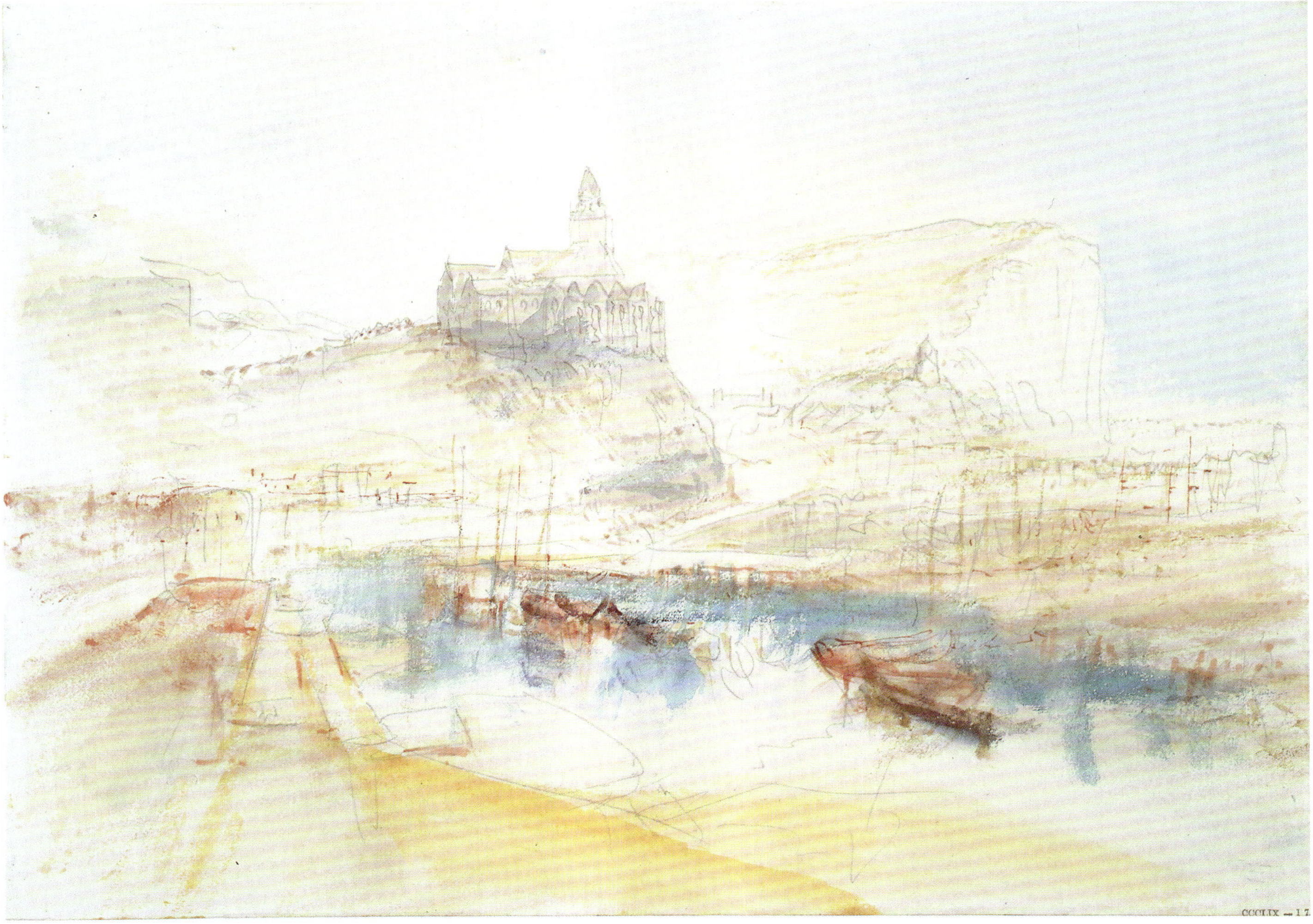

1 Tréport

Le Tréport, with the Church of St-Jacques 1845
Pencil and watercolour, with pen 231 × 330 (9⅛ × 13)
TB CCCLIX 17 D35452
EXH: NG (276); Paris 1981–2 (176, repr., p.546, in col.); Tate Gallery 1987 (21); Tate Gallery 1993 (48)
LIT: *Works*, XIII, pp.191, 623; *R on P*, pp.158–9

We land on the pier of Tréport, and are delighted by the pretty irregularity of the old church, with its gabled chapels, which we draw on the spot, with one bold zigzag touch for their roofs, and a wriggle for every window. Yet it will not be easy for any one coming after us to give a better idea of the standing of the grey walls on their sea-worn mound, and of the bright chalk cliff beyond them. This cliff is a masterpiece of drawing; it is not possible with the given number of touches to indicate more faithfully the form of a chalk precipice, or the way it breaks into the turf at its brow. The whole sketch is hasty, but very beautiful.

The economic presentation of only the essential elements in this view of the port belies the fact that Turner had made a number of pencil drawings of its principal features, such as the church of St-Jacques, in his *Dieppe and Kent* sketchbook (TB CCCLXI ff.55, 75). A drawing by one of the artists in Ruskin's circle, most probably Arthur Severn (1842–1931), depicts Le Tréport from a similar angle to this watercolour (Bembridge 1212).

2 Tréport

A Distant View of Le Tréport, from the East 1845
Pencil and watercolour, with pen 231 × 330 (9⅛ × 13)
TB CCCLIX 12 D35447
EXH: NG (Box Z); New York 1966 (97, as 'Eu, with Louis Philippe's Chateau, 1845'); Paris 1983–4 (254, repr. p.304); Tate Gallery 1987 (20, repr. p.15, fig.3)
LIT: *Works*, XIII, p.191; *R on P*, p.159 n.1; Cook 1905, pp.8–9, repr. p.53; Butlin 1968, pl.23

We set out for a walk about the town, retaining, however, our first interest in the chapel and cliff; and being disturbed by the military (a couple of lancers), we put them in revengefully in red outlines.

Turner's visit to Eu coincided with that of Queen Victoria and Prince Albert, so it could be that the soldiers in the foreground here and in other watercolours of Eu and Le Tréport are English troops. However, the style of the bearskin helmets suggests that these are French officers from Louis-Philippe's force.

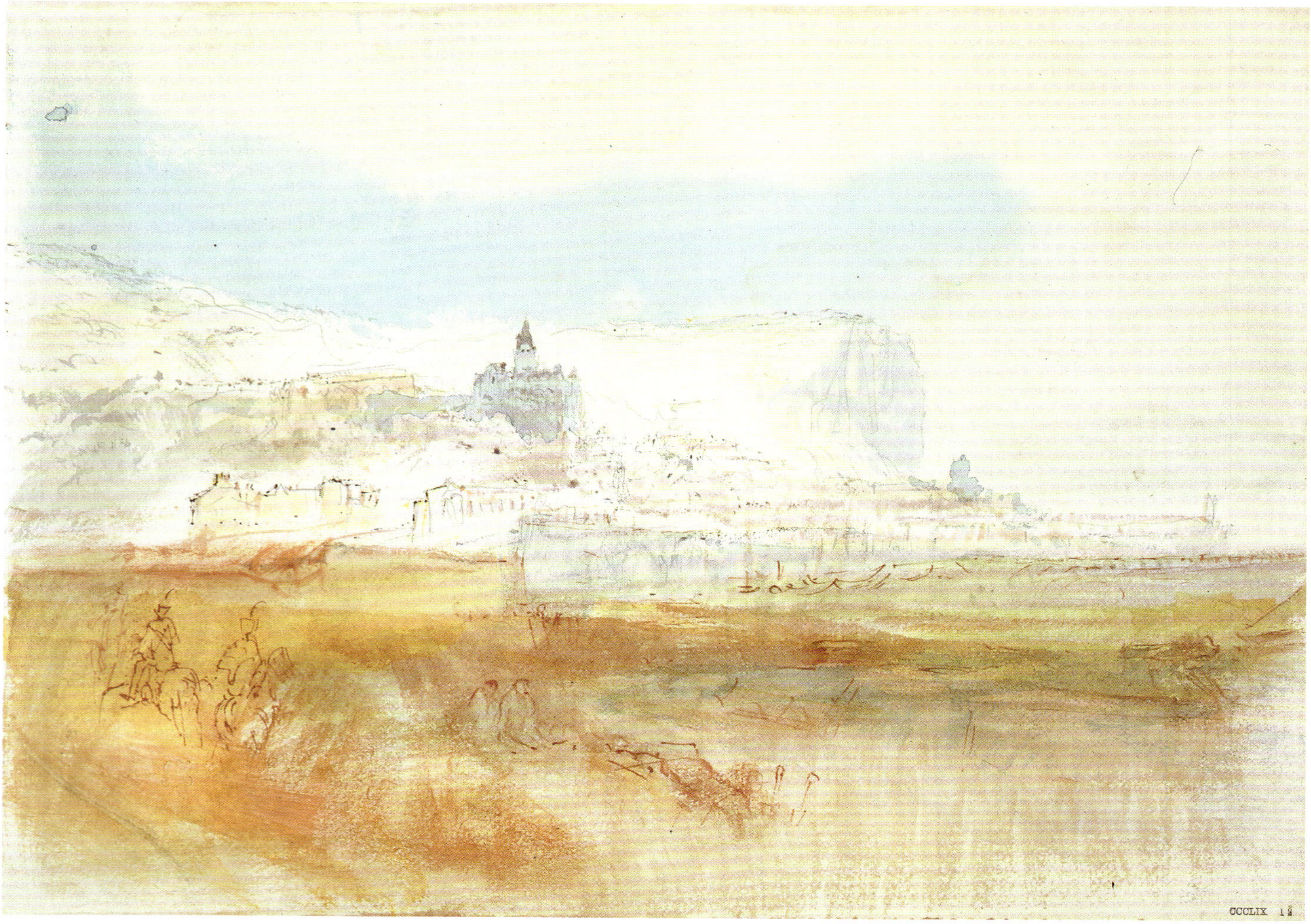

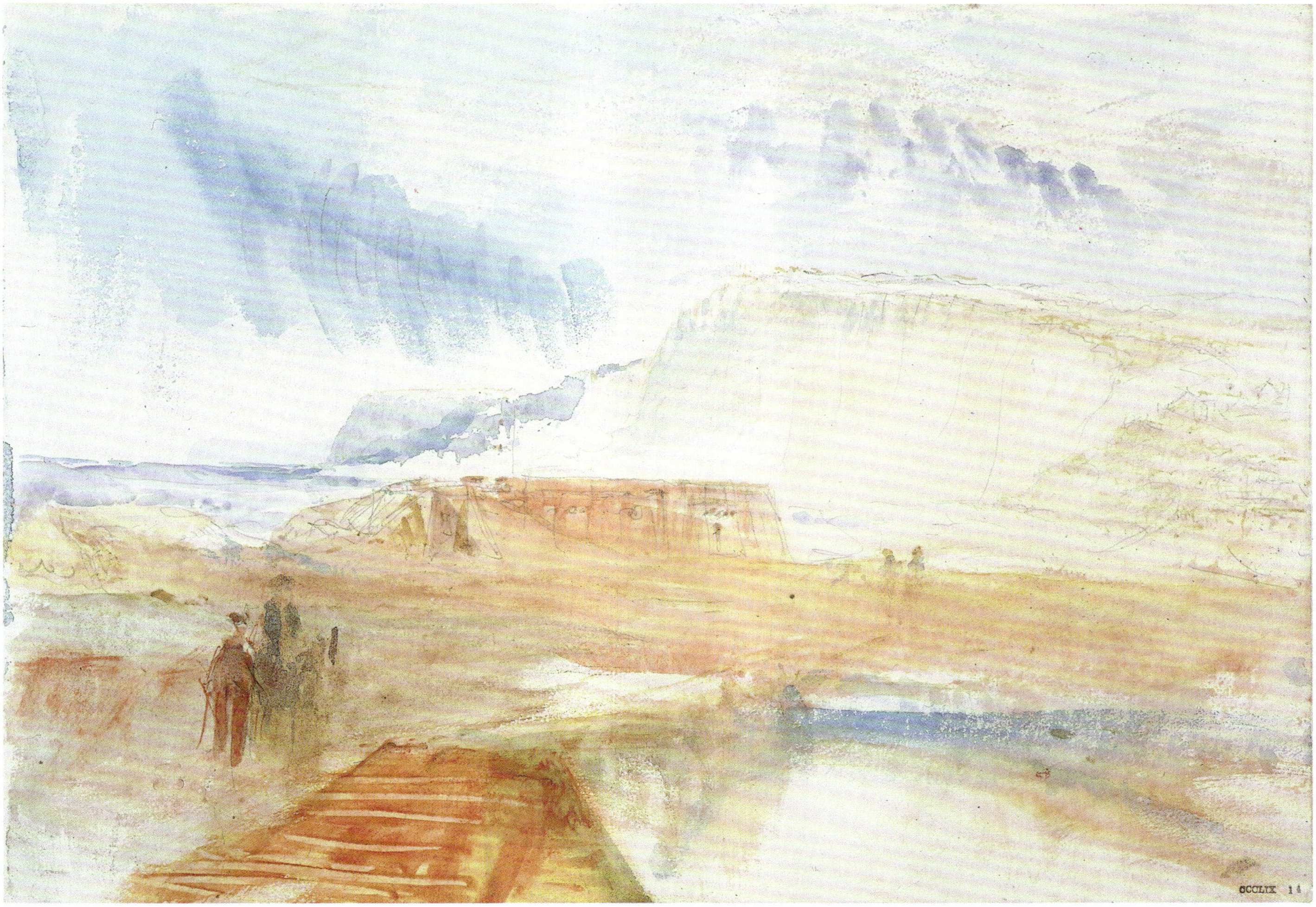

3 Tréport

The Cliffs at Mers-les-Bains, from Le Tréport 1845
Pencil and watercolour 231 × 327 (9⅛ × 12⅞)
TB CCCLIX 14 D35449
EXH: Oxford 1878 (249-19); Tokyo 1963–4 (49); New York 1966 (98); British Museum 1975–6 (300); Sofia 1978 (90); Athens 1981 (66); Tate Gallery 1983; Melbourne 1985; Tate Gallery 1992–3 (102, repr. p.80, fig.102)
LIT: *Works*, XIII, pp.191–2, 561; *R on P*, p.159 n.1; Wilton 1982, p.75, pl.128

We wander still farther from the town, and see old piers and fortifications under amazing effects. The military are still interested in our motions. The officer having held his sword in an unsatisfactory manner towards his legs, is obliged to change its position, and appears now to be carrying two.

Very hasty; but grand in arrangement of colour and interesting in execution. Note the vermilion in the pier in the foreground laid in very wet and the white lines scraped out with the wooden end of the brush towards the left, carrying the vermilion out at that side.

The object in the middle distance is a fortification with two gates of entrance, and a flagstaff, and the sweeping pencil lines to the right of the flagstaff mean, I believe, that the smoke of a gun was to be there if ever the picture were finished.

Mers-les-Bains is on the opposite side of the mouth of the River Bresle from Le Tréport. There are no records of there having been any fortifications on the quayside during the 1840s, unless they were of a temporary nature, erected at the time of Queen Victoria's visit. The structure Ruskin refers to seems to be one of the larger walls of the harbour.

4 Eu

Eu, from the South-east 1845
Pencil and watercolour, with pen
232 × 327 (9⅛ × 12⅞)
TB CCCLIX 13 D35448
EXH: NG (Box Z); Newcastle 1924 (151); Royal Academy 1974–5 (628); Paris 1981–2 (180, repr. p.552 in col.)
LIT: *Works*, XIII, p.192; R. and S. Redgrave, *A Century of Painters of the English School*, 1866, II, pp.86–7; *R on P*, p.159 n.1; Cook 1905, pp.8–9, repr. p.50; Finberg 1961, pp.410–11; Butlin 1962, pp.82–3, pl.32

Getting tired of the beach, we walk up the country, and obtain a general view of the town of Eu.

The part of the blue touch in the distance, on the left, with a spike to it, means our old friends, the hills and church of Tréport; the darker and level blue means the sea under a fresh breeze. The whole looks quite instantaneously done; but it is not; the dark crumbling touch was laid first, then water was put to it, and it was gradated into the church: lastly, a wet horizontal touch of blue has been added below, to give it more breadth.

The general character of the French cathedral churches, rising out of the towns like a broken but massive group of steep basalt rock, with small pinnacles above, is quite wonderfully seized in this sketch.

The five pink, square-topped cones under the blue sea are the roofs of Louis Philippe's palace.

Having got rid of the military, we are now annoyed by cows, and horses of diligences pulling uphill; which, nevertheless, we mean to make something of, some day.

The majority of Turner's views of Eu are taken from the lofty hill to the north-east (see TB CCCLIX 4, 6, 15). This eminence is crossed by the road from Abbeville and provides a wide panorama across the Bresle valley, with the town at its centre. Turner clearly walked all round the town, exploring the possible configurations of its buildings. The third building to feature prominently in the

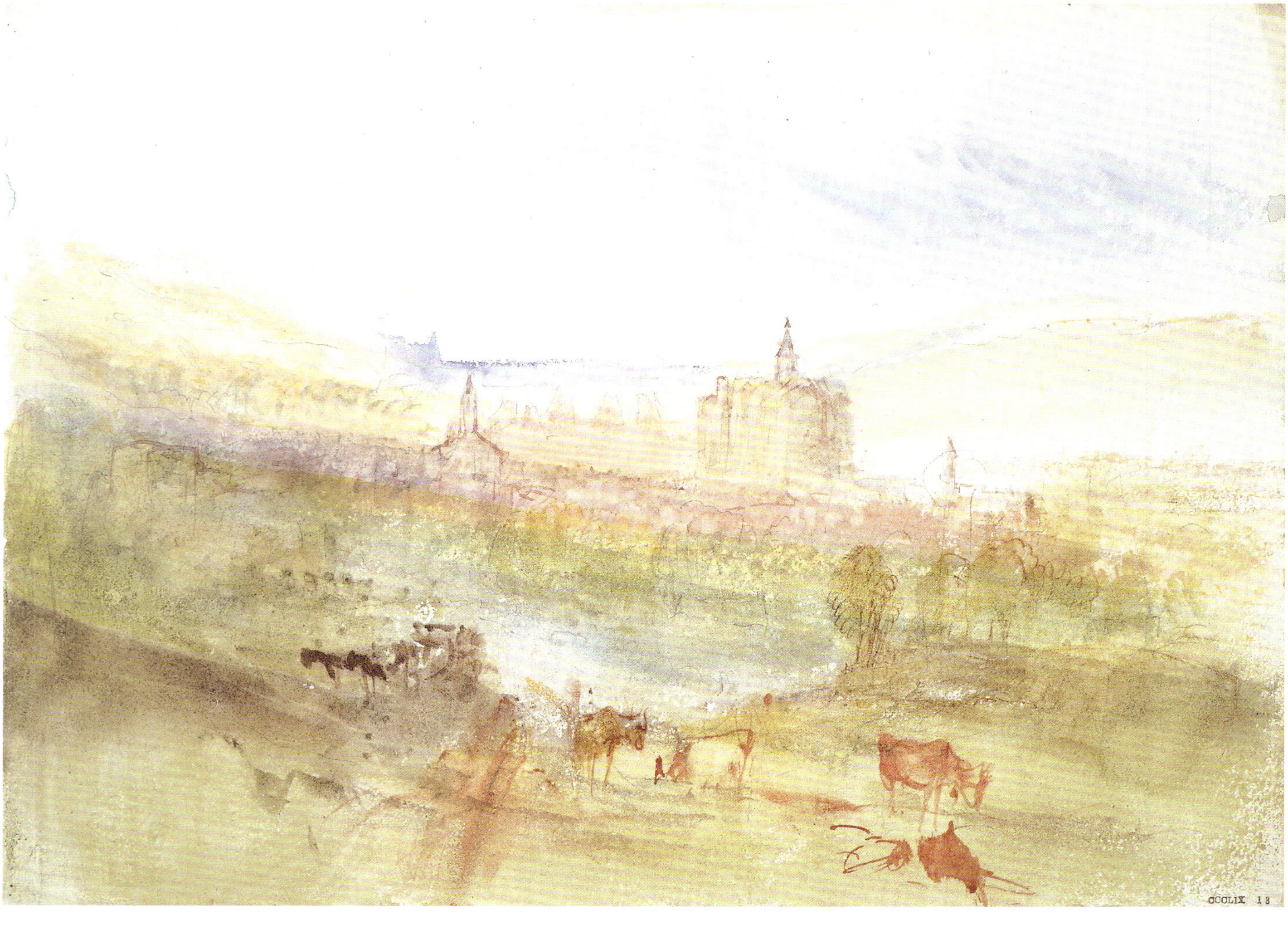

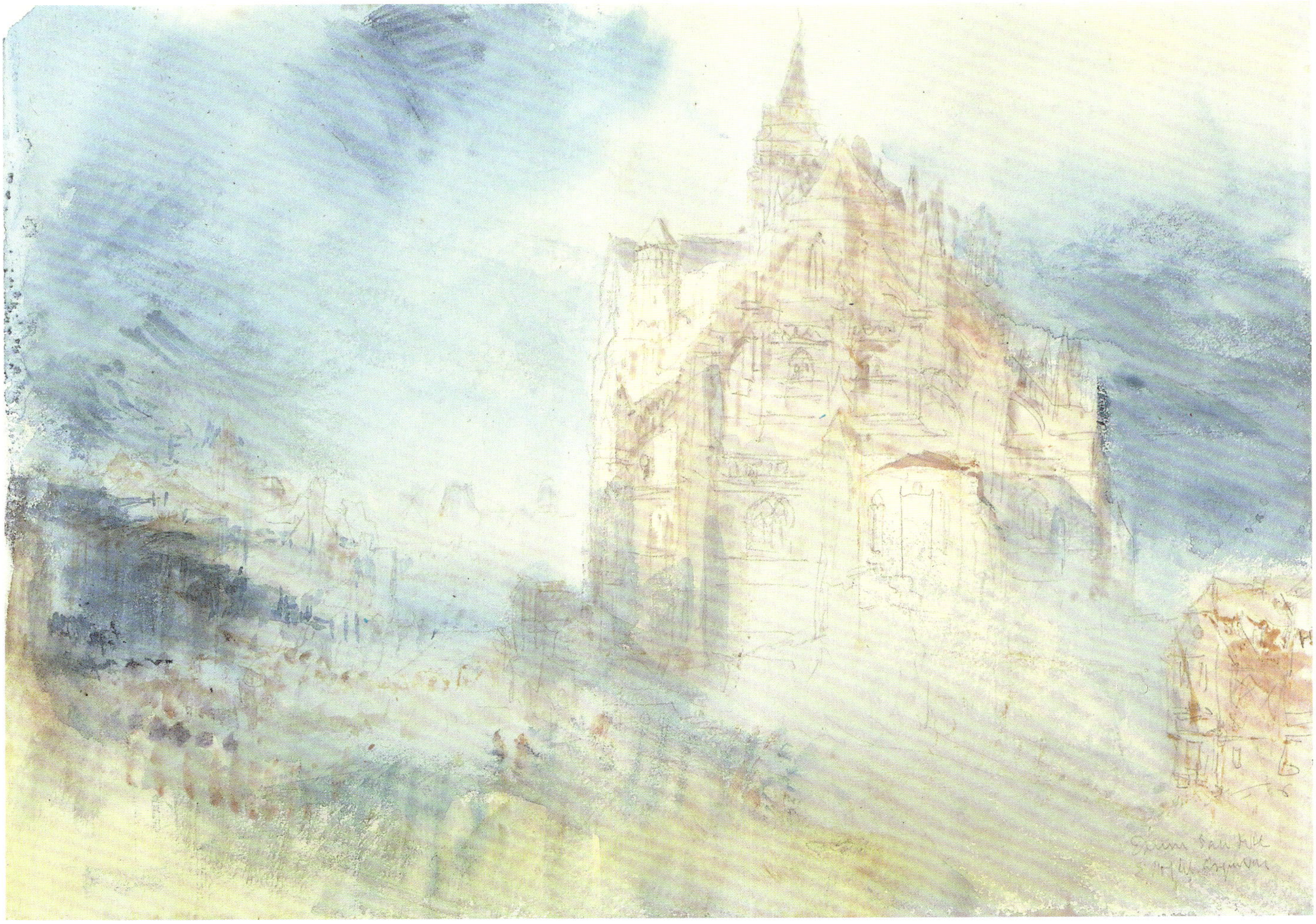

5

views of Eu (seen here to the left of the collegiate church of Notre-Dame and St-Laurent and the Château) is the seventeenth-century chapel of the Jesuit college, built by Catherine of Clèves. Another, more distant view, from the south-east was also in the sketchbook from which this leaf was taken (TB CCCLIX 2).

5 Church of Eu

Eu: The Church of Notre-Dame and St-Laurent, with the Château of Louis-Philippe beyond 1845
Pencil and watercolour 232 × 328 (9⅛ × 12¹⁵⁄₁₆)
Inscribed, bottom right: 'E[...] pine saw mill' | '[?EP of W Arqueville]'
Verso: Pencil sketch of ?the Chateau at Eu. Inscribed: [?'Sindai'] and [?'Eu']
TB CCCLIX 16 D35451
EXH: NG (277); British Museum 1933a; National Gallery 1936–9; Washington 1963–4 (78, repr.); Prague 1969 (142); Brussels 1970–1 (86); Munich 1972–3 (156, repr. colour, p.127); Royal Academy 1974–5 (629); Copenhagen 1976 (88); Hamburg 1976 (133, repr. p.166); Tate Gallery 1988 (50); Royal Academy 1993 (306, pl.266)
LIT: *Works*, XIII, pp.192–3 and p.623; *R on P*, pp.159–60; Wilton 1982, p.75, pl.127

We continue our walk till it is late, and, returning to town, see the church by moonlight, in the sea fog.

The apse of Eu is one of the most interesting in France in its bold pyramidical structure, being surrounded by a double range of chapels, with corresponding pinnacles and double flying buttresses. I am puzzled by the appearance as of a vineyard or hop-garden in the street below; and cannot venture positively to state, though I am decidedly under the conviction, that this remarkable appearance is presented by the good people of Eu going to evening service.

The collegiate church at Eu was begun in the twelfth century and completed in 1240. Turner had first noted the impressive building while travelling from Abbeville to Dieppe in 1824 (TB CCXVI f.203). Among the pencil drawings of his 1845 visit, there are a number of studies of both the external and internal features of the building

(TB CCCLXI ff.21 verso, 34 verso and 35 recto, 47 verso, 54 verso and 58 verso; see also TB CCCLIX 7, 10 for freely painted internal views). Another watercolour, probably once also in this sketchbook, depicts a nearer view of the château, with the mass of the church towering above to the right (TB CCCXXXIV 16). Ruskin had visited Eu, and what he called the 'pet church of Louis Philippe', the year before Turner made his visit. He was, however, disappointed by 'some modern glass, of the worst kind' (*Works*, XII, p.435). He later returned there with his young bride, Effie, on their honeymoon journey in 1848 (see Links 1968, pp.20–2).

6 Coblentz

A Steamer and Passengers at a Pier: ?Ehrenbreitstein from Coblentz *c*.1841
Watercolour and gouache, with pen
243 × 343 (9⁹⁄₁₆ × 13½)
Watermarked: J WHATMAN | TURKEY MILL | 18[?21]
TB CCCLXIV 284 D36137
EXH: NG (278); British Museum 1937–8 (frame 5); Washington 1963–4 (70, repr.); Prague 1969 (141); Tokyo 1970–1 (98); Munich 1972–3 (152, repr. p.129); Cologne 1980 (58, repr. p.109); Tate Gallery 1989 (48, repr. p.49); Tate Gallery 1990
LIT: *Works*, XIII, pp.193, 623; *R on P*, p.160

We have taken the railroad across to Cologne, and the steamer to Coblentz. We are landed here just opposite Ehrenbreitstein, and are anxious about our luggage.

I have framed this sketch chiefly for the sake of its curious composition; the boat with the large sails, behind the chimney of the steamer, giving massiveness to the group; – next, as an instance of the delight which Turner used to take in smoke of

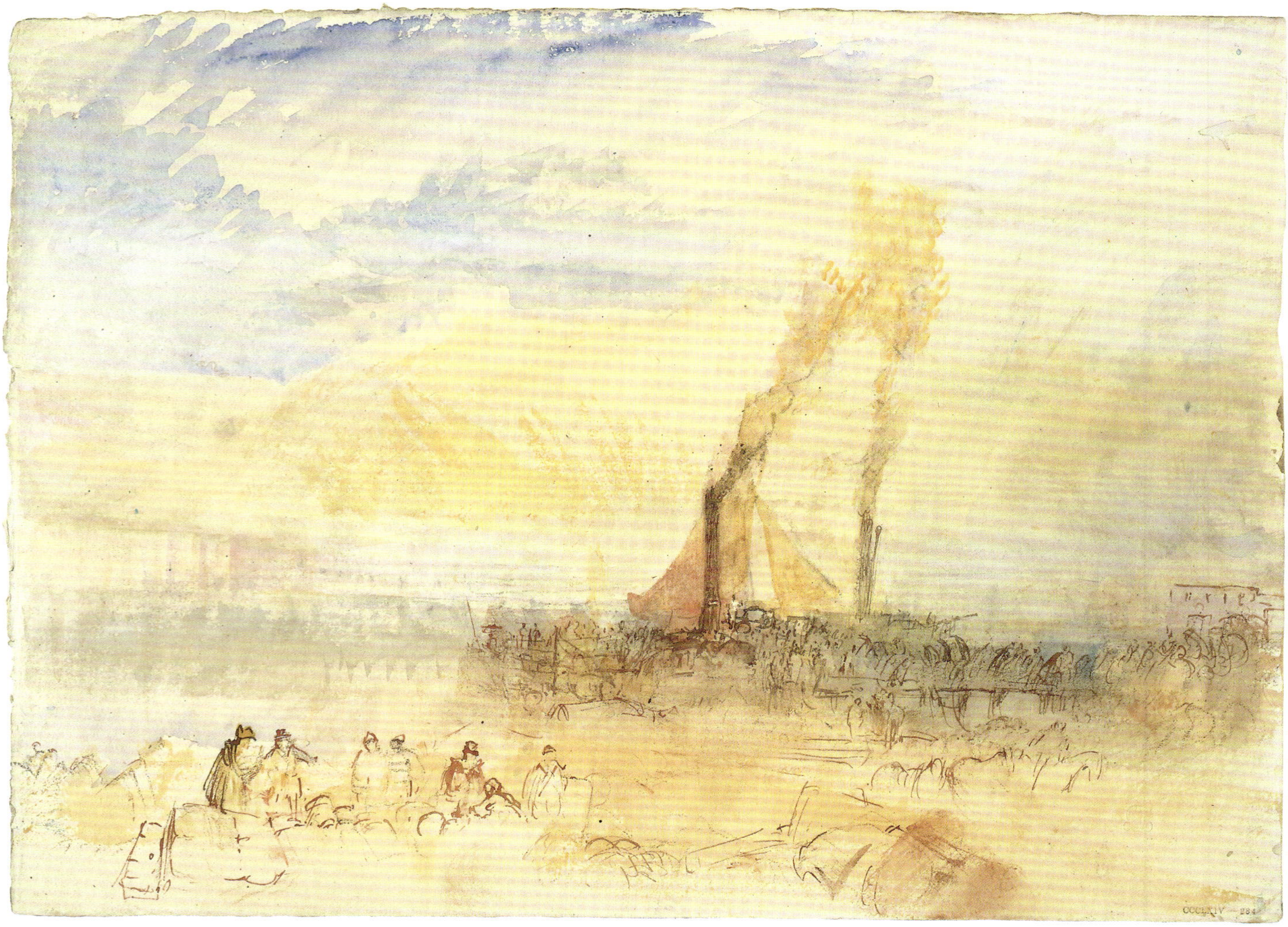

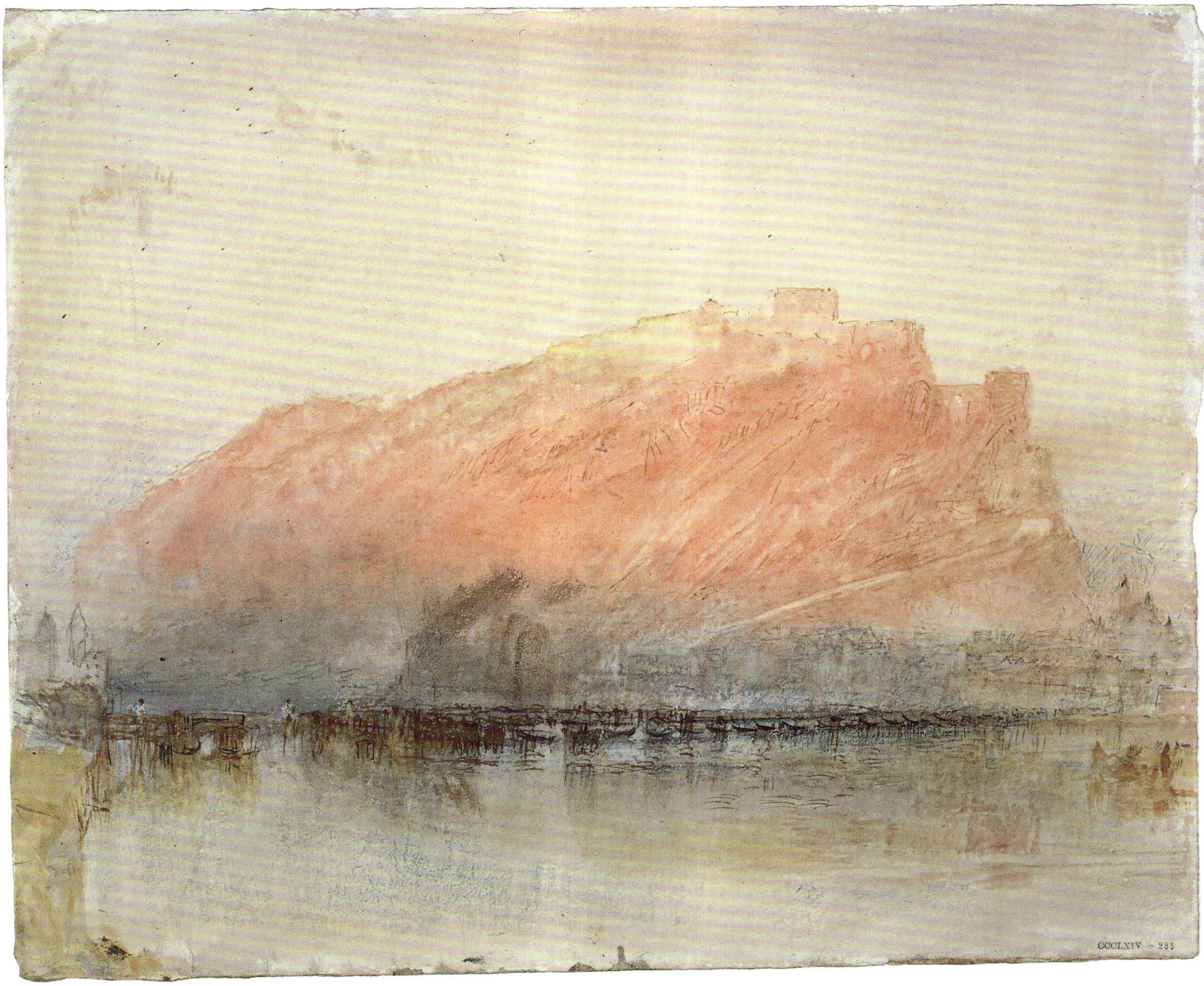

steamers, here seen under warm light; – lastly, because of its interesting indications of figures; the postillion with his two pairs of horses on the right, the crowd hurrying over the bridge above, and the group on the left busy with the luggage. Some carriages are waiting at the quay close to the steamer.

The topographical details evident in this view are not sufficiently distinct to confirm that the subject is definitely a view of Ehrenbreitstein; the outline of the castle could just as easily be that of Dover. However, Turner made a large group of watercolours of the view across the Rhine at Coblenz in 1841 (see Tate Gallery 1991–2, nos.128–36), as well as pencil drawings of the busy quayside there (TB CCCXVI ff.60 and 60 verso).

7 Ehrenbreitstein

1841
Watercolour, with pen 250 × 315 (9⅞ × 12 7/16)
TB CCCLXIV 285 D36138
EXH: NG (279); Amsterdam 1936 (238); Geneva 1955–6 (129); Tate Gallery 1959 (459); Washington 1963–4 (71); New York 1966 (90, repr. p.18); Royal Academy 1974–5 (23); Cologne 1980 (59, repr. p.110 in col.); Tate Gallery 1983; Melbourne 1985; Tate Gallery 1987; Tate Gallery 1991–2 (133, repr. p.186)
LIT: *Works*, XIII, pp.193–4, 372 [listed as No.79], 623; *R on P*, p.160; C. Clare, *J.M.W. Turner, his Life and Work*, 1951, p.106, repr. opp. p.64; Butlin 1962, pp.74–5, pl.28; M. Kitson, *J.M.W. Turner*, 1964, repr. p.66; Wilton 1982, p.57, pl.75

We dine at an hotel on the quay, and, after dinner, see Ehrenbreitstein by sunset from our window.

The expression of the strong Rhine current, as it rushes under the bridge of boats, is very perfect. This was a favourite subject of Turner's, there is another drawing of it under a different effect, in the series of unframed sketches. I could not frame it, because Turner had torn its edge half away in the sky [see TB CCCLXIV 309; Tate Gallery 1991–2, no.131, repr.].

The bridge of boats is opened on the left hand for a steamer to pass through, – her smoke is seen down the river. The white diagonal line is the ascent to the fortress.

Most interesting and beautiful.

In the group of watercolours of Ehrenbreitstein made in 1841, Turner depicts the fortress under a variety of sunset effects and from a number of different angles. The majority of these views are pervaded by a gentle atmospheric haziness from which this work stands apart. None of the others deploys quite such a striking use of a smeared wet-on-wet technique, nor such intense colour as this watercolour. This bold depiction of the fortress and its rock as a single area of colour anticipates the later series of views of the Rigi (see cat.nos.31, 35). Turner's viewpoint at Coblenz is some way up the Rhine from the church of St Castor's, whose twin towers can be seen on the left.

8 Coblentz, with the Bridge over the Moselle

The Mosel Bridge at Coblenz: Sample Study *c.*1841–2
Watercolour 236 × 295 (9⁵⁄₁₆ × 11⅝)
Verso inscribed in pencil, 'J. Ruskin Junr Esqr' and '9'
Watermarked: J WHATMAN | TURKEY MILL | 1822
TB CCCLXIV 286 D36139
EXH: NG (280); Manchester 1966 (46); British Museum 1975–6 (283, repr. p.156); Cologne 1980 (57, repr. p.108 in col.); Tate Gallery 1983; Melbourne 1985; Tate Gallery 1991–2 (136, repr. p.96 in col.); Tate Gallery 1993 (26, repr. p.46)
LIT: Not included in 1st ed., *Works*, XIII, pp.186, 194, 372, 623; *R on P*, p.161; Dillon 1902, p.332; Holme 1903, W42 repr.; Serota 1970, p.111; Wilton 1979, pp.483–4; Wilton 1982, p.66, pl.101

This drawing does not belong to the same series as those we have hitherto been examining: it was one of ten carried forward by Turner to a somewhat higher finish than his other sketches in the year 1842, in order to give an idea of a series of drawings which he proposed at that time to undertake in illustration to his Continental journeys, and which were to be finished realisations of the subjects shown in the sketches. Of these drawings he made twenty-seven; ten in 1842, five in 1843, ten in 1845, and two in 1850 [see Appendix II, pp.149–55]. *Many of the sketches for them will be found in the present series* [see cat.nos.20–4, 27–9, 31–35, 37, 39–40, 48, 75]. *This subject was realised for me in 1842* [fig.18], *and the composition of the resultant design is illustrated at some length in my* Elements of Drawing [see p.26, fig.14; and *Works*, XV, p.166–77, figs.32, 34–5].

Of the final commissioned watercolours made betwwen 1840 and 1851, there were only two which were not of Swiss subjects: the view of Constance (see cat.no.20) and the drawing based on this study. Its inclusion emphasises the importance to Turner of the German city on the route he favoured most often when travelling to Switzerland. Sadly, the finished view is now untraced. It was last recorded by Martin Hardie in his catalogue of the mezzotints of Sir Frank Short (*The Mezzotints and Aquatints of Sir Frank Short, R.A., P.P.R.E., other than those for the Liber Studiorum*, Print Collectors' Club, 1939). A quotation from Short reveals that the watercolour was on loan to the Victoria and Albert Museum (*c.*1912–13) from the collection of R.E. Tatham (p.32 no.95, pl.IV). This may have been an informal or temporary loan, since the watercolour is not documented in the Museum's records,

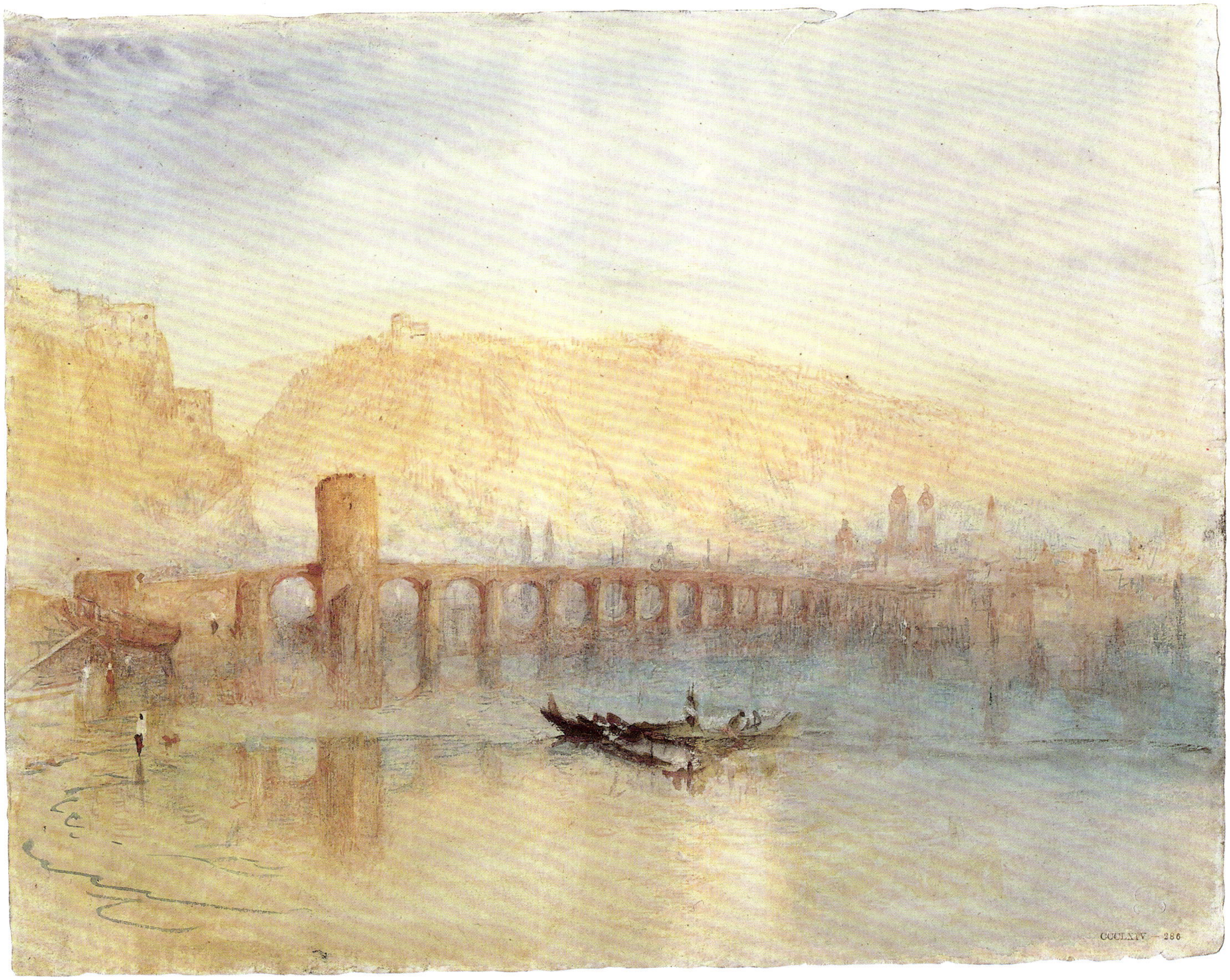

although Tatham is known to have lent other works by Turner. Another colour study of the Mosel Bridge from further upstream is TB CCCLXIV 308. Turner had thoroughly explored the Rhine's tributary, the Mosel, just two years earlier, in 1839 (see Tate Gallery 1991–2).

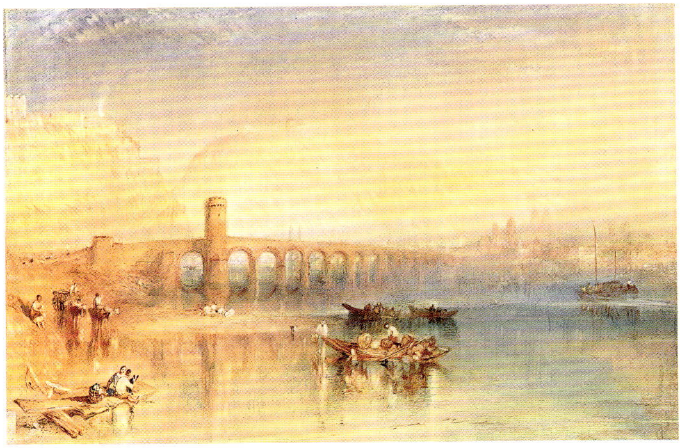

fig.18 William Ward, 'Coblenz', after J.M.W. Turner *c.*1876–82, watercolour. *Cincinnati Art Museum, Bequest by Mary Hanna*

9 On the Rhine

Zwingenberg, on the Neckar 1844
Pencil and watercolour, with pen 229 × 329 (9 × 13)
Watermarked: J WHATMAN | 1844
TB CCCXLIX 26 D35150
EXH: NG (Box Z); Tate Gallery 1990
LIT: *Works*, XIII, p.194; *R on P*, pp.161–2 n.2; Cook 1905, p.16, repr. as 'On the Rhine (?)'

The slightly indicated foreground is a terrace projecting into the river; one figure sitting, and another lying down at the edge of the terrace, a third standing; the whole group indicated by a few red penned lines.

The passage of cooler colour on the left of this drawing is very beautiful.

The following three subjects have been newly identified by Dr Cecilia Powell, and will be included in the forthcoming exhibition, *Turner in Germany* (Tate Gallery 1995). The town of Zwingenberg lies to the south of Eberbach, the point at which the Neckar abruptly changes its northwards course and flows west towards the Rhine. Zwingenberg was apparently the original setting for one of the Neckar legends, in which the Devil lured his victims to the glen below the castle (the 'Wolfsschlucht') and tricked them into participating in a game of chance wherein they risked their souls. By the time Turner made his visit in 1844, the story had already been immortalised in Carl Maria von Weber's opera *Die Freischütz* (1821).

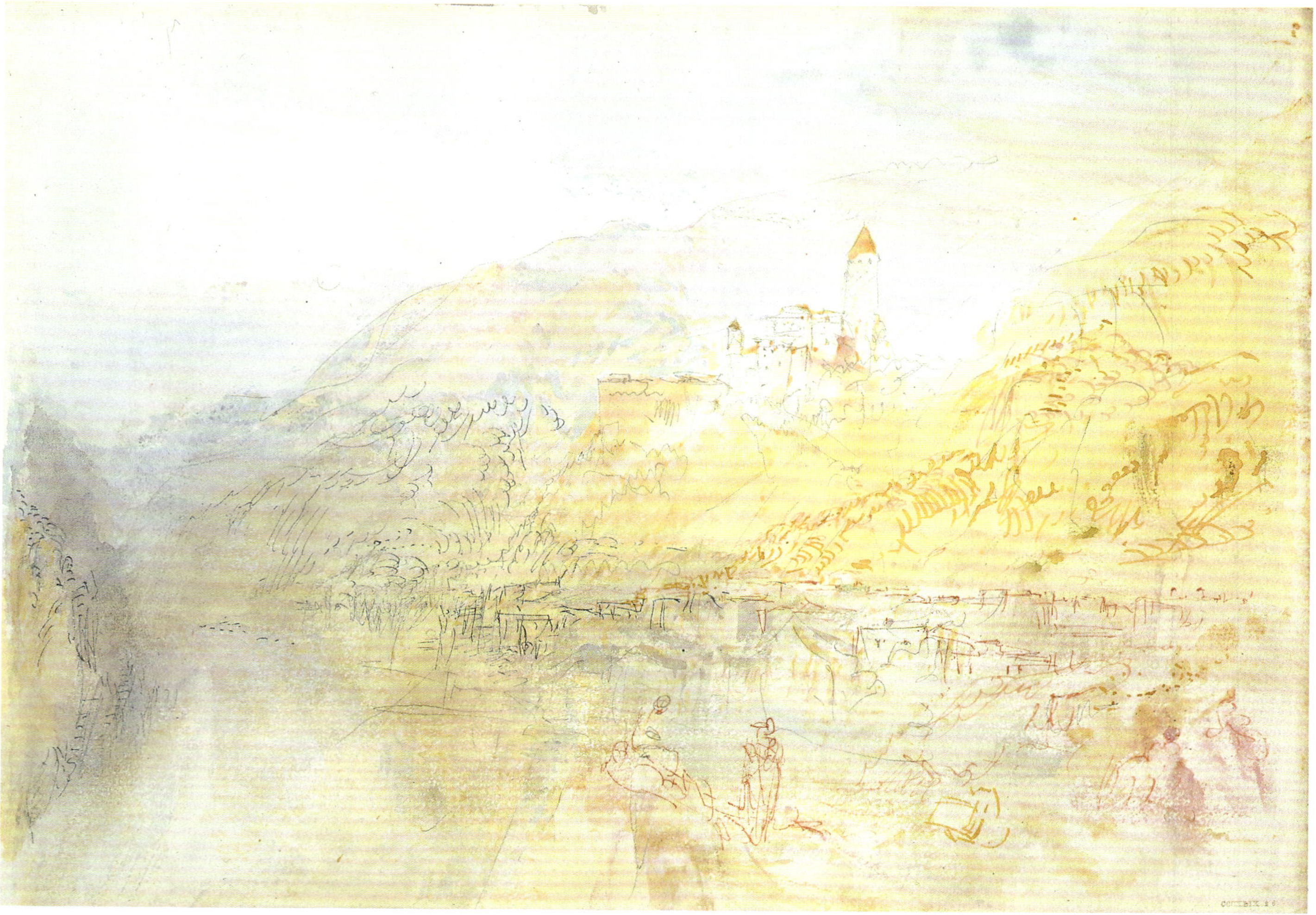

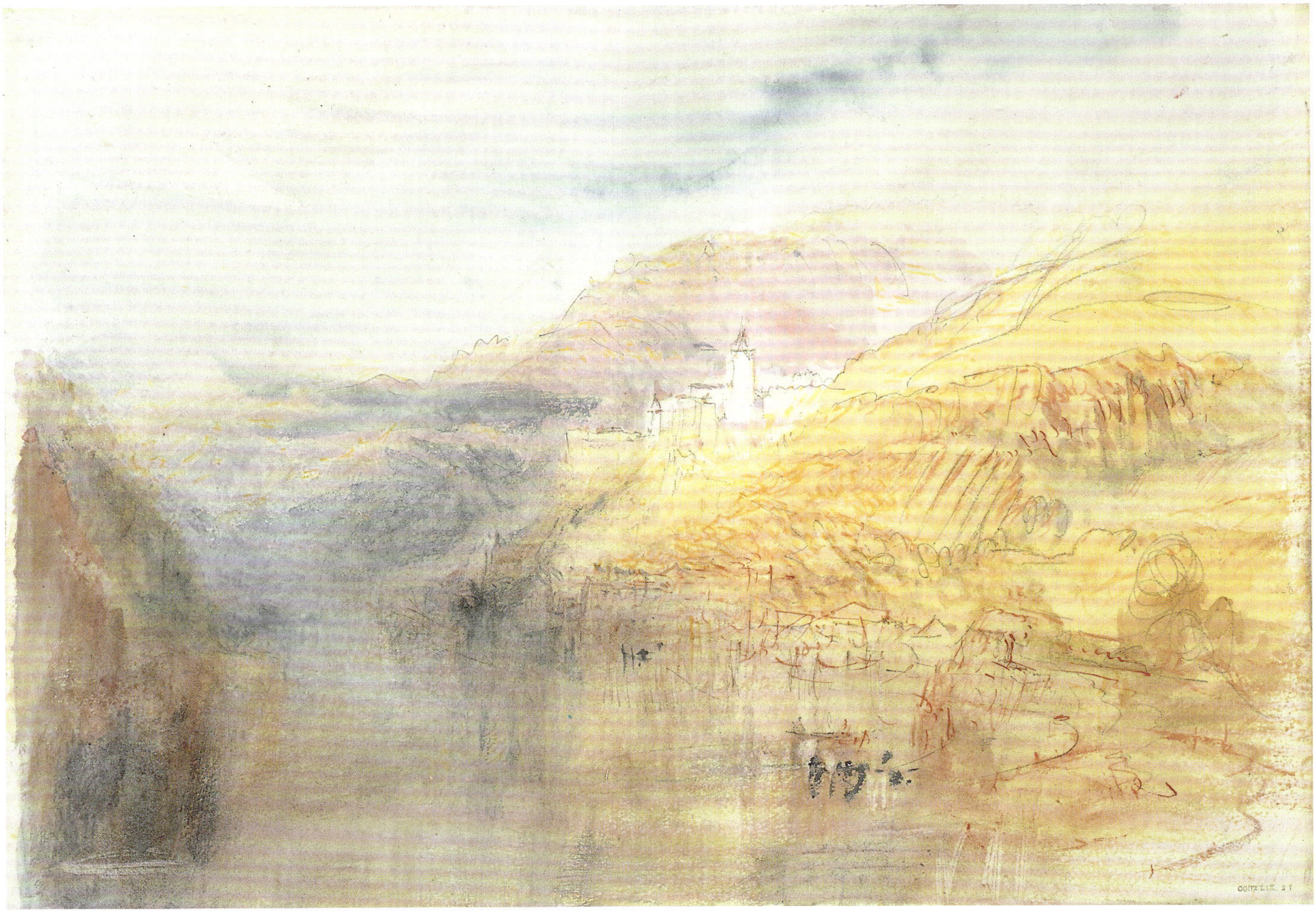

10 On the Rhine. The same subject from the river

A Distant View of Zwingenberg, on the Neckar 1844
Pencil and watercolour, with pen 229 × 328 $(9 \times 12\frac{15}{16})$
Watermarked: J WHATMAN | 1844
TB CCCXLIX 27 D35151
EXH: NG (Box Z); Sheffield 1964–5; Dresden 1972 (115); Lisbon 1973 (54); British Museum 1975–6 (294, repr. p.152 in col.); Tate Gallery 1992–3 (128, repr. p.96)
LIT: *Works*, XIII, pp.194–5; *R on P*, p.162 n.2; Cook 1905, p.24, repr. as 'Castle on Rhine'

Loose and unsatisfactory in treatment in most parts; but interesting in the drawing of the rocks on the hillside on the right; the pencil, and the paler violet touches, with the full and deep red penned work, being there combined with consummate skill. Note the rapidity of the first sketch, in the sweeping touch of pencil forming the loop above these crags.

In this more distant view of Zwingenberg, Turner draws the viewer's eye to the castle by the simple, but effective means of leaving that area of his paper blank, other than the pencil lines which describe the structure of the castle. In his later work, when using a pen to strengthen details, Turner tended not to use ink, but resorted instead to an assorted range of watercolours.

11 On the Rhine. The same subject, nearer

Hirschhorn, on the Neckar 1844
Pencil and watercolour, with pen 229 × 330 (9 × 13)
Inscribed, upper centre 'Blue' and upper right '[?Tower against the sky]'
Watermarked: J WHATMAN | 1844
TB CCCXLIX 20 D35144
EXH: NG (281); Paris 1937 (115); Tate Gallery 1953–9; Dresden 1972 (114, as 'Rheinfelden: am Rhein', repr. p.77, pl.25); Lisbon 1973 (53, repr. p.135); British Museum 1975–6 (293); Cologne 1980 (68, repr. p.119); Paris 1983–4 (251)
LIT: *Works*, XIII, pp.186, 195 (in the 1st ed. of Ruskin's catalogue, this work was no.8), 623; *R on P*, p.161; Finberg 1910, repr. pl.LXXXV, opp. p.148 as 'On the Rhine, 1844'; Wilton 1982, p.73, pl.124

A perfectly studied and splendid composition. Consider, one by one, the uses of the various passages of its colour, especially the introduction of the dark green touches at the river bank on the right side, as they complete and enclose the gloom cast down by the cloud, and bring out the bright colouring of the banks. I cannot determine the objects indicated by red outline on the extreme right. They were evidently of great importance in Turner's mind; I suppose them to be parts of a dyke of basalt.

Hirschhorn lies more than twenty miles up river from Heidelberg. As well as this watercolour, Turner recorded the castle and town on ff.27 verso and 28 of his *On the Neckar* sketchbook (TB CCCII). In comparison to the sketches, which were observed from waterlevel, the watercolour adopts a higher viewpoint to present a panoramic view of the river. In many of his late watercolours Turner seems consciously to seek out a vantage-point from where he can survey his chosen subject. The surface of the water in the bottom corner of the image suggests the current flowing around a sandspit or an island. This is the tip of a small island on which stands the Ersheimkapelle, a building that is clearly visible in the sketchbook drawings. For another view of Hirschhorn, see cat.no.82.

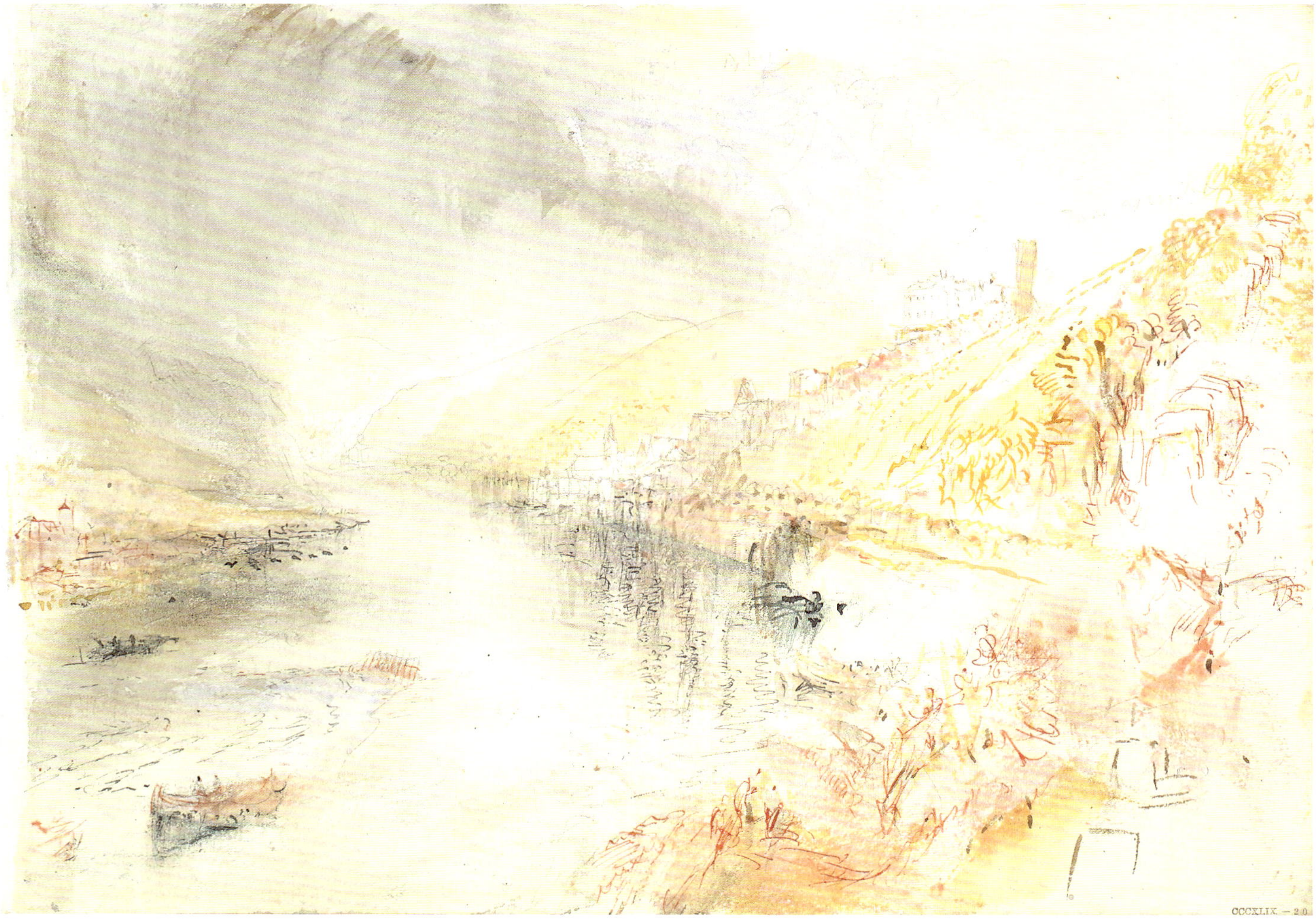

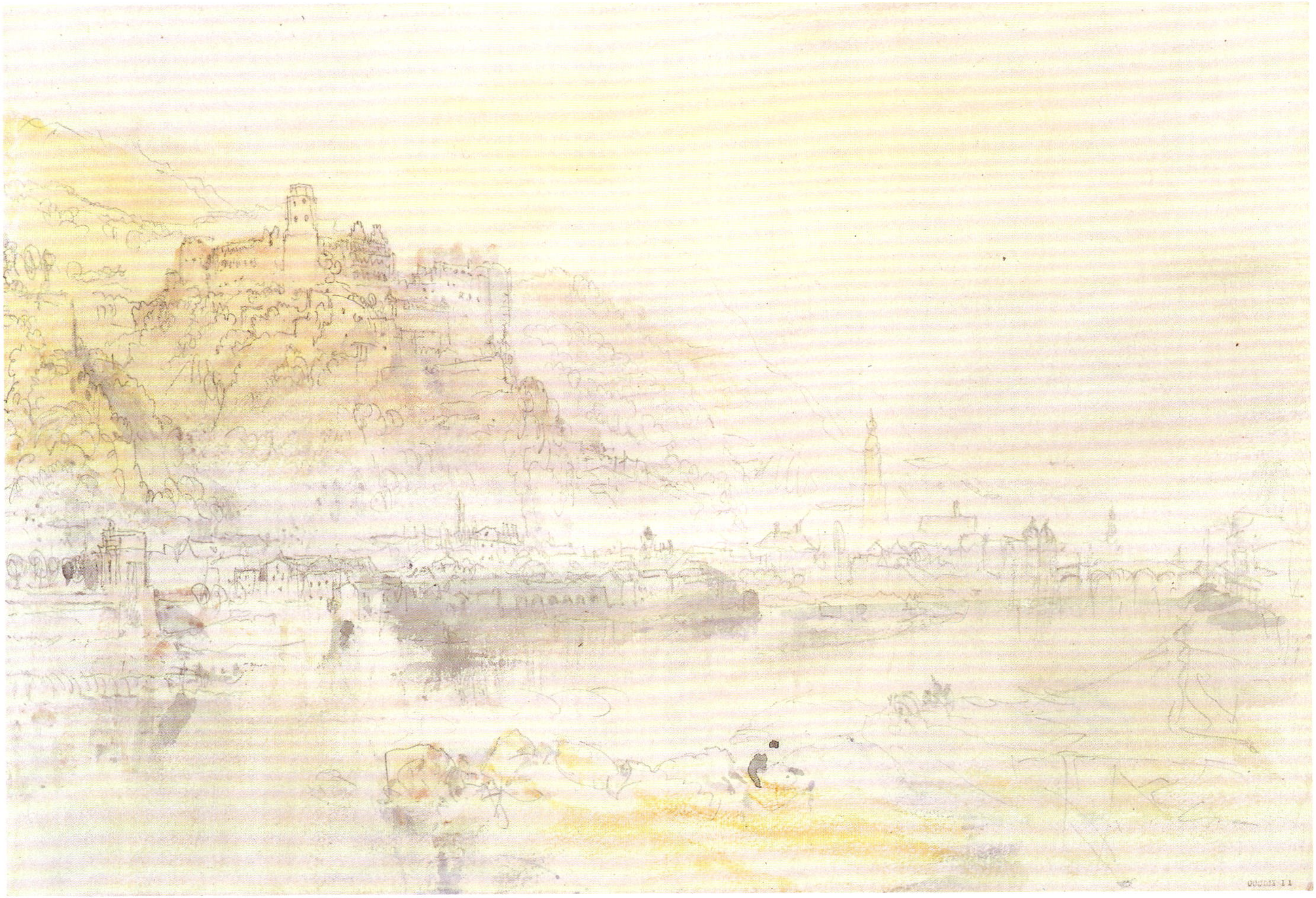

11A Heidelberg

Heidelberg from the North-east 1844
Pencil and watercolour 228 × 330 (9 × 13)
TB CCCLII II D35231
EXH: Oxford 1878 (248-33); Paris 1937 (116); Düsseldorf 1950 (34); Tate Gallery 1959–65; Adelaide 1961 (37, repr. p.27); Paris 1983–4 (252)
LIT: *Works*, XIII, pp.186, 195 (this work and its commentary were only included in the 1st ed. of Ruskin's catalogue) and p.562; *R on P*, p.163n; Schefold 1968, p.139, repr.

I have included this sketch in the series rather on account of the beauty of its subject than for its own merits; it being very slight, and not in effect much beyond what other people might have done. The mass of castle is, however, beautifully indicated. There seems a persuasion in Turner's mind that the gabled part of the castle should be rose-coloured, and the tower and wall on the left browner or warmer; as we find the same division of colour in the next sketch.

Heidelberg has long appealed to artists for the picturesque setting of its castle, high above the roofs of the old town. Turner's first visit seems to have taken place during the 1830s, and is recorded in his *'Heidelberg up to Salzburg'* sketchbook (TB CCXCVIII); the visit will be discussed in Dr Cecilia Powell's forthcoming study of Turner's travels in Germany, along with the following seven works (cat.nos.12–18). During the 1840s Turner painted several impressive watercolours of Heidelberg, seen from the west on the north bank of the Neckar (W 1376, City Art Galleries, Manchester; W 1377, private collection; W 1554, National Galleries of Scotland, Edinburgh), as well as a large unfinished painting (B&J 440, Tate Gallery). On his journey in 1844 he sought out many of the viewpoints he had already recorded. This view, looking along the river towards the bridge and the prominent tower of the Heiliggeistkirche, for example, repeats that preserved on ff.22 verso and 23 of the *'Heidelberg up to Salzburg'* sketchbook.

12 Heidelberg. From the front of the castle

1844
Pencil and watercolour 227 × 329 (8 15/16 × 13)
TB CCCLII 13 D35233
EXH: NG (Box Z); Tate Gallery 1953–9; Folkestone 1971–2 (19); British Museum 1975–6 (299); Madrid 1983 (96, repr. p.101); Tokyo 1986 (106, repr.); Tate Gallery 1988; Tate Gallery 1990
LIT: *Works*, XIII, pp.195–6; *R on P*, p.162 n.1; Cook 1905, pp.8–9, repr. p.23; Schefold 1968, p.133, repr.; Wilton 1987, p.227, fig.298

Very hasty; but highly interesting in its indication of the way Turner liked to lead his curves to the main points of his principal objects. The two large curves in the sky are outlines of hills, and are merely put there to indicate that in the finished drawing those curves should lead one to the main tower of the castle, and one to its first gable, while the second gable should be the only piece of the castle relieved against the sky. It is slightly touched with rose colour, to darken it for the sake of this relief. The tops of the battlements to the right of it would have been left in light against the yellow hills, thus connecting the light of the sky with the white mist on the wood on the right. You see the battlements are carefully left free from the rose tint which covers the rest of the castle.

Note, in the position of the dark side of the large tower just under the main angle of the fortress, Turner's frequent habit of sustaining his principal masses one by the other: also, the careful marking of the balcony to its central window, and of an interrupting shaft in the fourth of its six sustaining arches (the seventh arch belonging to a detached terrace in front). The apparently careless sweeps of purple colour in the water are meant to enclose white sails, in order to balance the broad light of this house; and the strong purple touch on the right is one dark sail, necessary to direct the eye out of the picture on that side; the castle being otherwise too isolated a mass.

Over thirty years after Turner's visit, Mark Twain acknowledged the castle's continuing power to ignite the viewer's imagination when he described it as 'the Lear of inanimate nature – deserted, discrowned, beaten by the

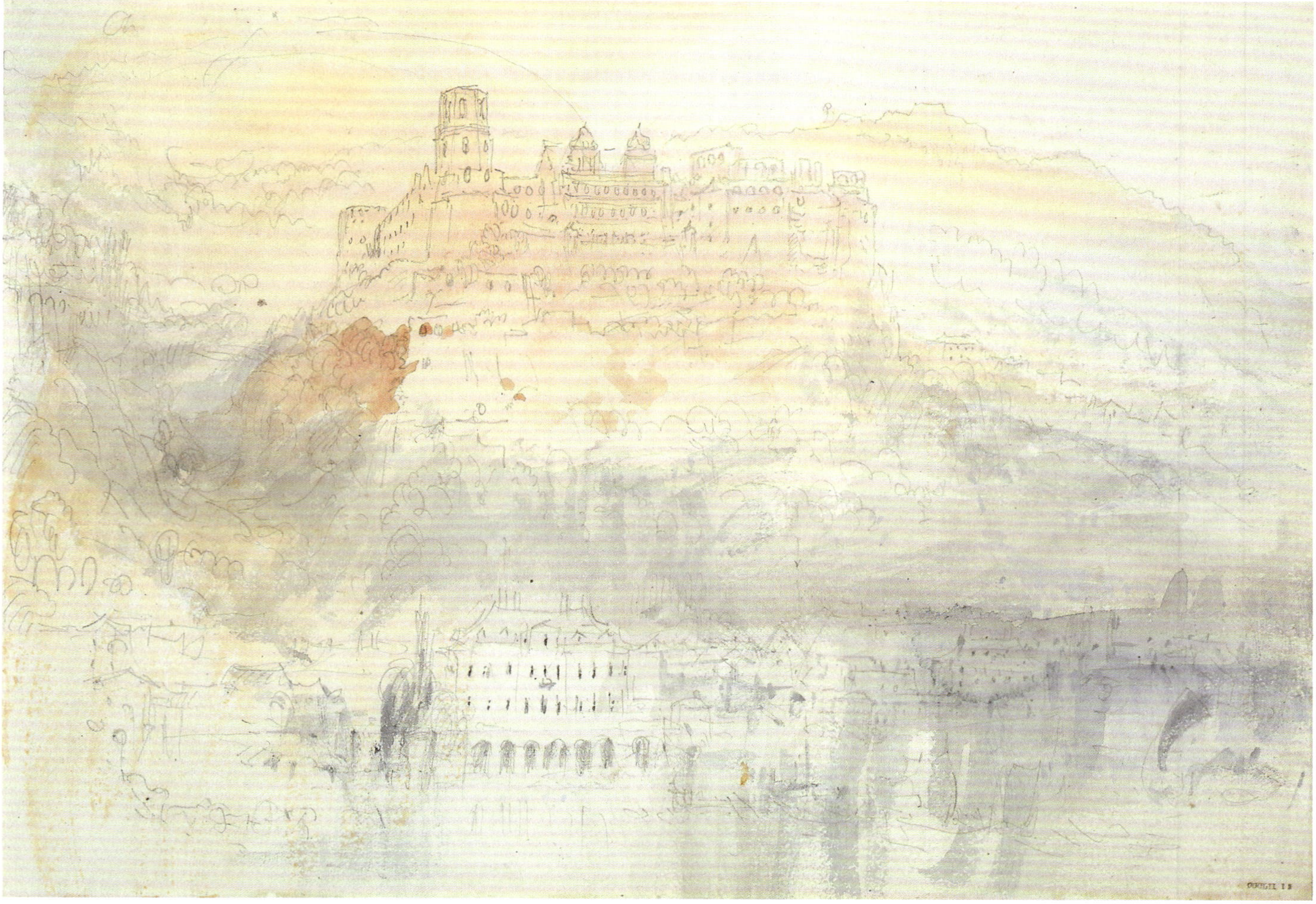

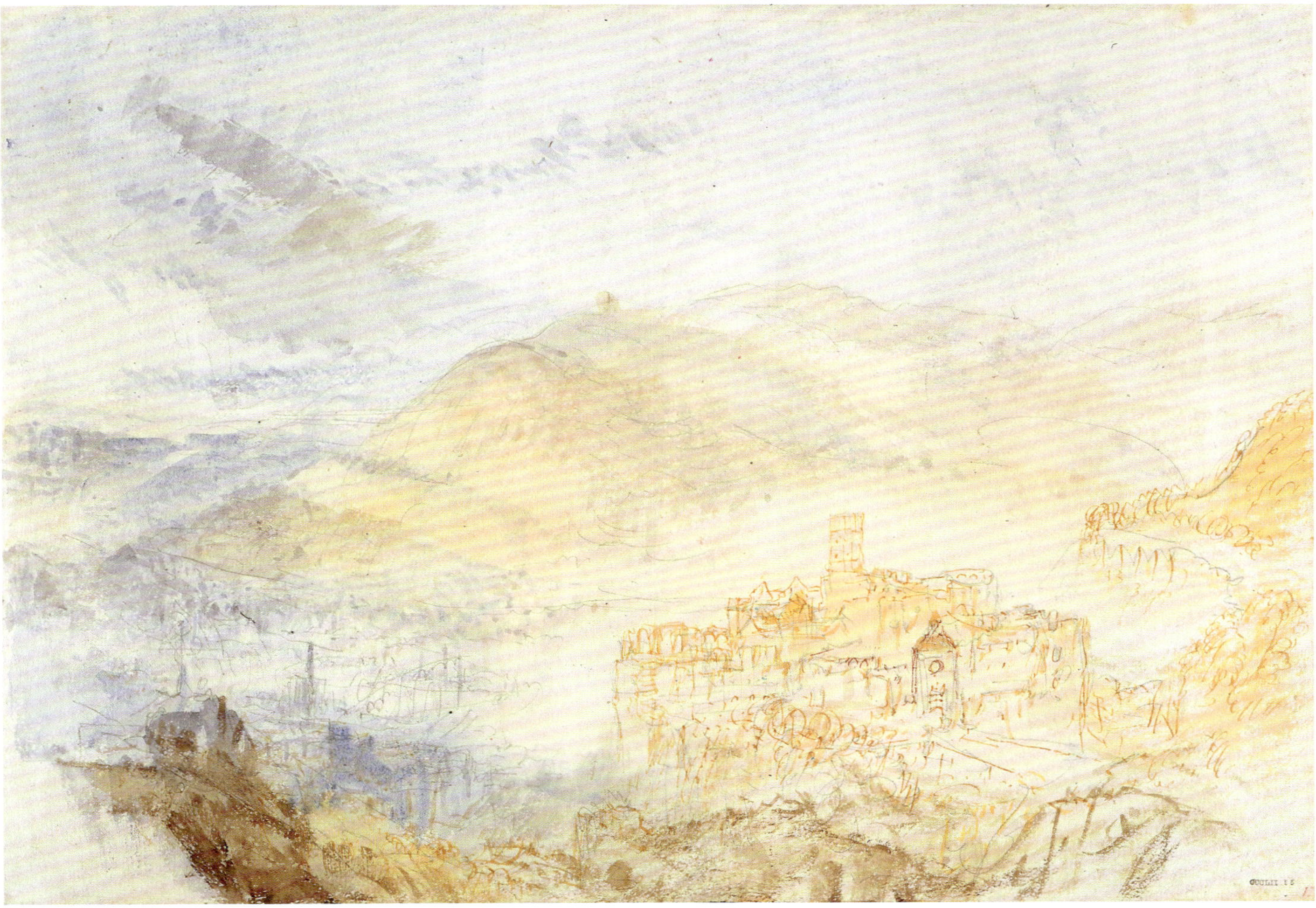

storms, but royal still and beautiful' (*A Tramp Abroad*, 1880). In this watercolour Turner repeats a composition he had drawn on his earlier visit (TB CCXCVIII ff.23 and 23 verso).

13 Heidelberg

Heidelberg from the South 1844
Pencil and watercolour, with pen 228 × 327 (9 × 12⅞)
TB CCCLII 15 D35235
EXH: Düsseldorf 1950 (36); Adelaide 1961 (39, repr. p.28); British Museum 1975–6 (298, repr. p.159, incorrectly identified as no.299); Copenhagen 1976 (81); Hamburg 1976 (116, repr. p.157); Cologne 1980 (64, repr. p.115)
LIT: *Works*, XIII, p.196; *R on P*, p.162 n.1; Cook 1905, p.49; Schefold 1968, p.124, repr.

View of the castle from above. Very grand in subject, but chiefly interesting from the use of the quantity of confused blue touches on the left. The castle, I have no doubt, was drawn first; Turner wished to make it a rich and complex mass, but it was so much broken up that it began to want solidity; first, therefore, a pure white cloud of mist is thrown round it, which gives it unity and substance; but, if you hide the blue touches with your hand, you will see that the building is still wanting in massiveness. The blue touches are then put on, purposely shapeless and confused, and the castle becomes solid at once by contrast.

14 Heidelberg

Heidelberg: Looking down on the Castle from the South
1844
Pencil and watercolour, with pen 229 × 328 $(9 \times 12\tfrac{15}{16})$
TB CCCLII 8 D35228
EXH: NG (282); Washington 1963–4 (75, repr.); Folkestone 1966; Brussels 1970–1 (84, repr.); Cleveland 1977–8 (72, repr. p.91); Cologne 1980 (65, repr. p.116)
LIT: *Works*, XIII, pp.197, 372, 623; *R on P*, p.162; Schefold 1968, p.142, repr.; Wilton 1982, p.73, pl.125

We go a little lower down the hill in the afternoon, and draw the castle from that side of it, now all bathed in golden light.

Very noble in its arrangement of massy form, and in its breadth of glow.

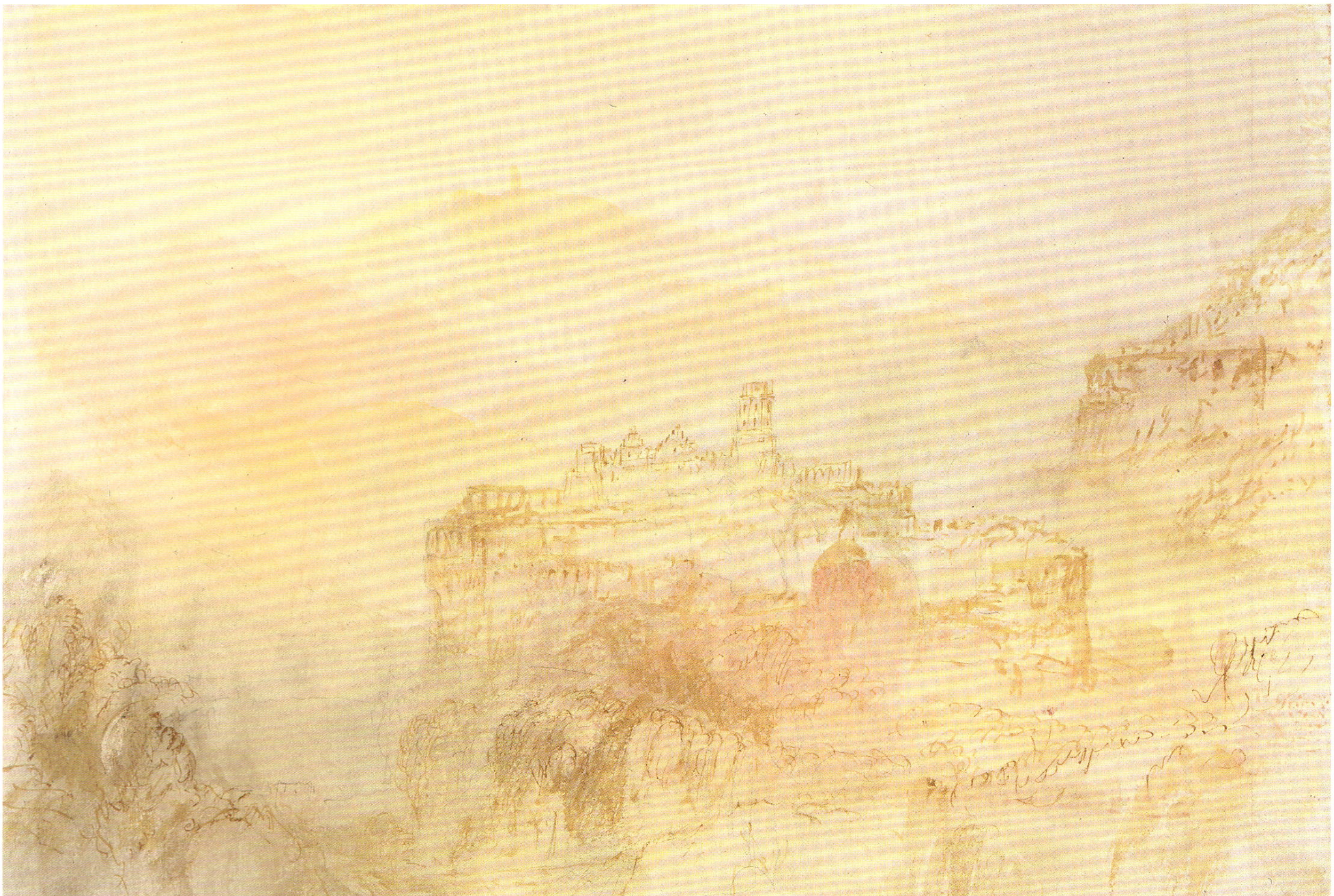

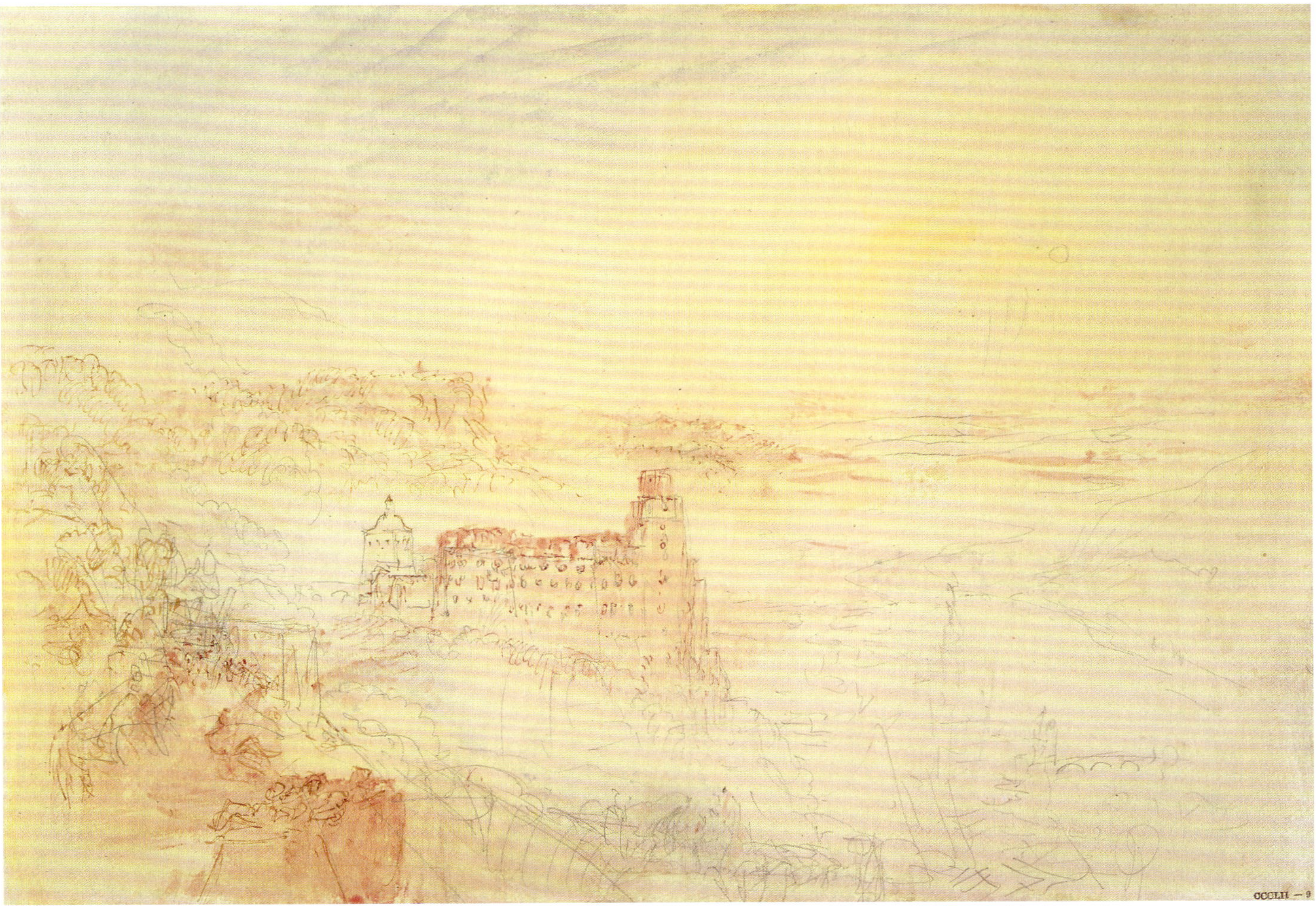

15 Heidelberg

Heidelberg: Looking West with a Low Sun 1844
Pencil and watercolour, with pen 228 × 327 (9 × 12⅞)
TB CCCLII 9 D35229
EXH: NG (283); Tate Gallery 1959–65; British Museum 1975–6 (296); Toronto 1980–1 (92, repr. p.85, col. pl.21)
LIT: *Works*, XIII, pp.197, 372, 623; *R on P*, p.163; Schefold 1968, p.132, repr.

And lastly, we go quickly round to the other side of the castle, and sketch it as seen against the sunset.

This is a perfectly composed picture, and exquisite as far as it goes. Note the beauty of tone in the stream of white mist behind the castle, and the delicate change from the rosy colour of its battlements to the warmer square mass of the foreground which throws it into distance.

The pencilling of the outline sketch is, observe, always treated by Turner as so much grey colour, and allowed for in the after tinting; thus here, the grey pencilling at the bottom becomes an expression of shadow in the middle distance.

The steeple of the tower church is marked in rose colour: one bridge in pencil beneath it, the other long bridge in faint blue beyond it. Our paper was provokingly greasy, in a most important place, just under the sun; we do the best with it we can.

During the visit to Heidelberg documented in the *'Heidelberg up to Salzburg'* sketchbook, Turner climbed up above the castle to take in the details of the view looking west, towards the Rhine (TB CCXCVIII ff.8 verso, 10 verso, 11). When he returned to Heidelberg in 1844, as well as this watercolour, he made a pencil drawing in which he once again recorded the view (*Spires and Heidelberg* sketchbook, TB CCXCVII f.14 verso).

16 [Untitled]

Heilbronn from the Neckar 1844
Pencil and watercolour 229 × 328 (9 × 12$\frac{15}{16}$)
Watermarked: J WHATMAN | 1844
TB CCCLII 16 D35236
EXH: Düsseldorf 1950 (37); Adelaide 1961 (40, repr. p.28); Tokyo 1963–4 (46, repr. in Japanese cat. only); Madrid 1983 (98, repr. p.102); Tate Gallery 1993 (32)
LIT: *Works*, XIII, p.197; *R on P*, p.163 n.1; Cook 1905, p.44, repr. as 'Coblenz from the Moselle'; Zink 1954, pp.225–8, repr. p.226; Schefold 1968, pp.142–3, repr. p.146

This and the two following subjects were in the same book as the preceding ones of Heidelberg. Their locality will eventually be quite ascertainable, but I have not yet had time to determine it. This is one of the slightest sketches of the series, but pretty and instructive in its simple succession of colour; – yellow, rose, and blue.

Although the subject of this view was identified by Fritz Zink in 1954, the watercolour has only recently been correctly exhibited as a view of Heilbronn on the Neckar. Zink's article identifies each of the buildings, some of which were destroyed by bombing in 1944. He also notes how Turner faithfully indicated the external spiral staircase in his depiction of the church of St Kilian (the furthest tower to the left) simply by means of a squiggle running down the building. The staircase is suggested in exactly the same way on a page of the *On the Neckar* sketchbook (TB CCCII f.15).

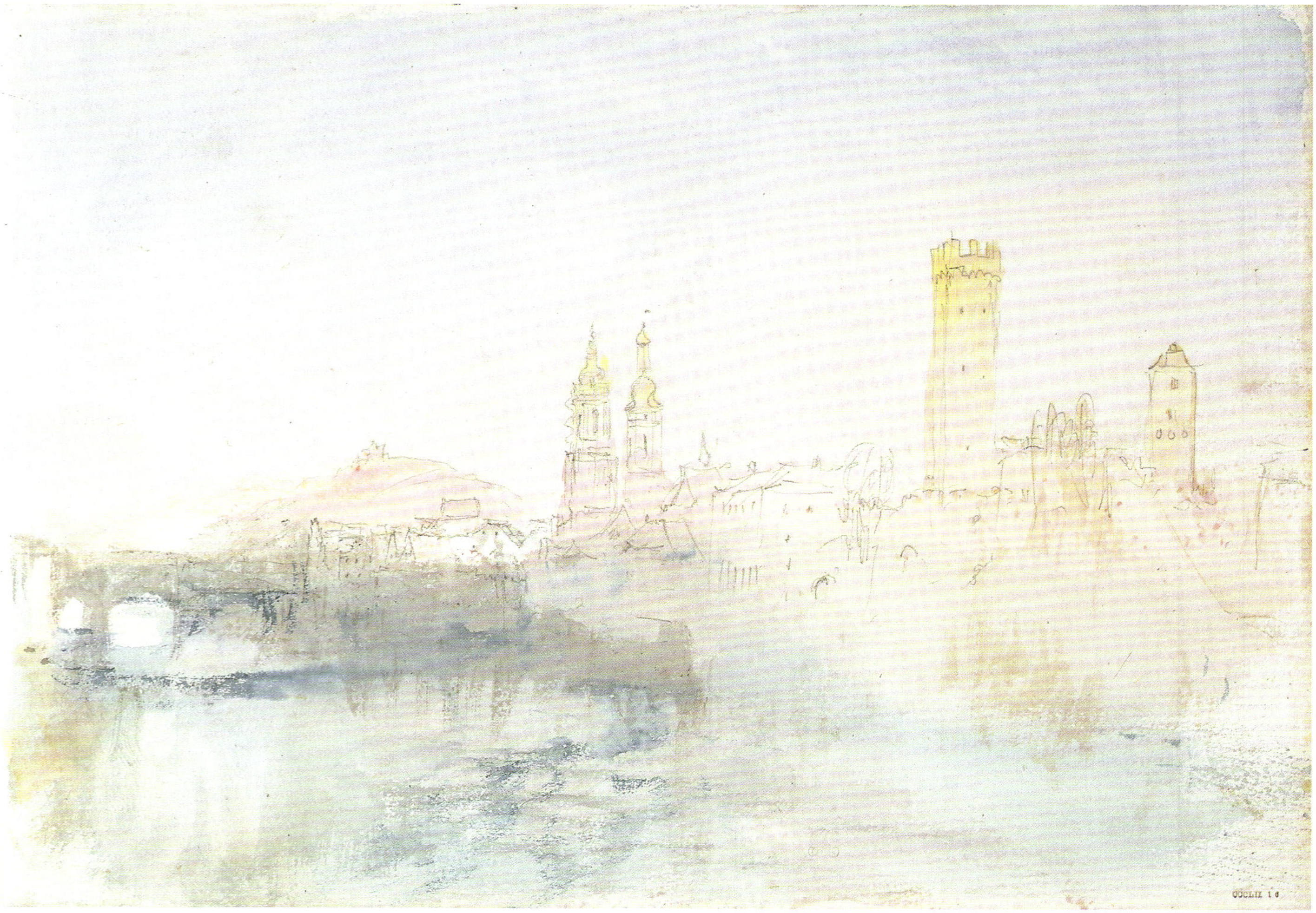

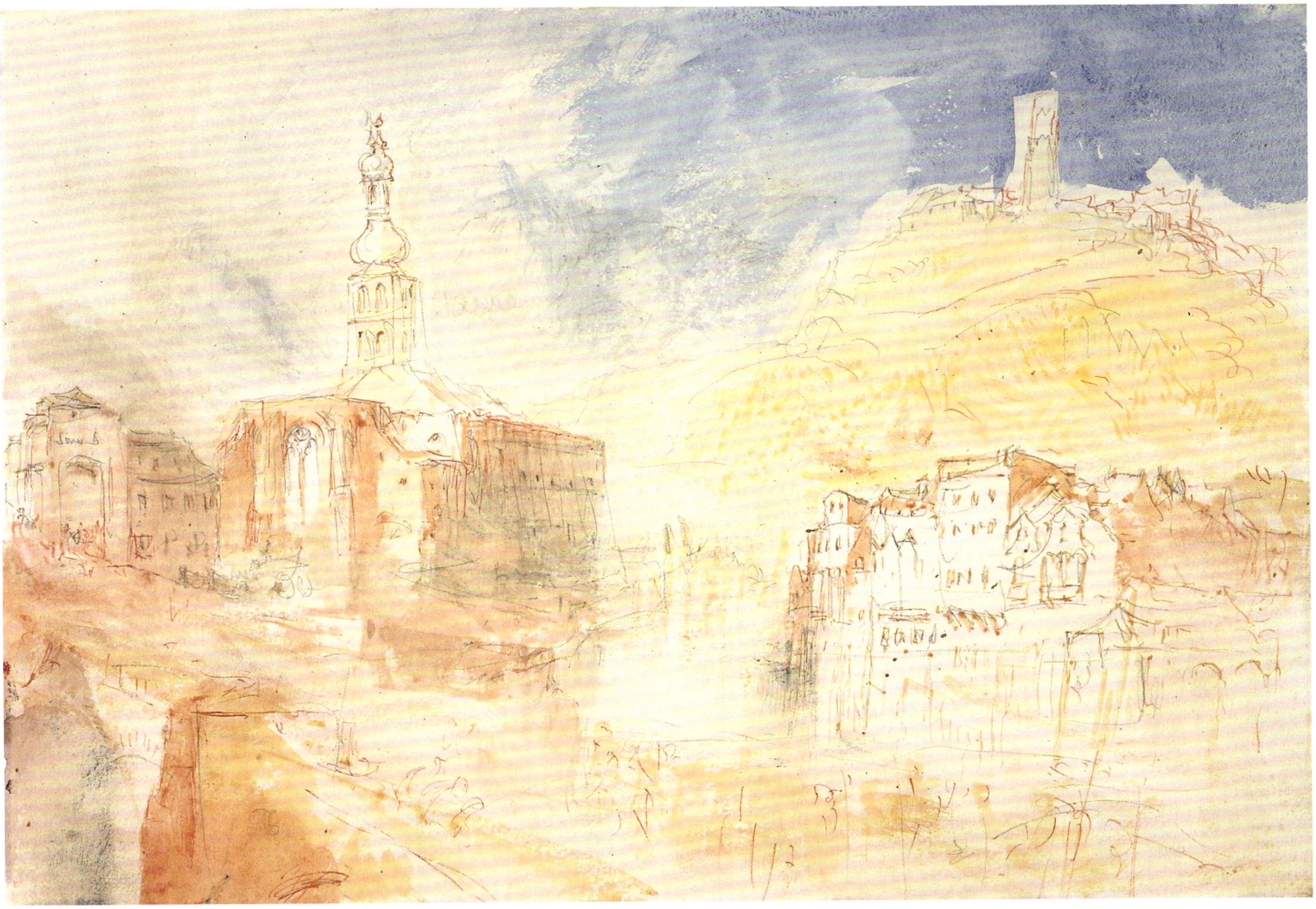

17 [Untitled]

Kreuznach, on the River Naar 1844
Pencil and watercolour, with pen 228 × 328 (9 × 12 15/16)
Watermarked: J WHATMAN | 1844
TB CCCLII 10 D35230
EXH: NG (284); British Museum 1933a. This subject will be discussed by Cecilia Powell, who identified the view depicted while pursuing research for the forthcoming exhibition *Turner in Germany*, Tate Gallery 1995
LIT: *Works*, XIII, pp.197–8, p.372 as 'Heidelberg', and p.623; *R on P*, pp.163–4

A composition of exquisite beauty, and drawn in Turner's most powerful manner; hasty, but not careless. The expression of the picturesque block of architecture about the old church is as perfect as it is possible to render it with the given quantity of work. Observe how the whole is centralised by the single touch of darker vermilion in the centre, and how carefully the dark side is gradated to the distance; terminating with one faint touch of blue at the bottom of the further angle. Cover this blue touch with your finger, and see how much you will lose. Then observe how the two poplars at the turn of the river are used to unite the two masses of buildings; hide them in like manner with the finger, and the picture is instantly cut into two parts.

The laying in of the sky at last is very curious. The tower on the top of the hill had first been outlined with pencil, and painted yellow. Then it was not high enough, and got a new top, with red battlements, and two dark red touches at the side. Not being high enough yet, it got a third top, fainter. Then it was not thick enough; and so when the blue sky was struck (dropped would be a more accurate word) over the whole, the painter left a good breadth of white beyond his outline, besides giving plenty more room for the top of the hill, which was too round, and had to be raised to the right.

The confused blue touches in the middle of the sketch mean hills.

In the past this drawing has been identified incorrectly as a view of Heidelberg. In associating it with other sheets from the *Heidelberg* sketchbook, Ruskin's comments suggest that it may be a Neckar subject. However, the town depicted is on the River Naar.

18 [Untitled]

Neckarsteinach 1844
Pencil, watercolour, with pen 229 × 330 (9 × 13)
Watermarked: J WHATMAN | 1844
Verso: Pencil sketch of Neckarsteinach, from further to the left of the view on the recto
TB CCCLII 14 D35234
EXH: Düsseldorf 1950 (35); Adelaide 1961 (38, repr. p.27); Tokyo 1963–4 (45, repr. in Japanese cat. only); Folkestone 1966; Paris 1972 (309); Madrid 1983 (97); Tate Gallery 1993 (31)
LIT: *Works*, XIII, p.198; *R on P*, p.163 n.1; Cook 1905, p.64 as 'Bellinzona'; Zink 1954, p.228; Schefold 1968, pp.139–41, repr

This drawing, though somewhat confused and unsatisfactory, contains much that will be interesting to artists in its execution. The finest part of it is the rounded hill in light behind the castle, and the winding valley and river under its cliffs.

Neckarsteinach stands at the confluence of the Neckar and the Steinach, about nine miles from Heidelberg. Another sketch of the town, taken from a viewpoint slightly to the left of this watercolour, is one of a number of views of Neckarsteinach in the *On the Neckar* sketchbook (TB CCCII f.29).

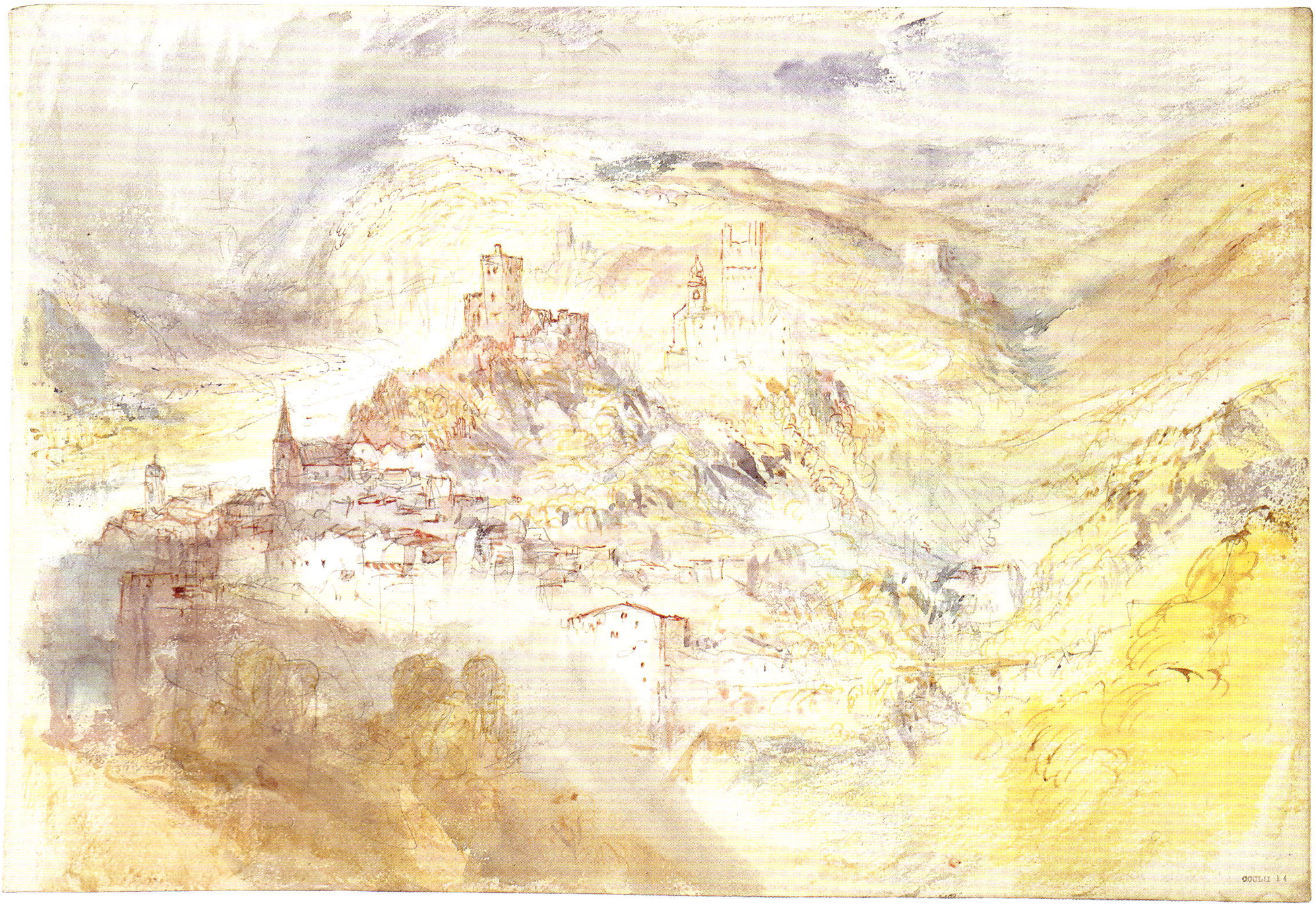

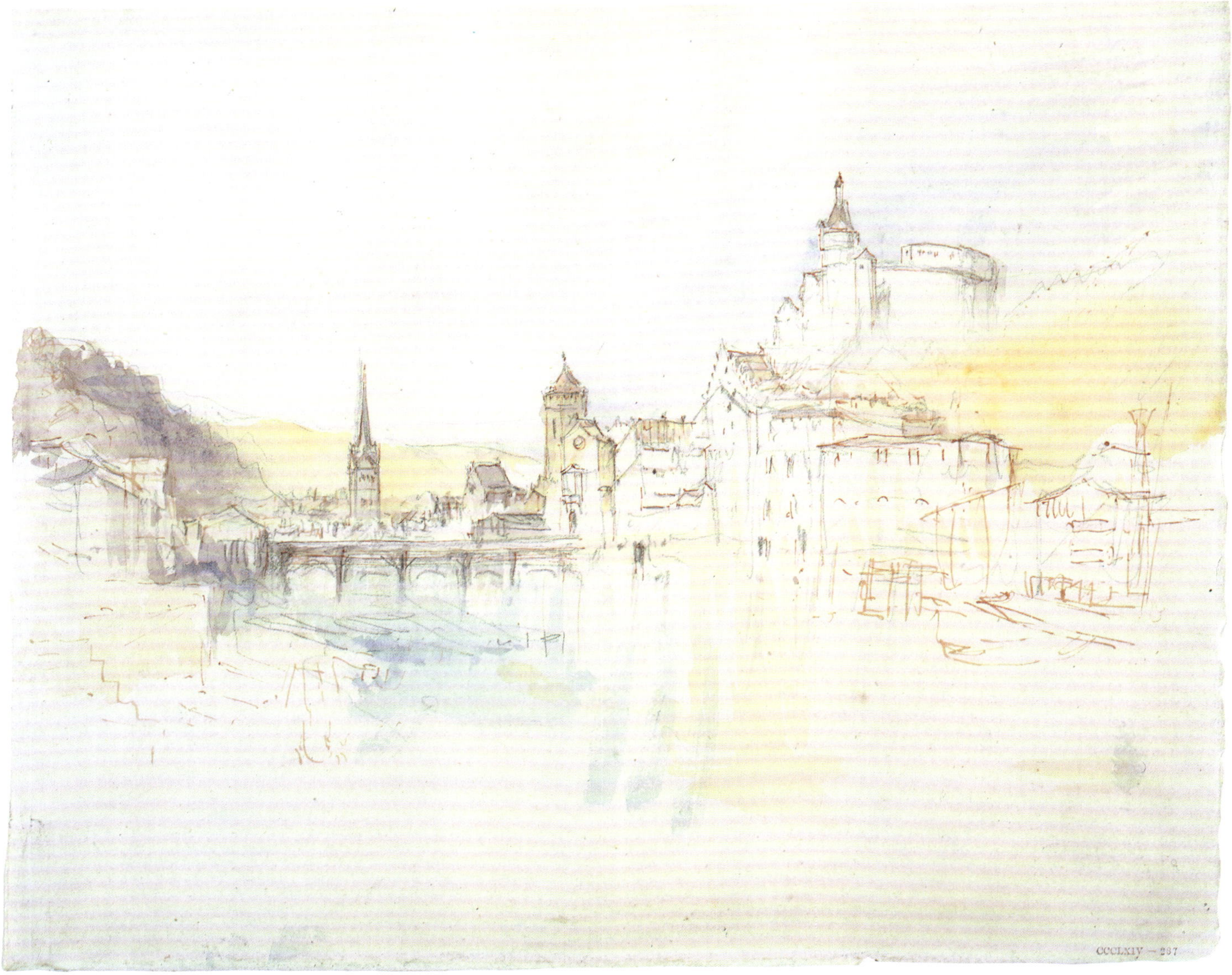

19 Schaffhausen

Schaffhausen: Looking Down the Rhine, from below Kastell Munot ?1841
Pencil and watercolour 237 × 294 ($9\frac{3}{8} \times 11\frac{5}{8}$)
TB CCCLXIV 287 D36141
EXH: NG (285)
LIT: *Works*, XIII, pp.198–9, 372, 623; *R on P*, pp.164–5

At last we enter Switzerland, and dispose ourselves to take pleasure in simpler and less superb masses of architecture, and in tones of clear and sweet mountain air.

This I believe to be rather a memorandum of the castle and bridge of Schaffhausen, by way of material likely to be of use in other compositions, than itself a design for a picture. But it is therefore all the more interesting, as showing how Turner could not but compose – even when he did not care to do so. The square house is put just under the castle, partly to sustain it, partly to set off its pretty outline; but these two masses being nearly equal, and attracting the eye as such, a third, the oblique sail, is added, and puts all right. But this sail is itself cut vertically into four, that it may carry down the divisions of the house just above, and give them importance enough to neutralise the formality of its central mass. The carrying down the dark right-hand side of the house into a curve, gathered up to the left by half of the sail, is especially Turneresque. Two gables and a chimney carry the diagonal of the sail out of the picture to the right.

In 1841 Turner made a large group of watercolours of the Falls of the Rhine at Schaffausen (W 1460–1467, W 1469), as well as a view of the town itself (W 1468, Fitzwilliam Museum, Cambridge); this last shares the spare use of colour found in this study. There are two other coloured drawings of Schaffhausen in the Turner Bequest (TB CCCLXIV 218, 337), and it is perhaps surprising that of the three watercolours Ruskin should have picked this example to catalogue in his first selection. Unlike many of the other Swiss views in this catalogue, it is not related to a finished watercolour. This is especially peculiar, since Ruskin owned the 1845 view of Schaffhausen at the time he wrote this catalogue (p.150, fig.48). In choosing this work, he seems to have been motivated by a desire to use the fact that it is not particularly finished in order to analyse Turner's painting and compositional techniques.

20 Constance

Constance: Sample Study *c.*1841–2
Watercolour 242 × 311 (9⁹⁄₁₆ × 12¼)
Verso inscribed in pencil, '8' and in red chalk '12'
TB CCCLXIV 288 D36142
EXH: NG (286); Düsseldorf 1950 (32, as 'c.1830'); Geneva 1955–6 (127); Tokyo 1963–4 (35, repr.); Brussels 1970–1 (98); British Museum 1975–6 (281, repr. p.141); Toronto 1980–1 (112, repr. p.183); Tate Gallery 1983; Melbourne 1985
LIT: *Works*, XIII, pp.199, 372, 623; *R on P*, p.165; Wedmore 1900, p.341; Dillon 1902, p.332–4, repr. pp.333; Serota 1970, p.112; Wilton 1979, p.484; Wilton 1982, p.66, pl.103

From the right bank of the Rhine; the Lake Constance in the distance.

The original sketch of a drawing made in 1842, at his own choice, for delight in the subject, and now in my possession [fig.19]. *The sketch is, however, of little importance, except on*

20

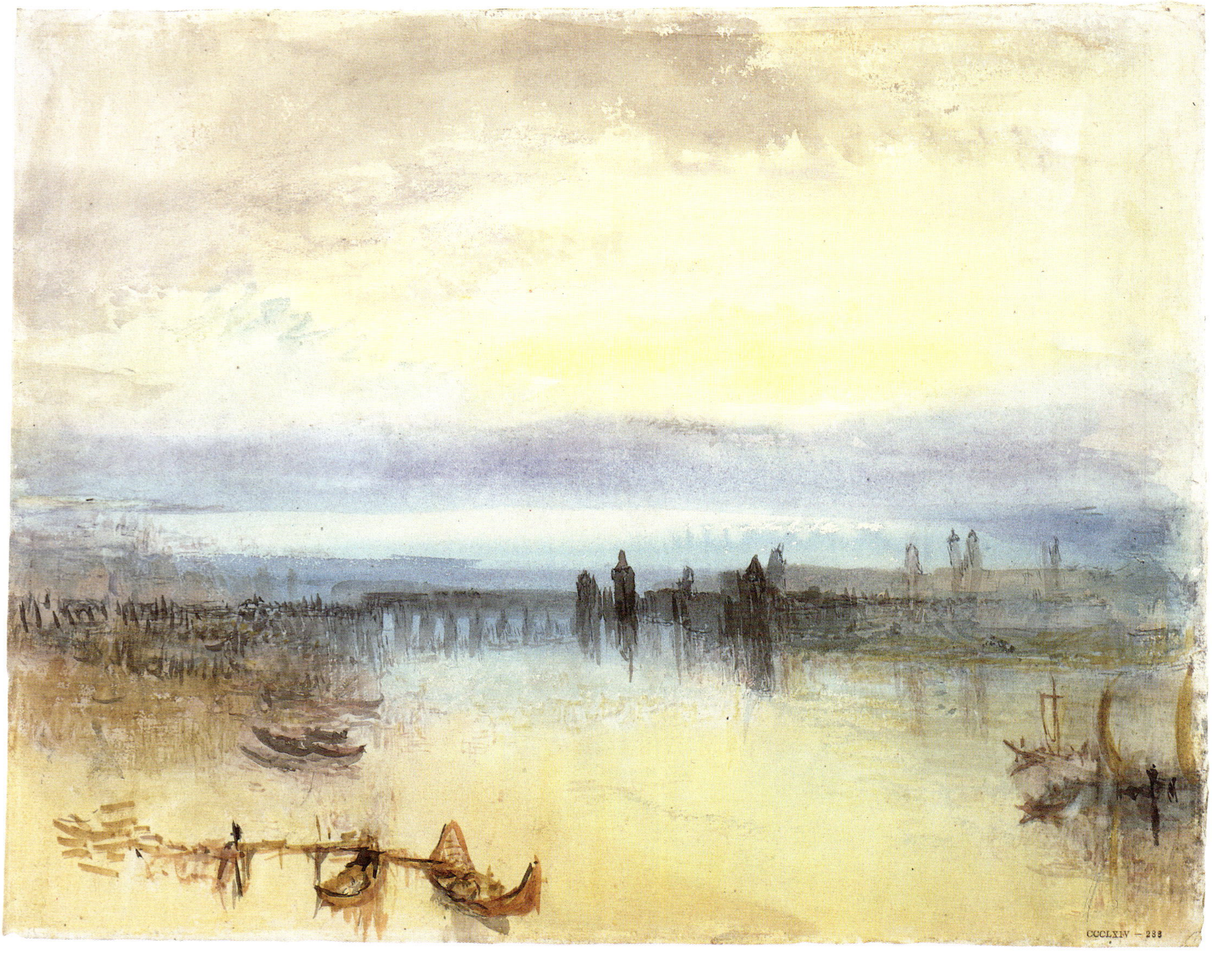

the ground of Turner's liking it himself. In the drawing made from it, he altered and enriched it exceedingly; the buildings being no more grey, but deep purple.

The introduction of the two boats in front is interesting, as an example of the way in which depth may be given to a picture by the perspective lines of its foreground objects. Remove these two boats, and the town at once loses all its distance, and the river all direction.

Ruskin's comments imply that this is actually a German subject, although he places it within the boundaries of Switzerland. Constance (or, more correctly, Konstanz) is indeed a German city and is divided by the Rhine as it flows out of Lake Constance. When this watercolour was shown to Turner's prospective clients as part of the 1842 group of 'sample studies', no one could be persuaded to select it (see Appendix II, pp.149–51). Turner, nevertheless, completed a finished watercolour based on this view as a means of paying Griffith for acting as his agent (fig.19). It was subsequently acquired by Ruskin, who noted that the day he brought it home was 'one of the happiest in my life' (*Works*, XIII, p.483). When cataloguing his watercolour, he later developed the comments he makes here, rightly noting that the finished work was 'unique in its luxury of colour' (*Works*, XIII, p.455). In the collection at Bembridge there is a squared-up pen and ink drawing by Ruskin, in which he has copied the foreground boats and distant towers of the finished watercolour (Bembridge, 1523). He perhaps intended to use his drawing to illustrate a lesson at the Working Men's College, where he taught from 1854.

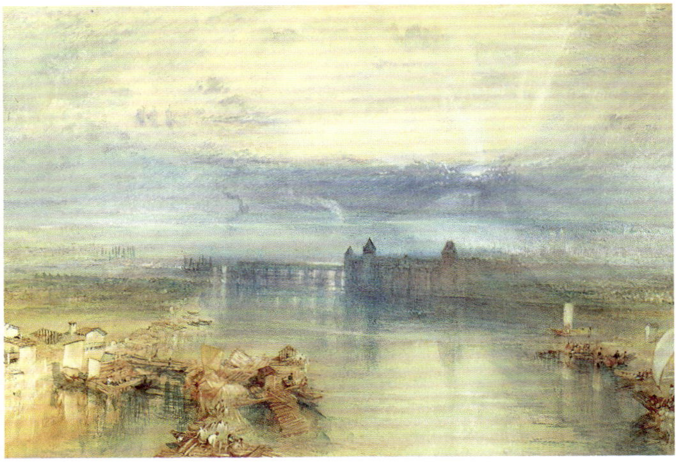

fig.19 'Constance' 1842, watercolour (W 1531).
York City Art Gallery

21 Zurich

A Fête Day in Zurich: Early Morning: Sample Study *c.*1845
Pencil, watercolour and scratching out
234 × 326 (9¼ × 12⅞)
Verso inscribed in pencil, 'Windus | Zurich | 7', and in ?Windus's hand, 'BGW'
TB CCCLXIV 289 D36143
EXH: NG (287); Tate Gallery, 1959–65; British Museum 1975–6 (291, repr. p.158); Zurich 1976–7 (89); Tate Gallery 1983; Melbourne 1985
LIT: *Works*, XIII, pp.199–200, 372, 623; *R on P*, p.165; Dillon 1902, repr. p.364; Rawlinson, Finberg and Holroyd 1909, p.37, pl.XXVII; Serota 1970, p.118; Russell and Wilton 1976, p.121; Wilton 1979, p.486; Wilton 1982, p.72, pl.121

We arrive at Zurich, after a long day's journey from Constance. The sun is setting beyond the lake, and the bridge over the Limmat is crowded with people, intent on aquatic affairs of an unintelligible kind. Realised for Mr. Windus of Tottenham, in 1845 [fig.20]. *The drawing has since been engraved* [27 May 1854; R 672, engraved by T.A. Prior].

In both of the commissioned watercolours of Zurich (figs.20, 21), Turner suggests the presence of huge crowds. Seen enjoying a fête on the waterfront, or going about their daily work, they are effectively bound together by the atmospheric sunset light created by Turner's watercolour washes. Andrew Wilton has suggested that these views of Zurich represent Turner's 'final important statement about the place of man in the cosmos, and it is an affirmative, indeed a joyous one' (Toronto 1980–1, p.171, no.93). As the spectator looks down the River Limmat in Turner's view, the city's principal features can be seen on either bank: the twin towers of the Grossmünster, on the left, and the spire of the church of St Peter, on the right, with the smaller tower of the Fraumünster Kirche, beyond. A less familiar watercolour view of Zurich is TB CCCLXIV 311, which focuses on the huge dial on the tower of St Peter's church.

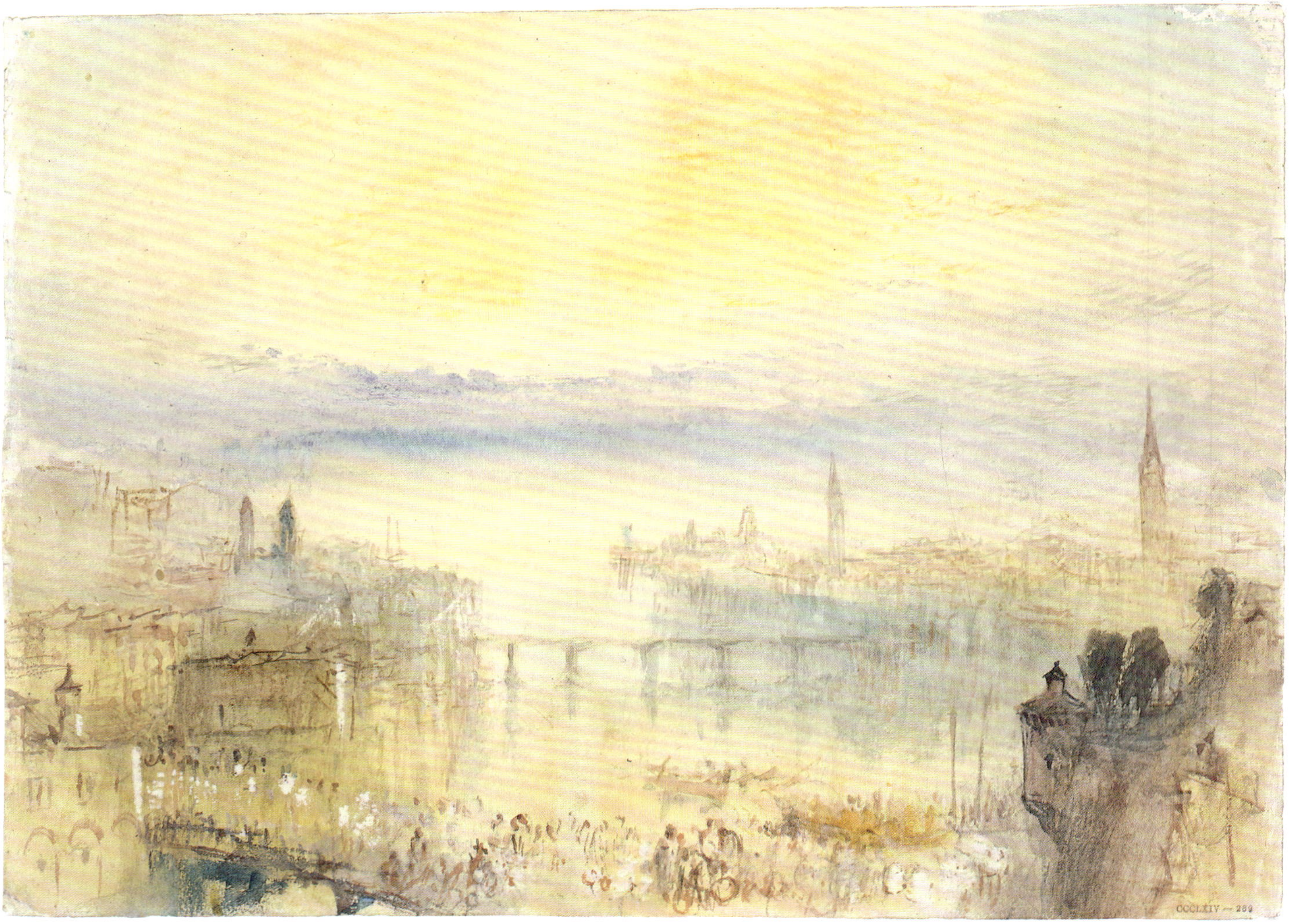

21

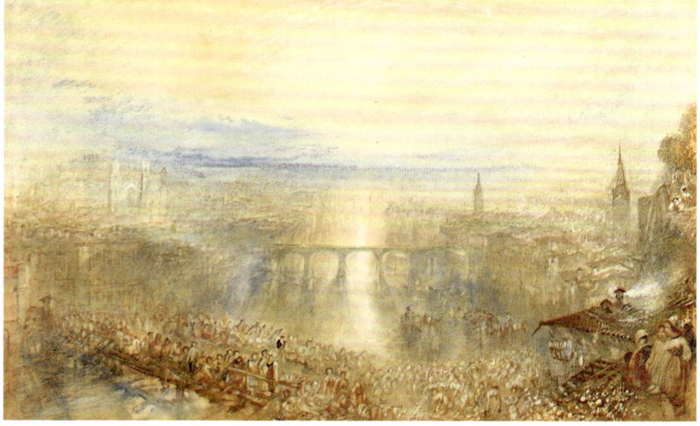

fig.20 'A Fête Day in Zurich: Early Morning' 1845, watercolour (W 1548). *Kunsthaus, Zurich*

22 Zurich

Zurich: Sample Study *c.*1841–2
Watercolour 241 × 304 (9½ × 12)
Verso inscribed in pencil, '<u>J A Munro Esqr</u> | 4', and in red chalk, '10'
TB CCCLXIV 291 D36147
EXH: NG (289); Tate Gallery 1959–65; Royal Academy 1974–5 (605); Copenhagen 1976 (84); Hamburg 1976 (113, repr. p.155, and p.80, pl.XVI); Zurich 1976–7 (42); The Hague 1978–9 (86, repr. 114); Mexico City 1979 (84, repr. in Mexican catalogue only)
LIT: *Works*, XIII, pp.200, 372, 623; *R on P*, p.166; Dillon 1902, pp.332, 362–6; Serota 1970, p.112; Wilton 1979, p.484; Wilton 1982, p.65, pl.98; Wilton, *Turner Watercolours in the Clore Gallery*, 1988 (2nd ed.), pp.144–5, pl.65

We get out of the crowd as soon as possible, and climb the bastions above the town. Blue and white mists gather over the lake as the sun descends.

Very beautiful in its way, though this belongs to an embarrassing class of Turner's sketches. It is not easy to see the use of carrying them so far, unless these views were to be ultimately completed, nor why the textures should be so highly laboured throughout, while the details wanted for completion are lost sight of.

Realised for Mr. Munro in 1842 [fig.21].

In this view Turner looks over the roofs of Zurich from a position near the River Sihl, on the west of the city. The use of watercolour here is very fluid. The movement of Turner's brush can be traced in the complex textures suggestive of the light falling across the surfaces of the densely packed houses that are only fully developed in the finished view. On 13 April 1844 Ruskin wrote in his Diary, 'Into town to see Munro's collection, and made myself very unhappy for two of them – the Splugen and Zurich. Would give the world for them; I shall have them some time however if I live.' [*Diaries*, I, p.273]. Although he did later possess the Splügen (see under cat.no.75), Ruskin never owned the finished version of Zurich, based on this work.

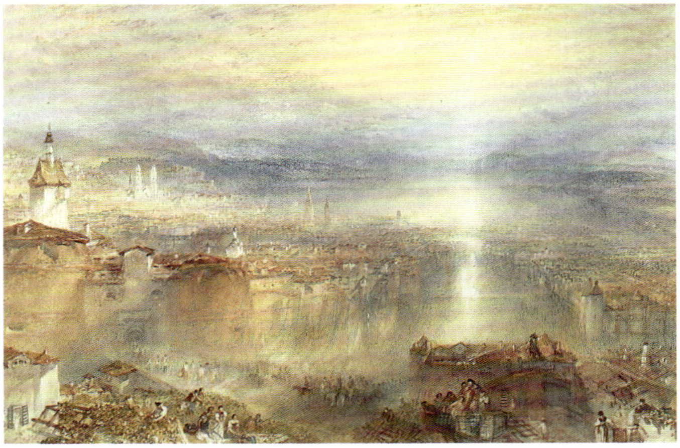

fig.21 'Zurich' 1842, watercolour (W 1533). *British Museum*

22

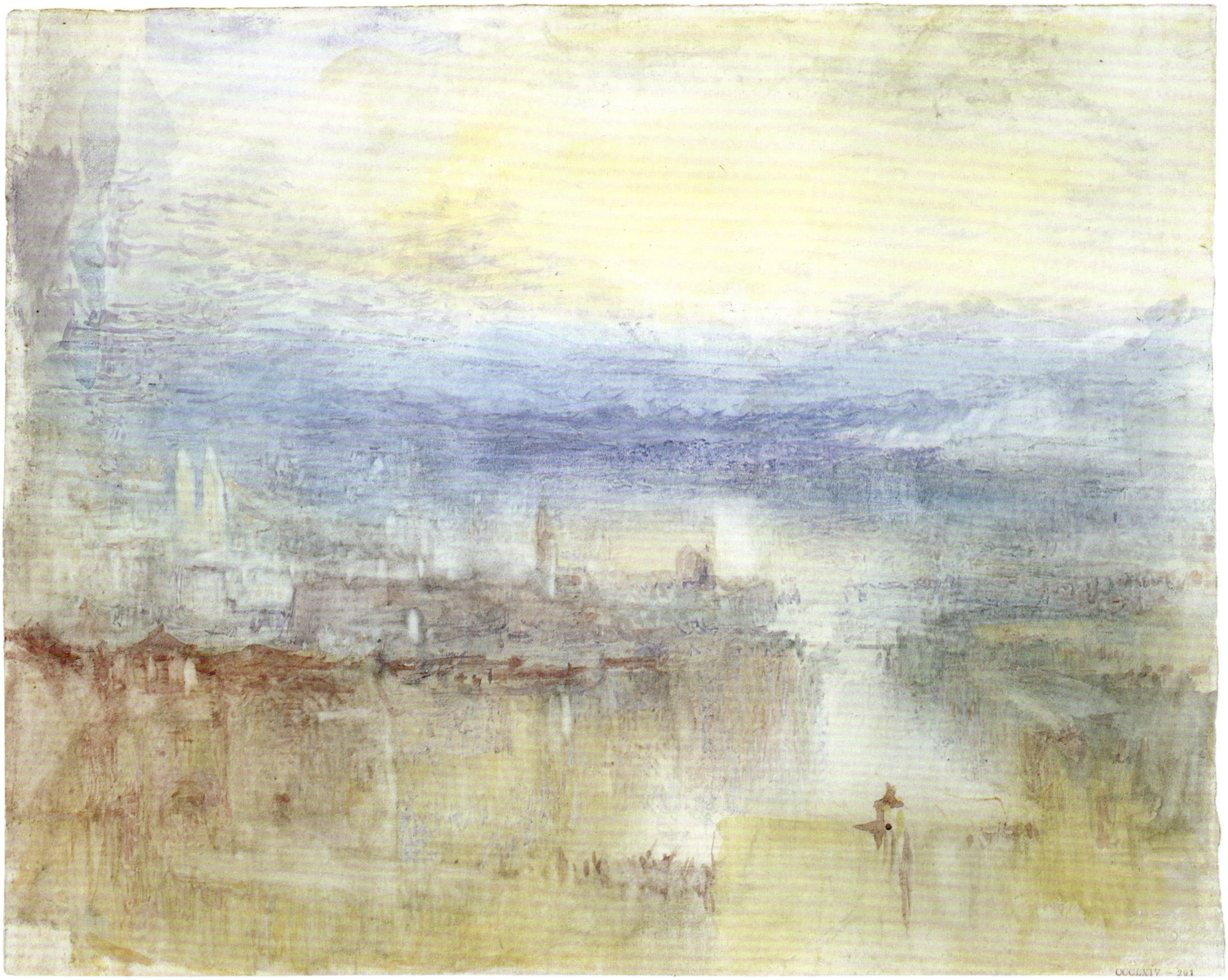

23 Lucerne

Lucerne from the Walls: Sample Study *c.*1841–2
Pencil and watercolour 234 × 312 (9¼ × 12⁵⁄₁₆)
Watermarked: ?fleur de lys
Verso inscribed in pencil, '<u>J Ruskin Jn^r Esqr</u>' and in red chalk, '17'
TB CCCLXIV 290 D36145
EXH: NG (288); Berne 1947–8 (84); Geneva 1955–6 (128); Tokyo 1963–4 (36, repr.); Brussels 1970–1 (99); British Museum 1975–6 (285); Zurich 1976–7 (74); Tate Gallery 1983; Melbourne 1985; Tate Gallery 1992–3 (148, as 'Lausanne from the walls, 1842')
LIT: *Works*, XIII, pp.200 (this work was no.21 in the first edition of the catalogue), 372, 623; *R on P*, pp.165–6, repr. opp. p.166; Wedmore 1900, p.354; Dillon 1902, pp.332–4, repr. p.331; Rawlinson, Finberg and Holroyd 1909, p.37, pl.XXI; Serota 1970, p.111; Wilton 1979, p.483; Wilton 1982, p.65, pl.100; Hayman 1990, p.95, repr.

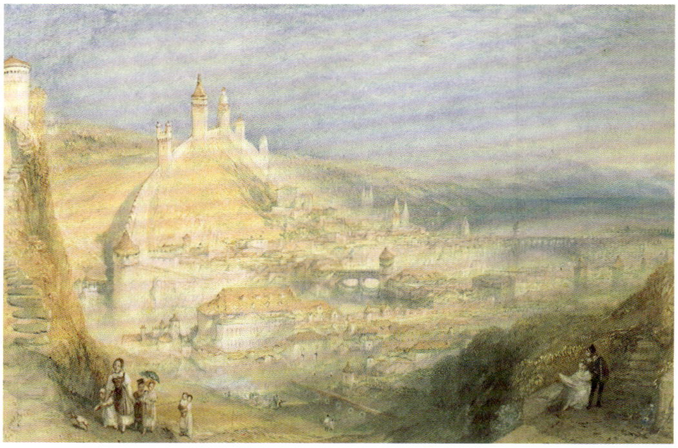

fig.22 'Lucerne from the Walls' 1842, watercolour (W 1529).
Board of Trustees of the National Museums and Galleries on Merseyside (Lady Lever Art Gallery)

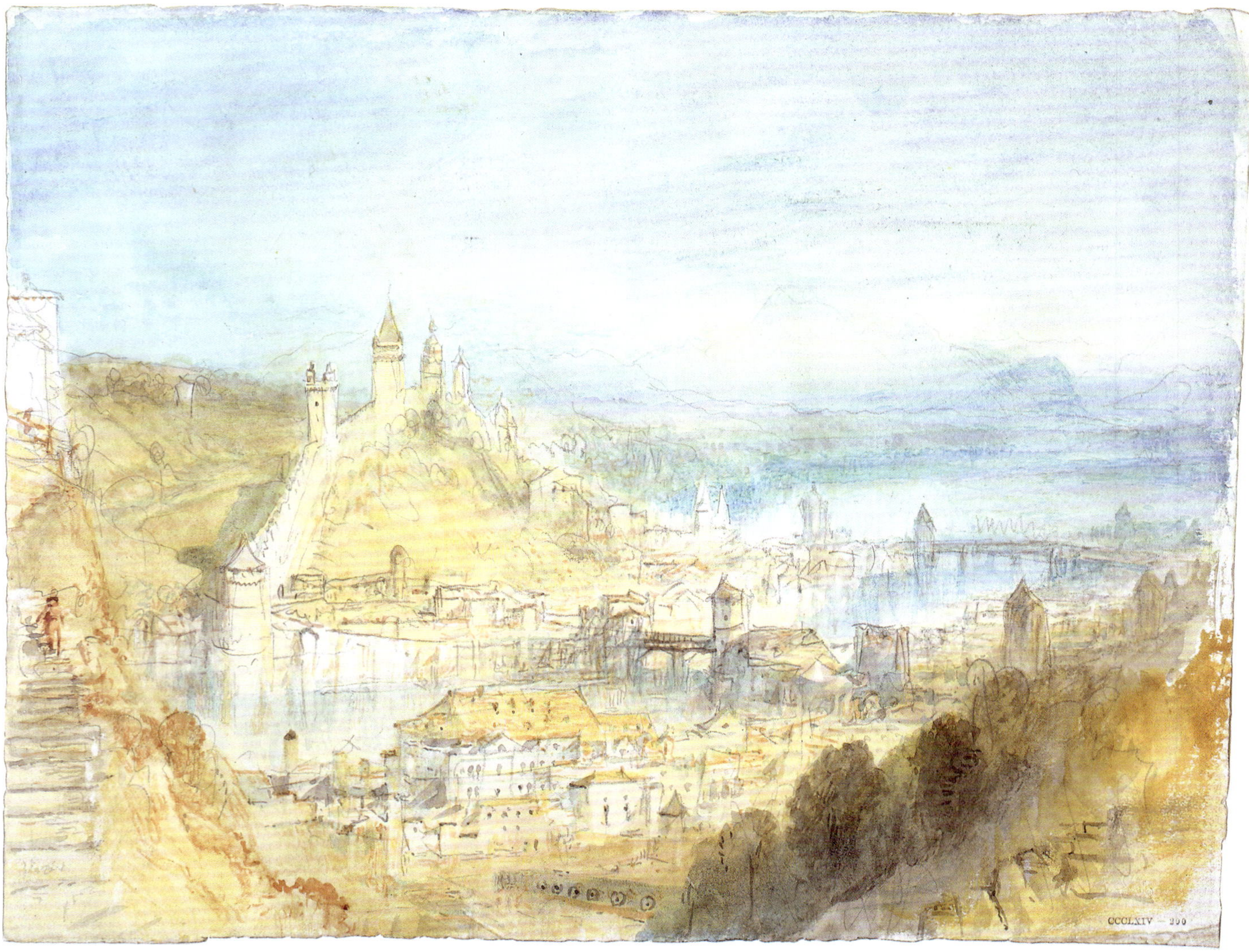

23

Arriving at Lucerne, we immediately climb the hill above the Reuss to try if we can see the Alps. No Alps to be seen, the day being grey and misty and disagreeably hot besides. The form of the Rigi is, however, dimly visible beyond the first branch of the lake; and the old town delights us, especially the wall and towers bent like a bow over the hill behind it, which defended it in the old times of Austrian spears from any attack on the land side.

An elaborate and most precious drawing, all the more valuable, as the characteristic features of Lucerne are now being rapidly destroyed.

Realised for me by Turner in 1842 [fig.22].

Turner made Lucerne his base on several of his late visits to Switzerland. He depicted the town and the view across the lake to the Rigi repeatedly, exploring in his watercolours the changes brought about by different light and weather effects (see here nos. 24, 31, 35, 36). This view encompasses the whole town from a position to the north-west, and looks up the Reuss, past the Spreuerbrücke and the famous Kapellbrücke, to the waters of Lake Lucerne. What Ruskin aptly likens to a strained 'bow' is the fourteenth-century Museggmauer, a protective wall punctuated by nine towers of different architectural styles. The way Turner depicted the wall fascinated Ruskin, who made his own outline on a visit to Lucerne in order 'to illustrate Turner drawing' (see p.18, fig.8). Similarly, in volume IV of *Modern Painters* (1856), he discussed Turner's tendency to produce only vague effects in his treatment of distances with reference to the towers in the finished watercolour of this view (*Works*, VI, pp.92–3, pl.26). There are very few changes between this 'sample study' and the watercolour first owned by Ruskin: the single figure climbing the walls is replaced by two groups of holiday-makers; and what is only a line of six round objects in the study is given greater substance as a shooting contest. At the time of writing this catalogue, Ruskin had already prophesied that Lucerne would be spoilt by insensitive changes (*Works*, VI, p.456). His worst fears were confirmed when he returned in 1866: 'Round by Turner's old view, all destroyed by barracks below, now, and Restaurants *every*where' (*Diaries*, II, p.591: 19 June 1866).

24 Lucerne. From the lake

Lucerne from the Lake: Sample Study *c*.1844–5
Watercolour 233 × 327 (9 3/16 × 12 7/8)
Verso inscribed in pencil: 'Lucerne | 8 | 10', and in another hand 'J.R.'
TB CCCLXIV 386 D36252
EXH: ?NG (Box Z); 4th Loan Collection 1891, no.18; Tate Gallery 1983; Melbourne 1985
LIT: *Works*, XIII, p.201; White 1896, p.22 no.24, as '1814'; *R on P*, p.166 n.3; Serota 1970, p.116; Wilton 1979, p.485; Wilton 1982, p.71, pl.115

After dinner we take a boat, and begin sketching the town from the water. The weather clears gradually, and as we watch the mountains come one by one out of the haze, we are much diverted from our work, and draw the town but carelessly.

Realised by his own choice in 1845. The drawing is now in my possession [fig.23].

During the spring of 1844, Ruskin remarked to Turner on the 'peculiar atmosphere' of his most recent watercolours. To this Turner replied, 'Yes ... atmosphere is my style' (*Diaries*, I, pp.273–4). This is one of many studies in which the desire to convey the sense of a fleeting impression has overtaken more formal requirements of topographical accuracy. The finished watercolour, by contrast, introduces a more precise architectural panorama, and includes the ancient Hofbrücke, running along the waterfront below the towers of the Museggmauer. Turner had recorded numerous details such as this in his *Between Lucerne and Thun* sketchbook, a page of which surveys the town from a viewpoint similar to that in this study (TB CCCXXIX f.3 verso, ?1841 or 1844; see Tate Gallery 1993, p.42 no.20, repr.). Although Ruskin was the first

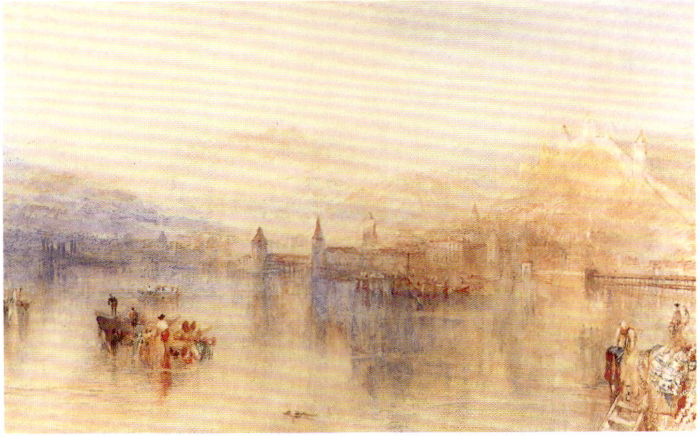

fig.23 'Lucerne from the Lake' 1845, watercolour (W 1544). *Mr and Mrs Eugene Victor Thaw, USA*

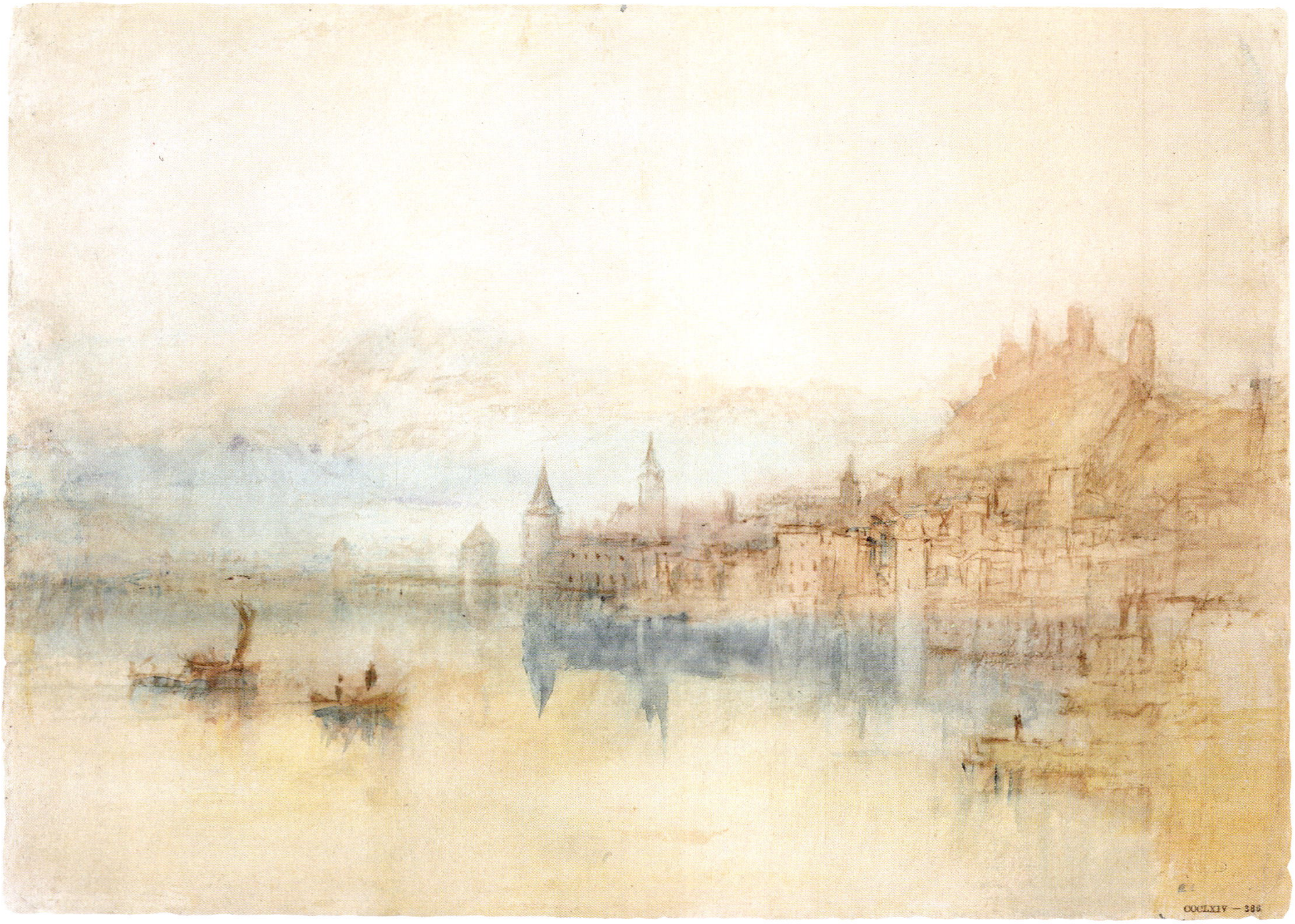

24

owner of the finished view, it was not one of the watercolours he commissioned from Turner in 1845 (see Appendix II, pp.152–4). While it hung on the walls of his home, he wrote about it in Volume IV of *Modern Painters*. There he noted how Turner had adjusted the outline of Mount Pilatus's peak to suit his own instinctive notions of mountain form (*Works*, VI, pp.277–8, fig.72, and pp.361–2, figs.106–7). In the mid-1860s, Ruskin eventually parted with the drawing 'because it was too sorrowful to me – after Lucerne itself was finally destroyed' (*Works*, XIII, p.476).

25 Mont Pilate

Mount Pilatus, from Lake Lucerne ?1841 or 1844
Pencil, watercolour and gouache 227 × 291 ($8\frac{15}{16} \times 11\frac{1}{2}$)
TB CCCXXXII 26 D33496
EXH: NG (290)
LIT: *Works*, XIII, pp.201, 372 as 'Mount Pilatus from Küssnacht', 623; *R on P*, pp.166–7; Serota 1970, p.130

The evening gets so beautiful that we give up our sketch of the town, and row out into the lake; Mont Pilate glowing in ruby red, as the sun sets.

Wonderfully beautiful. The perspective of the right-hand shore, which gives distance and magnitude to the Mont Pilate, the use of the oblique line of the boat to keep the eye from resting on the formal oblong of the lake boundaries, and the long reflections of the fragment of blue cloud are all intensely Turneresque.

Although this view of Mount Pilatus has been thought in the past to have been made from Küssnacht, it was more probably made from a position closer to Lucerne. The view from Küssnacht itself can be found in cat.no.30, where Mount Pilatus is only one of several peaks above the lake. Turner sketched the mountain in one of the small books he used in Switzerland, although it has not yet been possible to date the sketches precisely (*Between Lucerne and Thun*, ?1841 or 1844, see TB CCCXXIX f.10 verso). There is evidence at the left-hand edge of this sheet that it was formerly part of one of Turner's soft covered, or 'roll', sketchbooks. Sadly, the appearance of the watercolour itself has changed significantly since it was selected by Ruskin. The darkening of some washes of gouache is especially noticeable in the sky. This seems to be the result of a subsequent change in the pigment used or in the medium applied. A similar effect can also be found on other sheets of this sketchbook (TB CCCXXXII ff.29, 31). The drawing was included in the larger selection of Turner watercolours at the National Gallery during the nineteenth century, where it was one of many Turner subjects copied by Hercules Brabazon Brabazon (1821–1906); his version is also in the Tate Gallery ('Sunset: Mountain and Lake', NO3651). Brabazon, like many other young artists, would most probably have been encouraged to undertake such copies as a result of Ruskin's advice in publications such as *The Elements of Drawing* (1857, *Works*, XV).

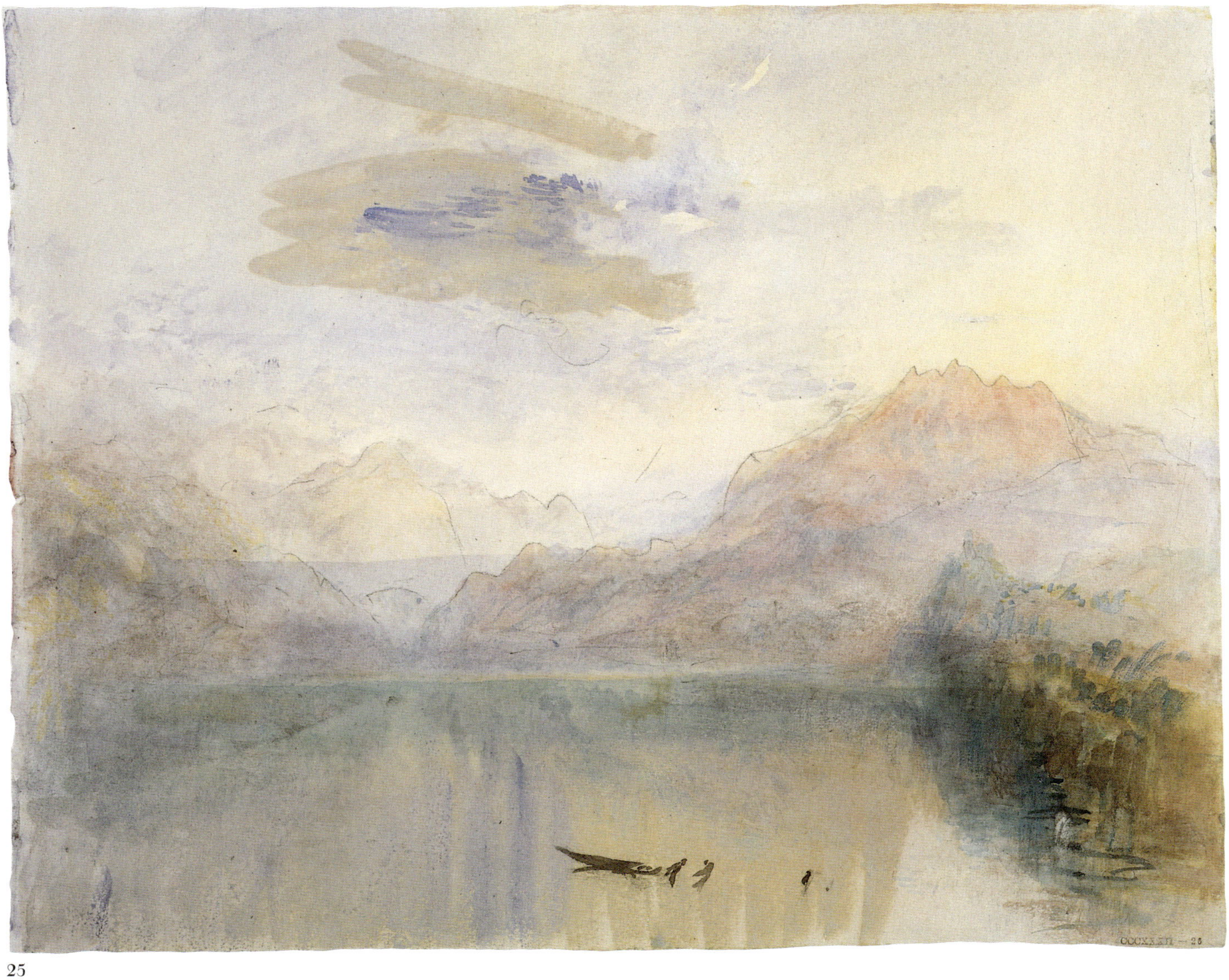

25

26 Lucerne Lake

Lake Lucerne: the Bay of Uri, from Brunnen *c*.1841–2
Watercolour 244 × 299 ($9\frac{5}{8} \times 11\frac{13}{16}$)
TB CCCLXIV 342 D36202
EXH: NG (769); Tate Gallery 1931–4; Coventry 1974 (36); Toronto 1980–1 (114); Paris 1983–4 (247)
LIT: *Works*, XIII, p.201 (no.22 in Ruskin's first edition of the catalogue); *R on P*, pp.123 n.1, 258; Russell and Wilton 1976, p.100, repr.

Having set out for an excursion among the hills, we sleep at Brunnen, and are sorry to find, next morning, on walking down to the quay, that bad weather is coming on; the lake looking very hazy, and mischievous clouds forming under the Rothstok on the right hand.

Brunnen was very little more than a small village when Turner first visited it in 1802. It did, however, offer spectacular views of Lake Lucerne in both directions, tempting Turner to revisit it on a number of occasions; other views at Brunnen in this catalogue are nos.32–4. Judging by the number of existing watercolours of this subject, Turner was particularly fond of the view south, looking down the Bay of Uri (see for example, TB CCCXXXII 32 and TB CCCLXIV 313, 348, 387). The boats in the foreground testify to Brunnen's importance at that time as a port for the area around Schwytz; goods were ferried south past Brunnen, towards the St Gotthard Pass, on their way to Italy. Another of Turner's watercolours of this view makes plain the range of goods that were transported on the lake, and is inscribed 'Cattle going in boat' (TB CCCLXIV 348).

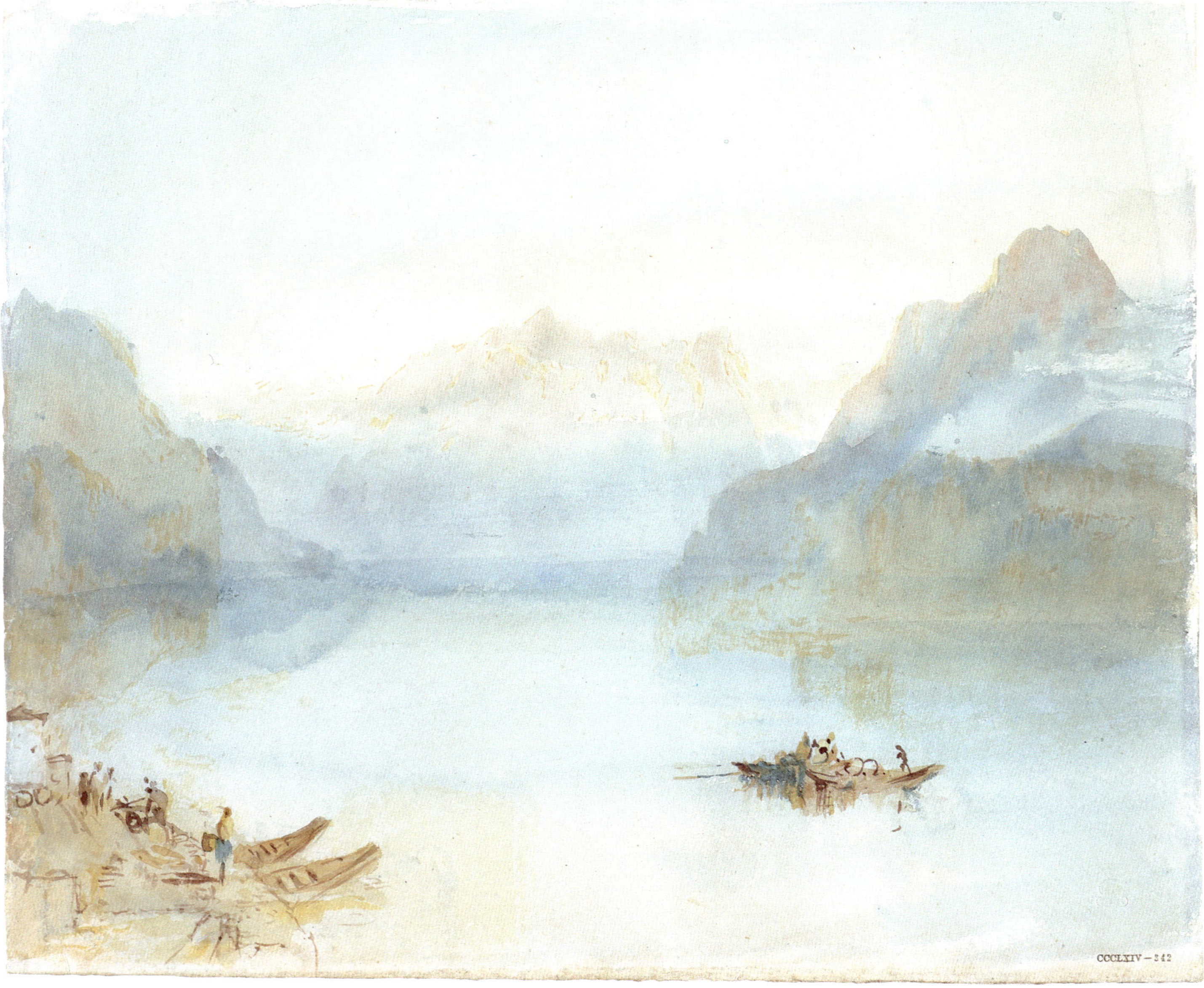

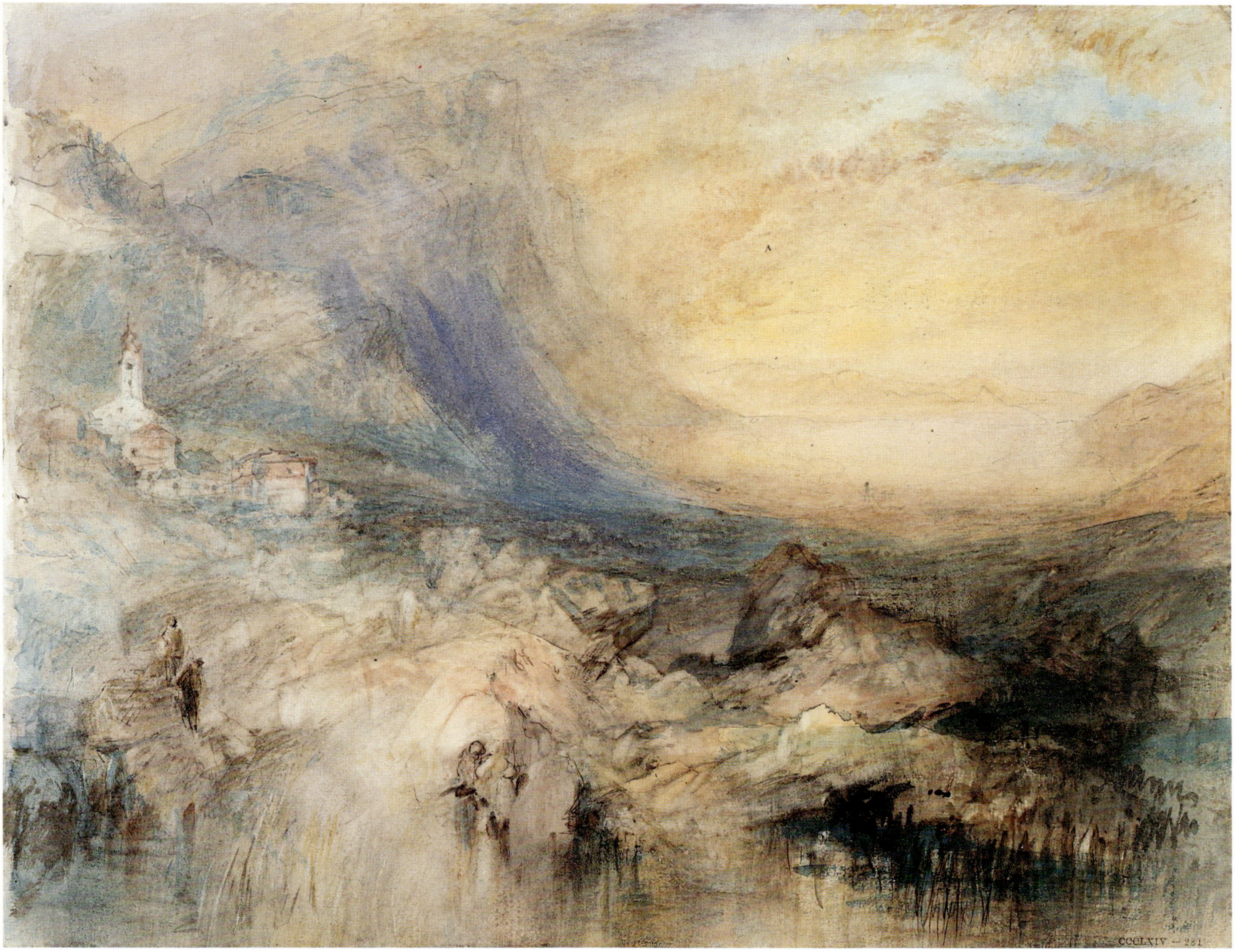

27 Goldau

Goldau, with the Lake of Zug in the Distance:
Sample Study *c.*1842–3
Pencil and watercolour, with pen 228 × 290 (9 × 11$\frac{7}{16}$)
Verso inscribed in pencil: 'Goldau – Rigi – and Lake of Zug | No.7 | x 05'
TB CCCLXIV 281 D36131
EXH: NG (98); Tate Gallery 1959–65; Dresden 1972 (113, repr. p.89, fig.31); Lisbon 1973 (55, repr. p.139); Royal Academy 1974–5 (610); Copenhagen 1976 (86); Hamburg 1976 (115, repr. p.157 and p.81, pl.XVII); Zurich 1976–7 (80); Toronto 1980–1 (105, repr. p.89 and pl.25); Tate Gallery 1987; Tate Gallery 1990
LIT: *Works*, VI, pp.378–84; XIII, pp.201–2 (no.23 in the 1st ed. of Ruskin's catalogue), 372, 612; *R on P*, p.123; Wedmore 1900, p.355; Dillon 1902, p.332; Holme 1903, repr. as W44; Serota 1970, pp.114, 131; Wilton 1979, p.484; Wilton 1982, pp.68–9, pl.108.

The bad weather does come on; but we persist in our excursion; and, after getting very wet at Schwytz, are rewarded by seeing the clouds break as we reach the ridge of Goldau, and reveal the Lake of Zug under a golden sky.
Realised for me in 1843 [fig.24].

The unexpected deluge of rock that fell from the Rossberg in 1806 and engulfed the entire village of Goldau, was well known to nineteenth-century Swiss tourists, and was even commemorated in Byron's verse drama *Manfred* (1817). Turner's view does not focus on the mountain which had wrought such devastation, but is instead, concerned with the new village on the lower slopes of the Rigi. Further down the valley, the spire of the church at Arth can be seen in the distance. Murray's *Hand-book for Travellers in Switzerland* records that the valley was filled with huge boulders, between which natural springs had formed enclosed pools (Murray 1838, p.44). Turner again visited the spot during his 1843 tour, making a number of pencil drawings of the outline of the Rigi (see especially *Lakes of Zug and Goldau* sketchbook, TB CCCXXXI f.11 verso). Although some modern scholars have challenged his opinion (see Wilton 1982), Ruskin believed 'Goldau' to be a tragic subject. He noted especially Turner's powerful use of red in the sky, a feature more marked in the finished version, and which he believed Turner used symbolically to suggest blood and death (see *Works*, VI, pp.378–81, pl.50). A painting in which Ruskin also connected a fiery scarlet sunset with a portentous message was 'Slavers Throwing Overboard the Dead and Dying – Typhon Coming on', which his father bought for him as a New Year present in 1844 (1840, Museum of Fine Arts, Boston; B&J 385). A copy by Ruskin of the finished 'Goldau' is in the Ashmolean Museum in Oxford (Walton 1972, p.84, repr).

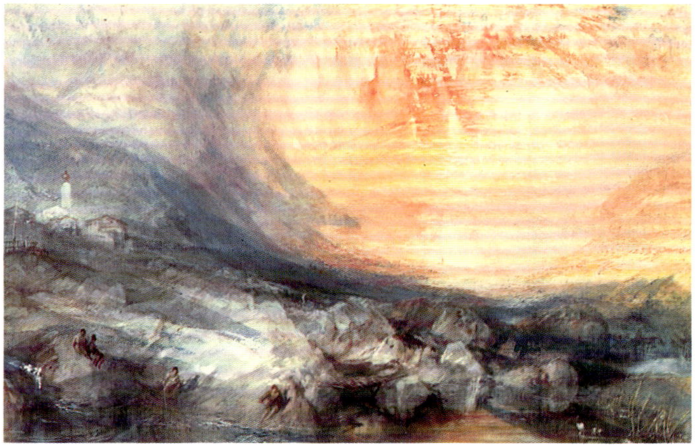

fig.24 'Goldau' 1843, watercolour (W 1537). *Private Collection, courtesy Richard L. Feigen & Co.*

28

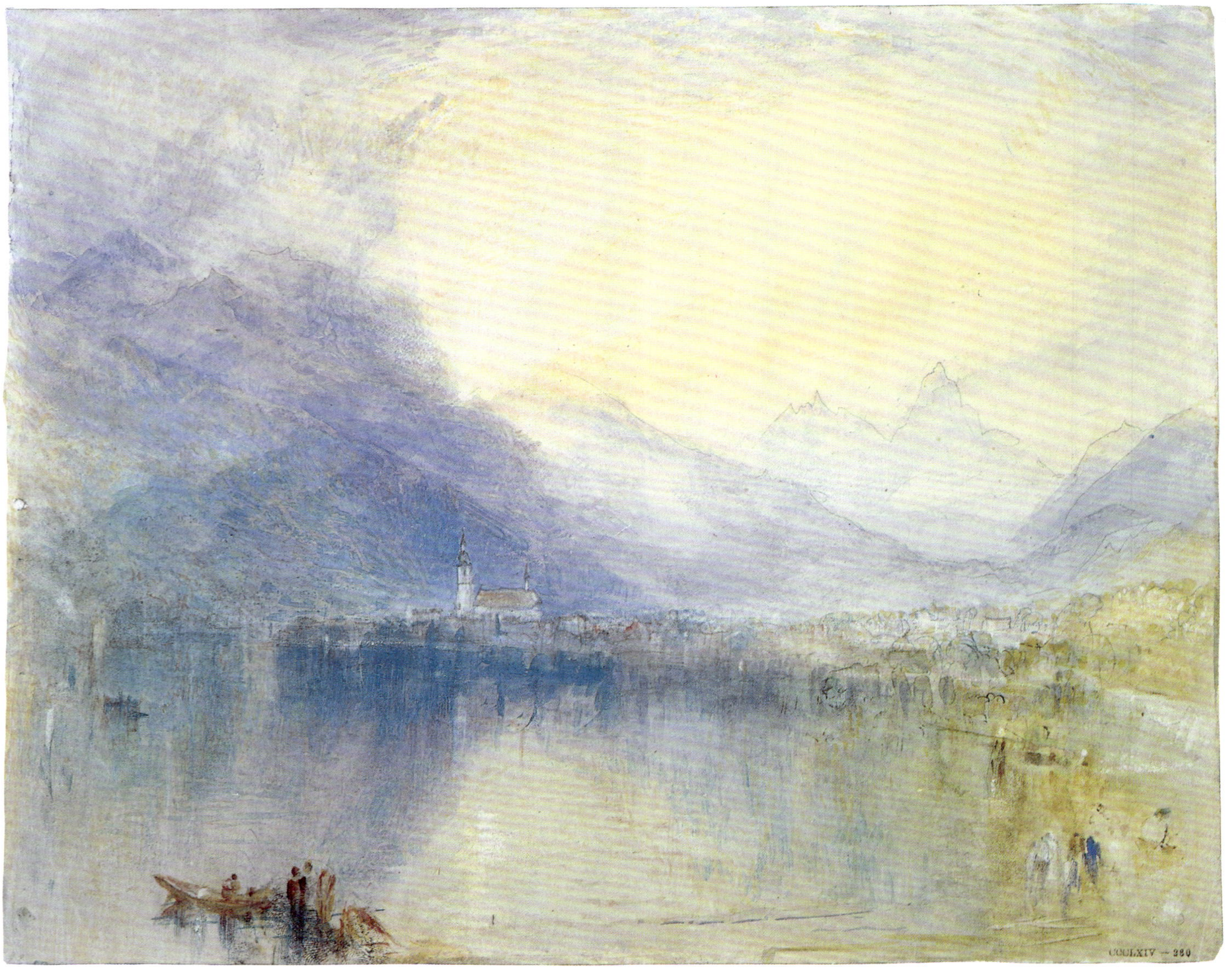

28 Arth

Arth, on the Lake of Zug. Early Morning: Sample Study *c.*1842–3
Pencil and watercolour, with pen and ink and scratching out
228 × 290 (9 × 11 7/16)
Verso inscribed in pencil: 'Art. Lake of Zug | No.9' 'x 810' and 'Mr Munro'
TB CCCLXIV 280 D36129
EXH: NG (97); National Gallery 1936–9; Amsterdam 1947–8 (66); Berne 1947–8 (75, as '*c.*1830'); Düsseldorf 1950 (27); British Museum 1958 (75–7); Adelaide 1961 (31, repr. p.24); Washington 1963–4 (73); Royal Academy 1974–5 (606); Leningrad 1975–6 (78); Copenhagen 1976 (85); Hamburg 1976 (114, repr. p.156); Tate Gallery 1983; Melbourne 1985; Lugano 1991–2 (60, repr. p.163); Tate Gallery 1993 (29, repr. pp.28, 47)
LIT: *Works*, XIII, pp.202, 372, 612; *R on P*, p.122; Dillon 1902, pp.332, 362, repr. p.363; Holme 1903, repr. W37; Serota 1970, pp.113, 131; Wilton 1979, p.484; Wilton 1982, p.67, pl.105

We sleep at Arth, and are up, and out on the lake, early in the morning; to good purpose. The sun rises behind the Mythens, and we see such an effect of lake and light, as we shall not forget soon.

Elaborate and lovely.

Realised for Mr. Munro in 1843 [fig.25].

Arth is situated at the southern end of the Lake of Zug in the valley between the Rigi and the Rossberg. In Turner's depiction, the only building to be clearly distinguished is the seventeenth century parish church of Sts Georg and Zeno, which rises up from the edge of the lake. Ruskin suggested that Turner thought of this tranquil morning scene as the contrasting pair to the sunset at Goldau (cat.no.27), and that both subjects record effects Turner had actually seen at the places depicted (*Works*, VII, p.438n, pl.87). Turner uses only gradations of blue and yellow in this work to create one of the richest tonal studies among his late watercolours, recalling similar treatments of the Rigi from this period. While the colours are perfectly balanced in the 'sample' study, the watercolour of Arth that Turner produced for Munro abandoned the subtle haze that makes the study so appealing, and instead adopted a much darker palette. This proved to be not to Munro's taste (*Works*, XIII, p.484), and so it was later sold to Ruskin, who had long coveted the work. At one time he had became greatly vexed when he thought Munro had sold it to Windus (*Diaries*, II, pp.490–1). In characteristic fashion, however, he soon tired of the watercolour, complaining that Turner had introduced 'coarse' figures in the foreground and had taken 'less care for the painting, and more for the facts' (*Works*, XIII, p.455).

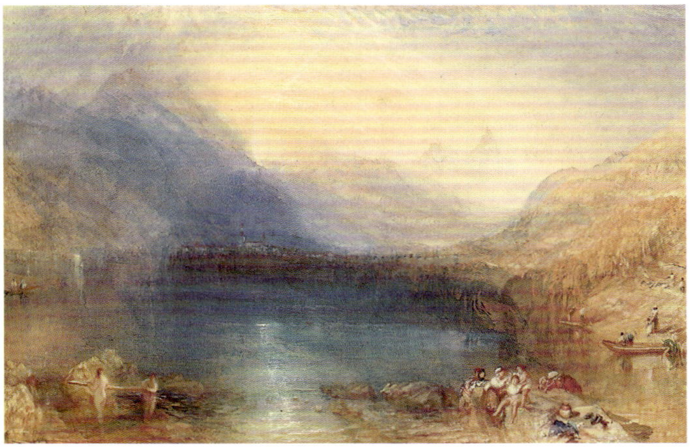

fig.25 'The Lake of Zug: Early Morning' 1843, watercolour, gouache, and coloured chalks, over traces of graphite; scraping with penknife (W 1535). *Metropolitan Museum of Art, New York, Marquand Fund, 1959*

29 Kussnacht

Küssnacht, Lake of Lucerne: Sample Study *c.*1842–3
Pencil and watercolour, with pen and scratching out
228 × 292 (9 × 11½)
Verso inscribed in pencil: 'Kusnacht and Tells Church and Gesler Castle | Lake of Lucern | No.2 | x 99 | * 6 | Mr.Munro'
TB CCCLXIV 208 D36053
EXH: Oxford 1878 (235–47); Eastbourne 1937 (Frame 12); Sheffield 1946–7 (Frame 12); Berne 1947–8 (77); Whitechapel 1953 (181); Wakefield 1960 (Frame 12); Washington 1963–4 (72, repr.); Manchester 1966 (49); Prague 1969 (140); Royal Academy 1974–5 (609); Zurich 1976–7 (79); Athens, Georgia 1982 (85); Tate Gallery 1983; Stockholm 1984 (45); Tate Gallery 1993 (27, repr. p.46)
LIT: *Works*, XIII, pp.202 (no.24 in the 1st ed. of Ruskin's catalogue), 562; Wedmore 1900, p.356; Dillon 1902, p.332; Serota 1970, pp.113, 130; Russell and Wilton 1976, p.101; Wilton 1979, p.484; Wilton 1982, p.67, pl.106.

We breakfast at Kussnacht, and afterwards go fishing on the Lake of Lucerne. The village, seen from the boat, presents this pleasant aspect; the clouds of last night melting away gradually from the hills.

Realised for Mr. Munro in 1843 [fig.26].

Küssnacht lies at the end of the most northerly arm of Lake Lucerne. Like much of the area around Lake Lucerne, its history is steeped in the legends associated with William Tell and his part in the liberation of Switzerland from Austrian rule. It was after a visit to Küssnacht that Goethe suggested the subject of Tell's heroic struggles to Schiller, resulting in the famous play (1804), and subsequently in Rossini's opera (1829). On the back of this watercolour an inscription by Turner refers to the little chapel just outside Küssnacht, near where Tell is supposed to have killed his enemy Gessler. He also mentions the ruined tower on a hill behind the town, which even in Turner's time was only romantically connected with Gessler. In this composition, and in those of Arth and Brunnen (cat.nos.28, 32), Turner uses the strong diagonal lines of the mountains as a natural framing device. The reflections floating out on to the lake give an echo to this underlying structure. At the centre of the image is the baroque church of Sts Peter and Paul, together with the town hall and the old schoolhouse. In the watercolour completed for Munro, Turner unified his design with a rich golden tone, before applying areas of vivid green gouache to suggest the woodland on the rising ground above the lake.

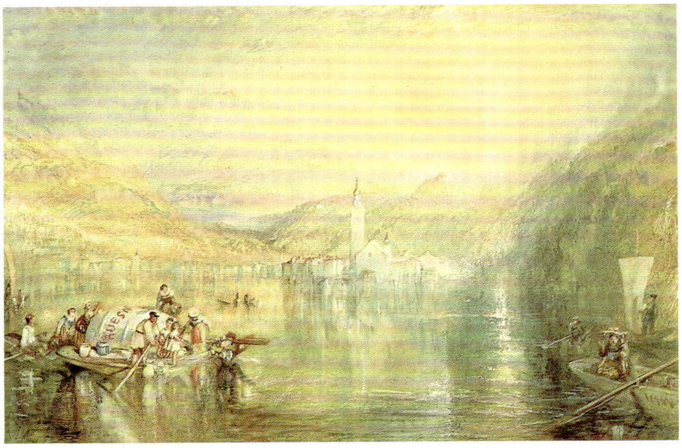

fig.26 'Küssnacht, Lake of Lucerne' 1843, watercolour (W 1534). *Manchester City Art Galleries*

29

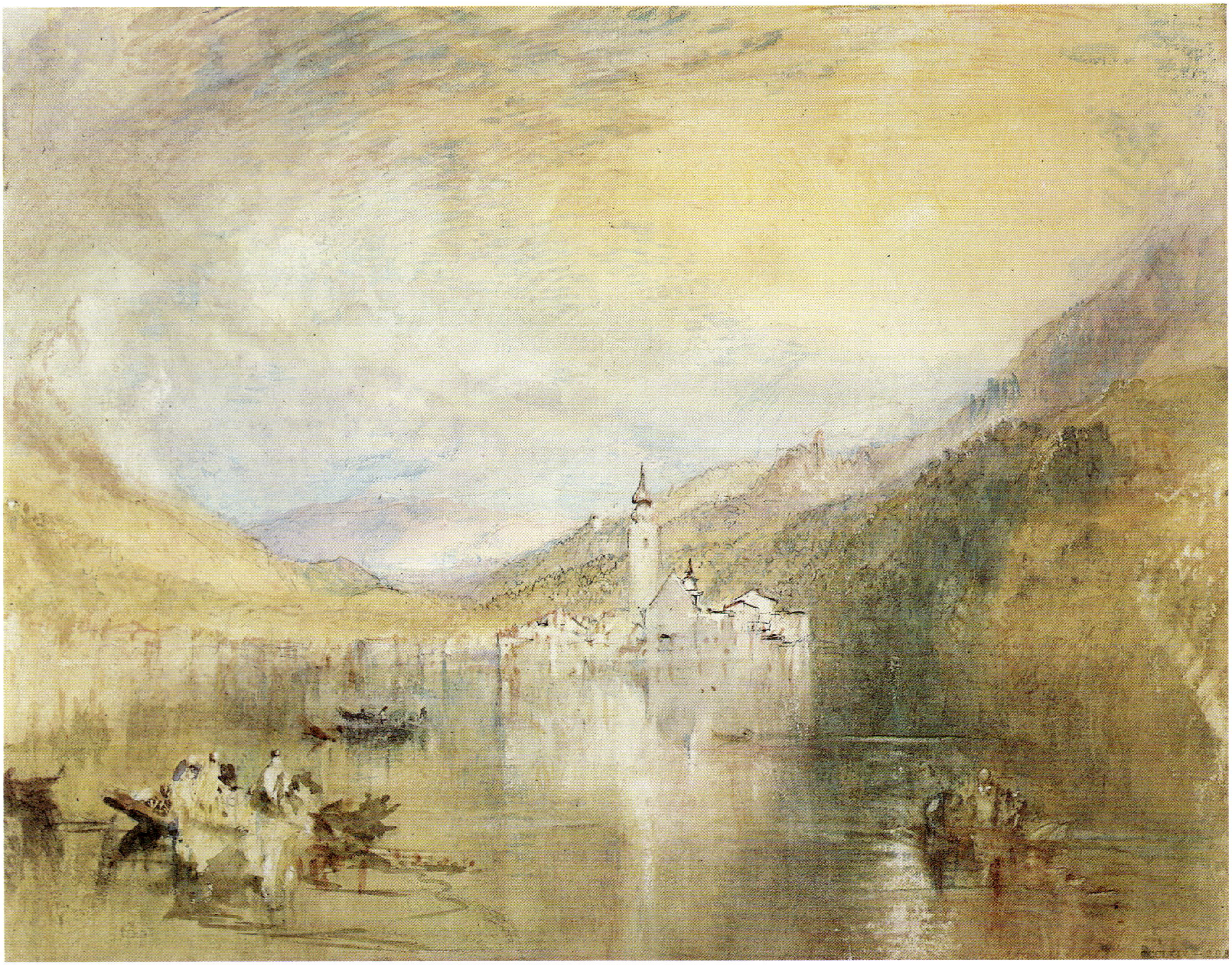

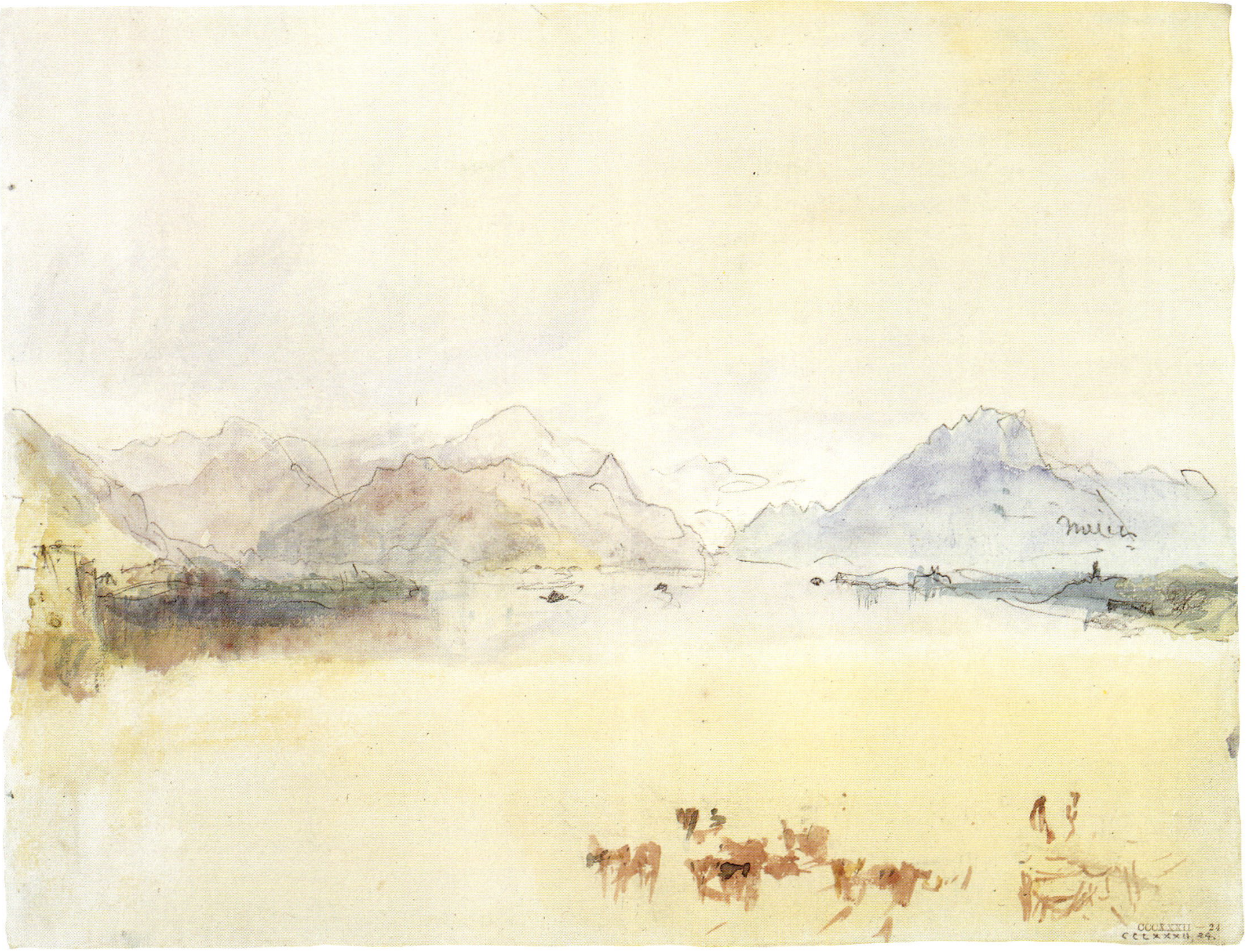

30 Meggen

Lake Lucerne, from near Meggen ?1841
Pencil and watercolour 227 × 292 ($8^{15}/_{16}$ × $11^{1}/_{2}$)
Inscribed, at right: 'Megen'
TB CCCXXXII 24 D33494
EXH: NG (43)
LIT: *Works*, XIII, pp. 202–3 (no.25 in 1st ed. of Ruskin's catalogue); pp. 372 as 'Lake of Lucerne, from Küssnacht', 610; *R on P*, pp.105–6; Serota 1970, p.130

The evening is quite cloudless and very lovely; the air clear, owing to the past storms. We much enjoy a walk on the Lucerne shore, Mont Pilate showing blue in the distance. Three large boats rowing from Lucerne show as dark spots on the golden lake. The cows, finding the flies troublesome, stand deep in the water.

Most instructive: the connection of the two dark banks by the boats giving continuity and quietness to the composition; the red cows completing its glow, and by their spottiness preventing the eye from dwelling too much on the three spots of boats.

Beyond Mont Pilate is the opening to the Lake of Lungern and Bernese Alps, indicated by the white light in the distance. The inscription on the right is, I believe, 'Megen', the name of a little town on the right bank of the lake, thus alluded to in Ebel's Guide: 'Hauteur, 10 myriametres; Chapelle de Meggen. Vue delicieuse sur les Alpes que cotoie la route, et sur les Alpes d'Engelberg, et de Berne' [first published Zurich 1793].

When cataloguing the Turner Bequest, Finberg thought that this sheet was originally part of a 'roll' sketchbook used by Turner around Lake Geneva (*Fribourg, Lausanne and Genevaz* sketchbook; TB CCCXXXII). More recent research, however, has suggested that it and other sheets (i.e. cat.no.25) can be grouped to form another sketchbook, focusing on Lake Lucerne (see Serota 1970).

31 The Rigi at Dawn

The Dark Rigi: Sample Study *c*.1841–2
Watercolour 231 × 322 (9⅛ × 12¹¹⁄₁₆)
Verso inscribed in pencil, 'H.A.Munro Esq[r] | K', and in red chalk, '11'
TB CCCLXIV 279 D36127
EXH: NG (96); Berne 1947–8 (83); Whitechapel 1953 (191); Geneva 1955–6 (126); British Museum 1958 (75–7); Tokyo 1963–4 (34, repr. in Japanese cat. only); Tate Gallery 1959–65; Brussels 1970–1 (97, repr.); Paris 1972 (306); Royal Academy 1974–5 (599, repr. p.164); Zurich 1976–7 (73); Cleveland 1977–8 (70, repr. p.89); The Hague 1978–9 (85, repr. pp.113, 96, captioned as cat.no.83); Mexico City 1979 (83); Madrid 1983 (91); Paris 1983–4 (245, repr. p.296); Tokyo 1986 (102, repr. p.251); Tate Gallery 1987; Tate Gallery 1990; Trento 1993 (19, repr.)
LIT: *Works*, XIII, pp.203, 372, 612; *R on P*, pp.121–2; Wedmore 1900, p.357; Dillon 1902, pp.332, 366, repr. p.365; Serota 1970, pp.110, 112; Wilton 1979, p.484; Wilton 1982, p.67, pl.104

We might imagine many excursions in the neighbourhood of Lucerne, before we exhausted Turner's sketches there; I have therefore only chosen five more from among about thirty executed between 1840 and 1843. This one is of Mont Rigi, seen from the windows of his inn, 'La Cygne', in the dawn of a lovely summer's morning; a fragment of fantastic mist hanging between us and the hill. Realised for his own pleasure in 1842. The drawing is in the possession of Mr. Munro [fig.27].

Even in Turner's day, Mount Rigi was the goal of tourists, who sought the beautiful views from its summit. The long back of the mountain rises to a peak of 5,700 feet, known as Rigi Kulm, at the northern end. Three of the watercolours that Turner completed and sold in 1842 were views across Lake Lucerne to the Rigi (see also cat.no.35 and p.150, fig.41). These are tranquil contemplations of the mountain at different times of day, in which much the same viewpoint is adopted for each work. In the 'Dark' and 'Blue' Rigi subjects (figs.27 and 41) its outline is seen against the rising dawn, where deep blue and mauve shadows are created through a careful accumulation of small brushstrokes. In the commentary for this study, Ruskin

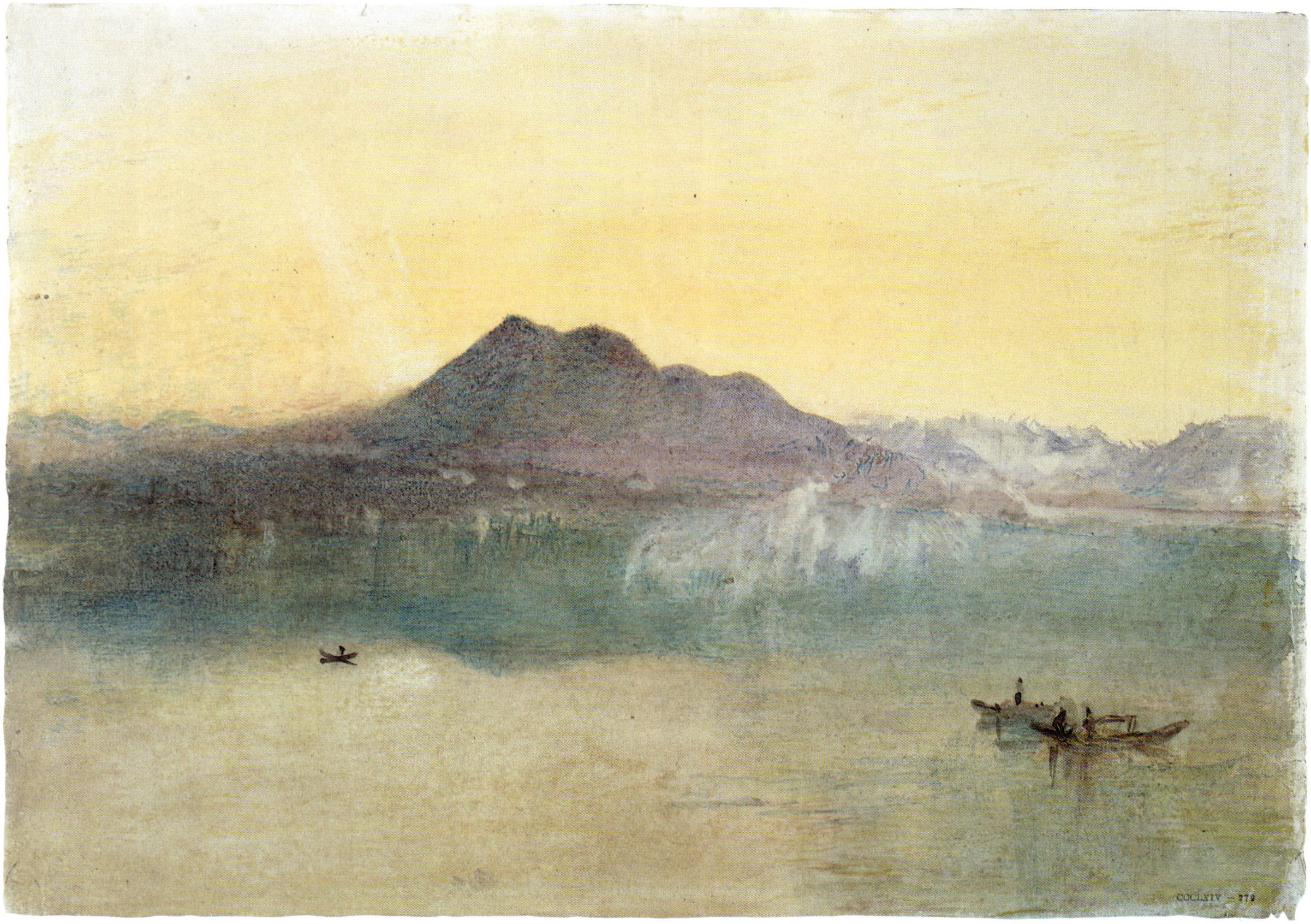

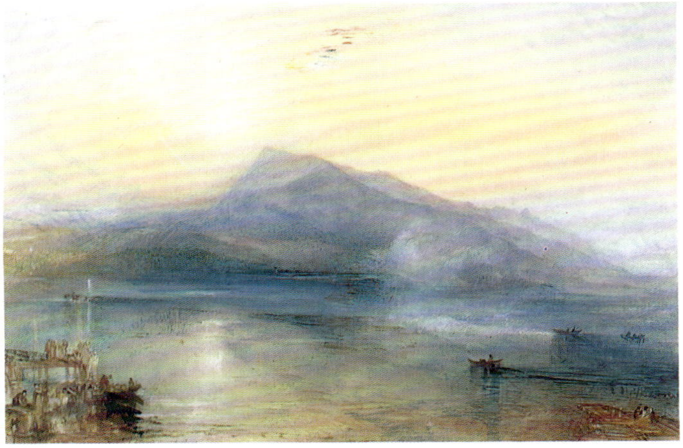

fig.27 'The Dark Rigi' 1842, watercolour (W 1532). *On loan from the Nivison Collection to the Laing Art Gallery, Newcastle upon Tyne*

implies that the watercolour based on it was one of the four works Turner presented as completed 'specimens' when the 'sample' studies were first offered by Griffith. He has here perhaps confused the provenance of the two dawn subjects; by his own account, it was Bicknell who bought the specimen drawing of the 'Blue Rigi', while Munro commissioned the watercolour based on this study as a companion to the sunset view he had already acquired (see cat.no.35 and *Works*, XIII, pp.477, 480). Turner's visits to the Swan Inn at Lucerne are discussed below (cat.no.36).

32 Brunnen, from Lake Lucerne

Brunnen, from the Lake of Lucerne: Sample Study, ?1843–5
Pencil and watercolour, with gouache
242 × 296 (9 9/16 × 11 11/16)
Verso: Pencil sketches of cloud effects and a lighthouse.
Inscribed: 'Ruskin' 'Lucerne looking towards | Schwitz'
Watermarked: J WHATMAN | TURKEY MILL | 1822
TB CCCLXIV 375 D36237
EXH: 4th Loan Collection 1891 (34); Berne 1947–8 (94); Cleveland 1977–8 (71, repr. p.90); Tate Gallery 1983; Melbourne 1985
LIT: *Works*, XIII, pp.203–4; White 1896, pp.31–2 no.41; *R on P*, p.122, n.1; Serota 1970, p.118; Wilton 1979, p.485; Wilton 1982, p.72, pl.120

We arrive at Brunnen early in the morning, and see the two Mythens above Schwytz, in clear weather this time.

Very elaborate and beautiful, the dark slope of the hills on the right especially. Note the value of the little violet touch of light behind their central darkest ridge. Realised for me in 1845 [fig.28].

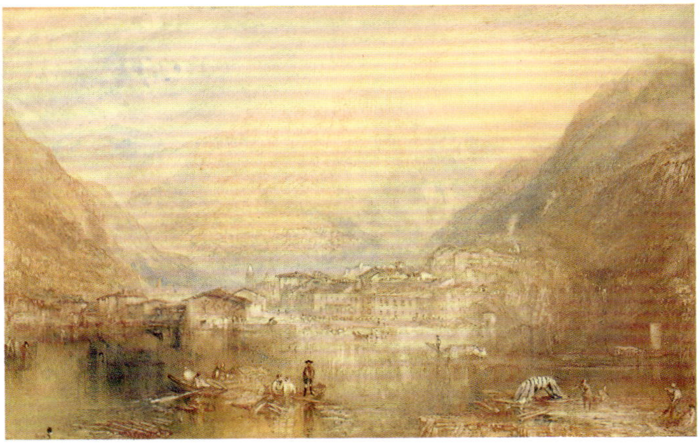

fig.28 'Brunnen, from the Lake of Lucerne' 1845, watercolour (W 1545). *Sterling and Francine Clark Art Institute, Williamstown, Massachusetts*

Turner explored Brunnen and Schwyz most extensively in 1843. One of the watercolours painted on the tour that summer is a view of the twin peaks of the Mythen, seen from the banks of the River Muota, with the town of Schwyz beyond (W 1487, National Gallery of Scotland, Edinburgh; see Campbell 1993, p.36, repr.). Turner also later worked up one of his 1843 sketches of the Mythen in his final group of finished watercolours, made around 1850 (see W 1488, private collection (c/o Agnew's) and W 1562, Victoria and Albert Museum, London). At the centre of this study is a rather generalised representation of the town of Brunnen, its form blurred and indistinct as it melts into its own reflection. Although Ruskin was ini-

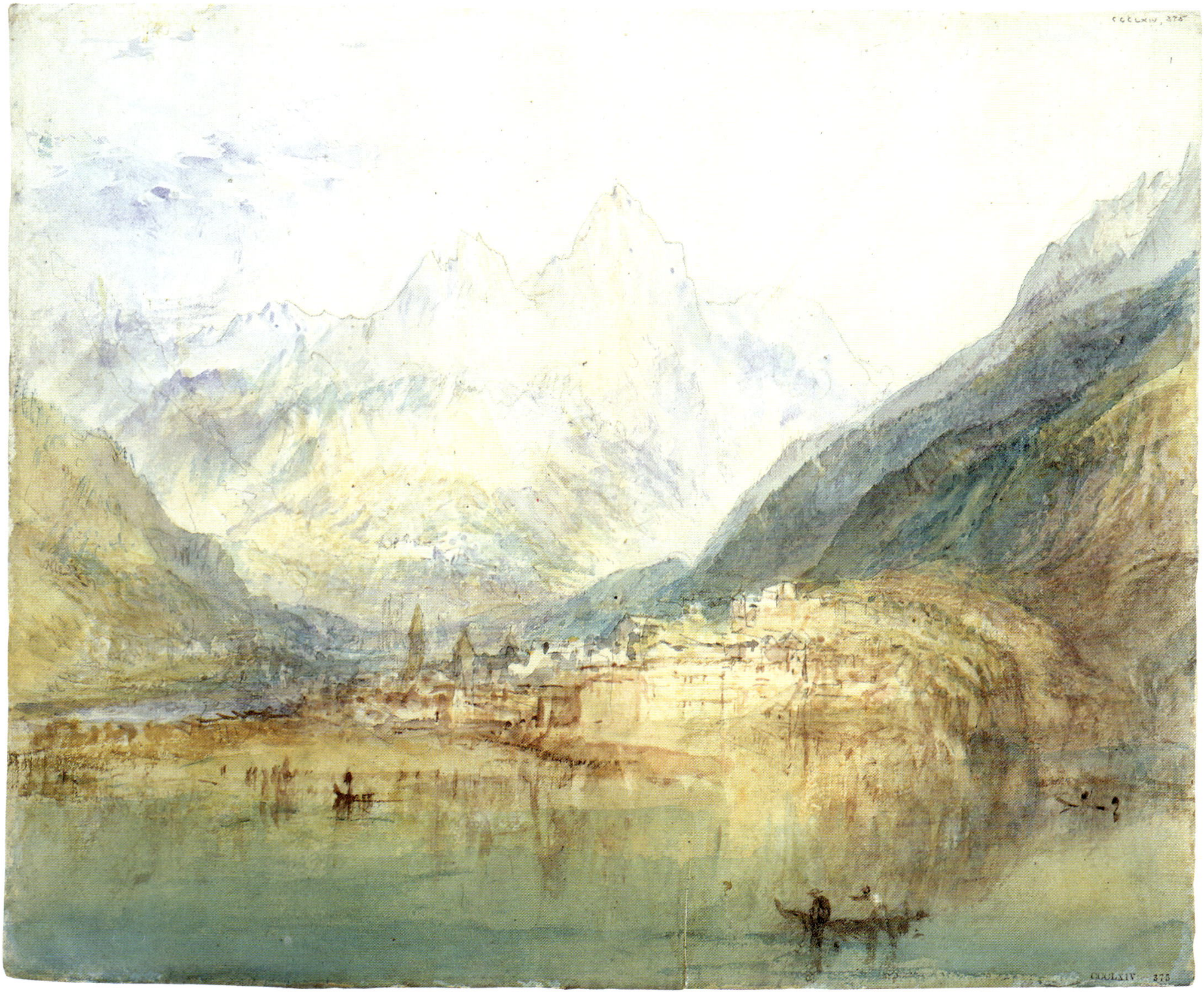

32

tially bemused by Turner's late style, he later stated that he generally preferred the Swiss sketches to the finished watercolours based on them. Writing to his father about the view of Brunnen, he lamented that 'In the sketch there were no ugly hotels; in the drawing he put them in and spoiled his subject' (27 November 1861; *Works*, XIII, p.206 n.1). Ruskin also owned one of two colour sketches of Brunnen outside the Turner Bequest. He presented it to the Fitzwilliam Museum, Cambridge, in May 1861 as part of a gift of twenty-five Turner watercolours (W 1486; the other view of Brunnen is in the Courtauld Institute of Art, London, W 1485).

33 Lake Lucerne

Lake Lucerne: The Bay of Uri from above Brunnen: Sample Study *c.*1841–2
Watercolour and gouache 242 × 297 (9⁹⁄₁₆ × 11¾)
Verso: Pencil sketch of boats under a cloudy sky, with a lighthouse. Inscribed, in pencil, 'Lucerne', and in red chalk '37'
TB CCCLXIV 354 D36216
EXH: NG (834); Toronto 1980–1 (115, pl.28); Tate Gallery 1983; Melbourne 1985
LIT: *Works*, XIII, p.204; *R on P*, pp.122 n.1, 263; Dillon 1902, p.332; Finberg 1909, p.1209 where TB CCCLXIV 387 is incorrectly identified as no.33 in Ruskin's catalogue; Serota 1970, p.111; Wilton 1979, p.483; Wilton 1982, pp.64–5, pl.97

The upper reach of it, looking towards Tell's Chapel, from the hill above Brunnen.

The delicate, light, and sharply drawn clouds of this sketch are peculiarly beautiful, and it was realised by Turner in

1842, with great care. The drawing is in the possession of Mr. Munro [fig.29].

It has already been noted that Turner was particularly fond of Brunnen's position on Lake Lucerne (see cat.no.26). While pausing there on his travels in 1858, Ruskin was able to verify Turner's perceptions when he stayed in one of the 'white houses in Turner's sketch' (i.e. cat.no.32), which offered him views 'looking up the northern & down the southern reach of the lake' (Hayman 1982, p.27). In 1842, and again in 1845, Turner produced watercolours that capture his awed reverence for the spectacular scenery. The two finished works dating from 1842 both focus on the view south, towards Fluelen (see fig.29, and p.150 fig.42). In comparing this study with the finished view, it is quickly apparent that Turner abandoned the limpid blue washes suggesting the Bay of Uri, replac-

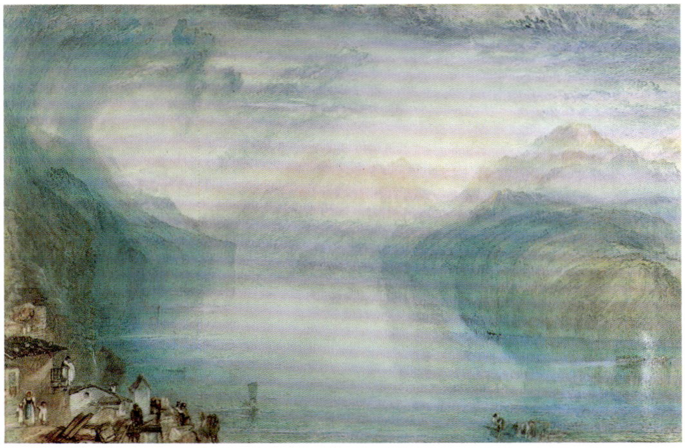

fig.29 'Lake Lucerne: The Bay of Uri from above Brunnen' 1842, watercolour over pencil (W 1526). *Private Collection, New York*

33

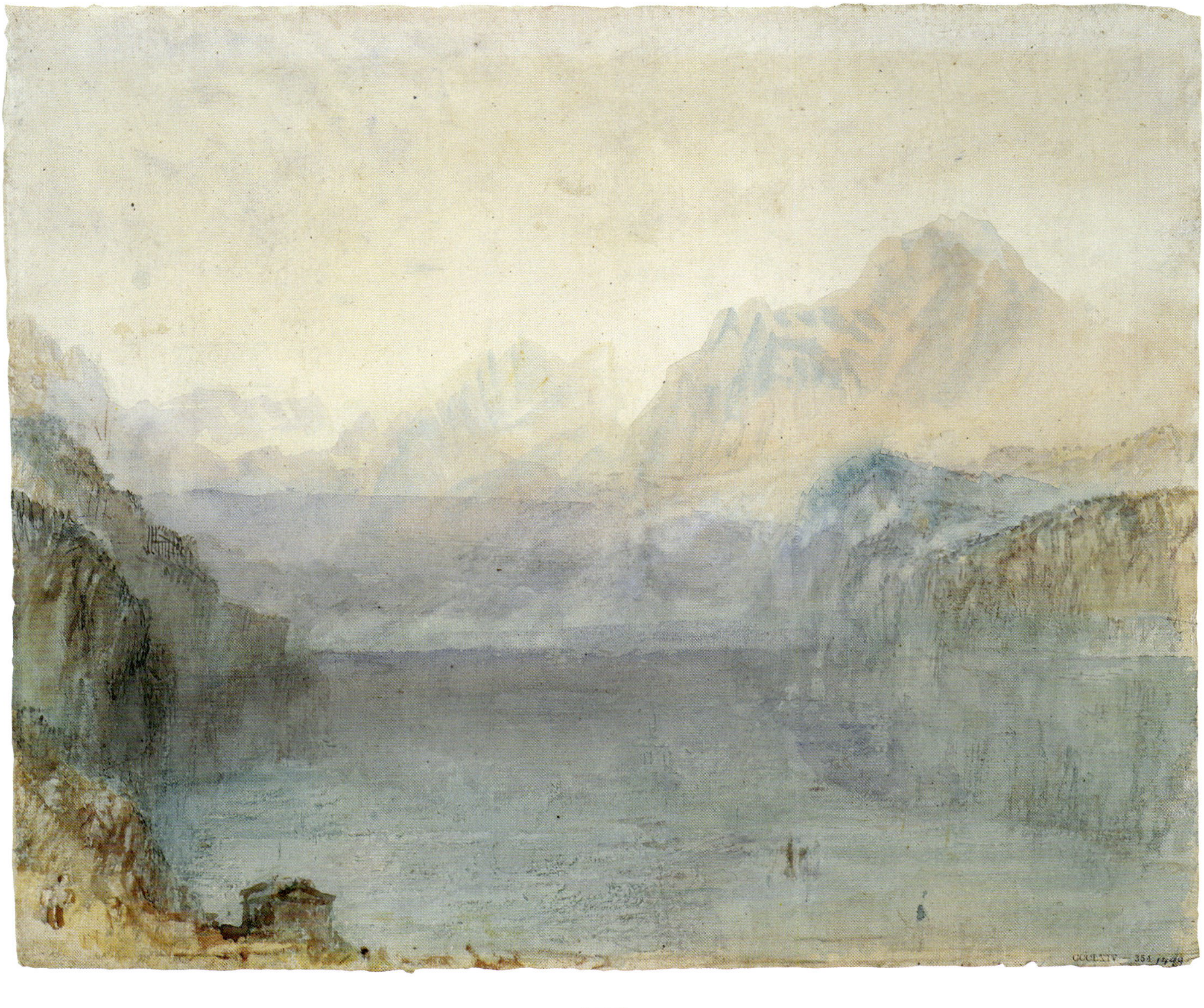

ing them with an expanse of brilliant white light reflected from the watery sunset. The shores along this stretch of the lake are dominated by sheer cliffs, which plunge deep into the water. Yet somehow, according to the legend, it was at this point that William Tell leapt from a boat to escape imprisonment by Gessler; the event is commemorated in the famous chapel situated under the last cliff on the left in this study. Another watercolour, also made as a result of the 1841 tour, focuses on Tell's Chapel itself (W 1480, Yale Center for British Art, New Haven). The verso of this sheet has a pencil sketch of shipping and the outline of a lighthouse (see also cat.nos.32, 37). It is possible that Turner made these hasty jottings once he was back in England, perhaps while at Margate.

34 Lake Lucerne

Lake Lucerne, from Brunnen: Sample Study *c.*1844–5
Watercolour and gouache, with pen
246 × 308 ($9\frac{3}{4} \times 12\frac{1}{8}$)
Verso inscribed in pencil, 'Lucerne', in another hand, 'J.R.', and in red chalk '29'
TB CCCLXIV 385 D36250
EXH: 4th Loan Collection 1891 (17)
LIT: *Works*, XIII, p.204; White 1896, pp.33–4, no.45; *R on P*, p.122 n.1; Serota 1970, p.119; Wilton 1979, p.486; Wilton 1982, p.70, pl.114

The lower reach of it, looking from Brunnen towards Lucerne. A careless sketch, but realised very beautifully for Mr. Windus in 1845 [fig.30]. *The drawing has been since engraved* [R 671, engraved by Robert Wallis, and published 27 May 1854].

34

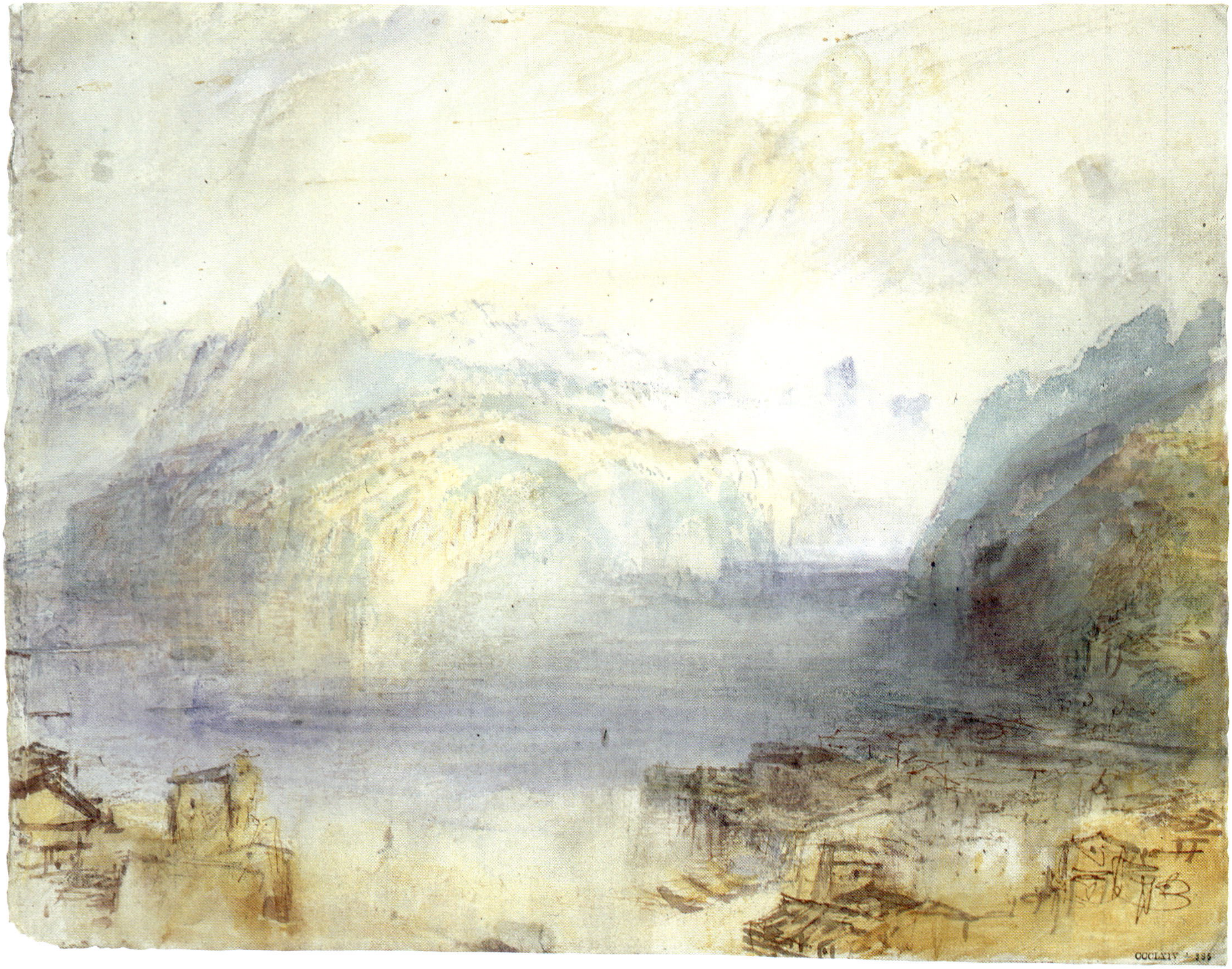

Two of the set of ten watercolours in 1845 were views from above Brunnen (see also W 1543; p.150 fig.49). Both drawings are handled in a considerably broader fashion than the earlier views from the town of 1842. This new-found expansiveness is even more evident in this preparatory study, where the roofs of the houses are indicated simply by an apparently random cluster of pen lines. This subject is the only one of the four completed views from Brunnen to look west along the lake. In Turner's depiction, the opposite shore appears to have a gentle rounded form, softened by the suggestion of dense woodland. All of which is quite different from the sublime cliffs on the southern arm of the lake. The finished watercolour was one that Ruskin longed to own. When the possibility arose of acquiring works from the Windus collection in 1858, he wrote to his father pointing out what a 'desirable' drawing it was, accompanying his list of Turner *desiderata* with a thumbnail sketch of the finished work (Hayman 1982, p.40).

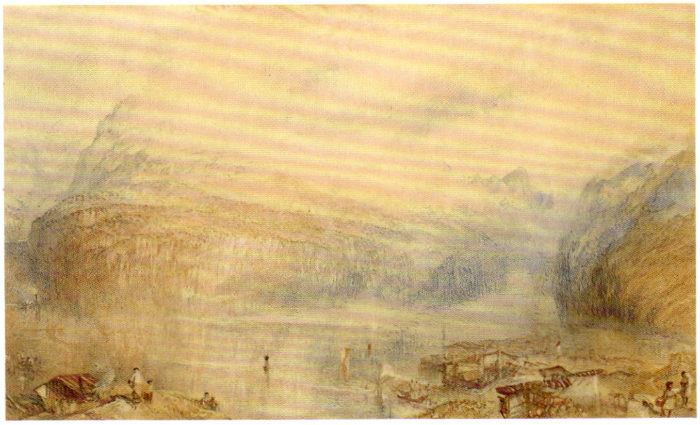

fig.30 'Lake of Lucerne, from Brunnen' 1845, watercolour (W 1547). *Indianapolis Museum of Art, Bequest of Kurt F. Pantzer, Sr*

35 The Rigi at Sunset

The Red Rigi: Sample Study *c.*1841–2
Watercolour 228 × 302 (9 × 11 15/16)
Verso inscribed in pencil, 'E', and in red chalk, '15'
TB CCCLXIV 275 D36123
EXH: NG (45); Royal Academy 1974–5 (602); Zurich 1976–7 (72); Tate Gallery 1983; Melbourne 1985; Tate Gallery 1987; Tate Gallery 1990
LIT: *Works*, XIII, pp.204, 372, 610; *R on P*, p.106 as 'The Rigi from Lucerne'; Wedmore 1900, p.358; Dillon 1902, p.332; Serota 1970, p.110; Wilton 1979, p.483; Wilton 1982, p.66, pl.102

The same view as No.31, by evening instead of morning light. I cannot tell why Turner was so fond of the Mont Rigi, but there are seven or eight more studies of it among his sketches of this period. This one was realised for his own pleasure in 1842. The drawing is in my possession [fig.31].

The warm sunset that illuminates the Rigi in this study and in the finished watercolour derived from it, was intended to balance the cooler views of the mountain by dawn light (see cat.no.31). Apart from his expressive use of colour, Turner seems particularly interested in the newly risen moon, floating above the Rigi. Its reflection as a solid path of light anticipates a similar representation of this effect by Edvard Munch (in paintings such as 'The Voice', 1893, Museum of Fine Arts, Boston, or 'Moonlight', 1895, National Gallery, Oslo). The inclusion of both the setting sun and the new moon is a frequent feature of Turner's later landscapes, where the condensed limits of the traditional view within the picture frame are extended to represent the elliptical expanse of sky seen by the eye. As Ruskin notes, there are many other views of the Rigi from Lucerne in the Turner Bequest, apparently recording several visits (i.e. TB CCCLXIV 320, 324, 327, 330 (fig.39), 331, 337, 338, 342, 354). A smaller group of studies of the Rigi can be found in collections outside the Bequest. These probably left Turner's collection via his agent Thomas Griffith (W 1472–4, W 1478 and the watercolour sold at Sotheby's, 10 March 1988, lot 109). Although the 'Red Rigi' was in Ruskin's possession at the time he wrote this catalogue, it was first owned by Munro, who bought it from the group of four 'specimens' in 1842.

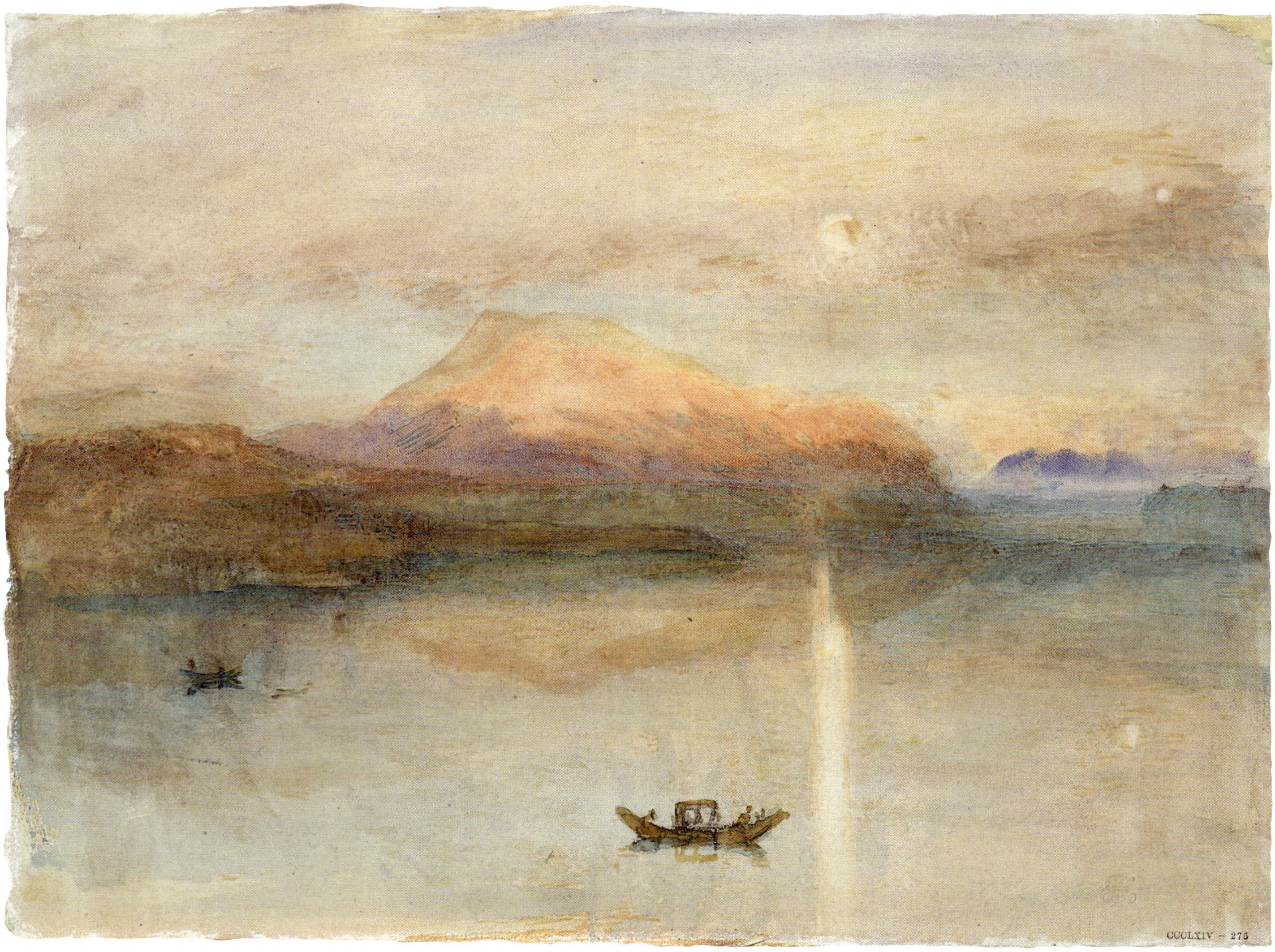

35

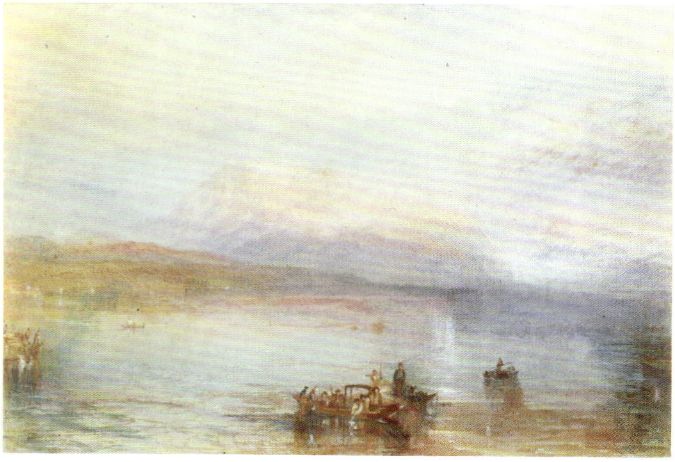

fig.31 'The Red Rigi' 1842, watercolour (W 1525).
National Gallery of Victoria, Melbourne, Felton Bequest, 1947

36 [Untitled]

Lucerne, with Mount Pilatus beyond *c.*1844
Pencil, watercolour and gouache 244 × 309 ($9\frac{5}{8} \times 12\frac{3}{16}$)
Watermarked: C ANSELL | 1828
TB CCCLXIV 341 D36201
EXH: NG (768); Tate Gallery 1931–4
LIT: *Works*, XIII, pp.204–5; *R on P*, p.258 as 'Lucerne and Mount Pilatus'; Dillon 1902, p.366

We bid farewell to Lucerne as the morning reddens Mont Pilate; hardly anything of the lake visible; and it is so early that no one is stirring except just about the boats. A blotted and careless drawing, but so pretty in subject as to be worth including in the series. There is body-colour white, touched in the mist beyond the lake, and over the second tower. This is very rare in Turner's water-colour sketches. I believe the second tower was meant to be the first, and when he put the other in farther to the left, he could not make up his mind to part with the first one.

The building in the foreground, discussed by Ruskin, is the Zier-Gilgen, a tower which was originally part of the fortifications alongside the Kapellbrücke; it is probably the tiled roof of the Wasserthurm on the covered bridge that appears as the second tower from the left. The lakeside area running from this point eastwards had been redeveloped in the years prior to Turner's visits of the 1840s. One of the new establishments to open was the Swan Inn ('La Cygne' or 'Schwan'), which stood close to the landing-place for the steamers. The first steamers on the lake had been introduced in 1837. As Ruskin suggested above (cat.no.31), the Swan was possibly the hotel Turner stayed at during his visits to Lucerne. However, with Turner's reputation for parsimony very much in mind, the moderately-priced Hôtel des Balances has also been put forward as a possible alternative (Dillon 1902, p.366), especially since Murray records other travellers' complaints that the Swan was 'dear'. But to look at the evidence of Turner's many views in pencil and watercolour suggests that the Swan is the most likely candidate. The white building on the right in this watercolour may even be part of the hotel. Turner recorded the essence of this view in the *Spires and Heidelberg* sketchbook of 1844 (TB CCXCVII f.20). This watercolour is one of two that adopt this viewpoint, perhaps from an upstairs window of the hotel; the other is TB CCCLXIV 400. The second work seems to have been made shortly afterwards, presumably from the motif, since there the orange cloud, which appears on the left here, has moved across towards the peak of Mount Pilatus.

36

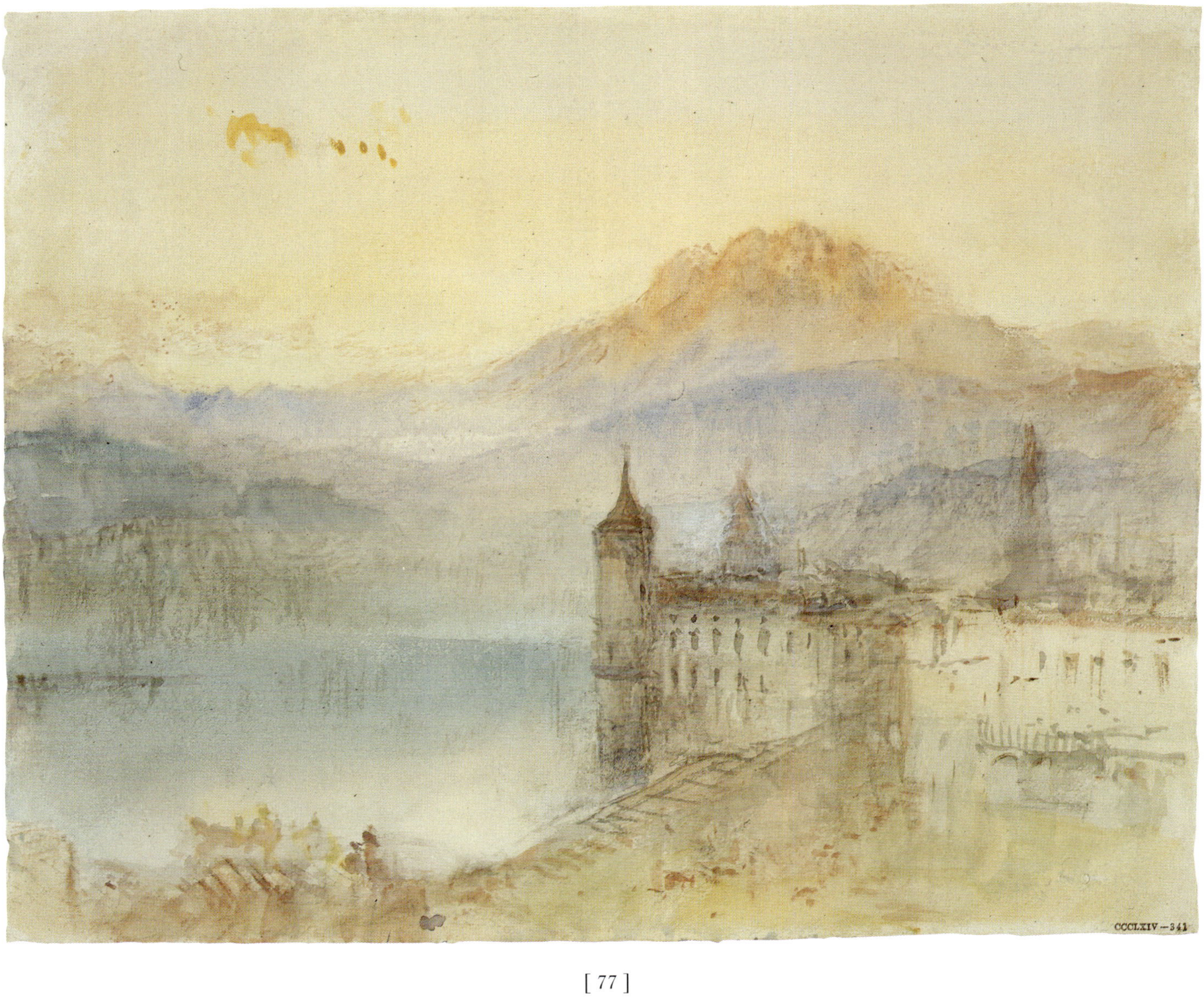

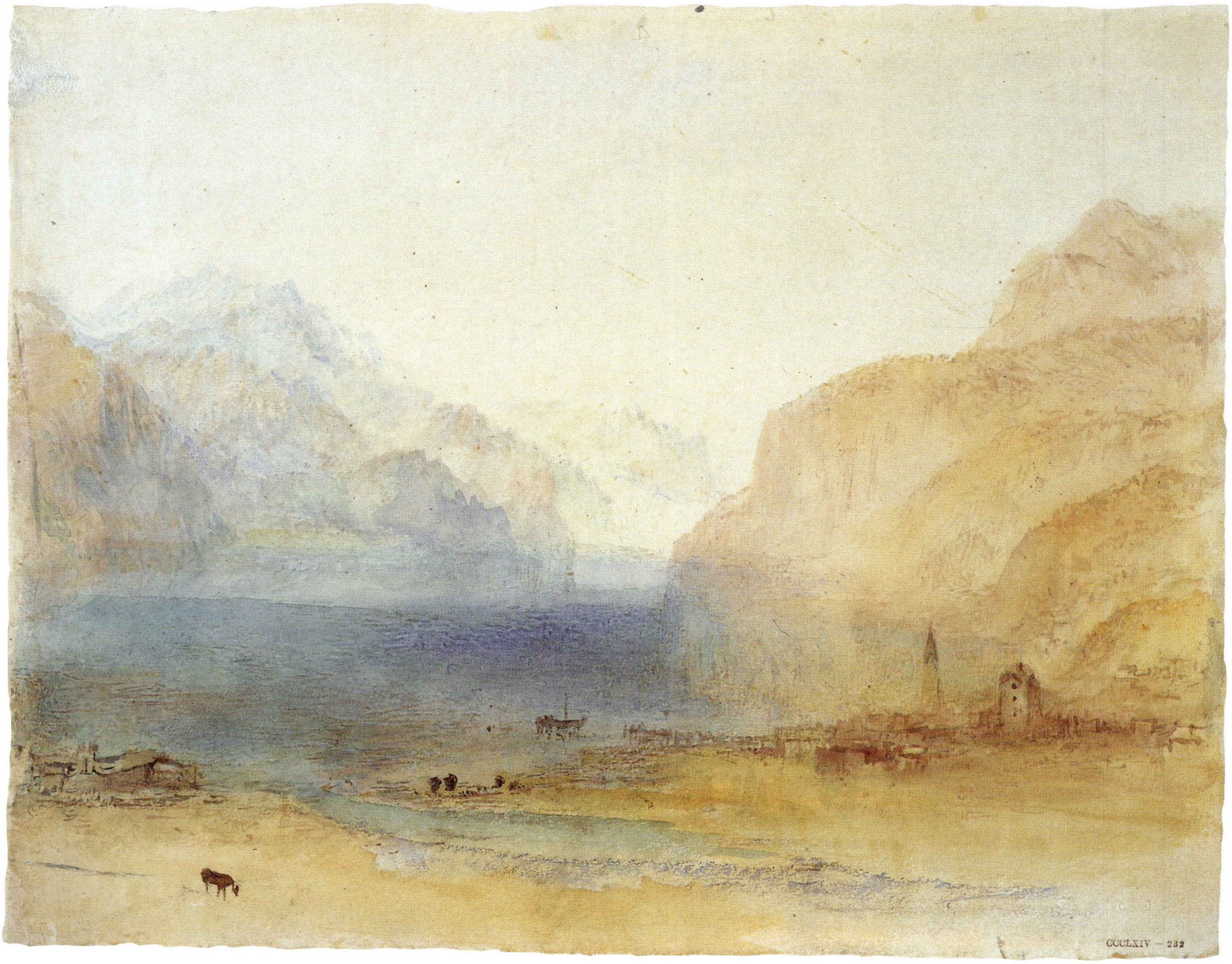

37 The Village of Fluelen

Fluelen: Morning (Looking towards the Lake of Lucerne): Sample Study *c*.1844–5
Watercolour 244 × 305 (9⅝ × 12)
Verso: Pencil sketch of sail boats and a steamer off the coast: ?Margate. Inscribed in pencil, 'Lucerne | Munro ' and in ?Munro's hand 'HAJM', and in red chalk '39'
TB CCCLXIV 282 D36133
EXH: NG (99); Tate Gallery 1983; Melbourne 1985
LIT: *Works*, XIII, pp.205, 372, 612; *R on P*, pp.123–4; Serota 1970, p.116; Wilton 1979, p.485; Wilton 1982, p.71, pl.118

We sleep at Fluelen; and going out for our usual walk before breakfast, find the effect of morning mist on the lake quite enchanting.

The blue touches in the foreground indicate the course of the river to the lake, through its marshy delta.

The massy square building is a large private house, almost

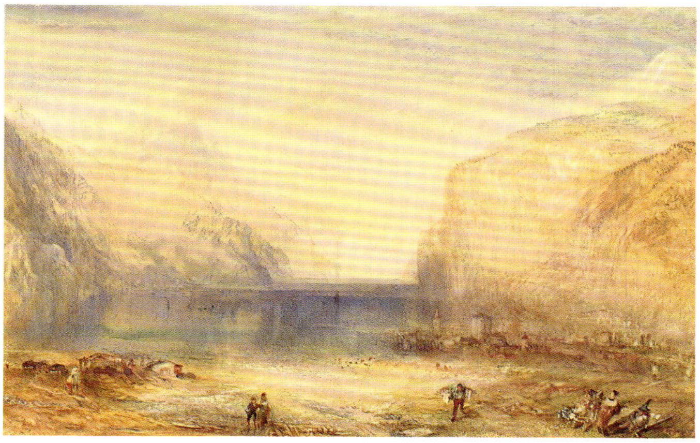

fig.32 'Fluelen: Morning (Looking towards the Lake of Lucerne)' 1845, watercolour and bodycolour (W 1541). *Yale Center for British Art, Paul Mellon Collection a tower, and perhaps in the shell of its walls ancient; but Turner has much exaggerated its elevation.*

Realised for Mr. Munro in 1845 [fig.32]. *The subject was one very dear to Turner, he having made one of his earliest and loveliest drawings (of great size also), for Mr. Fawkes of Farnley, from this very shore* ['Lake of Lucerne, from the Landing Place at Fluelen, Looking towards Bauen and Tell's Chapel', exh.1815; W 378, repr. in col. in Hill 1992, p.133].

Fluelen lies at the southern end of Lake Lucerne and was an important point on the route to Italy via the St Gotthard Pass. When Turner visited Fluelen in the early 1840s, the marshes surrounding the Reuss delta close to the town were considered a health hazard. Murray observed that this must account for the appearance of the people of the region, who were characterised by 'pale faces, crippled limbs, and goitred necks' (Murray 1838, p.94). In his watercolours of Fluelen Turner condenses the essence of the town into its two most prominent buildings: the baroque church of Sts George and Nikolaus (which he recorded in a separate pencil sketch, TB CCCXLIV 377) and the massy building noted by Ruskin. This is a medieval keep known as Schlösschen Rudenz, formerly the property of the Attinghausen family, who collected tarifs from those travelling up the lake. Ruskin visited Fluelen in 1852 and was able to confirm that the individual details of the view were all correct. However, he wrote in his Diary that 'there is no point from which he could have got his view. He supposes himself in the air' (*Works*, XIII, p.460, n.2). The existence of other colour studies of Fluelen, from a position closer to the town, suggests that Turner's composition was only finally arrived at in the watercolour after some hesitancy (see TB CCCLXIV 331; Serota also lists a watercolour of this view, formerly in the collection of Henry Vaughan, which is possibly that now at University College, London (W 1482); see Serota, p.116 and n.16). Ruskin considered the finished work 'the last Alpine drawing Turner ever made with loving power' and noted that its execution 'is in freshness and clearness unrivalled, the sky being laid in with one dash' (*Works*, XIII, p.459). See also cat.no.39.

38 The Lake Lucerne from Fluelen

?1843–5
Pencil and watercolour, with pen 241 × 297 (9½ × 11¾)
Verso, inscribed in red colour '8'
TB CCCLXIV 344 D36204
EXH: NG (773); Tate Gallery 1931–4; Cape Town 1936–7 (Frame 22); Berne 1947–8 (90); San Marino 1951–2 (Frame 34)
LIT: *Works*, XIII, p.205; *R on P*, p.260; Hind 1925, pl.XXXII

Just when we are going to start for St. Gothard, we find that the misty morning has broken into a cloudy day and that assuredly it is soon going to rain. We are much discomposed at this aspect of affairs, as seen from our inn window, but make a hasty blot of it, nevertheless, as the diligence horses are putting to; and the blot is a grand one.

Ruskin's assumption that Turner's visit to Fluelen coincided with an outburst of stormy weather is possibly justified, for the artist introduced thundery grey clouds in the majority of the existing studies of the town. The other view of Fluelen commissioned by Munro in 1845, for example, depicts the town from the lake with swirling lines of raincloud descending from further up the valley (p.150, figs.47, 50). Similarly, one of the studies by Turner

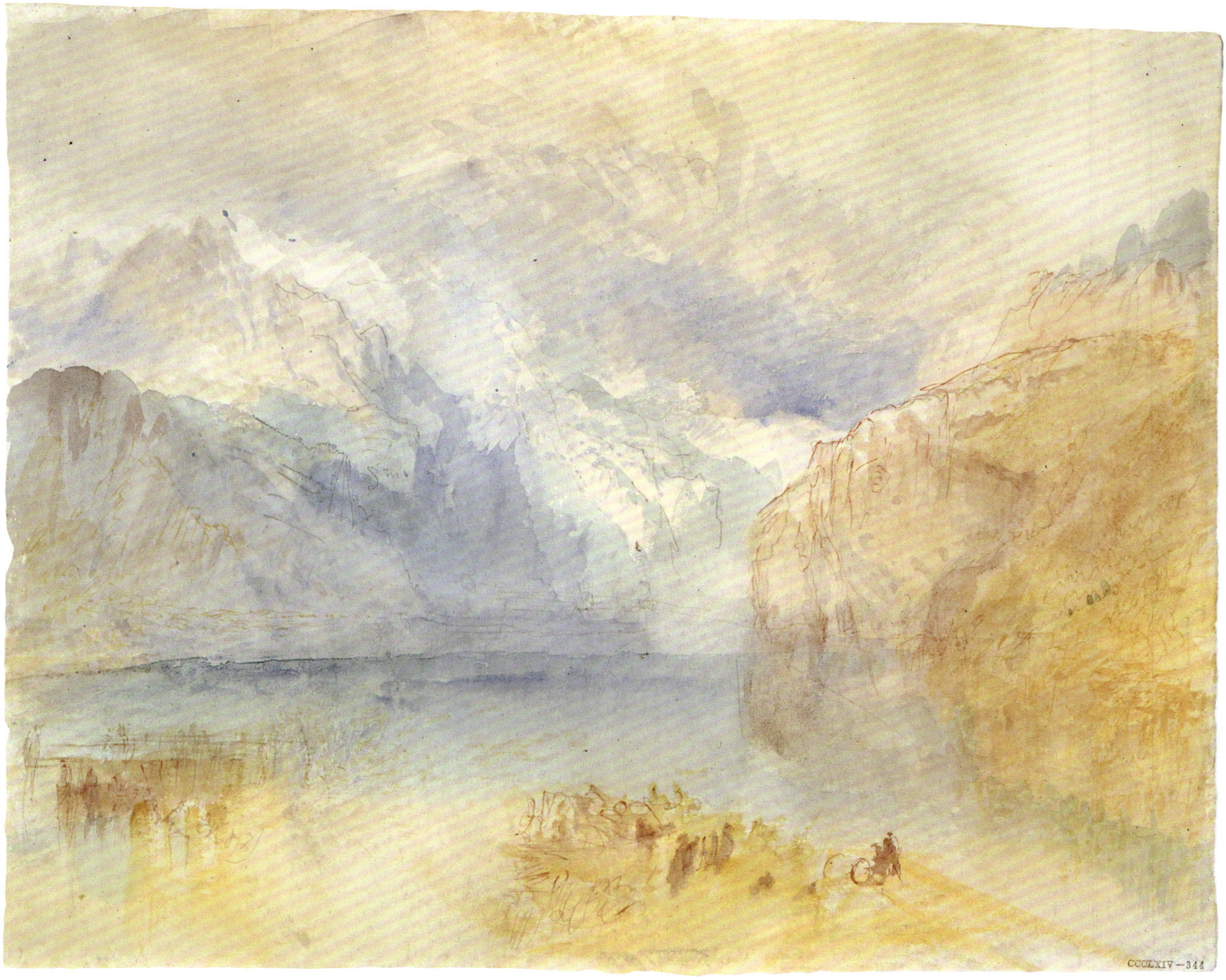

38

that Ruskin gave to the Fitzwilliam Museum in 1861 is taken from closer to the shore at a point when the storm has actually arrived in the town (W 1483). Ruskin may also be correct is assuming that Turner made studies from the window of his inn. As well as this subject, there are two works now in the National Gallery of Ireland with an identical viewpoint, looking north down Lake Lucerne (W 1476–7; Dawson 1988, pp.126–9, repr.). The latter view appears to have been taken from a raised position, since it includes a wide expanse of foreshore, very similar to that in this watercolour, where traders and boatmen are seen at work.

39 Scene on the St. Gothard

Storm in the St Gotthard Pass. The First Bridge above Altdorf: Sample Study *c.*1844–5
Pencil and watercolour, with pen 239 × 297 (9 7/16 × 11 3/4)
Verso inscribed in pencil: 'JR' 'Altorf'
TB CCCLXIV 283 D36135
EXH: NG (100); Royal Academy 1974–5 (614); Sofia 1978 (65); Athens 1981 (61); Tate Gallery 1983; Melbourne 1985; Tate Gallery 1993 (37, repr. p.51)
LIT: *Works*, XIII, pp.205–6, 372, 612; *R on P*, p.124 as 'Pass of the St Gothard: First Bridge above Altdorf'; Serota 1970, p.119; Wilton 1979, p.485; Wilton 1982, p.71, pl.117

And certainly, before we have passed Altorf, it comes on to rain to purpose. Fine things in the way of precipices and pines at this part of the road, as far as we can see them from under our umbrella. This sketch was realised by Turner for me in 1845 [fig.33], *but I having unluckily told him that I wanted it for the sake of the pines, he cut all the pines down, by way of jest, and left only the bared red ground under them. I did not like getting wet with no pines to shelter me, and exchanged the drawing with Mr. Munro for the realisation of No.37* [p.78, fig.32].

Just a short distance from Fluelen lies the village of Altdorf, the capital of the canton of Uri, and the place where William Tell allegedly shot an apple balanced on his son's head. Although it does not seem to have been suggested before, the subject of this view is possibly connected with the Tell legend. The finished work has sometimes been known as 'First Bridge above the Altdorf', a location confirmed by Turner's inscription on the verso of this study. According to Murray's *Hand-book*, after leaving Altdorf on the way up towards the St Gotthard, the traveller had to cross by bridge the fast-flowing stream in which

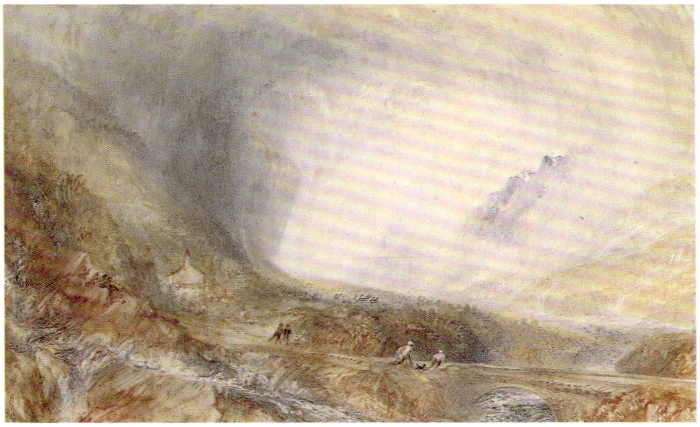

fig.33 'Storm in the St Gotthard Pass. The First Bridge above Altdorf' 1845, watercolour (W 1546). *The Whitworth Art Gallery, University of Manchester*

39

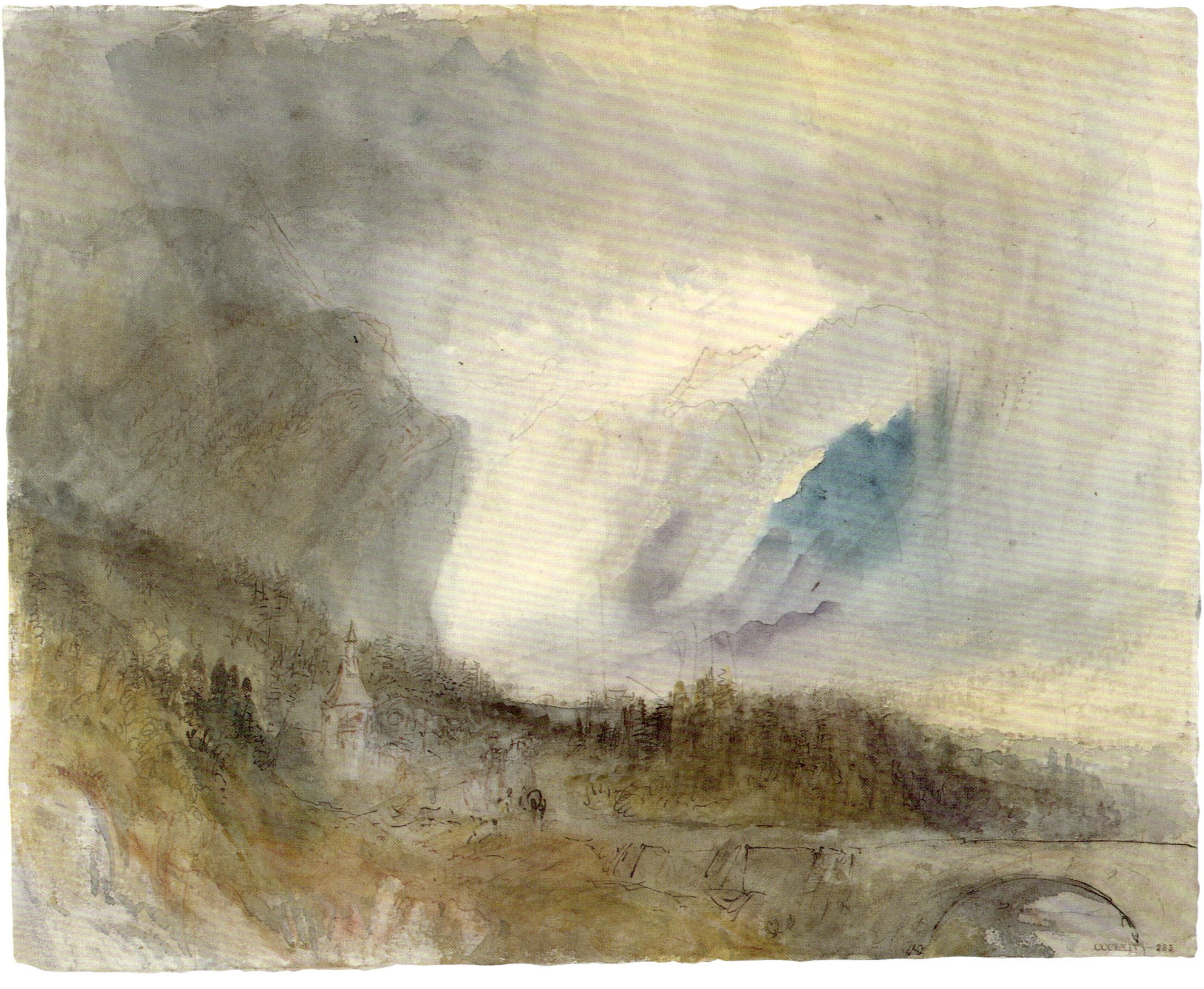

William Tell had lost his life trying to rescue a drowning child (Murray 1838, p.95). Near to the bridge stood a small chapel, built in 1522, which is perhaps the building on the left here. Turner may have worked up this study from a pencil outline he had sketched on the spot. Ruskin was travelling in Italy and Switzerland in the summer of 1845, but wrote home to his father for news of Turner's work on his commissioned subjects, at the same time speculating on how the artist would develop this sketch. He fancied, 'a forest scene would be very lovely & delicious, but I doubt if he will do any thing now but what pleases his fancy' (Shapiro 1972, p.207). He was not impressed with the resulting work, now in the Whitworth Art Gallery in Manchester, which by 1848 he no longer owned, merely referring to it as 'our bad Altdorf, with the crutches' (*Works*, XXXVI, p.92). He was, however, driven by a curiosity to check the actual topography of Turner's view, and jotted down his observations in a letter to his father from Altdorf during a visit in 1861:

> I walked three times yesterday to the bridge with the pines, which Turner cut away, when he made the drawing which I exchanged with Munro. In many respects, I find that the realised drawing was always liker the place than the sketch; though in this instance the pines were cut down; the bridge is really carefully drawn in the finished drawing; and being a formal and ugly one disappointed me – the sketch having suggested one far more picturesque [27 November 1861; *Works*, XIII, p.206 n.1].

40 The Pass of Faido

The Pass of St Gotthard, near Faido: Sample Study
*c.*1842–3
Pencil, watercolour, with pen 229 × 290 (9 × 11 7/16)
Verso inscribed in pencil: 'Pass Piolano | Tessin | No.14 | x o 12 | 29'
TB CCCLXIV 209 D36055
EXH: Oxford 1878 (239–29 as 'my Faido'); Paris 1937 (120); Berne 1947–8 (78); Geneva 1955–6 (130); Tokyo 1963–4 (43, repr.); Brussels 1970–1 (93); Folkestone 1971–2 (28); Zurich 1976–7 (81); Toronto 1980–1 (103, repr. p.178); Tate Gallery 1983; Melbourne 1985; Tate Gallery 1988; Tate Gallery 1990; Tate Gallery 1993 (30, repr. pp.29, 48)
LIT: *Works*, VI, pp.33–7, 378–9; XIII, pp.206–7, 562; *R on P*, p.124 n.2; Dillon 1902, p.332; Finberg 1910, repr. as frontispiece; Serota 1970, pp.114, 130; Wilton 1979, p.484; Wilton 1982, p.68, pl.107; Hayman 1990, p.34, repr.

We cross the St. Gothard in rain, very uncomfortably, the weather not beginning to clear till we are nearly half-way down the Italian side, close to Faido, when the sun comes out on the brown stones of the Ticino's bed in a most satisfactory manner; the Ticino is swoln with the rain, and threatens in many places to carry the road away, though its waters are still pure, having nothing but gneiss and granite to dash over.

This was a favourite sketch of Turner's. He realised it for me in 1843, with his fullest power; and the resultant drawing is, I believe, the greatest work he produced in the last period of his art [fig.34]. *It is etched, and copiously analysed in the fourth volume of* Modern Painters [*Works*, VI, ch.II, pls.20–21, 37].

By comparison of the etching with this sketch, it will be seen that the foreground on the right-hand side is much altered. In this sketch the turn of the road, and pillar at the angle of the wall, are drawn as they exist in reality; in the drawing a piece of road is introduced from a study of Turner's, made on the St. Gothard at least thirty years previously. The warm colour given to the rocks is exactly right; they are gneiss, with decomposing garnets, giving them the brightest hues of red and yellow ochre.

Ruskin's close analysis of the almost alchemical process by which Turner transformed the actual (or 'simple') topography of the Pass of Faido into one of the undisputed masterpieces of watercolour painting is rightly one of the set-pieces of *Modern Painters* (1856). There he described it as 'the last drawing' that Turner 'ever made with unabated power' (*Works*, VI, p.380). During the early days of August 1845, just three years after Turner's own visit, Ruskin had gone in search of the place that had inspired the subject he rated so highly. It was not immediately possible to establish the exact position of the view, and Ruskin had to explain what Turner had done to his manservant, John ('George') Hobbs, who exclaimed, '"Well – he *is* a cunning old gentleman to be sure"'. Ruskin himself was forced to admit that he 'should never have dreamed of taking such a subject' (Shapiro 1972, p.176). Although he was already aware that artistic licence was sometimes a part of Turnerian topography, it seems to have come as a real revelation that Turner could have created so forceful an image from such unpromising material. As he observed in a letter to his father, 'The Stones, road, and bridge are all true, but the mountains, compared with Turner's colossal conception, look pigmy & poor' (Shapiro 1972, p.172). More than twenty years after acquiring the watercolour, Ruskin was still deeply moved by what Turner had achieved; in 1869 he wrote to Charles Eliot Norton when visiting Faido a second time, stressing the important point that Turner had selected 'the Ticino as his exponent of Alpine torrent rage' (Bradley and Ousby 1987, pp.153–4; Ruskin's letter includes a thumbnail sketch of the watercolour).

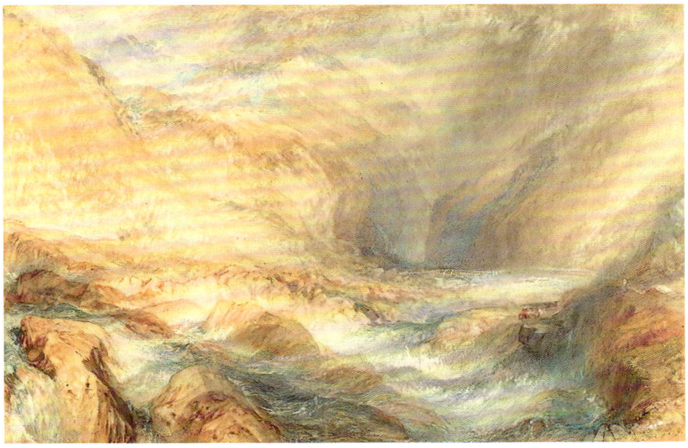

fig.34 'The Pass of St Gotthard, near Faido' 1843, watercolour (W 1538). *Mr and Mrs Eugene Thaw, USA*

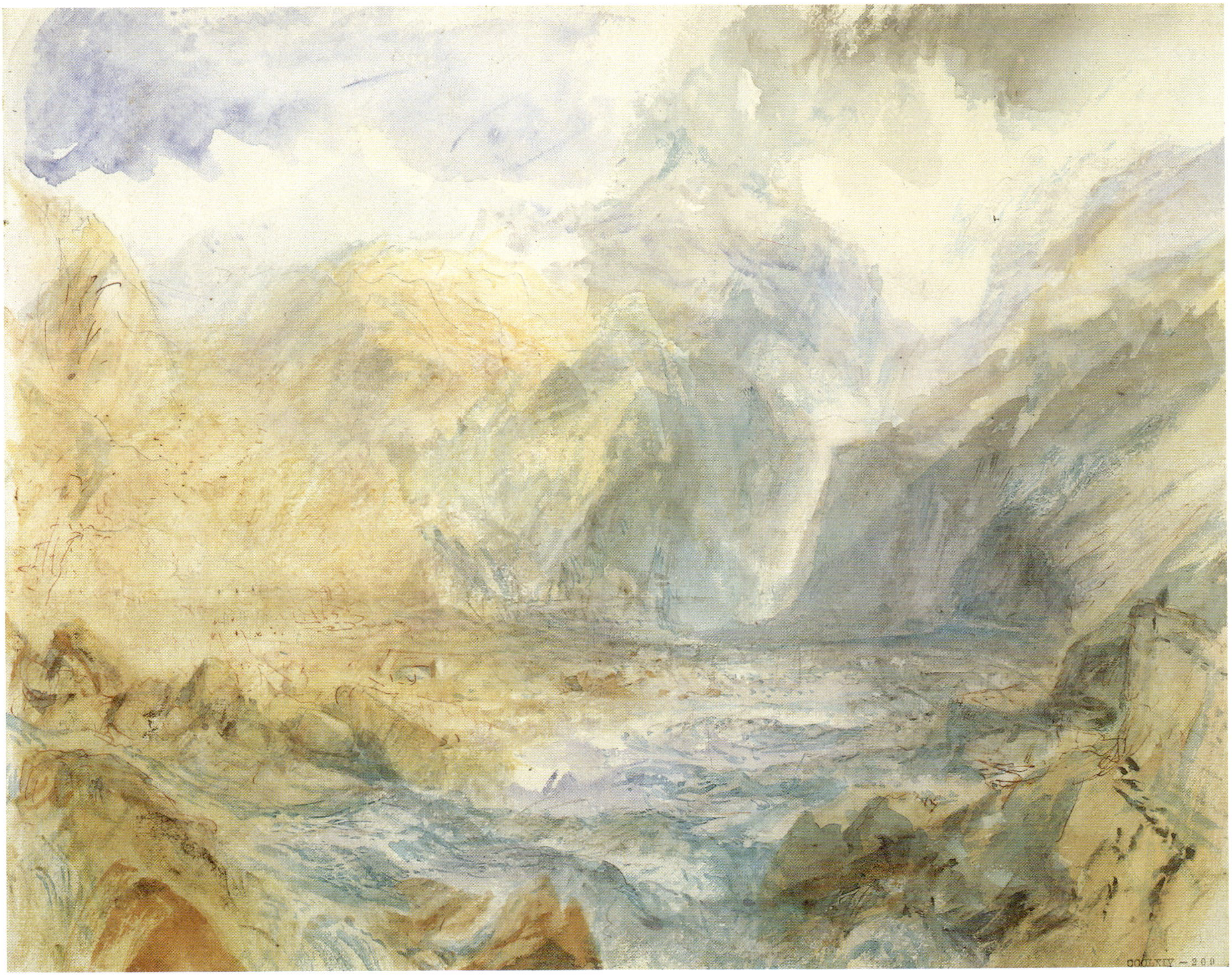

41 The Descent to Italy. (Bellinzona)

Bellinzona from the North ?1842
Pencil, watercolour and gouache, with pen
228 × 286 (9 × 11¼)
TB CCCXXXII 27 D33497
EXH: NG (453)
LIT: *Works*, XIII, pp.207, 315, no.336; *R on P*, pp.201–2; Serota 1970, p.130; Gilardoni 1978, no.3

The weather having completely cleared, we approach Bellinzona in the glowing light of a cloudless evening.

Nothing can possibly be more wonderful than this study, either in truth of mountain line, or beauty of composition. I do not know one which shows the difference between Turner and all other painters more completely; for instance, assuredly any other artist would have made the buildings on the hill in the middle distance as dark, or darker than the hill on which they stand, in order to show them better against the mist; but how tenderly Turner has marked that, though all are in shadow, (the ray of light over the hill striking quite above them,) the buildings are a little paler and warmer, as well as more exposed to diffused light, than the rock they stand upon.

The figures are wonderfully put in, directing the eye to the towers above, and giving distance to the road. The piece of quiet light river on the right is quite wonderful in effect at a little distance. The sketch is in all respects one of a thousand.

Turner visited Bellinzona on both his Swiss tours of 1842 and 1843. Further research is needed before it is possible to state with any confidence which watercolours relate to which trip. However, Ruskin provides a date for the 'sample study' of Bellinzona (cat.no.48), which is on a similar type of paper to this and cat.no.45, thereby suggesting 1842 as the most likely year for all three. As well as a group of about fifteen views in the Turner Bequest, there are other Bellinzona subjects in the collections at Dublin, Manchester and in the British Museum (W 1489–91).

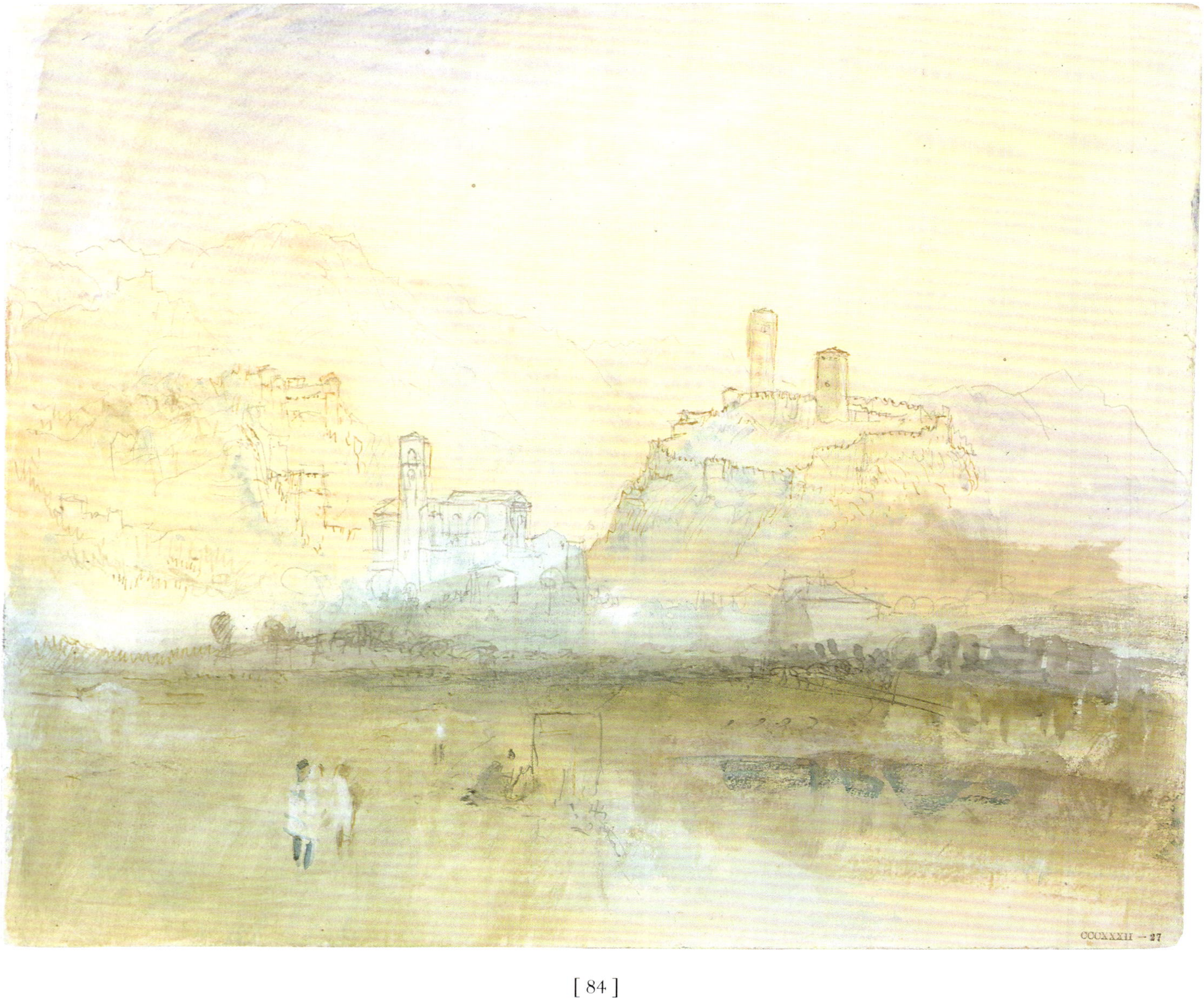

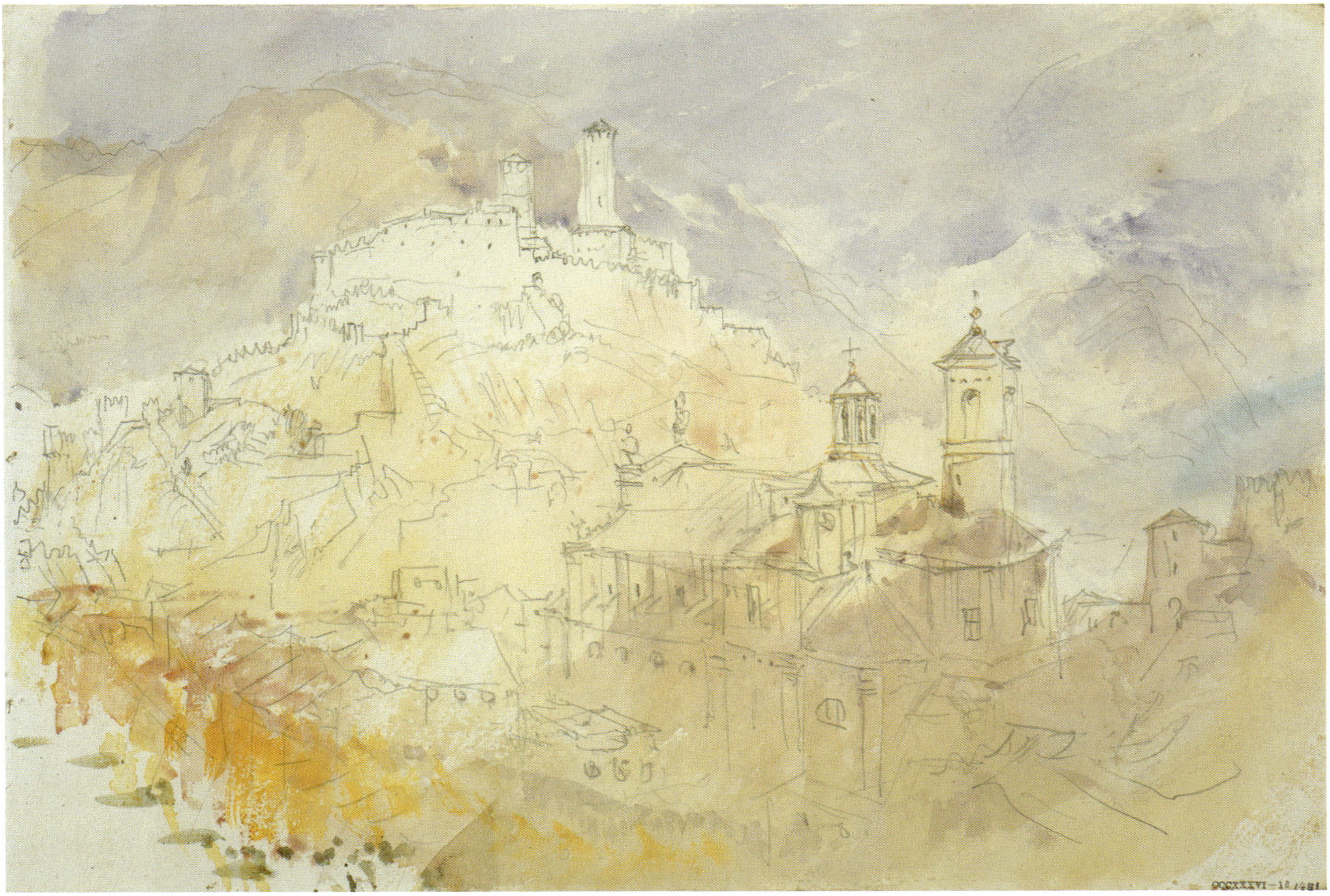

42 Bellinzona, from the North

Bellinzona: The Church of SS Pietro e Stefano, and the Castello Grande, from the East ?1843
Pencil and watercolour 227 × 335 (8$^{15}/_{16}$ × 13$^{1}/_{4}$)
TB CCCXXXVI 16 D33595
EXH: NG (784); Tate Gallery 1931–4; Tate Gallery 1988 (47); Tate Gallery 1990
LIT: *Works*, XIII, pp.207–8; *R on P*, pp.260, 259n.; Russell and Wilton 1976, p.116, repr.; Gilardoni 1978, no.9

The town of Bellinzona is, on the whole, the most picturesque in Switzerland, being crowned by three fortresses, standing on isolated rocks of noble form, while the buildings are full of beautiful Italian character. Turner went to the place several times, and made many studies there; but on the occasion of this visit, he seems to me to have been not in his usual health. The valley beneath the rocks is marshy and hot; and there is an indolence in the way this and the three following subjects are executed, which exactly resembles the character of work done under the languor of slight malaria fever. They were all in one book: and two of them (44 and 45) are more elaborate than most of the other subjects in it, but sickly and heavy in elaboration.

In this subject, note the colour used in spots for the tiled tops of the battlements under sunshine. Most artists paint tiles much too red; this peculiar amber hue is their exact colour. Compare No.62.

Each of the three castles at Bellinzona is associated with one of the cantons of the region: the largest and oldest is Castello Grande (Uri); to its east is Castello Montebello (Schwyz); and high above them both is Castello di Sasso Corbaro (Unterwalden). This view looks across the mass of ramparts leading up to Castello Grande from a position just below Castello Montebello. Although slightly obscured by the latter castle's shadow, the foreground is filled by the collegiate church of SS Pietro e Stefano, a Renaissance building which has been much altered over the years. Ruskin speculates here (and in the succeeding catalogue entries) that the colouring of Turner's views of Bellinzona indicates that the artist had fallen prey to malarial sickness. This was a hazzard that contemporary guidebooks warned travellers to be wary of in the lower Ticino valley. Indeed, during his first visit to Switzerland without his parents in 1845, Ruskin frequently wrote home about his fears of sleeping at Bellinzona because of the potential danger to his health (see Shapiro 1972, pp.166, 178, 179). It is possible, therefore, that, unless Ruskin had specific knowledge that Turner had been ill while at Bellinzona, he has simply transferred the reasons for his own anxiety to Turner's visits. Furthermore, his assumption is significantly weakened by his claim that cat.nos.42–5 all reflect this sickness; as is suggested below, cat.no.45 seems to come from a different tour and sketchbook. Ruskin developed the idea that an artist's well-being affects his (or her) use of colour in the manual *The Elements of Drawing*, which was written at much the same time as this catalogue (*Works*, XV, pp.156–7).

43 Bellinzona

Bellinzona from the South-east ?1843
Pencil and watercolour, with pen 228 × 326 (9 × 12⅞)
Verso: rough pencil sketches
TB CCCLXIV 384 D36249
EXH: 4th Loan Collection 1891 (16); Berne 1947–8 (97); Tate Gallery 1989
LIT: *Works*, XIII, p.208; White 1896, p.35 no.49; *R on P*, p.259n; Serota 1970, p.134; Gilardoni 1978, no.7

Beautiful as a subject, but less interesting as a sketch than most of the series. It is a good example, however, of Turner's architectural touch when he was careless. The opalescent peak of mountain behind the central castle is well given, however.

This view from the southern side of Bellinzona forms a pair with cat.no.44, where the Castello Grande is given only its simplest form. Both works are unified by the warm southern sunlight, which Turner recreates as layered veils in glowing washes of orange and pink. He seems to have particularly relished the way Bellinzona sprawls across the bottom of the valley, surrounded on all

43

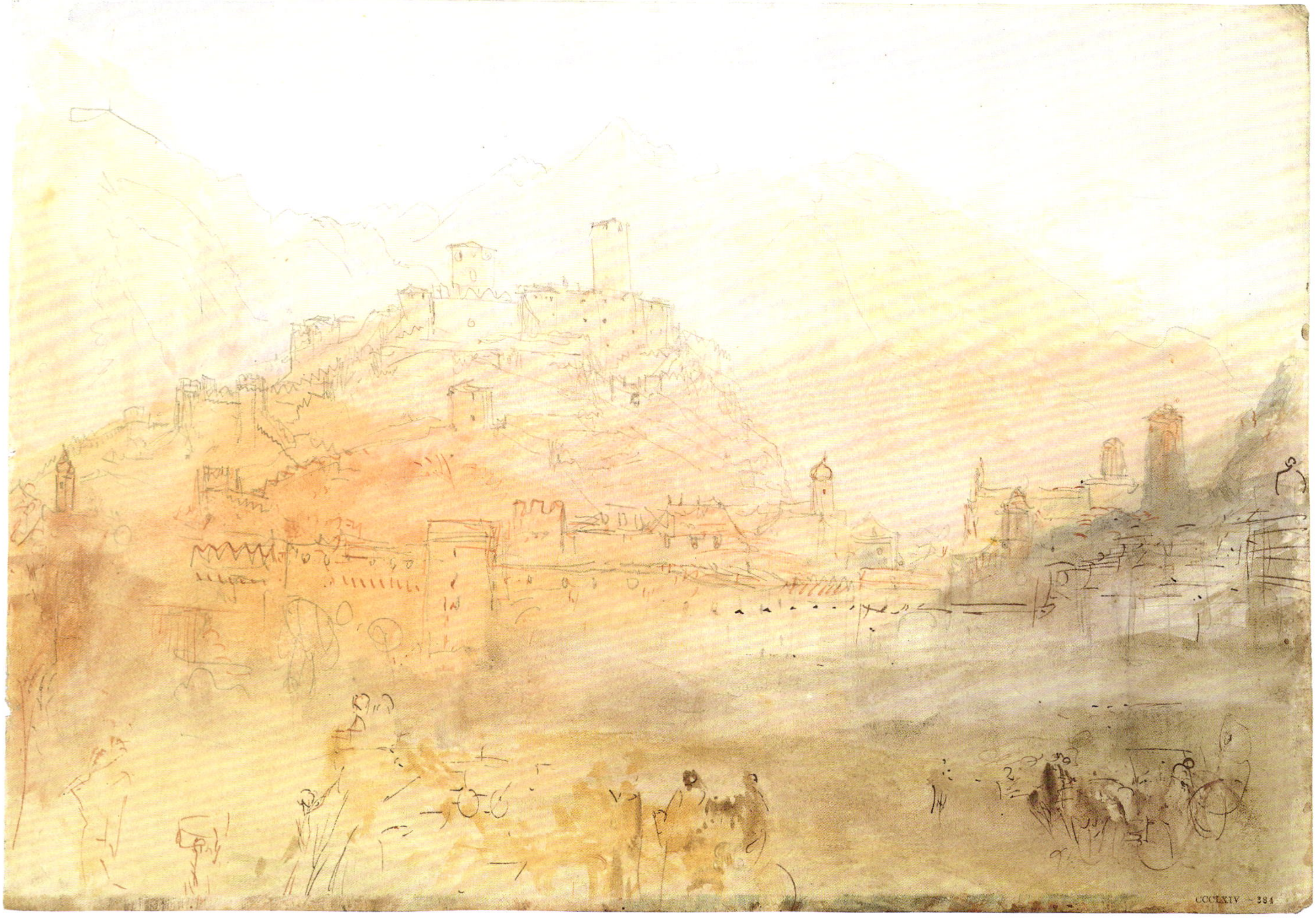

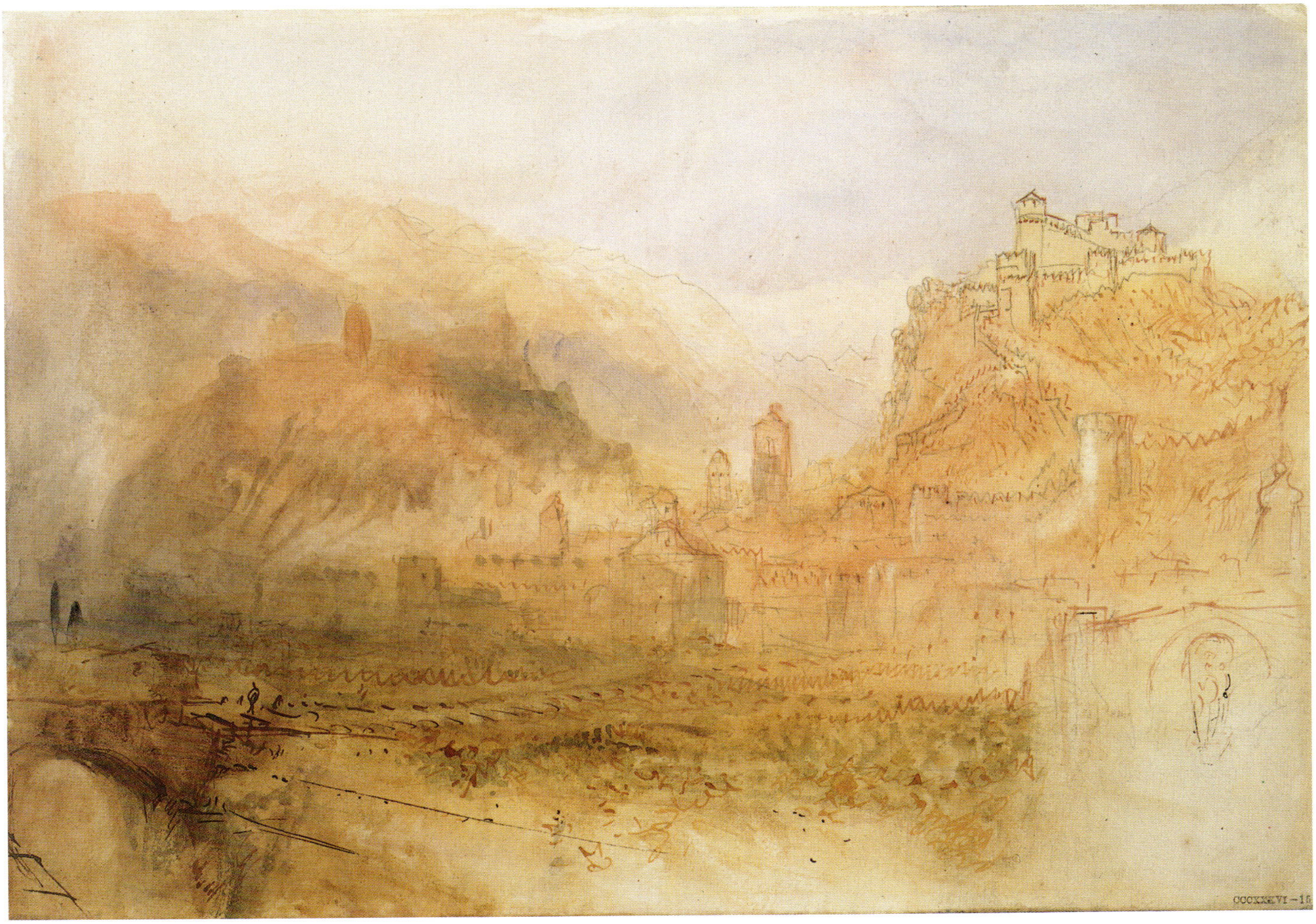

but one side by mountains. In spite of Ruskin's fears of catching malaria, he did visit Bellinzona briefly in 1845, concluding in a letter to his father that 'neither you nor I need trouble ourselves hereafter about Bellinzona or the head of the lago Maggiore. It is ugly and unhealthy' (Shapiro 1972, p.178). However, many years later, in 1858, he returned again on a sketching expedition, only to change his opinion completely. He then wrote home claiming, 'My sketching place here is the pleasantest without exception I have ever had to work in' (Hayman 1982, p.64; a selection of Ruskin's watercolours of Bellinzona is reproduced in Hayman 1990, pp.49–58).

44 Bellinzona

Bellinzona from the South-east ?1843
Pencil and watercolour, with pen 227 × 324 ($8\frac{15}{16} \times 12\frac{3}{4}$)
Watermarked: J WHATMAN | TURKEY MILL | 1839
Verso: rough pencil sketches
TB CCCXXXVI 15 D33594
EXH: NG (764); Tate Gallery 1931–4; Athens, Georgia 1982 (88)
LIT: *Works*, XIII, p.208; *R on P*, p.258; Rawlinson, Finberg and Holroyd 1909, pl.XXIII; Serota 1970, p.134; Gilardoni 1978, no.6; Wilton 1982, p.70, pl.112

Grandly fancied; but poor Turner has been quite ill, and could not draw the distant fortress; having got it into a great mess, he redeems it very nearly by the two dark cypresses, quite marvellously put in, and giving depth and largeness to all that purple-grey distance.

In this watercolour, the emphasis falls on the Castello Montebello, on the right. In the foreground is a bridge over a small tributary of the Ticino, known as the Dragonata. The bridge is reached from the Porta Lugano, at the right of this view. In contrast with the detailed outlines of the Castello Montebello, Turner has not developed the pencil underdrawing of the Castello Grande other than by applying a dab of his brush to convey the Torre Bianca. All three castles at Bellinzona were already partly ruined at the time of Turner's visit, but the Castello Grande still functioned as an arsenal and prison.

45 Bellinzona

Bellinzona: A Procession, Seen from the North ?1842
Pencil and watercolour, with pen 230 × 290 ($9\frac{1}{16} \times 11\frac{7}{16}$)
TB CCCLXIV 343 D36203
EXH: NG (772); Tate Gallery 1931–4; British Museum 1937–8 (Frame 6); Berne 1947–8 (89); British Museum 1975–6 (280, as a view 'from the south'); Zurich 1976–7 (83); Tate Gallery 1983; Melbourne 1985; Tate Gallery 1989 (26, as 'Bellinzona from the North', repr. p.38)
LIT: *Works*, XIII, p.208; *R on P*, pp.259–60 as 'Bellinzona from the South'; Serota 1970, p.131; Russell and Wilton 1976, p.112, repr. (image reversed); Gilardoni 1978, no.2; Wilton 1982, p.70, pl.113

Though we are not well, we mean to make a nice sketch of this, and take more pains than usual about the green banks of rock under the walls, besides drawing an Italian gentleman's house on the right, and his trellis of vines, and above all, his gateposts, which remind us of home, in our best manner; and we put some nice trees, and mist under them, beyond. But it is

45

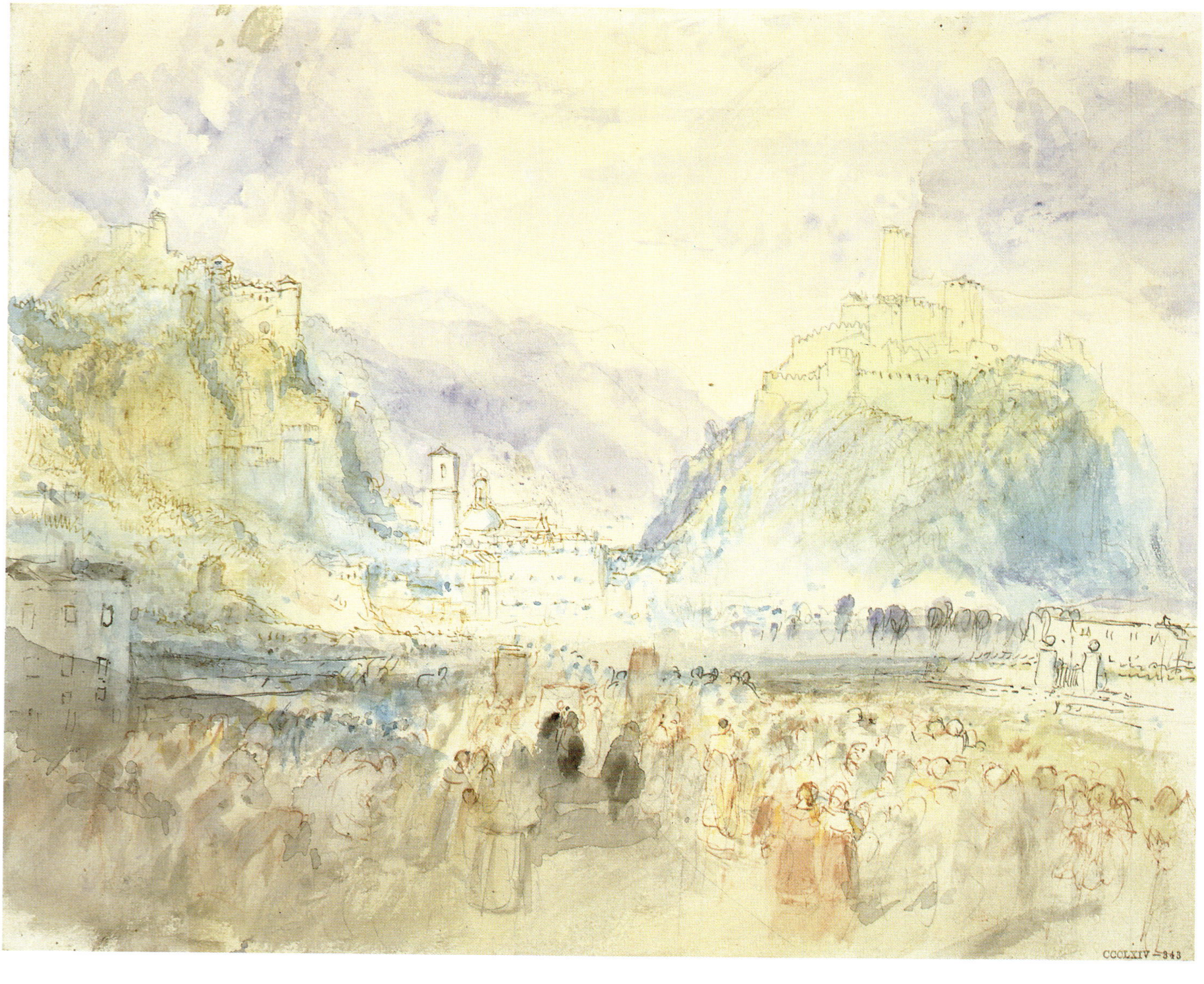

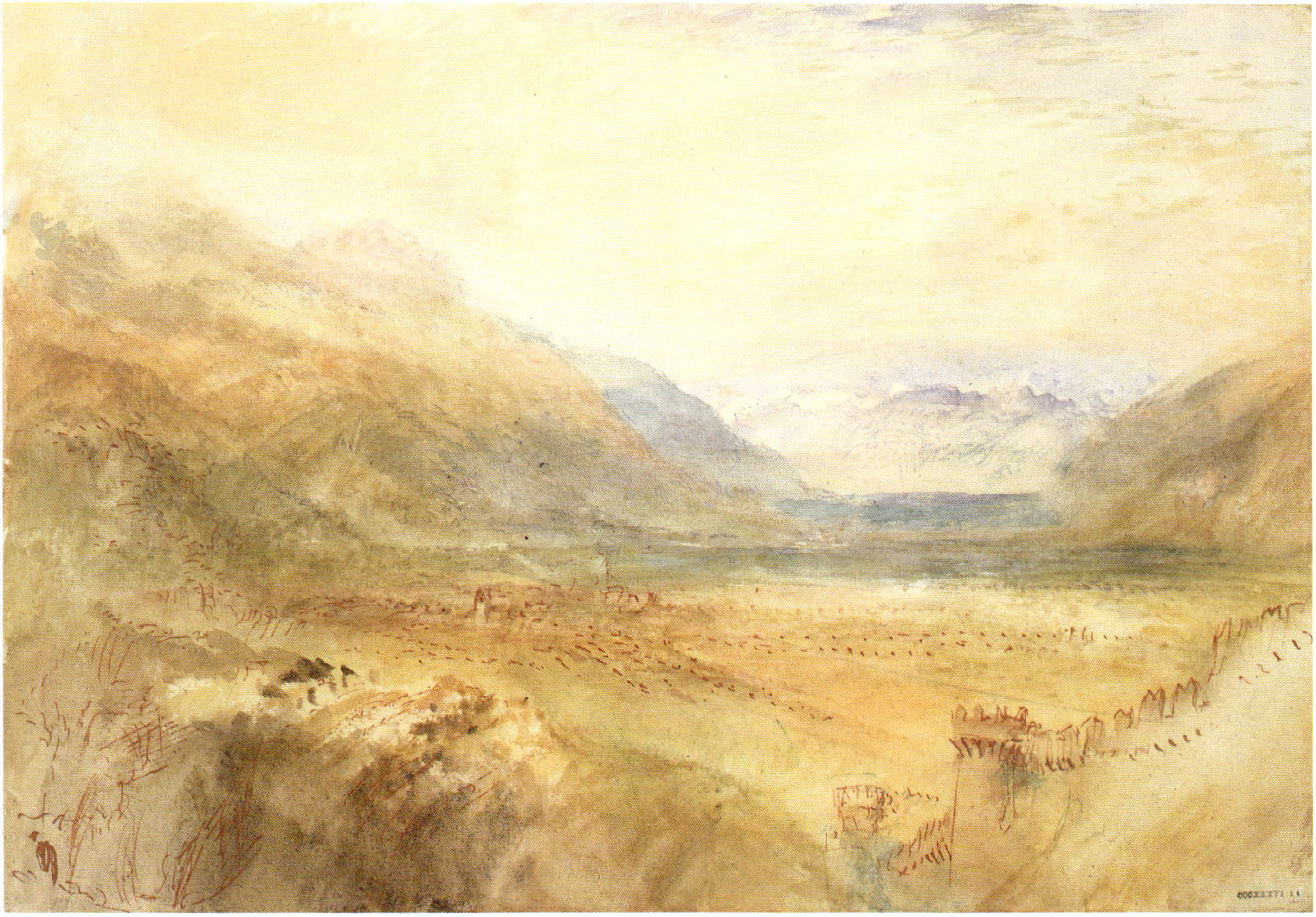

46

all of no use; the illness gets the better of us; we get quite wearied in the crowd, leave the kneeling figures in despair, and, when the time comes for us to put in our sky, make a complete mess of it.

It is not clear in this watercolour whether the procession is moving towards or away from the viewer. The underlying perspective suggests, however, that the focus lies on the collegiate church at the centre of the view. If the direction of movement can be tentatively surmised, there seem to be no real clues as to the nature of the event. It could possibly represent the traditional procession of 15 August, with which the feast of the Assumption is marked in Catholic areas of Switzerland; Turner was certainly abroad throughout August in 1842. The inclusion of a trellis with vines, noted by Ruskin, seems particularly appropriate, since the Ticino valley around Bellinzona has always been well cultivated, with many vineyards and small villas surrounding the town. Ruskin's assertion that Turner was ill when he made this study is examined under cat.no.42, above. His statement there that nos.42–5 were 'all in one book', also needs to be questioned, since the paper on which this watercolour is painted is noticeably smaller than the others in the group (see also cat.nos.41 and 48). Moreover, the cool colouring here is quite distinct from the temperate oranges and pinks deployed on the sheets taken from the *Bellinzona* sketchbook (TB CCCXXXVI).

46 View from the Castle of Bellinzona

Bellinzona: Looking South-west from Castello Montebello
?1843
Pencil and watercolour, with pen 227 × 327 ($8^{15}/_{16}$ × $12^{7}/_{8}$)
Watermarked: J WHATMAN | TURKEY MILL | 1839
Verso: rough pencil sketch
TB CCCXXXVI 14 D33592
EXH: NG (765)
LIT: *Works*, XIII, p.209; *R on P*, p.258; Serota 1970, p.134; Gilardoni 1978, no.15

Early next morning, feeling a little better, we climb to the top of the castle, and try to draw the valley as it opens to the Lago Maggiore. We cannot manage it, and rub the colours about till all assume an expression of malaria fog, which we did not intend. We try to brighten matters by touches of raw vermilion without any better success, and go down sulkily to breakfast.

In his *Hand-book for Travellers in Switzerland*, John Murray recommended the view down the wide, flat-bottomed Ticino valley from the heights of Castello Grande, which he claimed was 'very striking' (Murray 1838, p.217). This watercolour could have been taken from the favoured position, but seems more probably to be a view from Castello Montebello. The range of subtle earth colours deployed in this work has been achieved by a succession of washes, apparently rapidly applied. The overlapping areas of colour, which are sometimes almost muddy, are unlike the traditionally precise techniques of translucent English watercolour painting. As in Turner's other late Swiss watercolours, particularly those of Fribourg (TB CCCXXXV), a pen dipped in red watercolour has been used to give form to significant details, the dotted lines here suggesting a path across the valley. Another sheet, with a similar view down the valley, is no longer catalogued as part of the *Bellinzona* sketchbook, but is on paper of the same type and date (TB CCCLXIV 389; watermarked J WHATMAN | TURKEY MILL | 1839).

47 Bellinzona, from the South

Bellinzona from the South-west, on the Road to Locarno
?1843
Pencil and watercolour, with pen 228 × 327 (9 × 12⅞)
Verso: hasty sketch of a ?mountain pass; inscribed by a later hand, '48, used as 47' [i.e. as cat.no.47 here]
Turner Bequest; [no Inventory number given] D40516
LIT: *Works*, XIII, p.209; *R on P*, p.259n.; Cook 1905, p.18, repr., as 'A Swiss Pass (?)'; R.Yardley, *Turner Studies*, vol.4, no.1, 1984, p.60 (Yardley assumes that TB CCCXXXVI 13 was the subject described in cat.no.47)

47

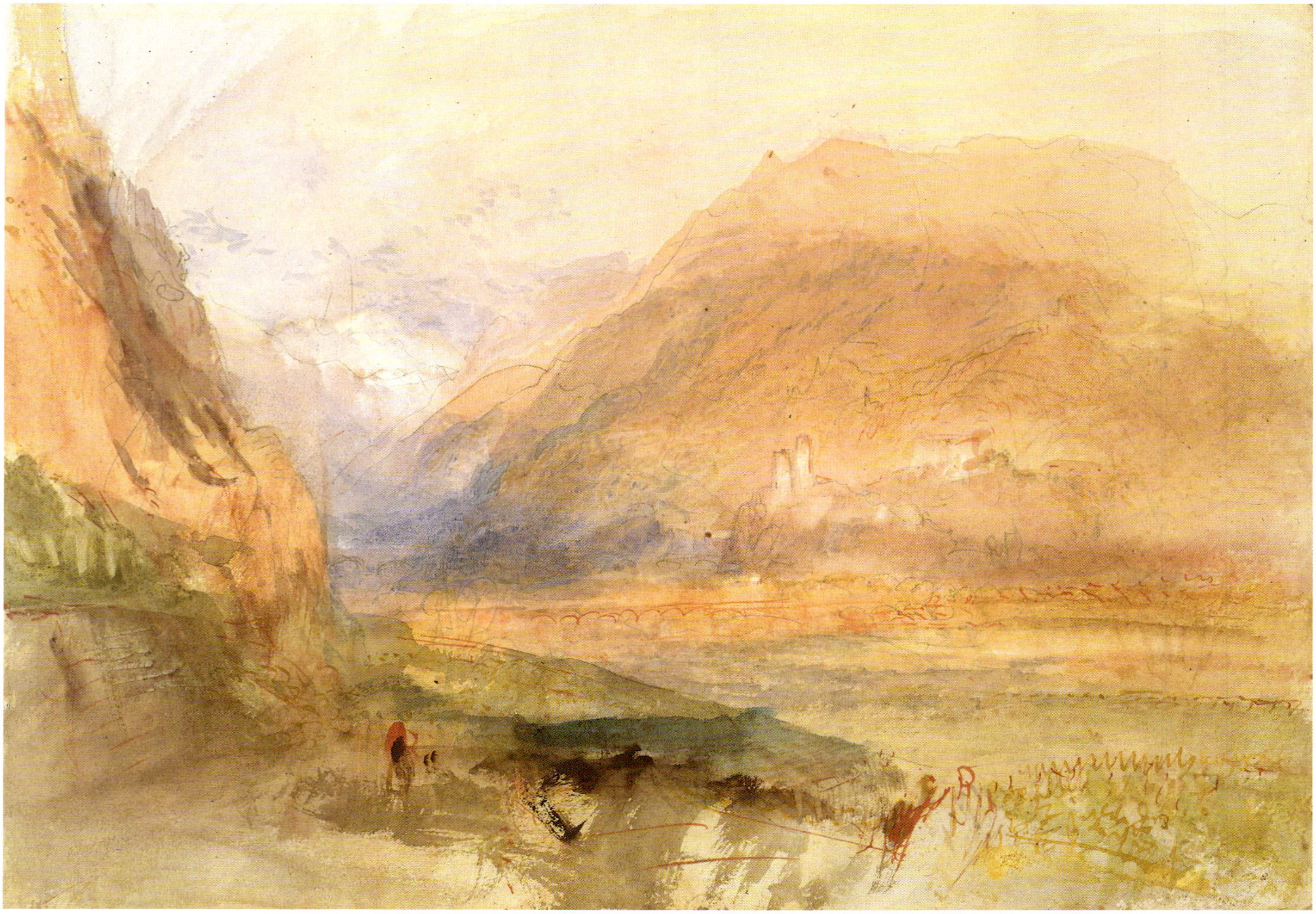

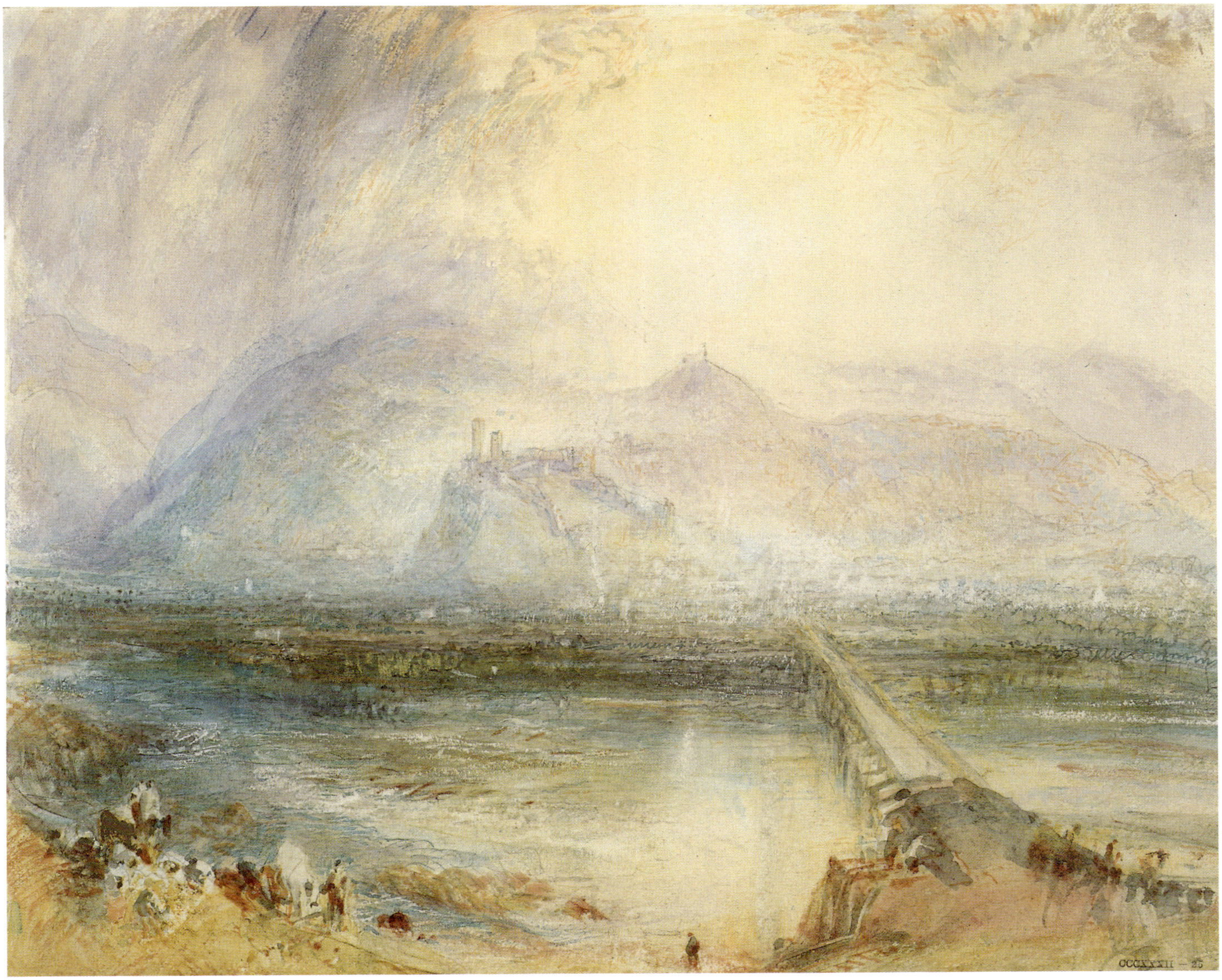

Our morning walk has nevertheless done us good; and as we leave the town, and look back to it, we get a vigorous memorandum of the bridge over the Ticino.

After writing this catalogue, Ruskin seems to have returned this watercolour to the tin boxes in the basement of the National Gallery, and it is probable that it has, therefore, never been exhibited. Certainly, it does not seem to have been catalogued by A.J. Finberg in 1909, perhaps on account of confusion between the various views of Bellinzona. Other watercolours which adopt a viewpoint from the west bank of the Ticino, looking back to Bellinzona, are TB CCCXXXVI 4, 13, and TB CCCXXXVII 7. The impressive bridge spanning the Ticino at the centre of these views had been completed in 1815. A recently identified watercolour of the bridge can be found in the Art Gallery and Museum at Oldham (Yardley 1984, p.60, repr.; W 1339).

48 Bellinzona, from the West

Bellinzona from the Road to Locarno: Sample Study
?1842–3
Pencil, watercolour and gouache, with scratching-out
229 × 289 (9 × 11⅜)
Verso inscribed in pencil: 'Bellinzona | No.12 | 13 | x o 14 | Mr Munro'
TB CCCXXXII 25 D33495
EXH: NG (84); Dresden 1972 (106, repr. p.78, pl.26); Lisbon 1973 (50, repr. p.129); British Museum 1975–6 (279); Zurich 1976–7 (82); Tate Gallery 1983; Stockholm 1984 (48); Melbourne 1985
LIT: *Works*, XIII, p.209 and p.611; *R on P*, p.118; Rawlinson, Finberg and Holroyd 1909, p.37, pl.XXIV; Serota 1970, pp.114, 130; Gilardoni 1978, no.12; Wilton 1979, pp.484–5; Wilton 1982, pp.69–70, pl.111; Hayman 1990, p.50, repr.; M. Davies, *Turner as Professor*, exh. cat., Tate Gallery 1992–3, p.65, fig.75

This beautiful drawing belongs to another series, and has no connection in point of time with the group we have just reviewed. I do not know when this drawing was executed, but it was shown by Turner, among others, in the year 1842, and was realised for Mr. Munro in 1843; but the realisation was not equal to the sketch [fig.35].

Ruskin's list of the watercolours completed by Turner in 1843 was drawn up more than thirty years later. It did not include a view of Bellinzona, and the comments here are the principal evidence for accepting that Munro of

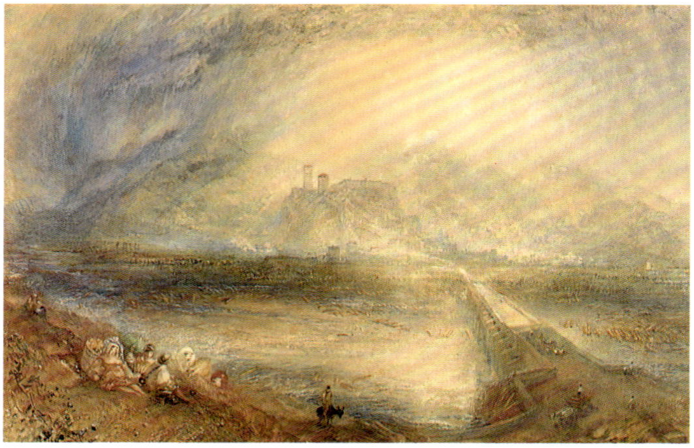

fig.35 'Bellinzona, from the Road to Locarno' 1843, watercolour (W 1539). *City of Aberdeen Art Gallery & Museums Collections*

Novar's 'Bellinzona' was based on a 'sample study' dating from 1842. The Turner Bequest contains a detailed pencil study of Bellinzona from the west on another sheet of the smaller paper associated with the 1842 tour (TB CCCXLIV 423), although the view there is taken from further to the right of the bridge. Both subjects set out the three fortresses on the opposite side of the river in much the same way. But in this watercolour Turner manages to suggest a greater sense of distance through the use of an atmospheric mist and the presence of lifting rainclouds. After he had built up an elaborate surface of exquisite flecks of colour, including rich purple shadows under the castle walls, Turner scratched at his paper to introduce effects of light falling on the water. In the finished drawing, however, he was not always able to recreate the finesse of these nuances so successfully. Of the two works, it was the sketch that Ruskin valued most highly. After his brief visit to Bellinzona in 1845, he wrote to his father somewhat dismissively: 'Bellinzona fine in form, but Turner's single sketch worth the whole valley with all the towns in it' (Shapiro 1972, p.178). The number '12' inscribed on the verso of this sheet links it with another view of Bellinzona, in Manchester City Art Gallery, which is inscribed '11' (W 1489). These numbers are possibly related to the group of 'sample studies' put together after the 1842 tour.

49 The Approach to Lago Maggiore from Bellinzona

A Storm over Lago Maggiore, from near Magadino ?1842
Pencil and watercolour, with coloured crayon
222 × 272 (8¾ × 10¾)
TB CCCXXXVII 28 D33631
EXH: NG (93); British Museum 1975–6 (277, repr. p.155); Zurich 1976–7 (63); Madrid 1983 (85, repr, p.95); Tokyo 1986 (103, repr. p.253); Tate Gallery 1988; Tate Gallery 1990; Tate Gallery 1993 (18, repr. pp.27, 41)
LIT: *Works*, XIII, p.209 and p.612; *R on P*, p.121 (the cross-reference to the 1857 catalogue incorrectly suggests the work was placed as no.93); Serota 1970, p.136

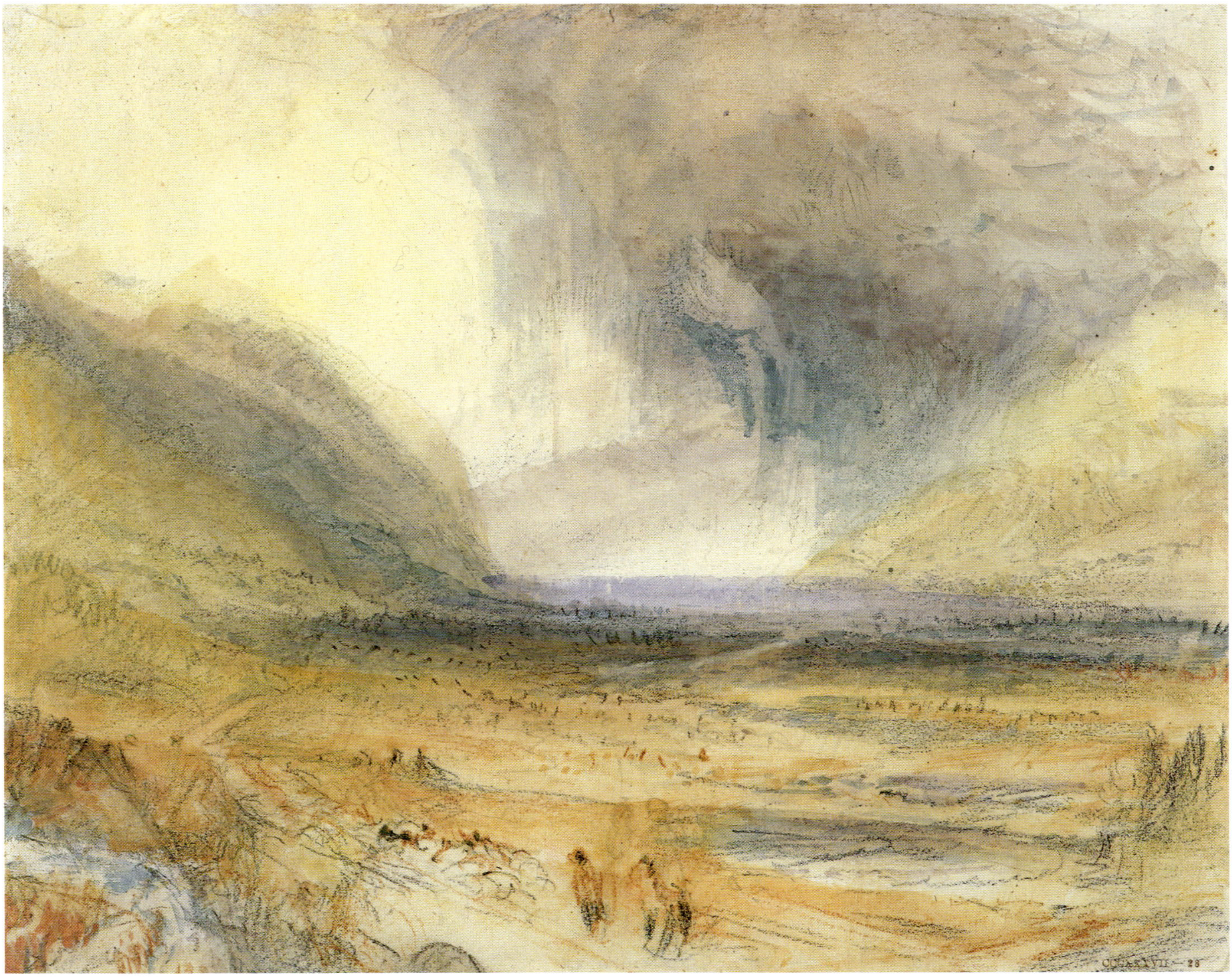

49

This wonderful study, one of the most perfect in the series, is done on paper as thin as that of a bank-note. Note how the vermilion on the rocks in the torrent, in the lowest left-hand corner, gives sunshine to all the mass of warm colour in the rest of the foreground. A flock of sheep are passing the bridge; and the Ticino zigzags irregularly through the plains below, leaving logs of pine scattered on its sand-banks.

Every way admirable and instructive.

What is most striking about both this view and cat.no.50, is Turner's use of coloured crayons over his washes of watercolour. He appears to have used something resembling a Conté crayon, in which chalk was combined with a greasy medium, making the artist's marks less fugitive. As a result, the surface of his paper has a rich, lively texture.

Although Turner has here produced an accurate representation of the broad plain of the lower Ticino valley, his subject is the raincloud that partly obscures the afternoon sunshine. Both these sheets were catalogued as part of the group of loose leaves that A.J. Finberg described as the *Bellinzona, Sion &c* sketchbook (TB CCCXXXVII). This tentative assemblage has since been challenged by Nicholas Serota, who suggested these drawings should be brought together with others variously scattered in the Turner Bequest to form a book he calls the 'Sihl' sketchbook of 1842.

50 Head of the Lago Maggiore

?1842
Pencil and watercolour, with coloured crayon
219 × 271 (8⅝ × 10¹¹⁄₁₆)
TB CCCXXXVII 29 D33632
EXH: NG (94)
LIT: *Works*, XIII, pp.210, 372 as 'Bellinzona', 612; *R on P*, p.121 as 'Mountains of Bellinzona, from Magadino'; Serota 1970, p.136

At Magadino the steamer is waiting for us to take us down the Lago Maggiore to Sesto Calende.

This study is drawn on the same thin paper as No.49, and yet the drawing of the distant mountain is more complete than in any other of these hundred sketches.

I can find no memoranda made lower down, on the Lago Maggiore, nor at Milan, nor at Verona, so that we must go on to Venice without any farther pause.

During the early 1840s the Lake Maggiore steamer service embarked at 5 o'clock in the morning and returned in the evening. Steamers appear on the lakes of many of Turner's late Swiss subjects, and are sometimes introduced in the finished drawings when there is no indication of them in the sample studies (see figs.46, 49), suggesting this was not an innovation he despised. Ruskin is correct in believing Turner did not push further south to the northern cities of Italy as part of last tours. Turner's principal tours to Italy took place in 1819 and 1828 (see C. Powell, *Turner in the South: Rome, Naples, Florence*, 1987). He did, however, travel through the Italian lakes on one of these final journeys; there are studies at Lugano and of Lake Como, mostly in pencil (TB CCCXXXVIII).

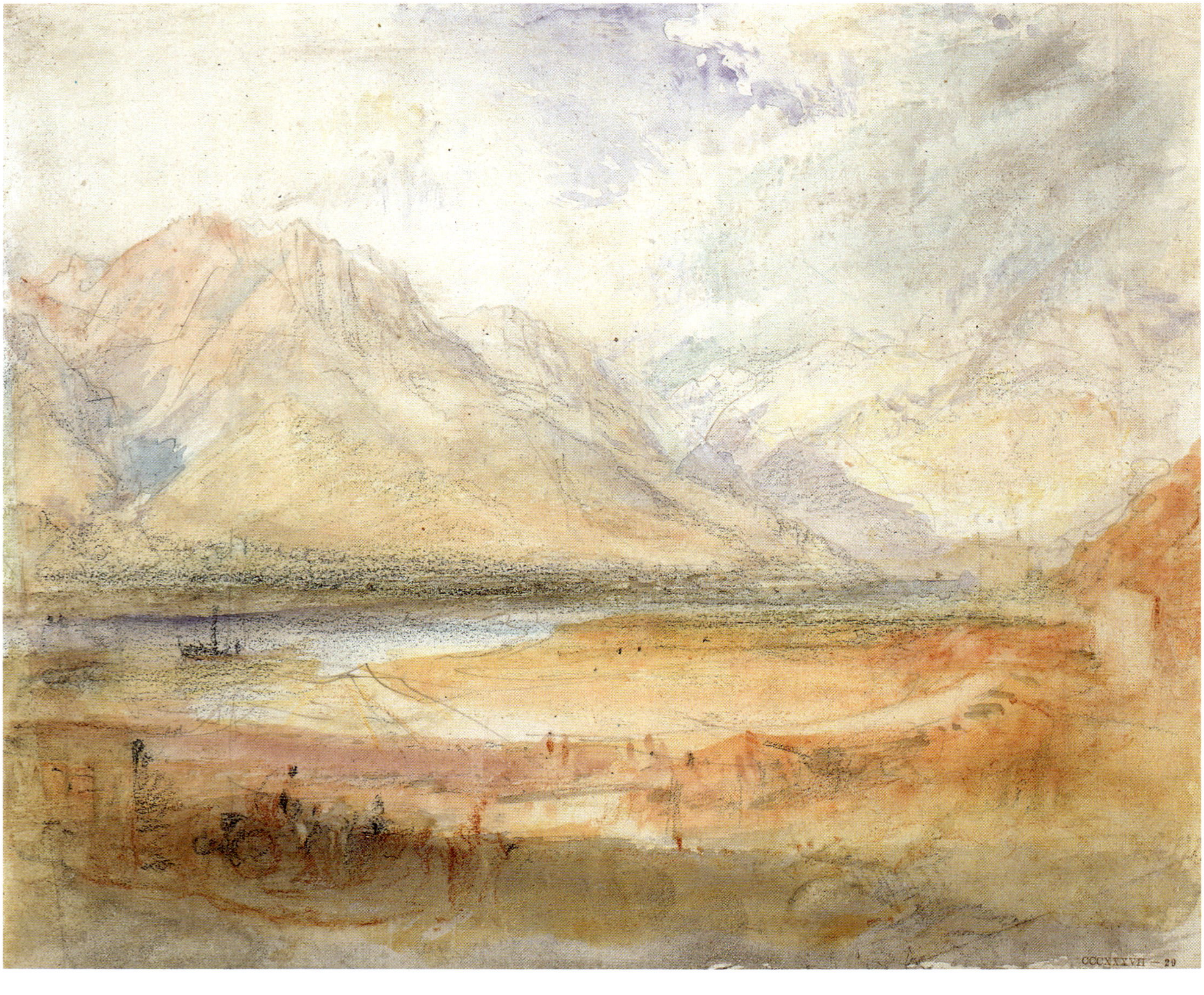

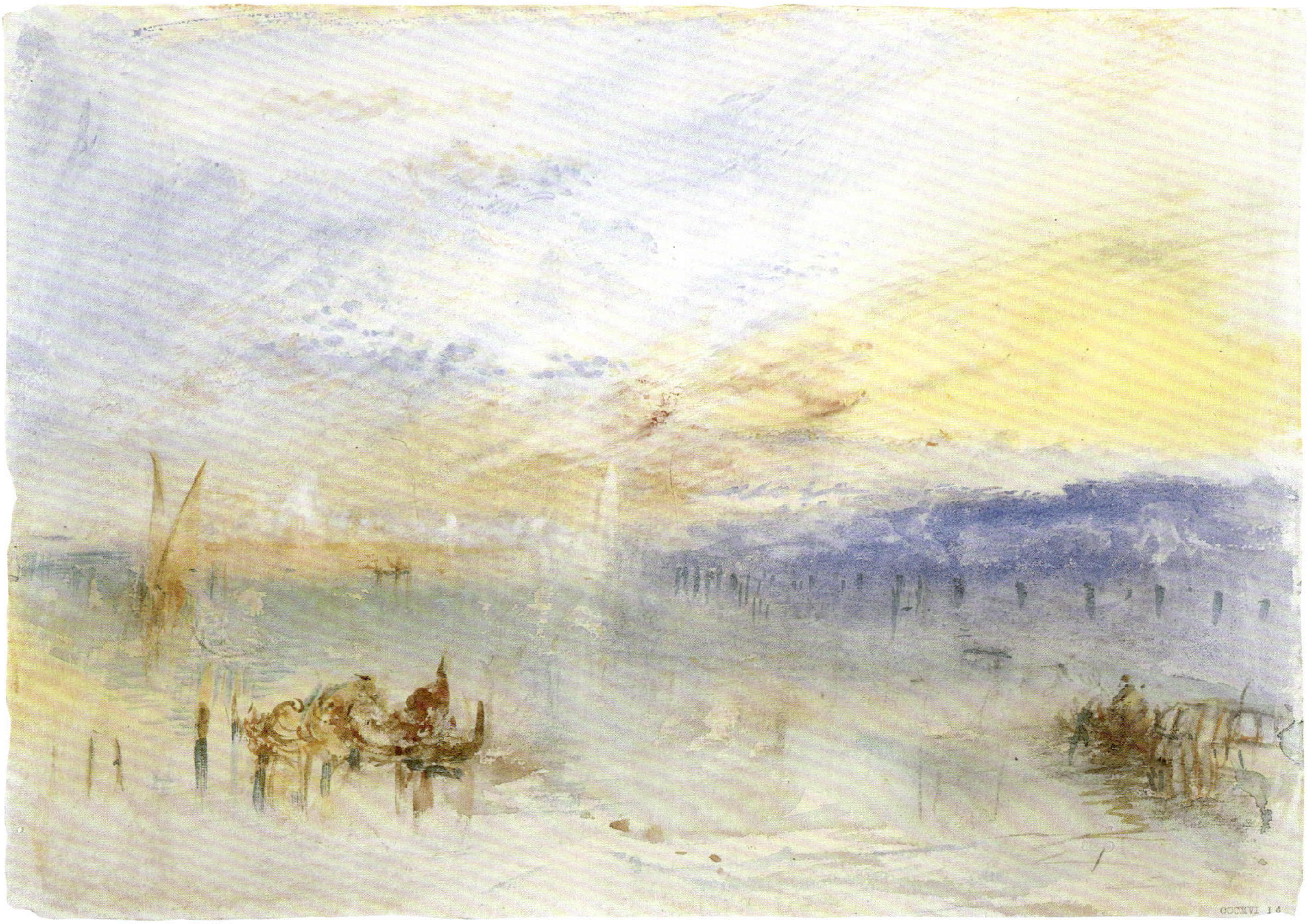

51 The Approach to Venice. From the land side, before the railroad bridge was built

1840
Watercolour and gouache, on off-white paper
230 × 323 (9 1/16 × 12 3/4)
TB CCCXVI 16 D32153
EXH: NG (51); Tate Gallery 1959–65; British Museum 1975–6 (241, repr. p.143)
LIT: *Works*, XIII, pp.210, 373, 611; *R on P*, p.108; Finberg 1910, repr. pl.LXXIX, opp. p.132 as 'About 1839'; Finberg 1930, pp.126 pl.XXIII (lower), p.174; J. Rothenstein and M. Butlin, *Turner*, 1964, repr. pl.114(b); Stainton 1985, p.60, pl.70

The line of green posts marks the edge of the deep water channel which led from Mestre to the opening of the Grand Canal. Very noble.

Turner's views of Venice have always been warmly admired by collectors and the public alike, but, surprisingly, there have only been two extended surveys of this aspect of his work: A.J. Finberg's *In Venice with Turner* (1930), and Lindsay Stainton's more recent account, *Turner's Venice* (1985). Both are valuable contributions which help to supplement Ruskin's comments on these watercolours. Other Venetian subjects not in the Turner Bequest are listed by Andrew Wilton (W 1352–75). Ruskin recognised that Venice held a special place in Turner's affections. In the catalogue of his own collection of Turner watercolours, he stated his belief that 'The Alps brought him always sadness, but Venice delight' (*Works*, XIII, p.497). Turner had first visited the floating city in 1819, after which he painted a watercolour of a group of travellers at Fusina, waiting to be ferried across the lagoon (W 721, private collection; repr. Wilton 1979, p.146). The towers and spires of Venice are set out along the line of the horizon much as they are in this later watercolour of 1840, instilling in the viewer the excited anticipation of soon reaching the enchanted palaces and waterways. The approach to Venice by water is something that is memorably invoked by Ruskin himself in his three-volume work *The Stones of Venice* (*Works*, IX–XI, 1851, 1853). Ruskin presented a signed copy of the first volume to Turner in 1851 (private collection).

52 The Ducal Palace and Riva dei Schiavoni. From the water

1840
Pencil, watercolour and gouache, with pen and scratching out 243 × 304 (9 9/16 × 12)
Inscribed, lower right: '[?lagoon]' or '[?green]'
TB CCCXVI 17 D32154
EXH: NG (52); Victoria and Albert Museum from 1934 (Frame 21); Tate Gallery 1993 (4, repr. p.25 and p.35)
LIT: *Works*, XIII, pp.210, 373, 611; *R on P*, pp.108–9 (misnumbered 'No.53'); Finberg 1930, p.174; Stainton 1985, p.58, pl.63

Careless, but rich in subject, and showing attention to little things which escape artists who make more elaborate drawings: the exact look of the foreshortened lion on the pillar, for instance, and the depression of the two last windows of the facade of the Ducal Palace.

This watercolour is one of two views of Venice in the Turner Bequest that are taken to a more finished state than the majority of these colour studies; the other work is the view of the Arsenal, which was already on display at Marlborough House when Ruskin made this selection in 1857 (TB CCCXVI 27; see Appendix I). Although there is no existing evidence to suggest that Turner actually received commissions for watercolours of Venice, several Venetian subjects are comparable in their handling to the completed Swiss drawings of the 1840s (W 1352–74; see also the unlisted view of S. Giorgio Maggiore, sold at Christie's, 15 June 1982, lot 182). The early history of these works is mostly obscure, but it is possible that they were produced for sale through Thomas Griffith, who is revealed in the provenances as one source for the works outside the Turner Bequest. The idea of commissioning Turner to produce finished Venetian views certainly

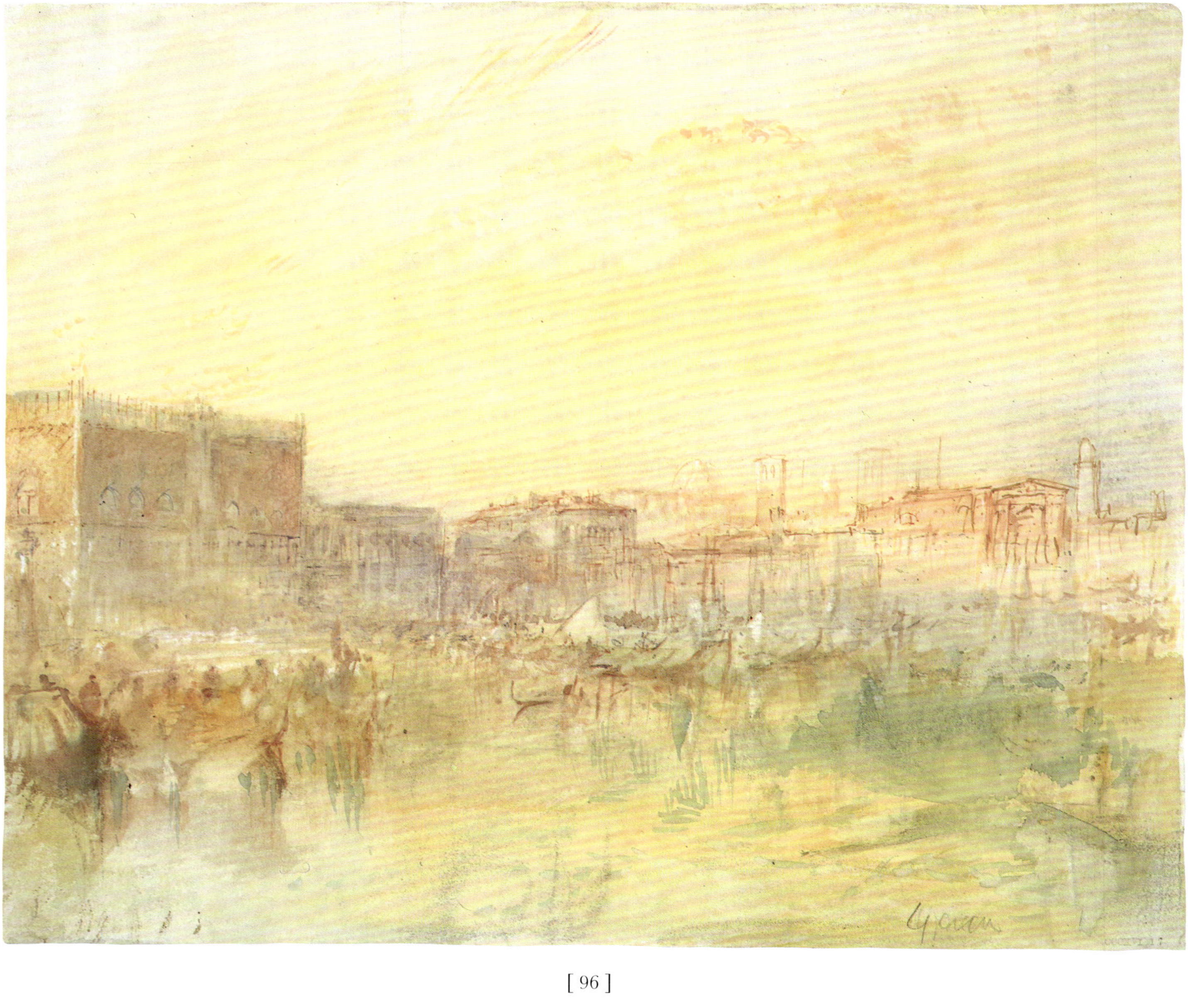

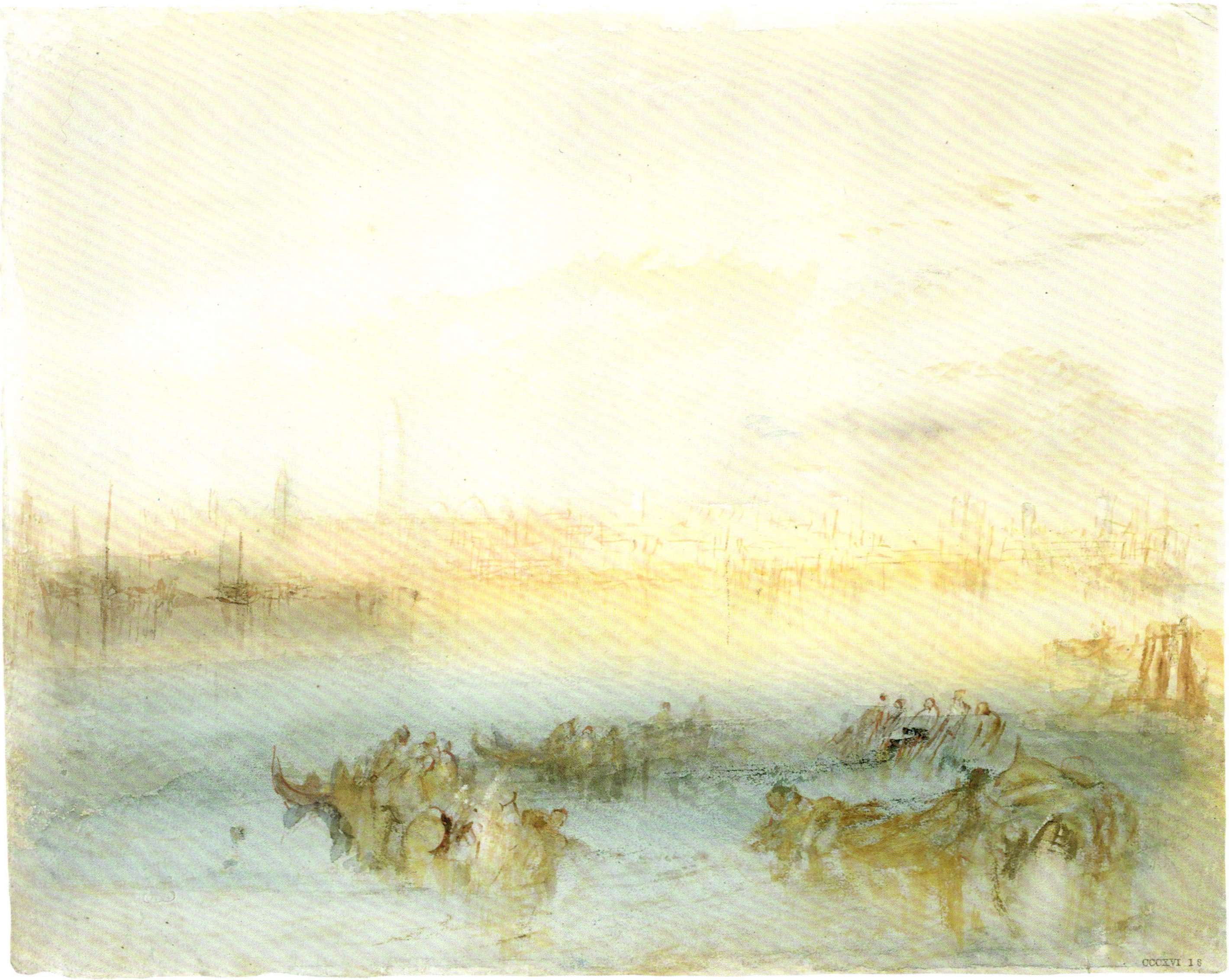

occurred to Ruskin in 1845 while he was waiting for the artist to complete his latest batch of Swiss subjects. In a letter to his father from Venice, Ruskin wrote, 'I wish he would make one a little water colour of Venice – his ideal of it is superb – it makes me quite pine for it *here*, that I may feel it more. Venice *itself* is now nothing, barring always fishing boats' (Shapiro 1972, p.207).

53 Riva dei Schiavoni, from San Giorgio Maggiore

Venice: The Riva degli Schiavoni from the East 1840
Watercolour, with pen 245 × 306 (9⅝ × 12$^{1}/_{16}$)
TB CCCXVI 18 D32155
EXH: NG (53); Tate Gallery 1934–7; Brussels 1970–1 (78, repr.); British Museum 1975–6 (237, repr. p.115); Tate Gallery 1992a (69, repr. pp.40, 69); Royal Academy, London 1993 (300, repr. pl.265)
LIT: *Works*, XIII, p.210, p.373 and p.611; *R on P*, p.109, as 'Riva degli Schiavoni from the Channel to the Lido'; Finberg 1930, p.174; Stainton 1985, p.59, pl.64

Very exquisite in colour and gradation, and the placing of the boats, and drawing the nets.

In his panoramic views of the city, Turner sets out the image by painting several horizontal bands of colour, building up form with both his brush and pen, yet generally resisting a literal representation of precise details. Because this technique is readily apparent here, this watercolour proved especially popular with copyists during the nineteenth century, many of whom had been exhorted to attempt the academic exercise by Ruskin. A copy by Isabella Lee Jay (fl.1868–96), one of his pupils, is in the collection at Bembridge (Bembridge 281; the collection also includes her copies of cat.nos.35, 66, 74); another copy of this work, by an unknown hand, is in the Courtauld Institute of Art (Spooner 71).

54 Riva dei Schiavoni, from the Traghetto per Chioggia

Venice: The Zitelle, S. Maria della Salute, the Campanile and S. Giorgio Maggiore from the Canale di S. Giorgio
1840
Pencil and watercolour, with pen 243 × 305 (9⁹⁄₁₆ × 12)
TB CCCXVI 19 D32156
EXH: NG (54); British Museum 1934–5; Amsterdam 1947–8 (62); Düsseldorf 1950 (21); Adelaide 1961 (25, repr. p.21); Royal Academy 1974–5 (548); Leningrad 1975–6 (72); Athens, Georgia 1982 (66); Tate Gallery 1983; Melbourne 1985; Tate Gallery 1988; Tate Gallery 1990; Bankside Gallery 1990 (6, repr, p.35); Tate Gallery 1993 (5, repr. p.35)
LIT: *Works*, XIII, pp.211, 373, 611; *R on P*, p.109 as 'The Salute, from S. Giorgio Maggiore'; Rawlinson, Finberg and Holroyd 1909, pl.XIX; Finberg 1930, p.174; Wilton 1982, p.61, pl.84; Stainton 1985, p.58, pl.62

It is low water, and the exposed beach is carefully expressed in the middle distance. Note that even in the apparently hasty passage on the left the painter has carefully marked the separate knots of the furled felucca sail. Any one else, in a hurry, would assuredly have drawn one continuous line for the sail, and then the dots or lines across it; it is much more difficult, and implies more deliberate purpose, to draw the sail itself in broken dots all the way down, implying that, where it is tied to the yard, the yard and sail together are so slender as to be lost sight of.

The economic representation of the felucca mast and its lateen sail, picked out by Ruskin, is exactly the sort of detail that Turner absorbed and transcribed in the pencil sketches he made while travelling (see TB CCCXIV ff.7 verso, 12, 13 verso, 14). A group of felucca and other boats, anchored in front of the Riva degli Schiavoni, is the focus of another of Turner's Venetian watercolours ('The Sun of Venice'; W 1374, National Gallery of Scotland, Edinburgh; Stainton 1985, pl.95). Turner's viewpoint in this subject is from the entrance to the canal which runs between the island of S. Giorgio Maggiore and the long arm of the Giudecca. The 'exposed beach', described by Ruskin, is presumably the point at which the main current of the Canale della Giudecca meets the smaller canal. In one of the watercolours that Ruskin gave to the Fitzwilliam Museum in Cambridge, Turner adopts the same viewpoint to depict storm clouds building over the lagoon, with a felucca chased by the wind (W 1353; Stainton 1985, pl.86).

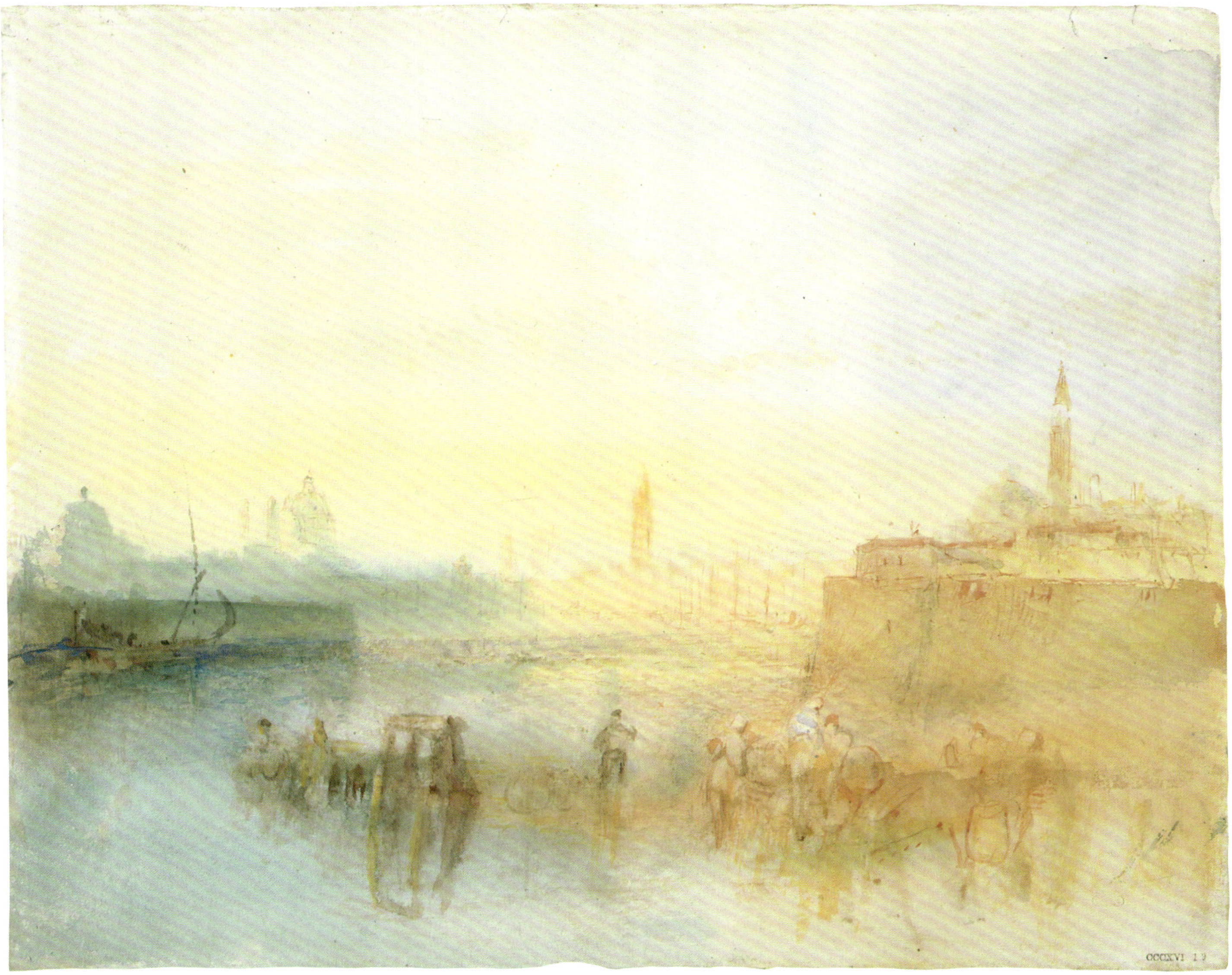

54

55 Riva dei Schiavoni. Looking towards the Madonna della Salute, which is seen in the extreme distance; the Church of San Giorgio between the two sails on the left

Venice: Shipping off the Riva degli Schiavoni, from near the Ponte dell'Arsenale 1840
Watercolour 243 × 306 ($9\frac{9}{16} \times 12\frac{1}{16}$)
TB CCCXVI 20 D32157
EXH: NG (55); British Museum 1934–5; British Museum 1937 (Frame 7); Tokyo 1963–4 (27, repr. in Japanese cat.only); Sheffield 1964–5; Royal Academy 1968–9 (561); British Museum 1975–6 (236); Tate Gallery 1977–8; Athens, Georgia 1982 (67); Tate Gallery 1987
LIT: *Works*, XIII, pp.211, 373, 611; *R on P*, p.109; Finberg 1910, repr. pl.LXXVIII, opp. p.129 as 'About 1839'; Finberg 1930, pp.125, 174; Stainton 1985, p.59, pl.67

The composition of these sails and groups of ships leading the eye into the distance is very beautiful.

Judging from the watercolours both inside and outside the Turner Bequest, the focus of Turner's trip to Venice in 1840 was the Bacino S. Marco. This is the anchorage in front of the principal buildings of the city, where the Canale della Giudecca meets the Grand Canal. Apart from the obvious interest of this part of Venice, which had inspired Canaletto and numerous other artists, there was a more personal reason for Turner's absorption. This lay chiefly in the fact that during this visit he stayed at the Hotel Europa, situated opposite the Dogana in the former Palazzo Giustiniani. Consequently, the sights surrounding the commercial pool were visible from his hotel, or were accessible by a short gondola ride. Ruskin brings together here a series of views along the rambling Riva degli Schiavoni, which suggest that Turner explored its length by foot, as well as from the water (cat.nos.55–8, 60). Among the sheets that Ruskin did not select, there is another watercolour that adopts a viewpoint very similar to that in this work (TB CCCXVI 13; Stainton 1985, pl.79). In both views, topography is subservient to the general vaporous effect, so that the form of the Campanile of S. Marco thrusts upwards, with the details of its balconies and peak left unresolved.

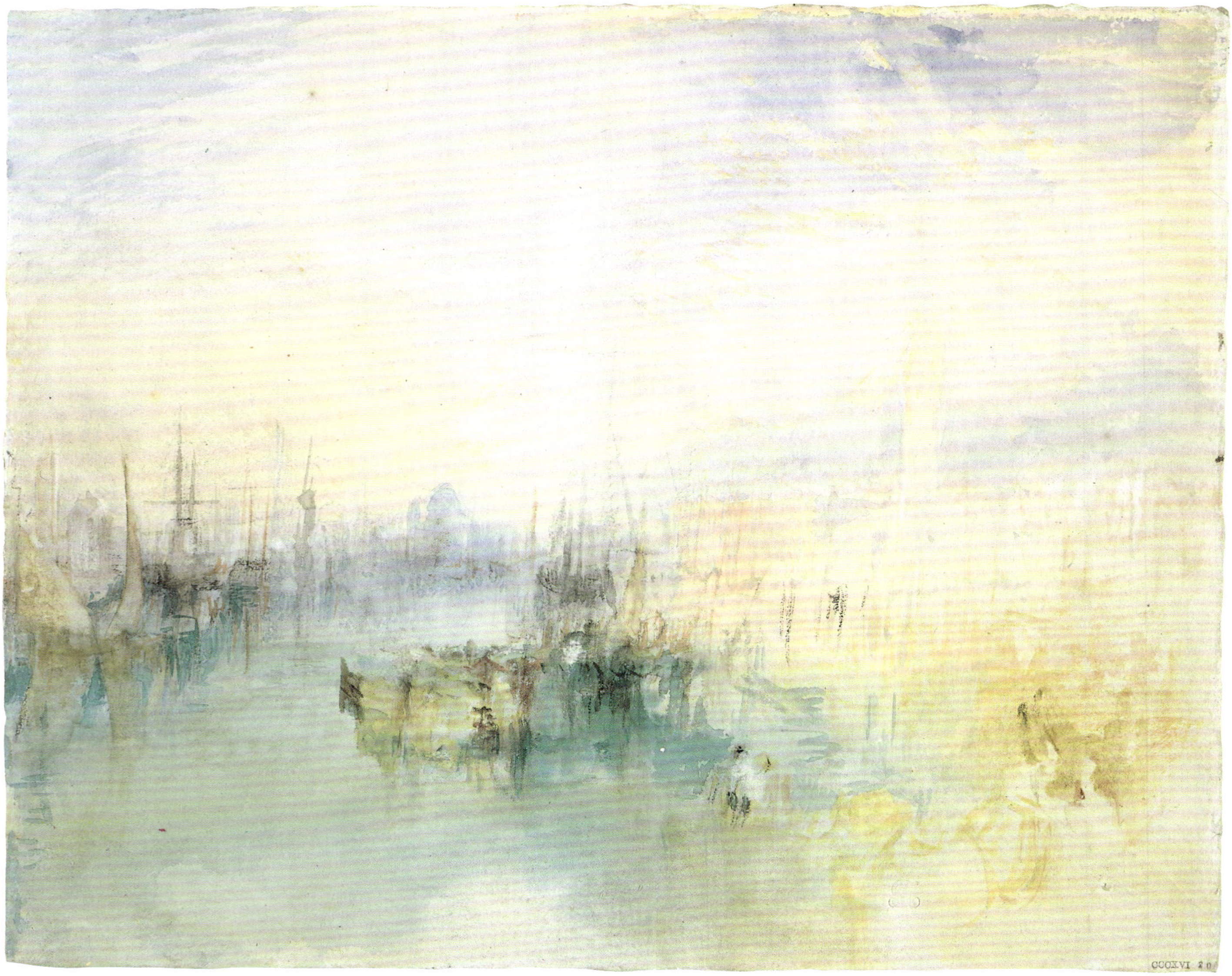

55

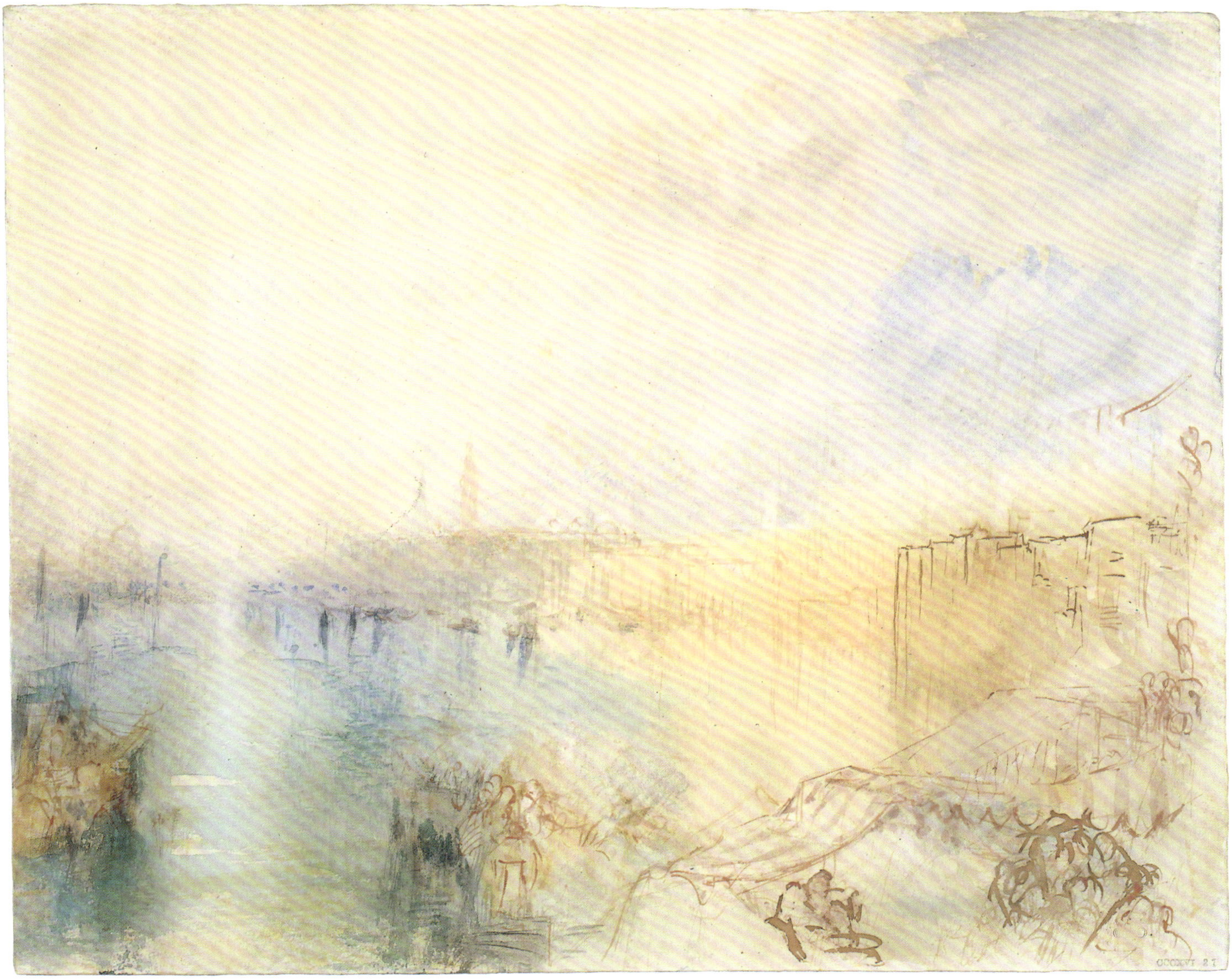

56 Riva dei Schiavoni. From the Fondamenta Ca'di Dio

Venice: The Riva degli Schiavoni, from near S. Biagio 1840
Watercolour, with pen 244 × 304 ($9\frac{5}{8}$ × 12)
Watermarked: C ANSELL | 1828
Verso inscribed in pencil: '[?Belike Club]'
TB CCCXVI 21 D32158
EXH: NG (56); Amsterdam 1947–8 (63); Düsseldorf 1950 (22); Adelaide 1961 (26, repr. p.21); Washington 1963–4 (62); Brussels 1970–1 (79); Folkestone 1971–2 (8); British Museum 1975–6 (238, repr. p.142)
LIT: *Works*, XIII, pp.211, 373, 611; *R on P*, pp.109–10 as 'Riva degli Schiavoni, from near the Public Gardens'; Finberg 1910, repr. pl.LXXX, opp. p.133; Finberg 1930, p.174; Stainton 1985, p.59, pl.65

This sketch is very beautiful, and to be noted especially for the way the two gleams of light on the water are left, portions of an under colour, which is prepared to receive the cool darker tint above, and to shine through it waveringly, while these fragments of it are left in luminous opposition.

It is to the painter's decisive use of these preparatory tints, and his perfect knowledge of the result which the superimposed tint is to produce, that his colouring owes a great part of its effect.

Another view along the Riva degli Schiavoni, looking towards S. Maria della Salute and the Campanile of S. Marco. The pen work in this study seems only partly finished; the transition between foreground and distance is too sudden, interrupting the recessions suggested in the washes. An example of the way Turner could provide greater detail by using a network of pen lines, while still preserving a unified design, is the watercolour known as 'The Riva degli Schiavoni' in the Ashmolean Museum, Oxford (W 1364; Stainton 1985, pl.69).

57 Riva dei Schiavoni. In the first twilight,* with the Bridge over the Rio dell'Arsenale

Venice: The Riva degli Schiavoni from near the Rio dell'Arsenale 1840
Pencil and watercolour 246 × 304 (9¾ × 12)
TB CCCXVI 22 D32159
EXH: NG (57); National Gallery 1938–9
LIT: *Works*, XIII, pp.212, 373, 611; *R on P*, p.110; Finberg 1930, p.174

The beak of a gondola shoots out from beneath the bridge. I have chosen this sketch chiefly for the sake of this incident; for a gondola is in nothing more striking to a stranger than in the unexpected dart of its beak – apparently by its own impulse, (the rower not being seen until the stern of the boat appears) – from under the arch of a bridge, seen as this is in strong light, while the boat's beak is always dark, if not black; and it is interesting to find Turner fixing on this as the leading incident of a composition.

**I call the 'first' twilight that which immediately precedes the sunset; the 'second' twilight, a peculiar flush, like a faint reflection of the sunset, which succeeds the first twilight, after some minutes.*

This view may have been taken from the bridge over the Rio dell'Arsenale, or from one that crosses the Rio della Tana. In seeking out the prospect from the eastern end of the Riva degli Schiavoni, Turner was able to give expression in a small group of watercolours to the relationship of the city to the surrounding influences of water and light. The spare colouring and the dazzling simplicity of this work recall the intensity of his first watercolours of Venice, painted on his way to Rome in 1819 (TB CLXXXI 4–7; Stainton 1985, pls.2–5). Ruskin is right to draw attention to the impact made on the composition by the prow of the gondola. In other Venetian subjects, Turner sometimes renders these boats in an incomplete manner,

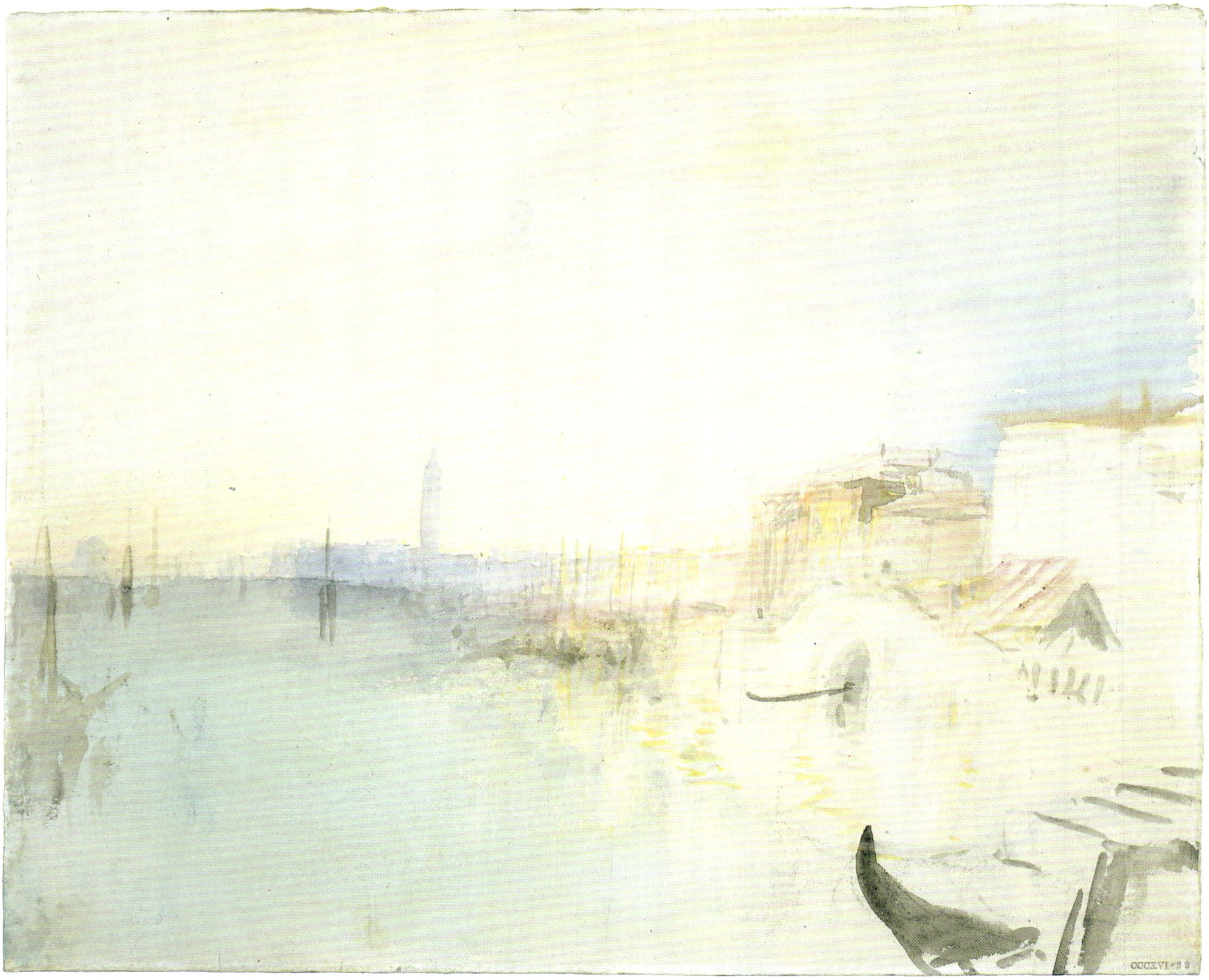

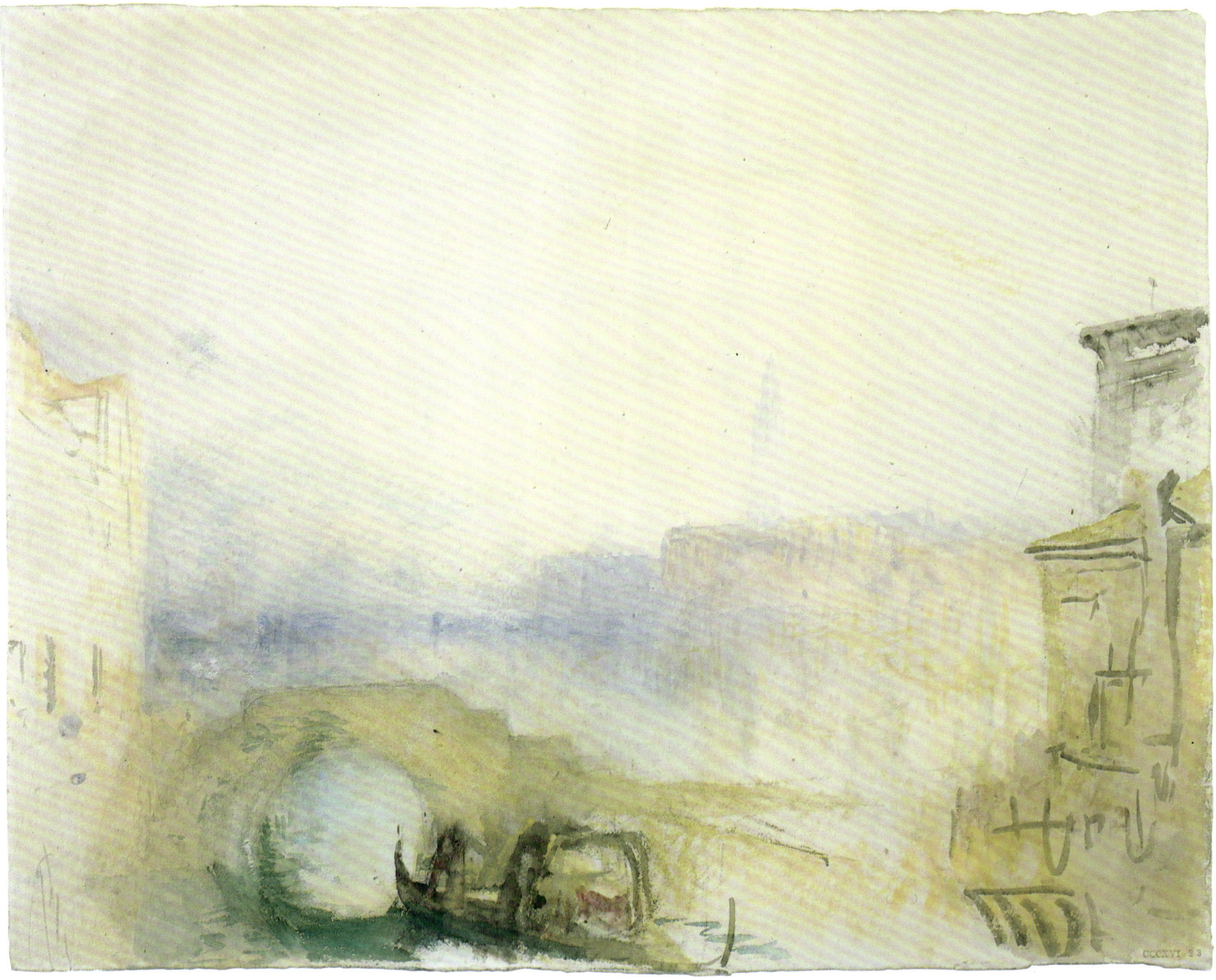

so that it is not always obvious what he has depicted. For example, the canopy of a gondola floats truncated in the foreground of one view, before disappearing under a bridge (TB CCCXVI 30; Stainton 1985, pl.71).

58 Bridge over the Rio dell'Arsenale

Venice: ?The Ponte Ca'di Dio 1840
Watercolour, with scratching-out 245 × 305 ($9\frac{5}{8}$ × 12)
TB CCCXVI 23 D32160
EXH: NG (58); Cape Town 1936–7 (Frame 18); Paris 1938 (246); Amsterdam 1947–8 (64); Düsseldorf 1950 (23); Adelaide 1961 (27, repr. p.22); Washington 1963–4 (63); Brussels 1970–1 (80); Folkestone 1971–2 (9); Munich 1972–3 (154); Cleveland 1977–8 (62, repr. p.81)
LIT: *Works*, XIII, pp.212, 373 (misnumbered '59'), 611; *R on P*, p.110, as 'Bridge on the Riva degli Schiavoni'; Finberg 1930, p.174; Stainton 1985, p.61, pl.72

A companion to the last sketch, only the gondolier is here entering instead of going out. The gondolier's head is rubbed out; the painter evidently sketched his figure as standing, and then remembered that he must have stooped to go under the bridge, and, at the short distance of the boat's stern from it, could not yet have risen. This is part of the expression of motion; the boat which has entered at speed is always at least ten feet within the bridge before the gondolier can completely rise.

In this view along the Riva degli Schiavoni, the drawn-out form of the Fondamenta has been made to turn a sharp angle of ninety degrees. This distortion allows the picturesque incident of a gondola passing under a bridge to be seen against the backdrop of such instantly recognisable features as the campanile of S. Marco and the principal dome of S. Maria della Salute. Turner took similar liberties in the first oil painting of Venice that he exhibited at the Royal Academy ('Bridge of Sighs, Ducal Palace and Custom-House, Venice: Canaletti Painting', 1833, Tate Gallery, B&J 349). It has been suggested that the bridge depicted is that over the Rio di San Martino, but as there is such a strong sense of design about this subject, it is unlikely that the topography can be identified precisely.

59 The Cemetery and Church of St. Michelle di Murano

Venice: S. Giorgio Maggiore at Sunset from the Hotel Europa 1840
Watercolour 244 × 306 (9⅝ × 12¹⁄₁₆)
TB CCCXVI 24 D32161
EXH: NG (59); National Gallery 1936–9; Manchester 1966 (41); Tokyo 1970–1 (100); Paris 1972 (103); Coventry 1974 (38, repr. p.39); Cleveland 1977–8 (61, repr. p.80)
LIT: *Works*, XIII, pp.212, 373 (misnumbered '60'), 611; *R on P*, p.110 as 'San Giorgio Maggiore'; Finberg 1930, p.174; Stainton 1985, p.62, pl.77

In a full flushed second twilight. Exquisitely beautiful for tender colour and atmosphere.

Ruskin initially believed this watercolour to be a view of Murano, which he also identified as the subject of an oil painting exhibited by Turner in 1842 ('Campo Santo, Venice', Toledo Museum of Art; B&J 397). Ruskin often expressed his opinion that this part of the lagoon was one of Turner's favourite subjects (see Shapiro 1972, p.205; Bradley 1955, p.112). In fact, this watercolour seems to show Palladio's church, S. Giorgio Maggiore, which could be seen across the Bacino from Turner's hotel; it is included in another of Turner's 1842 exhibits, 'The Dogano, San Giorgio, Citella, from the Steps of the

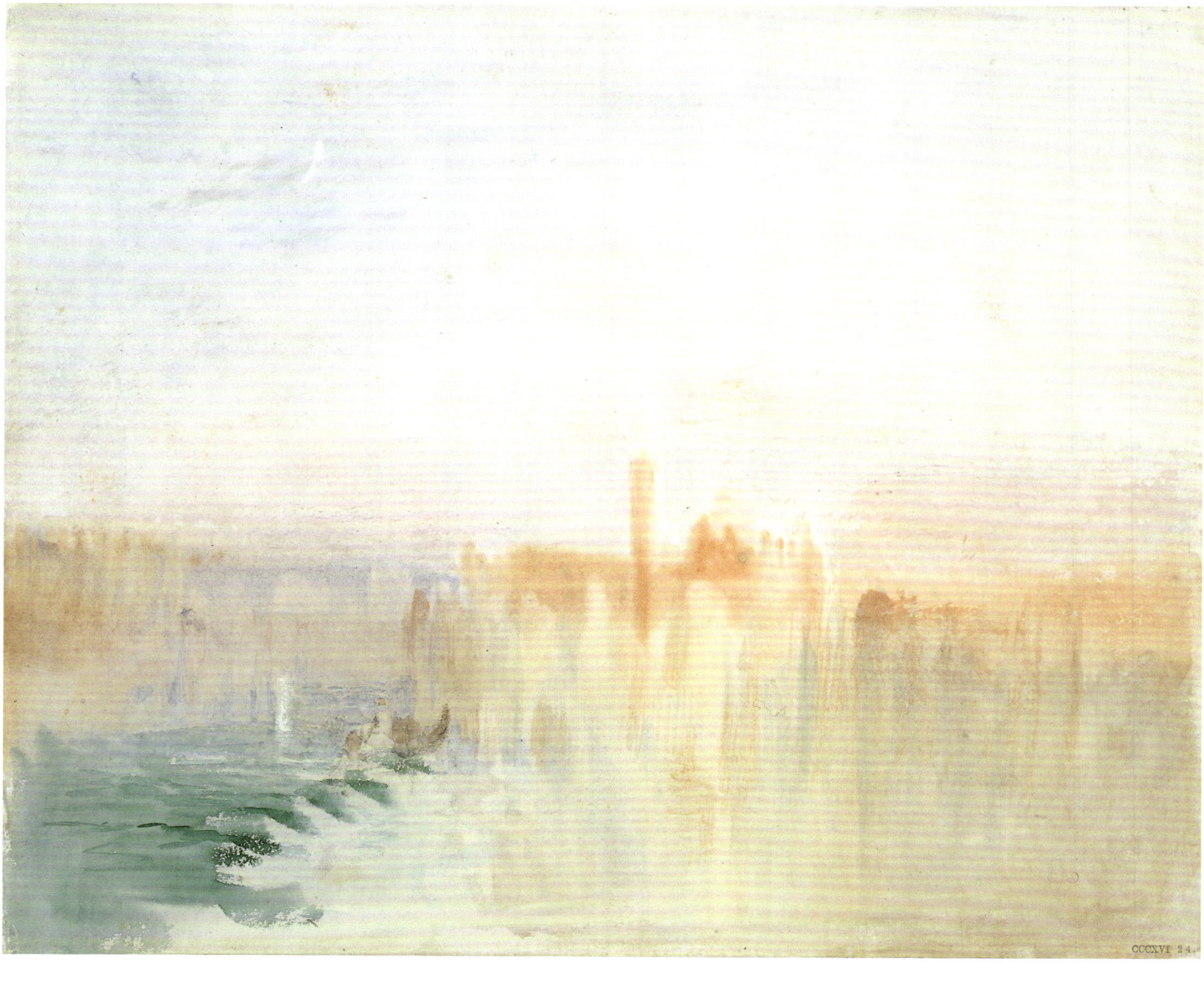

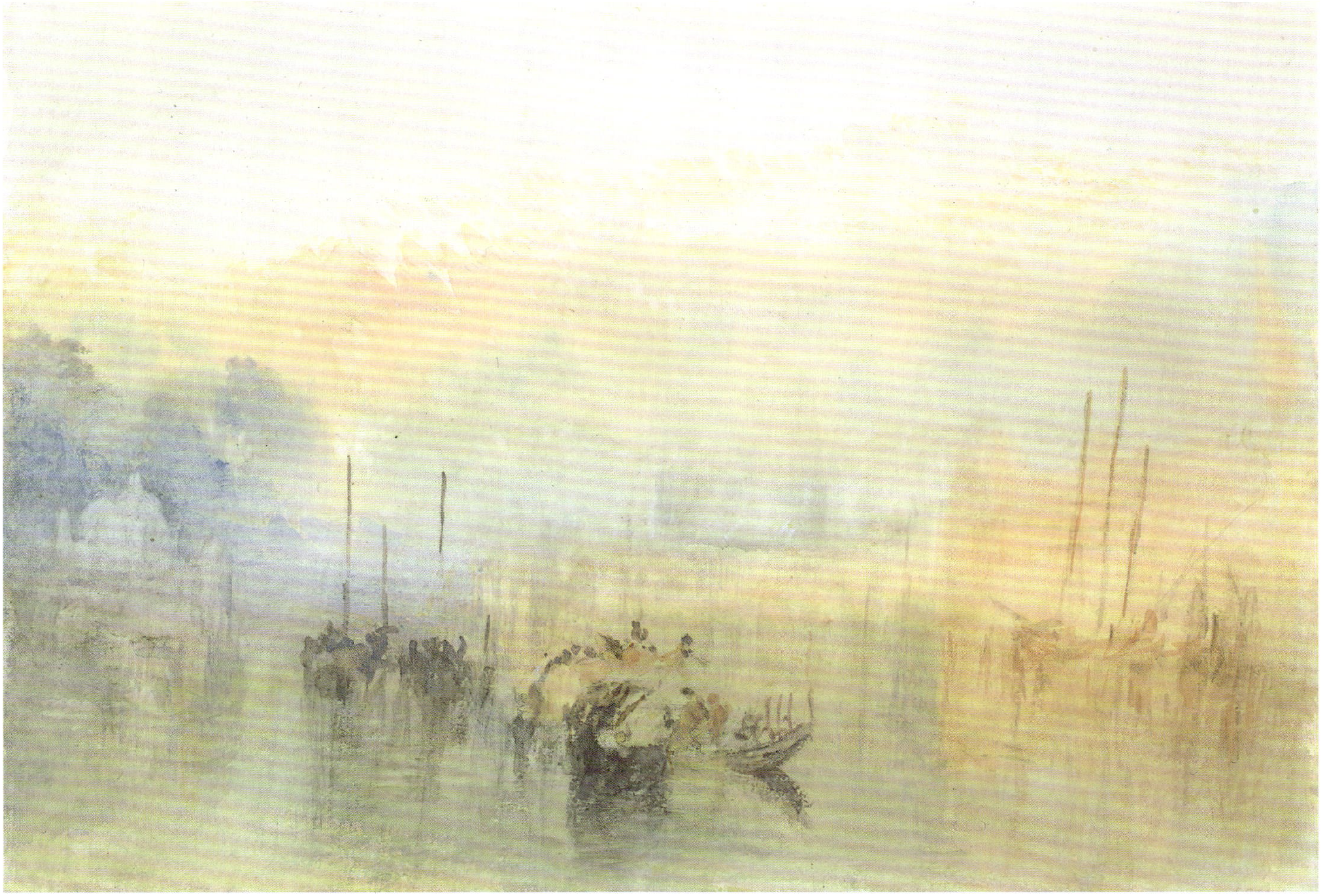

60

Europa' (B&J 396, Tate Gallery). During his 1840 visit, Turner was seen by William Callow at work in a gondola, sketching S. Giorgio lit up by the golden light of sunset (his account is quoted in Stainton 1985, p.22). It is not clear whether the sketches he was making were in pencil or in watercolour. In this study, however, it is most probable that Turner later recorded a strong impression, once he had returned to his hotel room.

60* The Head of the Grand Canal. Afternoon. Bad weather coming on

Venice: Entrance to the Grand Canal 1840
Watercolour 221 × 321 (8¾ × 12⅝)
Watermarked: J WHATMAN | 1834
TB CCCXV 4 D32120
EXH: NG (60); Paris 1937 (101); Tate Gallery 1937–52; Tate Gallery 1959–65; Dresden 1972 (95, repr. p.67, fig.15); Lisbon 1973 (42, repr. p.113); British Museum 1975–6 (230); Madrid 1983 (74, repr. p.87); Phoenix 1993 (29, repr. p.38)
LIT: *Works*, XIII, p.213 and p.611; *R on P*, p.111; Holme 1903, repr. W43; Finberg 1930, p.171

**These next sketches (60 to 69 inclusive) were on leaves of one drawing-book, apparently consecutive, and made in the course of two or three days. The other Venetian ones were on separate pieces of paper.*

Like cat.no.55, this is a view of the shipping anchored in the Bacino S. Marco. The domes on the left are those of S. Maria della Salute. Ruskin selected this and the following nine leaves from an intact roll sketchbook containing twenty-two subjects (TB CCCXV; endorsed in Ruskin's schedule as '13. Book of 22 coloured sketches of Venice'). By 1909 the book had long been broken up and the sheets mounted for display, so that A.J. Finberg was able to link only twenty-one watercolours with this book. The twenty-second subject could be TB CCCXVI 41. This is painted in the same diluted turquoise washes found in many of the Grand Canal subjects, whilst the architecture is similarly blocked-in over pencil outlines; the watercolour is also on the same size sheet as the roll sketchbook leaves.

61 The Steps of the Council of La Salute

Venice: The Grand Canal with S. Maria della Salute on the Left 1840
Pencil and watercolour, with pen 221 × 323 (8¾ × 12¾)
TB CCCXV 5 D32121
EXH: NG (61); National Gallery 1936–9
LIT: *Works*, XIII, pp.213, 373, 611; *R on P*, p.111; Finberg 1930, p.171; Stainton 1985, p.54, pl.45

The first idea of the engraved picture of 'The Grand Canal,' and interesting as a vigorous memorandum of the dark green reflection of the gondola.

The painting referred to by Ruskin is 'Venice, from the Porch of Madonna della Salute' (exh. 1835, B&J 362, Metropolitan Museum, New York). Ruskin's collection contained an impression of William Miller's 1838 engraving of the picture (*Works*, XIII, p.498). Since the painting was exhibited five years before Turner's 1840 visit, it is not probable that the watercolour is in any way preparatory to it. In fact, whilst the painting looks down the Grand Canal towards the Dogana, the watercolour depicts the opposite view, from the Salute looking up towards the point at which the Accademia bridge now crosses the canal. The Salute is the focus of three of Turner's more developed Venetian watercolours. The first is a general view of the church, seen as the sun sets over the Grand Canal, and is the view Turner must have had from the Hotel Europa (W 1368, private collection; Stainton 1985, pl.94). The Salute also appears in a view looking down towards the Dogana (W 1363, Ashmolean Museum, Oxford; Stainton 1985, pl.93). The third subject is a close-up study of part of the facade, with its pediments decorated by ornamental sculptures, looking in turn down the Rio della Salute (W 1370, National Gallery of Scotland, Edinburgh; Stainton 1985, pl.92).

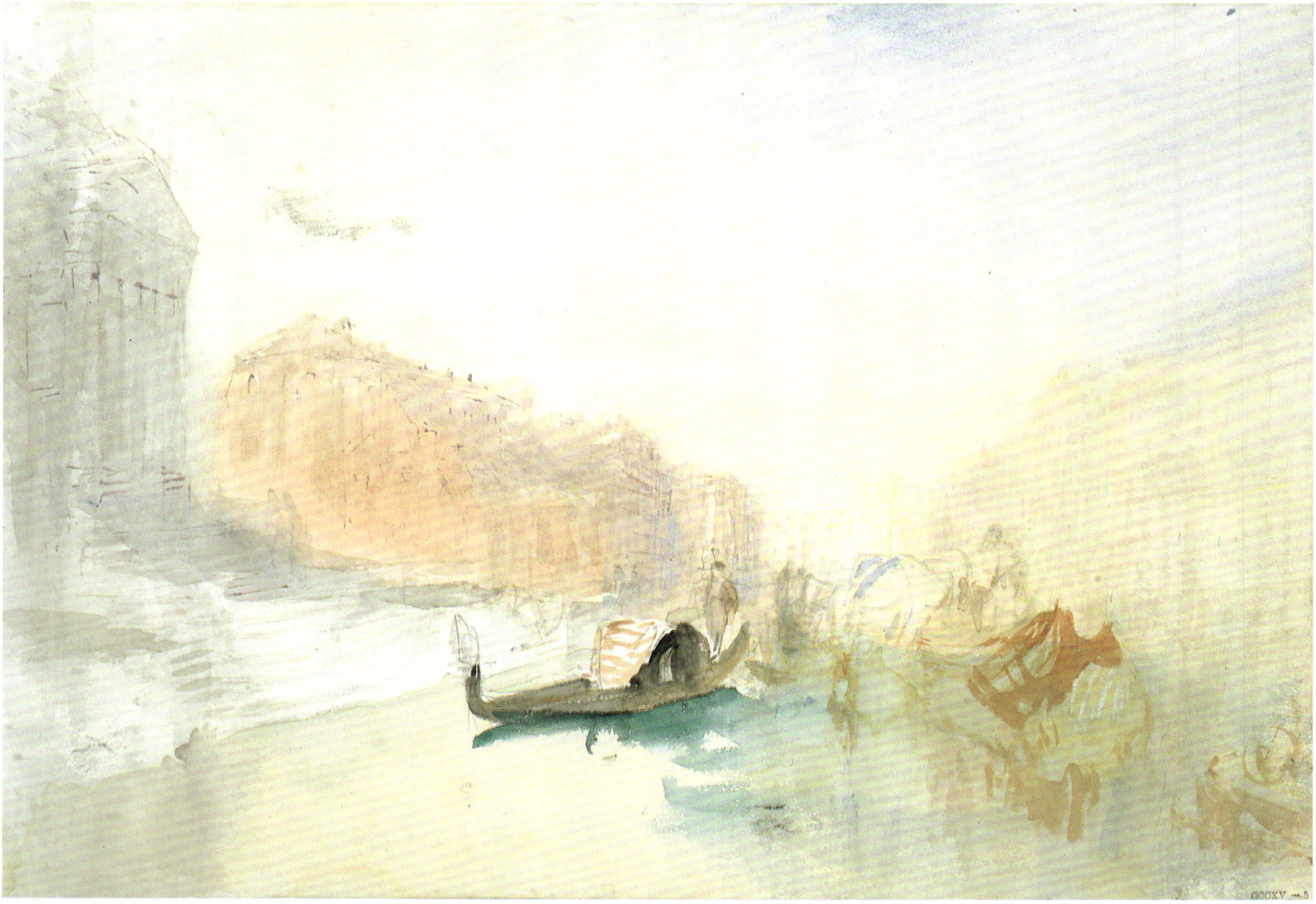

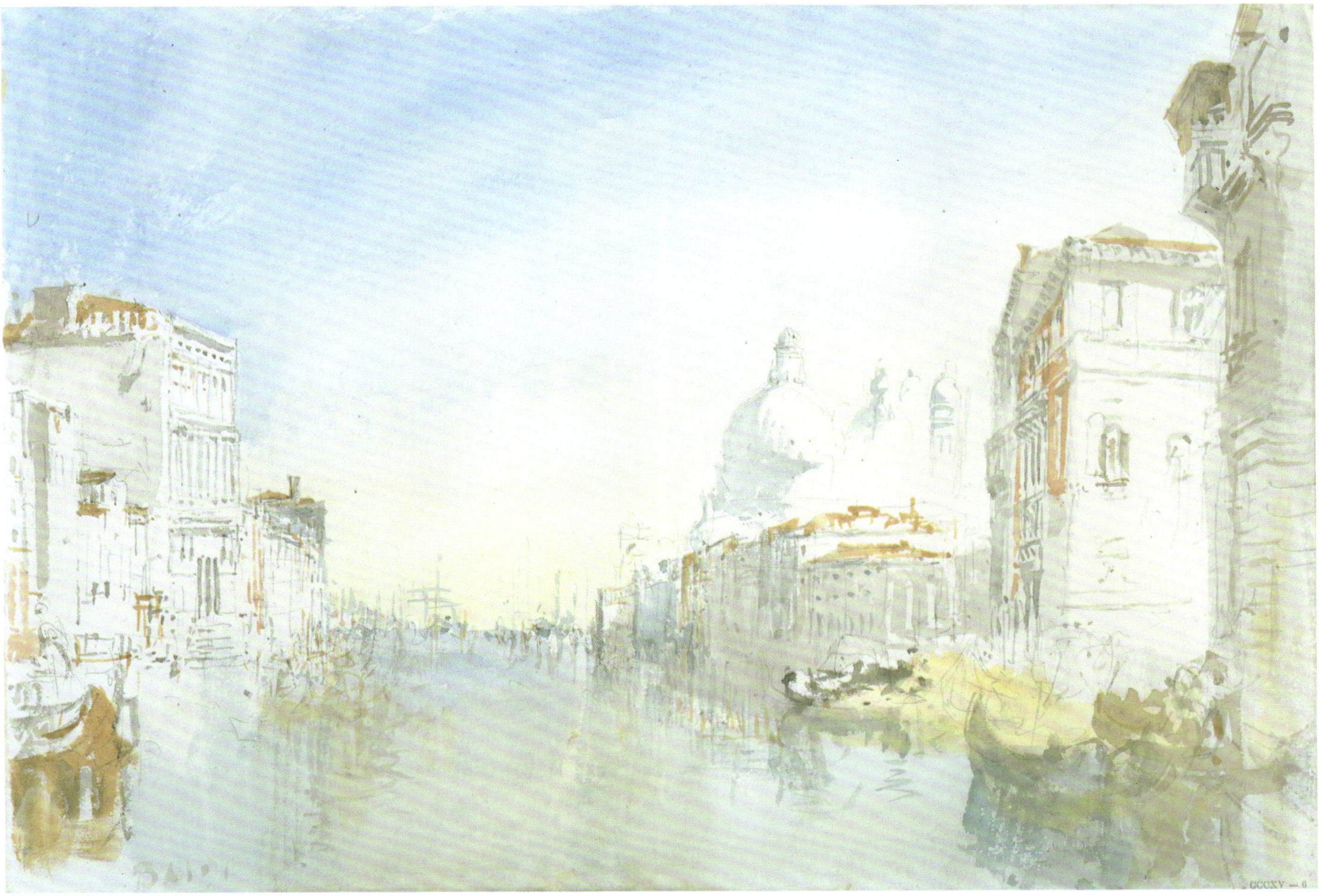

62 The Grand Canal, Looking back to the Salute

Venice: Looking down the Grand Canal to Palazzo Corner della Cà Grande and S. Maria della Salute 1840
Pencil and watercolour 221 × 325 (8¾ × 12¹³⁄₁₆)
Inscribed, bottom left: '[?BAIDI]'
TB CCCXV 6 D32122
EXH: NG (62); Hove 1934–5 (Frame 18); Hull 1948–9 (Frame 18); Cardiff 1951 (Frame 18); Royal Academy 1974–5 (549); Cleveland 1977–8 (58, repr. p.77); Madrid 1983 (75, repr. p.88); Tate Gallery 1983; Melbourne 1985; Tate Gallery 1990
LIT: *Works*, XIII, pp.213, 373, 611; *R on P*, p.111; Holme 1903, repr. W46; Finberg 1930, p.125, pl.xxii (top), and p.171; Wilton 1982, p.59, pl.80; Stainton 1985, p.55, pl.47

A study of local colour, showing the strong impression on the painter's mind of the opposition of the warm colour of the bricks and tawny tiles to the whiteness of the marble, as characteristic of Venice. He is not, however, right in this conception. When, in ancient days, the marble was white, the brick was covered with cement and frescoes; and the lapse of time, which has caused the frescoes to fall away, has changed the marble to a dark or tawny colour.

The colour of the tiles in this sketch is exactly true, when seen under afternoon sunlight. Painters are apt usually to represent them of too pure a red.

In their footnote to this entry, Cook and Wedderburn link Ruskin's specific comments about Turner's use of colour here with his more general observations on the Venetian paintings: 'I have noticed elsewhere that Turner's later Venices, when introducing much architecture, were often spoiled by his leaving the buildings too white. This was a morbid result of his feeling that he never could get them bright enough in their relation to the blue or green of the sea, and black of the gondolas' (*Works*, XIII, p.499). Turner made another study of this view in which he almost completely dispenses with colour (TB CCCXVI 1; Stainton 1985, pl.58). In both watercolours the domes and towers of the Salute are defined more by what has been omitted than by a slavish realisation of their actual appearance.

63 The Casa Grimani on the Grand Canal

Venice: The Palazzo Grimani and Rio S. Luca on the Grand Canal 1840
Pencil and watercolour 221 × 324 (8¾ × 12¾)
TB CCCXV 7 D32123
EXH: NG (63); Eastbourne 1937 (Frame 9); Sheffield 1946–7 (Frame 9); Whitechapel 1953 (212); Wakefield 1960 (Frame 9); British Museum 1975–6 (257, repr. p.148); Tate Gallery 1988 (43)
LIT: *Works*, XIII, pp.213, 373, 611; *R on P*, p.111; Finberg 1930, p.171; A. Wilton, *Turner Watercolours in the Clore Gallery*, 2nd ed., 1988, pp.138–9, pl.62

Very careless; but admitted into the series as being one of those used for the materials of the oil picture of 'Shylock,' and as showing a different method of study from most of the others.

As in cat.no.61, Ruskin mistakenly assumed that this watercolour was a preliminary design for an exhibited picture, in this case 'The Grand Canal' (1837, Huntington Library and Art Gallery, San Marino, California; B&J 368), one of the two oil paintings by Turner in his collection. In fact Turner probably used a sketch he made in 1819 for the painting (TB CLXXV 73). The focus of this watercolour is the Palazzo Grimani, on the left, which was designed by the architect Michele Sanmicheli in the mid-sixteenth century for the Procurator Girolamo Grimani. The palace remained in the Grimani family until 1806, when it was bought by the state and used as a post office; it is now the Court of Appeal. On the other side of the Rio S. Luca is the Palazzo Corner Contarini dei Cavalli. Other watercolours in the Bequest adopt viewpoints above and below the Palazzo Grimani, looking back at its elegant façade (TB CCCXVI 32 and TB CCCXVII 27; Stainton 1985, pl.36). In contrast with the majority of the watercolours in the Venetian roll sketchbook, this sheet is expressly concerned with architecture. For this catalogue, Ruskin selected no other depictions of the central part of the Grand Canal. However, the sketchbook contains many other views of the long canyon of palaces flanking the canal (TB CCCXV 1, 15, 16, 18, 19, 20, 21), as well as two watercolours of the Rialto Bridge (TB CCCXV 2, 3).

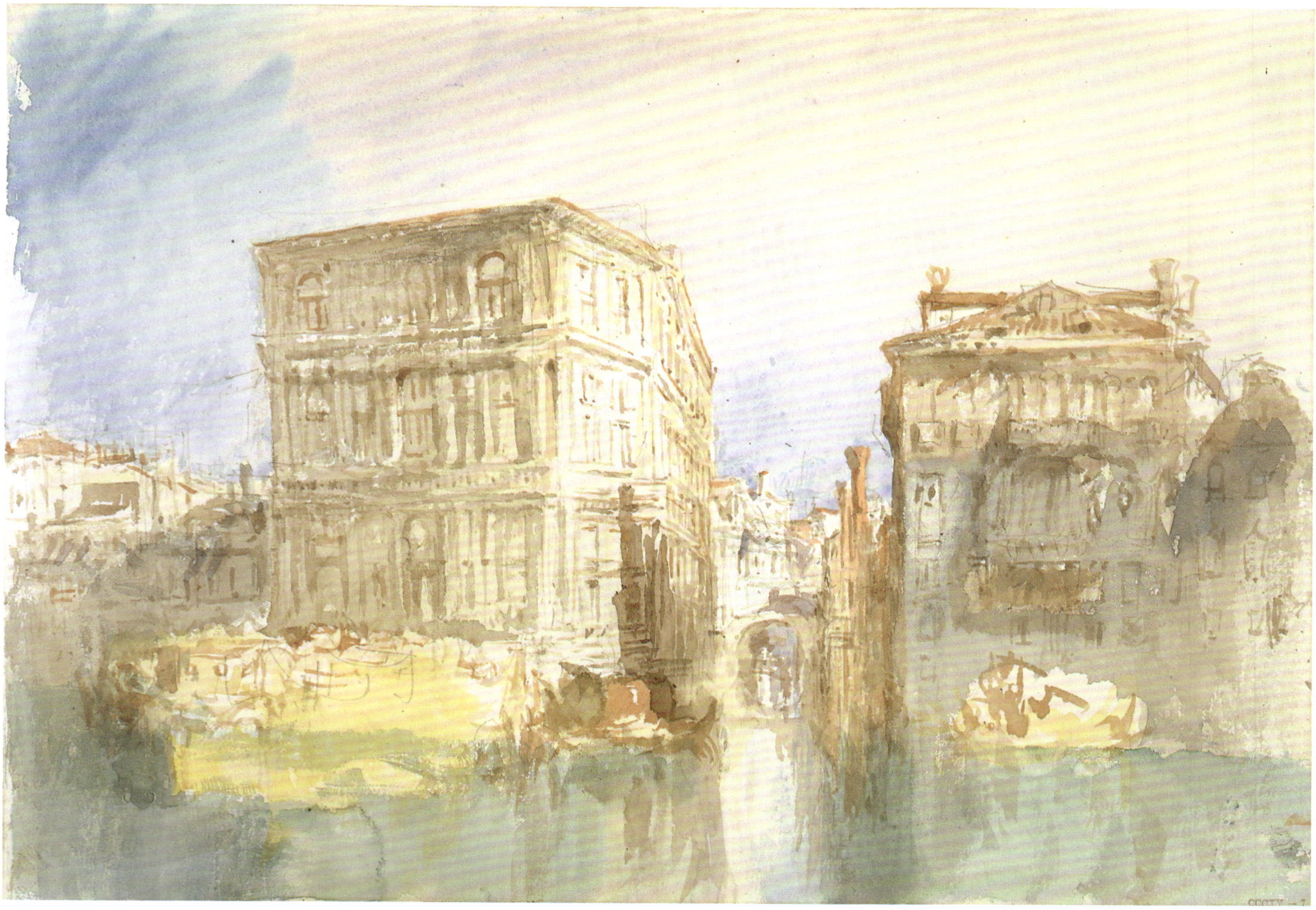

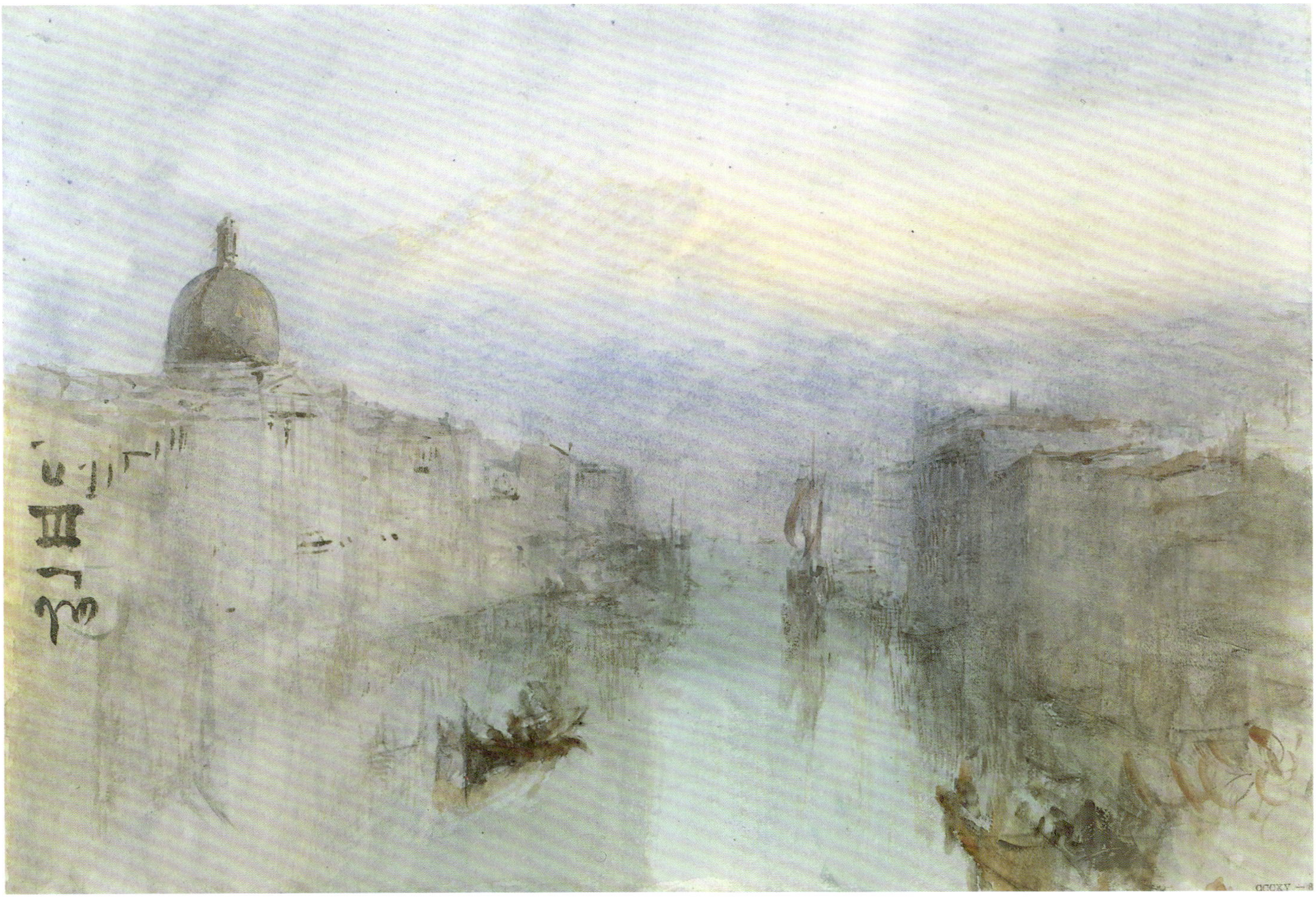

64 The Lower Extremity of the Grand Canal at Twilight, with the Dome of the Church of San Simeon Piccalo

Venice: the Grand Canal, with S. Simeone Piccolo; Dusk
1840
Watercolour and gouache, with pen and ink
219 × 320 (8⅝ × 12⅝)
TB CCCXV 8 D32124
EXH: NG (64); Paris 1937 (102); Tate Gallery 1937–52; Sheffield 1964–5; Folkestone 1966; Dresden 1972 (96); Lisbon 1973 (43, repr. p.115); British Museum 1975–6 (250, repr. p.146)
LIT: *Works*, XIII, pp.214, 373, 611; *R on P*, p.111; C. Lewis Hind, *Turner*, 1925, pl.v; Finberg 1930, p.171; Wilton 1979, p.232, fig.241; Stainton 1985, p.54, pl.46.

A noble sketch; injured by some change which has taken place in the coarse dark touches on the extreme left.

Visitors to Venice by train will be familiar with the church of S. Simone e Giuda, generally known as S. Simeone Piccolo, which lies directly across from the railway station at the northern end of the Grand Canal. The church was built between 1718 and 1738 by Giovanni Scalfarotto, whose design is derived from the Pantheon in Rome. His reverent classicism did not impress Ruskin, however, who considered it 'One of the ugliest churches in Venice or elsewhere. Its black dome, like an unusual species of gas-ometer, is the admiration of modern Italian architects' (*Works*, XI, p.433). Turner had made pencil sketches of this area during a previous trip to Venice; S.Simeone Piccolo appears on the right-hand side of a group of views in the *Venice* sketchbook (TB CCCXIV ff.79 verso, 81 verso, 85 verso). Where Turner applied his pen and ink to suggest a balcony at the left-hand side of the image, the ink (probably iron gall ink) has seeped deep into the paper, possibly arresting any further penwork Turner may have intended.

65 Venetian Fishing Boat

Venice: A Fishing Boat 1840
Watercolour 222 × 321 (8¾ × 12⅝)
TB CCCXV 9 D32125
EXH: NG (65); Paris 1937 (103); Tate Gallery 1937–52; Royal Academy 1974–5 (556); Cleveland 1977–8 (59, repr. p.78); Tate Gallery 1983; Melbourne 1985; Tate Gallery 1993 (3, repr. pp.25, 34)
LIT: *Works*, XIII, pp.214, p.373, 611, as 'Venice: Suburb towards Murano'; *R on P*, p.112; C. Lewis Hind 1925, pl.XLVIII; Finberg 1930, p.171; C. Clare, *J.M.W. Turner: His Life and Art*, 1951, repr. p.94, as a work of 1839; Wilton 1982, pl.81; Stainton 1985, pp.53–4, pl.43

I am not certain of the locality of this sketch; but it is a very interesting one in the distinctness and simplicity of its forms. The reason of the great prominence given to the sail of the boat is, that its curved and sharp characters may give the utmost possible amount of opposition to the absolutely rectangular outline of the building. The sky is very beautiful.

The topography depicted in this sketch has resisted the best attempts of scholars to identify Turner's location. Andrew Wilton suggested that the principal campanile is that of S. Giuseppe di Castello, at the eastern side of the island. This idea was challenged by Lindsay Stainton, who believed the campanile at the centre to be that of S. Giorgio dei Greci, with the dome and campanile of S. Pietro to its right, and the campanile of S. Giuseppe di Castello at the far right. Another watercolour which seems to depict the buildings in this view is cat.no.66.

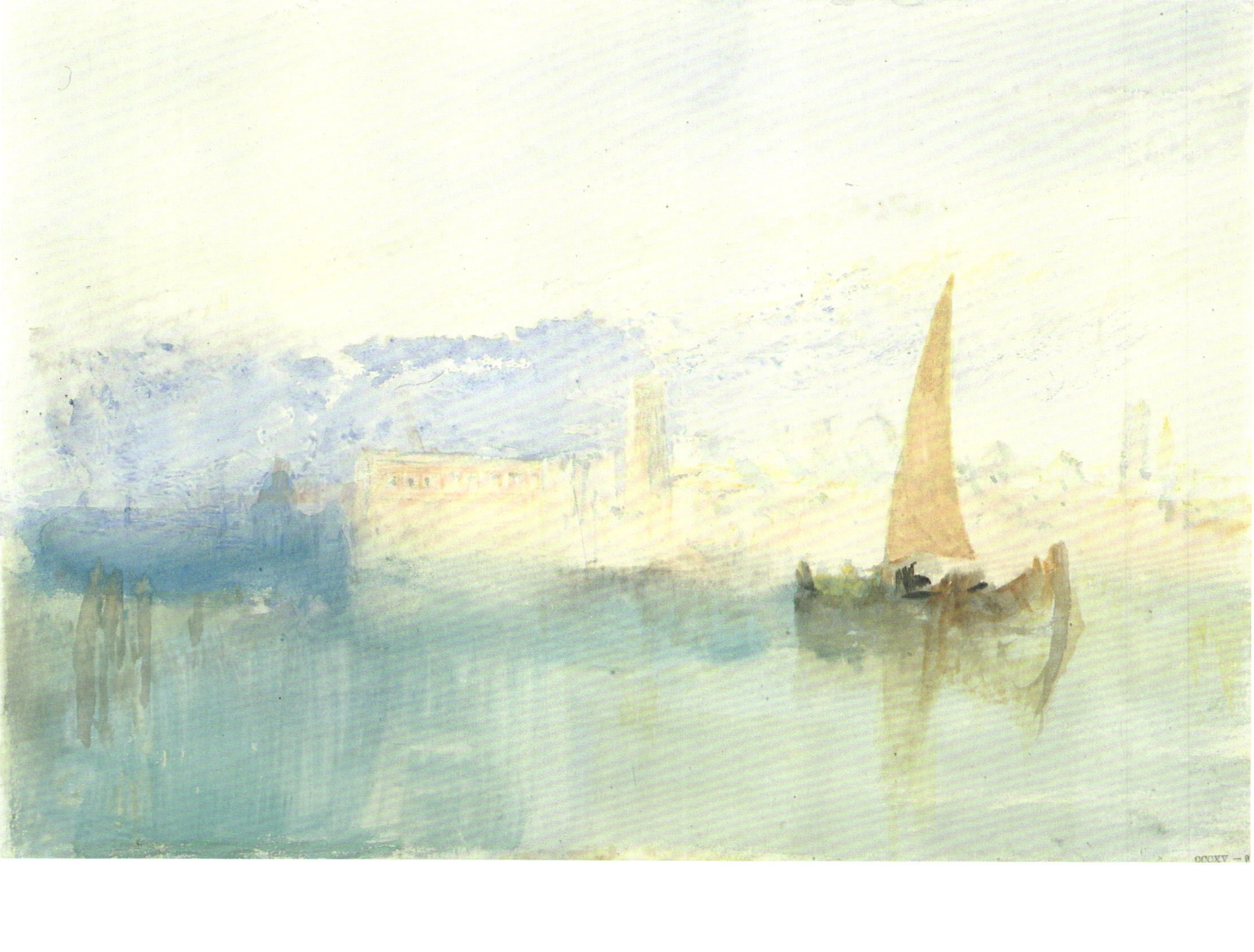

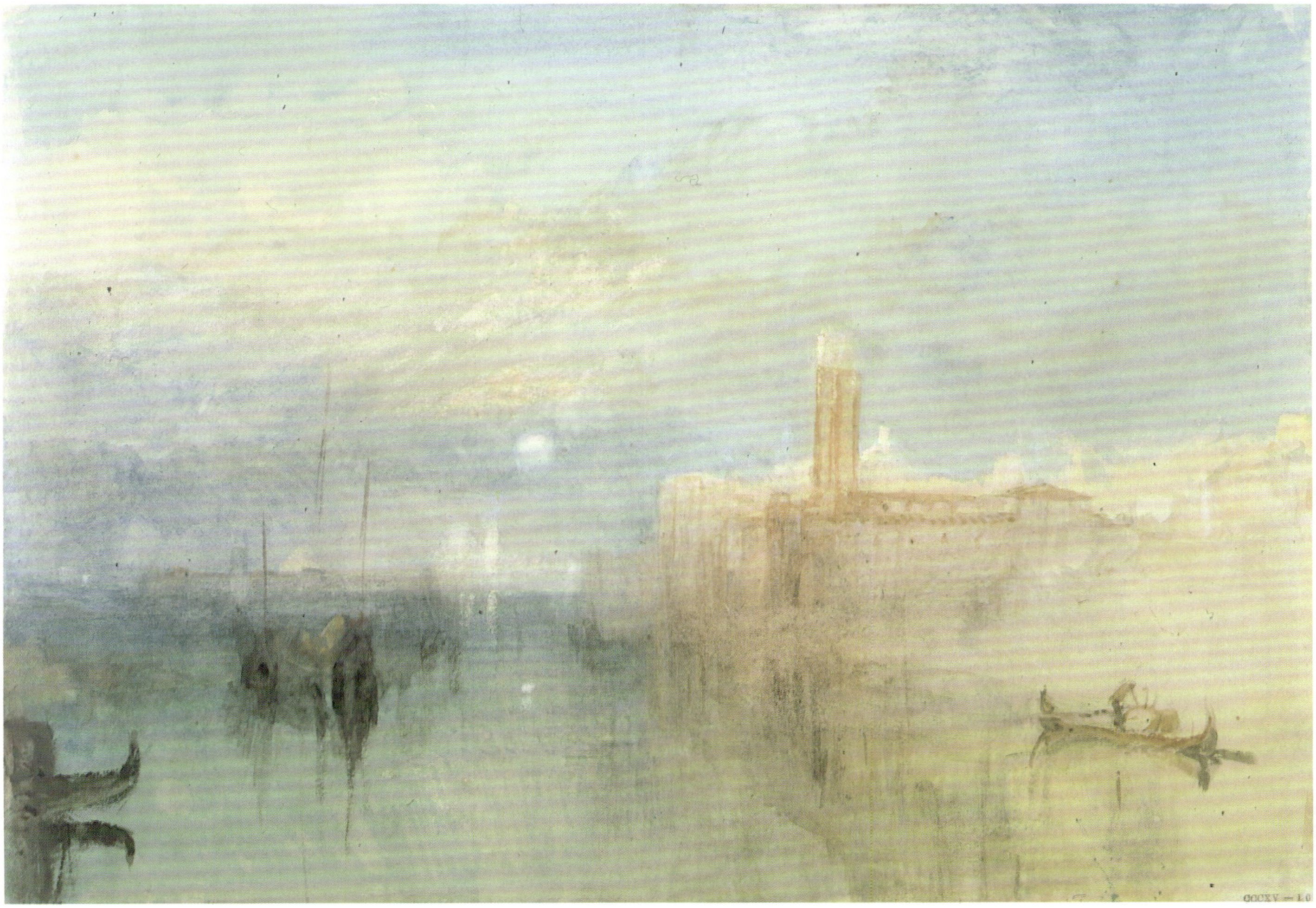

66 Moonrise

Venice: Moonrise 1840
Watercolour 220 × 319 ($8\frac{11}{16} \times 12\frac{9}{16}$)
TB CCCXV 10 D32126
EXH: NG (66); Cape Town 1936–7 (Frame 17); Tate Gallery 1937–52; Tokyo 1963–4 (26, repr. in Japanese cat. only); Sheffield 1964–5; Folkestone 1966; Folkestone 1971–2 (5, repr.); British Museum 1975–6 (231, repr. p.140); Tate Gallery 1992a (70 as '*c.*1840', repr. pp.40, 83); Phoenix 1993 (31, repr. p.38)
LIT: *Works*, XIII, pp.214, 373, 611, as 'Venice: Suburb'; *R on P*, p.112, repr.; Finberg 1930, p.171; Stainton 1985, p.55, pl.48; Wilton 1987, p.175, pl.238

A highly-finished study, but the locality is here also uncertain. There are so many campaniles in Venice of the class to which this tower belongs, that it is almost impossible to identify one of them under Turner's conditions of mystery, especially as he alters the proportions indefinitely, and makes the towers tall or short just as it happens to suit the sky.

It has been suggested that the campanile depicted here is that of S. Zaccaria seen from the Riva degli Schiavoni, and that the moon is setting in the early morning rather than rising (Stainton 1985, p.55). Even allowing for the kinds of distortion noted by Ruskin, none of the other architectural features really supports this identification.

67 General View of the Giudecca

Venice: The Giudecca, Looking towards S. Maria della Salute 1840
Watercolour and gouache, with pen 222 × 321 ($8^{3}/_{4}$ × $12^{5}/_{8}$)
TB CCCXV 11 D32127
EXH: NG (67); Paris 1937 (104); Sheffield 1964–5; Folkestone 1966; Brussels 1970–1 (75); British Museum 1975–6 (234)
LIT: *Works*, XIII, pp.214, 373, 611; *R on P*, p.112; Finberg 1930, p.171; Stainton 1985, p.55, pl.49

With the churches of the Redentore and St Giorgio. Very beautiful.

The great dome of S. Maria della Salute glows above the surrounding houses. At the centre of the composition are the campanile and dome of S. Giorgio Maggiore; the other details of the church are swathed in a haze of shimmering sunlight. As the viewer's eye travels down the expanse of the Giudecca on the right it is met by two domes: the first is that of the Redentore, while the more distant one belongs to the Zitelle.

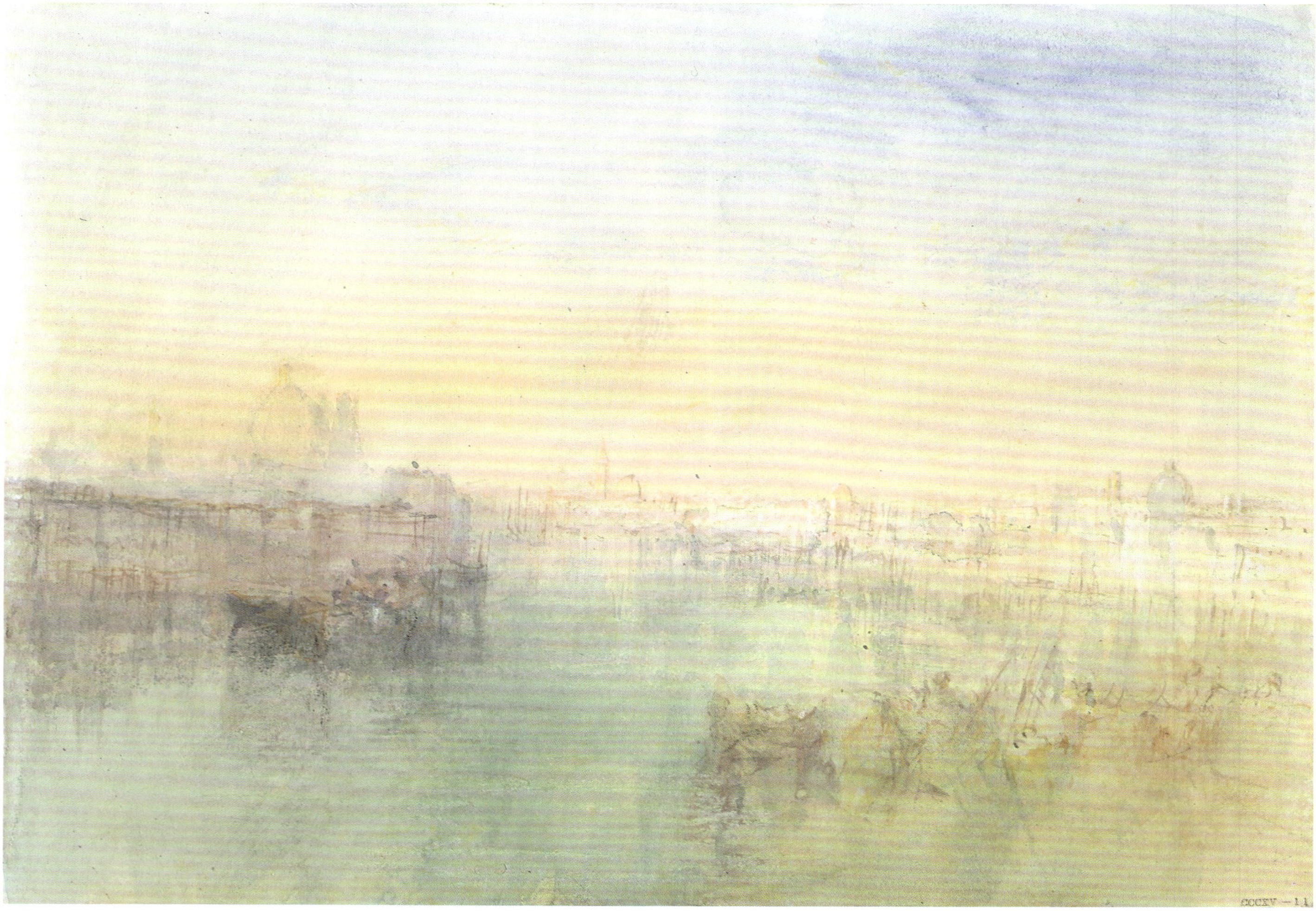

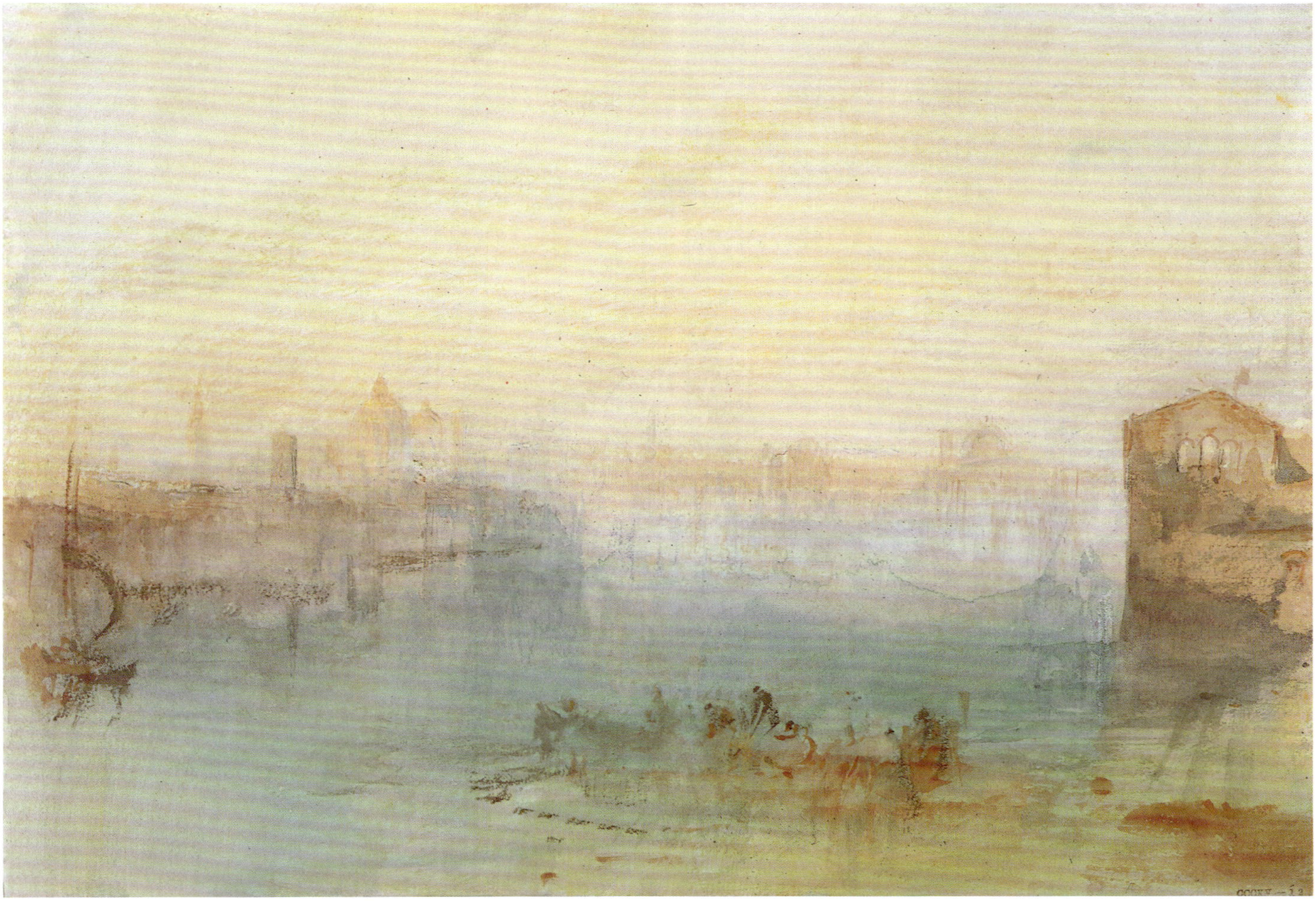

68 Looking down the Giudecca

Venice: The Giudecca from the Lagoon 1840
Watercolour, with pen 221 × 322 ($8\frac{3}{4} \times 12\frac{11}{16}$)
TB CCCXV 12 D32128
EXH: NG (68); Amsterdam 1936 (239); San Marino 1951–2 (Frame 17); Washington 1963–4 (59); Tokyo 1970–1 (99); British Museum 1975–6 (232); Madrid 1983 (77, repr. p.89); Tokyo 1986 (97, repr. p.241); Tate Gallery 1993 (7, repr. p.36)
LIT: *Works*, XIII, pp.214–5, 373, 611; *R on P*, p.122; Finberg 1930, p.171; Finberg 1961, p.381; Butlin 1962, pp.66–7, pl.24; Stainton 1985, p.55, pl.50

That is to say, looking from the lagoon into this great thoroughfare of Venice, the way its current runs. As we are here at the outskirts of the city, and looking towards its centre, we should perhaps say in any other town we were looking 'up' the street of it; but the direction of the current must, I suppose, regulate our mode of parlance in Venice.

The absolute tranquility that Turner managed to instil in so many of his late works, whether of Venice or of the Swiss lakes, was derived from his need to reflect the essence of the places he loved so deeply. In this view, the city is possessed completely by coloured mists, which float up off the lagoon to dissolve the buildings in an atmospheric blur. All seems sultry and still, but the billowing sail at the left suggests a gentle breeze. The composition is balanced simply by the turquoise and dark amber colours that Turner has selected, which he runs together in places to produce deep mauve shadows and reflections.

69 Looking up the Giudecca. Sunset

Venice: The Giudecca, Looking towards Fusina 1840
Pencil, watercolour and coloured crayon
221 × 323 (8¾ × 12¾)
TB CCCXV 13 D32129
EXH: NG (69); British Museum 1933b; Tate Gallery 1953–9; Folkestone 1966; Folkestone 1971–2 (6); British Museum 1975–6 (239); Tate Gallery 1993 (14, repr. p.39)
LIT: Works, XIII, p.215, p.373 and p.611; *R on P*, p.112; Finberg 1930, p.171; Wilton 1982, p.60, pl.82; Stainton 1985, pp.55–6, pl.51

The original sketch of the oil picture of 'San Benedetto, looking towards Fusina' [fig.36].

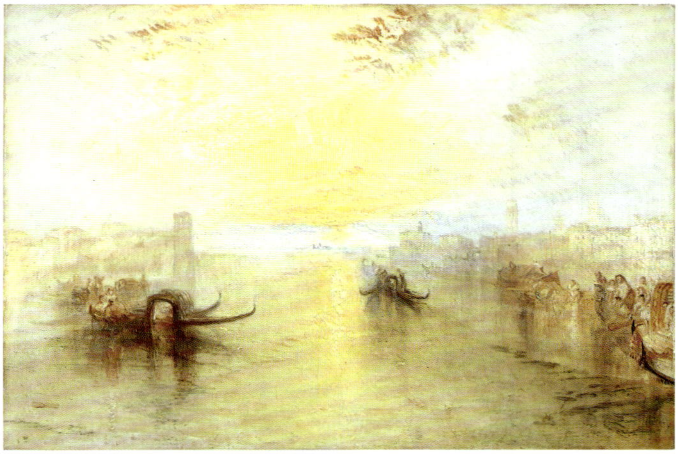

fig.36 'St Benedetto Looking towards Fusina' 1843, oil on canvas (B&J 406). *Tate Gallery. Bequeathed by the artist 1856* (N00534)

Ruskin connects this watercolour with one of the oil paintings Turner exhibited in 1843. Yet it is unlikely that Turner was entirely dependent on this study for a view he knew so well. Moreover, the view in the painting is more distant and includes a wider range of buildings on either side. Both works are most closely linked by the rich glow of the sunset above Fusina at the edge of the lagoon. Ruskin long considered 'St Bendetto, looking towards

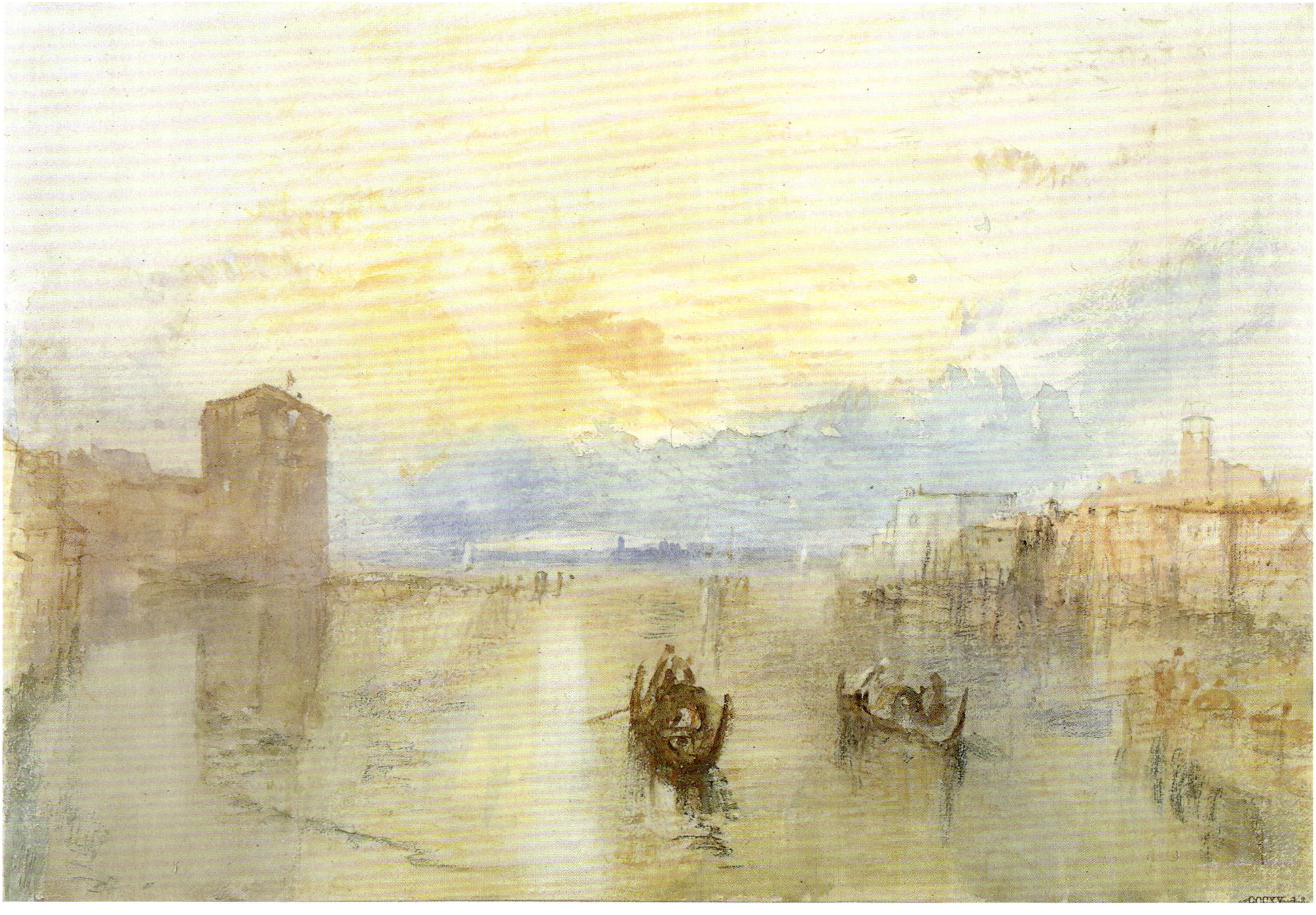

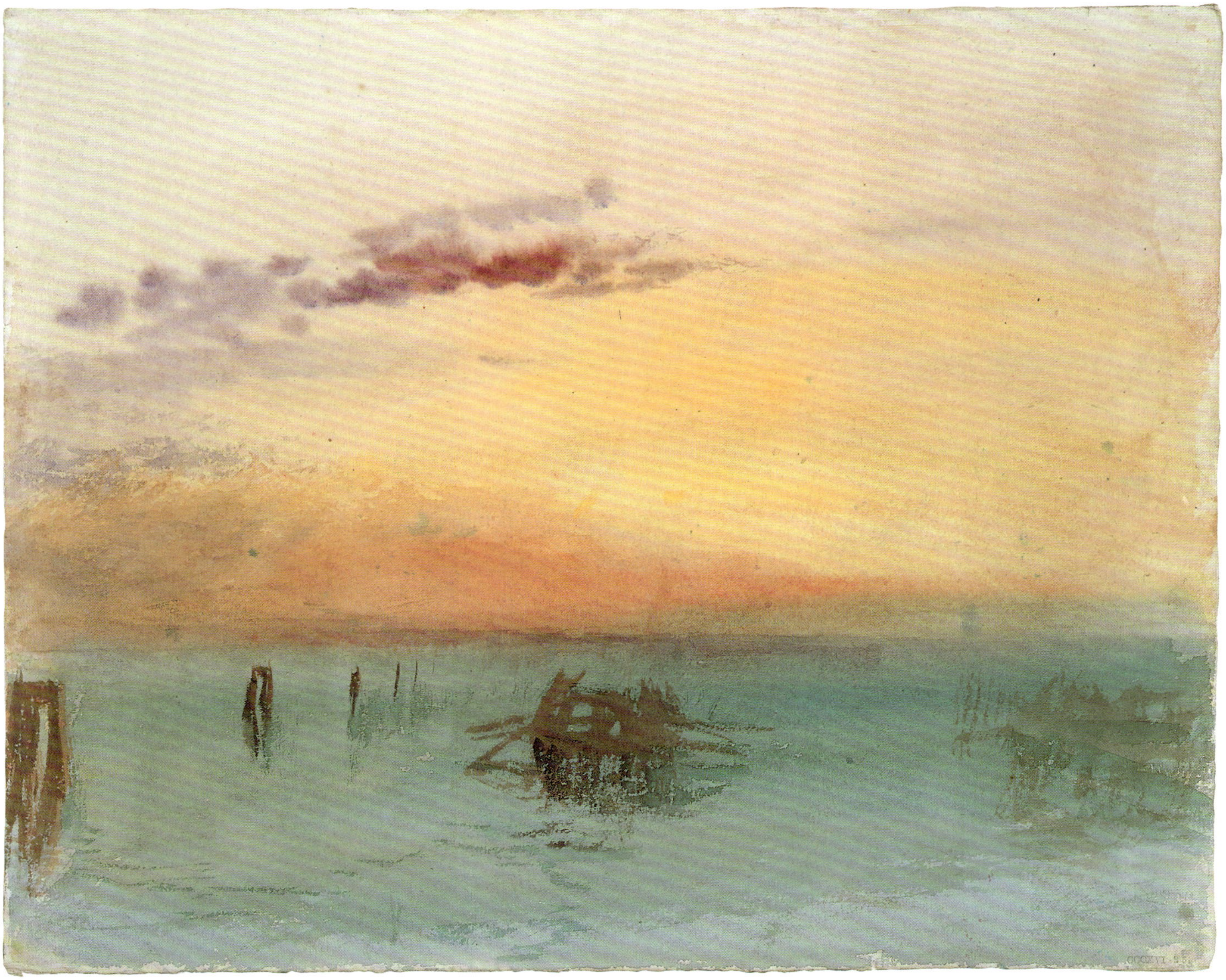

70

Fusina' Turner's 'best Venetian picture' (*Works*, XIII, p.166). His comments on it could just as easily be applied to this subject: 'The buildings have, in reality, that proportion and character of mass, as one glides up the centre of the tide stream: they float exactly in that strange, mirage-ful, wistful way in the sea mist - rosy ghosts of houses without foundations' (*Works*, XIII, p.165). Despite the title of Turner's oil painting, there is no church dedicated to S. Benedetto on the Giudecca; the only church in Venice by that name is situated behind the Palazzo Grimani, close to the Grand Canal. The building on the left, however, is possibly part of the church and convent of S. Biagio, which was destroyed in the nineteenth century and is now the site of the Mulino Stucky.

70 Venice

Venice: Looking across the Lagoon 1840
Watercolour 244 × 304 (9⅝ × 12)
Watermarked: C ANSELL | 1828
Verso: Inscribed with three lines of partly intelligible poetry about the sunset
TB CCCXVI 25 D32162
EXH: NG (70); Tate Gallery 1959–65; New York 1966 (73, as 'Sunset, Returning from Torcello', repr. p.17); Tate Gallery 1977–8; Athens, Georgia 1982 (68); Tate Gallery 1988; Tate Gallery 1990
LIT: *Works*, XIII, pp.215, 373, 611, as 'Venice, from Fusina'; *R on P*, pp.112–13; Finberg 1930, p.174; Butlin 1962, pp.56–7, pl.19; Stainton 1985, p.63, pl.83

Just after sunset. The position of the city is indicated by the touches of white in the vermilion cloud.

I cannot make out the long purple object like a wall in the middle distance. But I imagine, from the position of the sun, that the subject is a reminiscence of a return from Torcello towards Venice.

The clouds are remarkable as an example of Turner's frequent practice of laying rich colour on a wet ground, and leaving it to gradate itself as it dried, a few subsequent touches being, in the present instance, added on the right hand. Although the boat in the centre seems a mere scrawl, the action of the gondolier (at the left-hand side) is perfectly given in his forward thrust.

Although this watercolour was for many years listed as a view from Fusina, Lindsay Stainton has pointed out that if this were the case the effect captured would have to be a sunrise. This interpretation is contradicted by Turner's inscription on the verso, which seems to be a description of a sunset. The strong sunset colours used in this watercolour resolve themselves into several distinct fields, almost as if seen through a prism. In another work in the Bequest, Turner suggested the distant form of the city on the horizon amid predominantly blue and pink washes (TB CCCLXIV 332).

71 Scene in the Tyrol

The Entrance to the Via Mala ?1843
Watercolour and gouache 243 × 310 (9⁹⁄₁₆ × 12¼)
TB CCCLXIV 361 D36223
EXH: NG (71)
LIT: *Works*, XIII, pp.215–6, 611, as 'Ravine and Tower'; *R on P*, pp.113–4; Wilton 1982, p.58, pl.78

The twenty sketches which are above selected from the series which Turner made at Venice, are generally characterised by a depth of repose, and a delicacy of colour which would cause any one who had not seen other examples of Turner's work to suppose that tranquility and tenderness were the only characters of nature which the artist would ever care to express. I have, therefore, arranged in immediate sequence upon them some of his mountain drawings, in which force of colour, and energy both of form and effect, might induce us, in like manner, to suppose that these qualities had been the principal objects of his aim throughout his artistical life.

The subject which now introduces us to the Tyrolese defiles is indicated in colour only, without any of the pen-drawing or elaboration of texture which Turner always gave to the sketches he cared much for. Many such memoranda of colour exist among his loose papers; but their subjects are usually so little defined, that I have only admitted this one into the present series as an example of the class. It is, however, a very interesting one in its simplicity of gradation. It is curious how much of its glow depends on the two rude dashes of green in the bottom at the left; and how much of its size and distance on the mere indications of the level bed of the stream in the hollow.

There is, of course, too little detail to admit of the locality being verified; there are hundreds of such places among the Tyrolese Alps.

In spite of the doubts that Ruskin expressed as to whether the subject of this watercolour could be identified, he later suggested a connection with the Via Mala (*Works*, XIII, p.490 and n.3). The tower at the top of the crag on the left would therefore be part of the ruined castle of Hohenrätien, which also features in other watercolours (see also cat.nos.74, 80). It has been suggested that the strong earth colours can be most closely linked with the watercolours Turner produced during his journey through the Val d'Aosta with Munro of Novar in 1836 (see Wilton 1982, p.58). While this remains a possibility, the watercolours of the 1836 tour have yet to be fully documented, so no precise comparisons can be made. The topography, however,

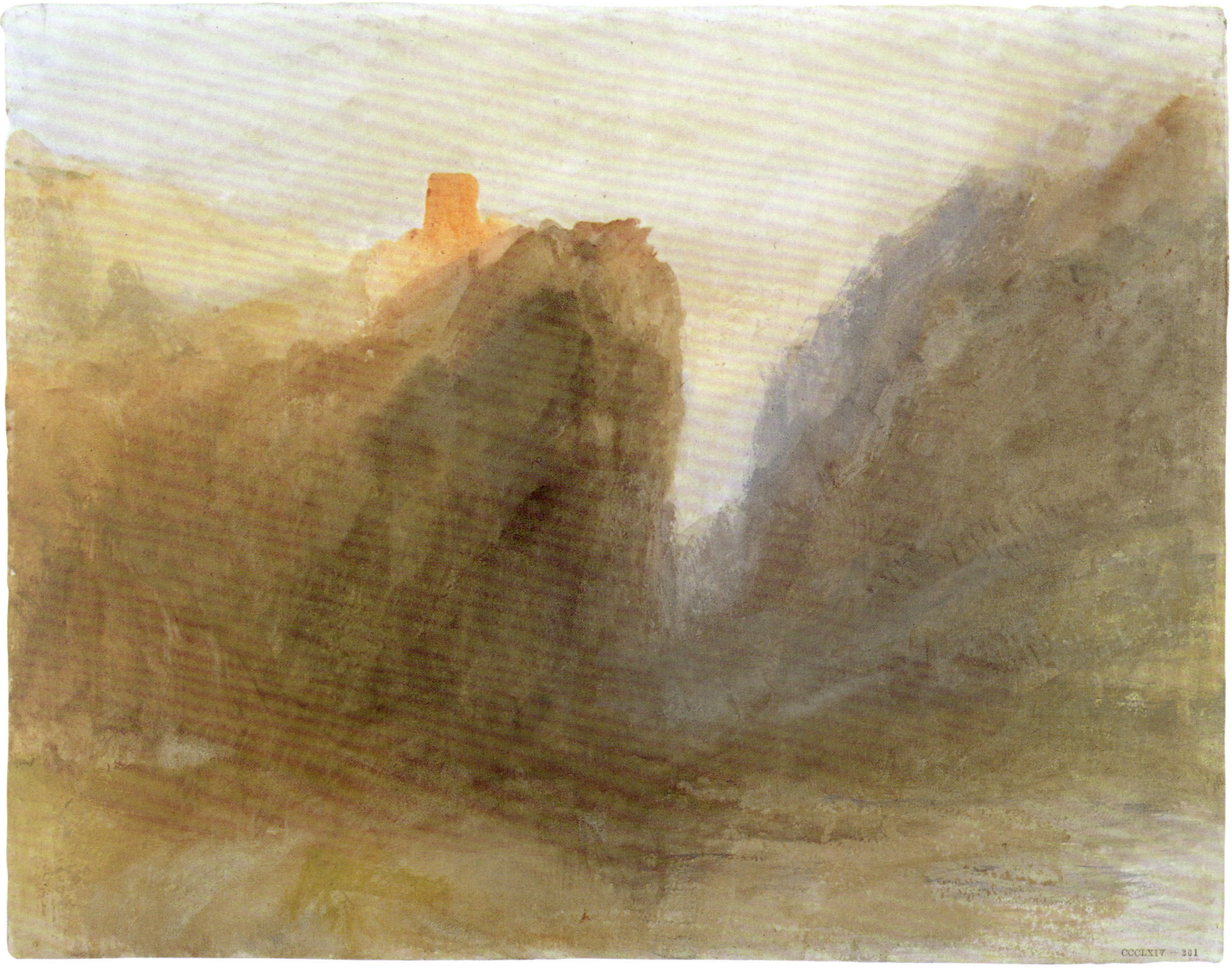

suggests that the watercolour is from a later tour, particularly since Turner is not known to have visited the Via Mala until 1843. Other watercolours linked with that Swiss tour do, in fact, demonstrate a very similar use of colour, although sometimes Turner applied a pen to his textured brushwork (see especially cat.no.47). A final point rests on the fact that all the other watercolours selected by Ruskin for this display date from after 1840, so it would perhaps have been unusual for him to have introduced a much earlier work; however, see also cat.no.97.

72 Scene on a Pass of the Higher Alps

Near the Pass of S. Bernardino: A Bridge over a River in a Gorge ?1843
Pencil and watercolour, with pen and some scraping out
227 × 327 ($8\frac{15}{16} \times 12\frac{7}{8}$)
Verso: rough pencil sketch of ?a gorge
TB CCCXXXVI 17 D33596
EXH: NG (72); National Gallery 1936–9; Washington 1963–4 (68, as 'Devil's Bridge in the Grisons, Switzerland, *c.*1841'); Brussels 1970–1 (83, repr.); British Museum 1975–6 (289, repr. p.158); Tate Gallery 1987; Tate Gallery 1990
LIT: *Works*, XIII, pp.216, 372 as 'The Red Gorge', 611 as 'Bridge, Alpine Pass'; *R on P*, pp.114, 284; Holme 1903, repr. W39; Serota 1970, p.134; Russell and Wilton 1976, p.113, repr.

I consider this, take it in all, the grandest sketch in the whole series, and purpose, therefore, to discover its subject, and then to illustrate it at length. I will say no more of it at present than that it deserves the spectator's closest attention, and the artist's most reverent study. I rather believe the subject to be on the St. Gothard, as the drawing was on a leaf of the book which furnished Nos.41, 44, 46 and 47.

The white object on the right of the bridge, with the sloping roof, is a gallery built to protect the road from an avalanche.

A fuller analysis of the strengths of this watercolour was never completed by Ruskin, nor did he subsequently discover the locality of the bridge depicted. Wilton proposed that it was a view of the Ganterbrücke on the Simplon Pass, near Brig, noting that a gallery still existed a little distance above the bridge. A more recent informal suggestion from Sr Franchino Giudicetti is that the bridge is situtated south of the Pass of S. Bernardino. There is some logic to this idea, since Ruskin notes that this sheet came from a book used mainly in the Ticino valley around Bellinzona; however, Ruskin is wrong is suggesting that cat.no.41 was once part of this book, see above.

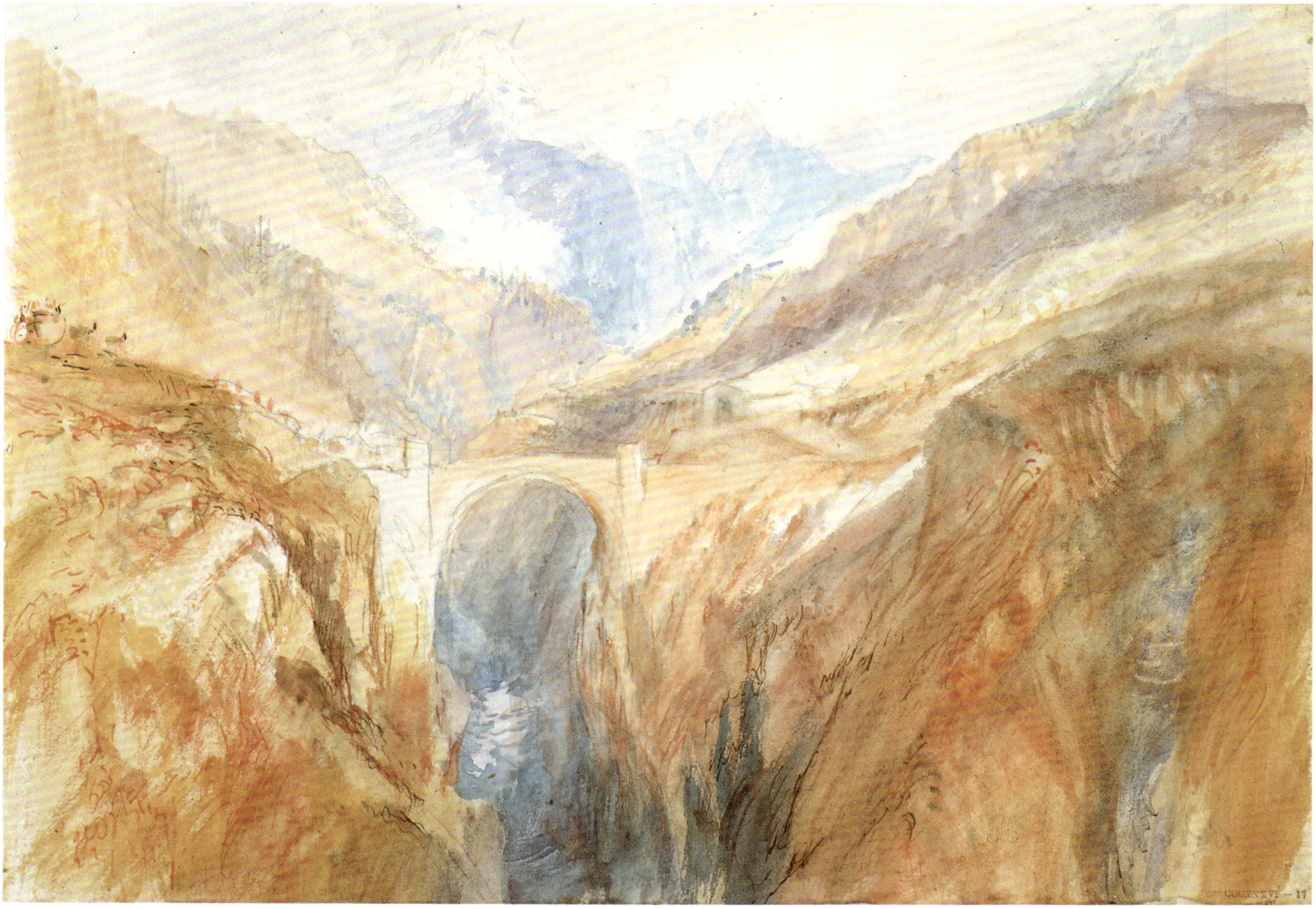

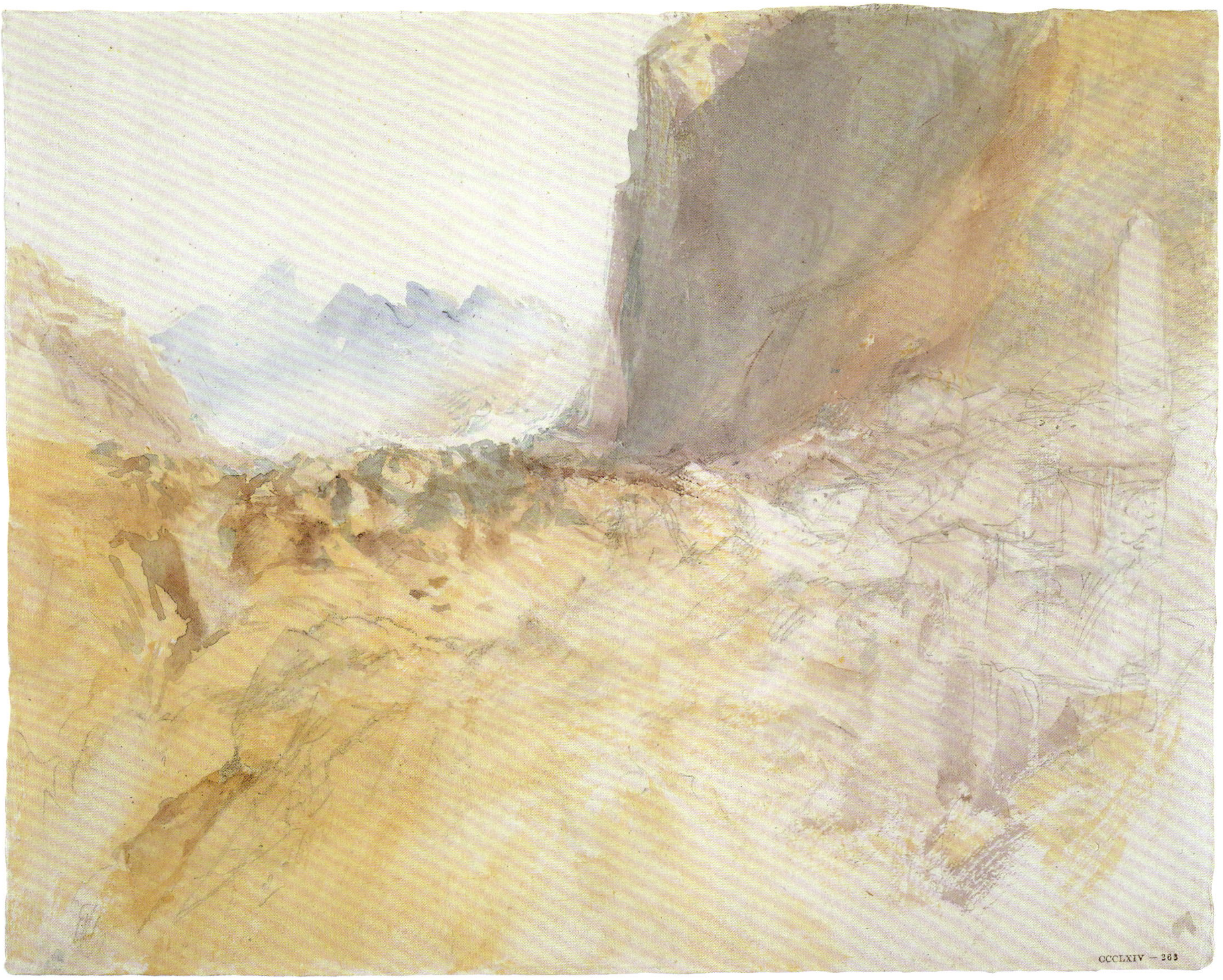

73 Village in the Higher Alps

?1843
Pencil and watercolour 242 × 300 ($9\frac{9}{16} \times 11\frac{7}{8}$)
TB CCCLXIV 363 D36225
EXH: NG (74); Berne 1947–8 (93 as 'Bergdorf, 1841')
LIT: *Works*, XIII, pp.217, 611 as 'Alpine Village Under Precipice'; *R on P*, p.115 as 'No.73'

I do not know the subject of this sketch; but there is enough detail to enable me to make it out some day: it follows at present sufficiently well in our series, as an expression of the look of the grey villages of the higher Alps in the midst of the stony débris of their passes. A considerable torrent descends under two bridges, between the mills on the right; and the breadth of effect in the half-grey, half-rosy light which touches the village is very beautiful.

I have no doubt that this study was made on the same journey as No.97, though I found it in another parcel; but it is not, I think, any Allée Blanche or Col de Ferret village.

Another watercolour in the Turner Bequest also depicts this village, dominated by its church tower, in complementary blue and orange washes (TB CCCLXIV 3). Neither view has yet been convincingly identified. Ruskin suggests that this sheet dates from the same tour as cat.no.97. Although it has been tentatively suggested that that watercolour relates to Turner's 1836 tour, it has been dated here to 1843. Similarly, this subject has more in common with Turner's use of colour in the early 1840s.

74 Fortress

The Via Mala, Looking towards Thusis *c.*1843
Pencil and watercolour, with scraping out
245 × 305 (9⅝ × 12)
TB CCCLXIV 362 D36224
EXH: NG (73); Amsterdam 1947–8 (67); Berne 1947–8 (76); Düsseldorf 1950 (28); Tate Gallery 1959 (461); Adelaide 1961 (32); Tokyo 1963–4 (40, repr. in Japanese cat. only); British Museum 1975–6 (290); Toronto 1980–1 (102, repr. p.177); Lugano 1991–2 (62, repr. p.167)
LIT: *Works*, XIII, pp.217–18, 373, 611; *R on P*, pp.114–15, as 'No.74'; Finberg 1910, repr. pl.LXXXIV, opp. p.141 as 'About 1844'; Russell and Wilton 1976, p.105, repr.; Wilton 1987, p.214, pl.282

This, next to No.72, is the noblest study in the series, displaying all Turner's power of modulation in subtle colours, and all his power of drawing, in the work in the rocks. In certain conditions of granitic rock, one of the chief characters of its water-worn mass is to divide into steps, – long and continuous, as in limestones, but in narrow vertical bands or columns, – of which two are seen here in high precipice on the right, and another has been taken possession of by the small secondary stream, whose undulations over the steps of it, exquisitely drawn and touched with blue reflections of the sky, are seen in the middle of the grey shadow; the water is hardly traceable above, its own spray forming a visible mist where the sun strikes, and hiding the stream. His strong sense of such granite structure in this particular rock is shown chiefly by the pencilling along the edge of the farthest precipice, where sloping lines in an almost equi-distant succession, indicate the jags of the cliff at its most exposed angle: I have no doubt that if Turner had ever realised this, he would have completely developed this structure through the mist, though he could not do so in his sketch without making that part of it inharmoniously conspicuous.

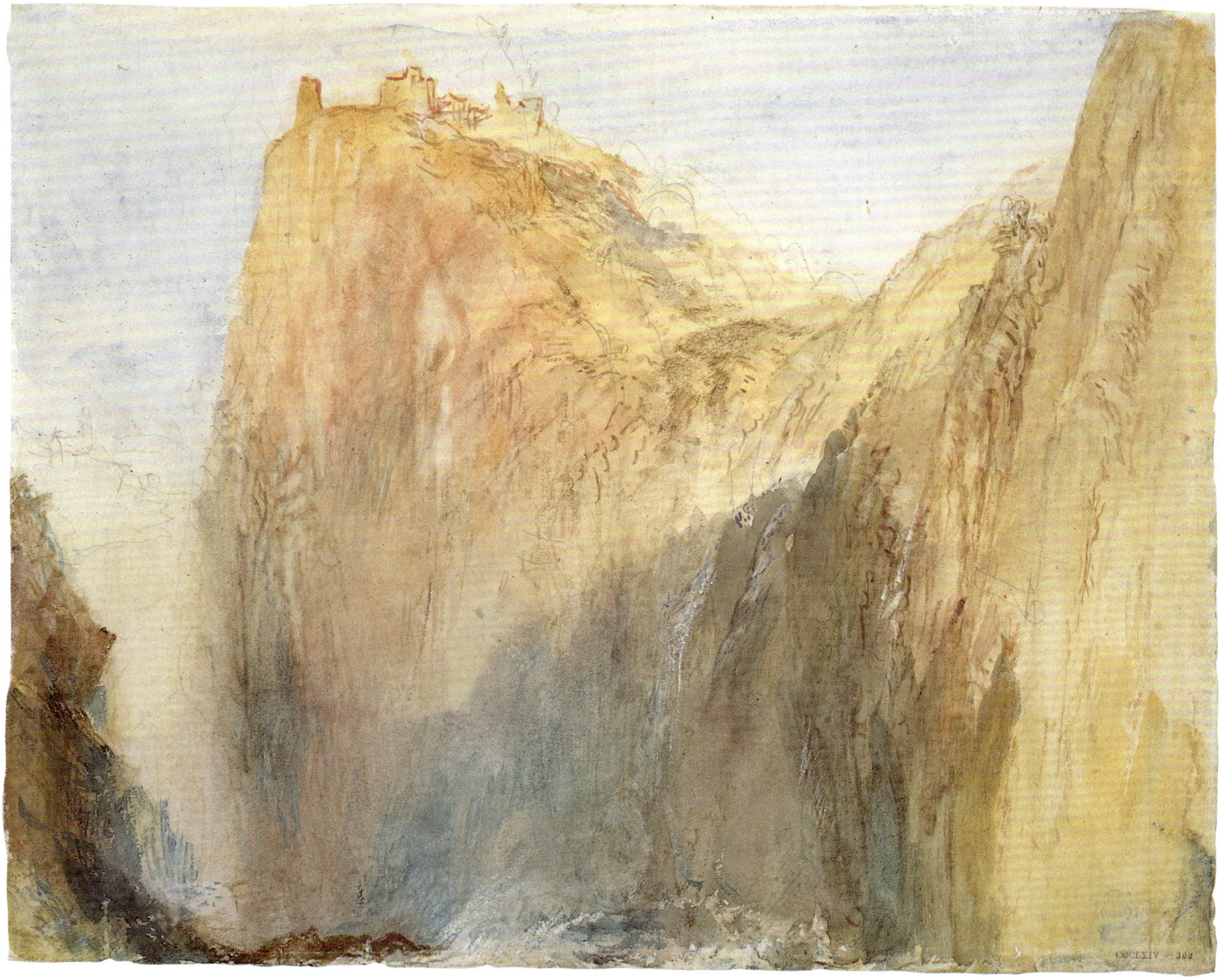

I was obliged, in mounting this drawing, just to catch its lower edge and no more; for Turner had actually used the white jags at the margin of the paper as part of the expression of the foam. As a composition, the drawing is remarkable for containing the utmost expression of height which it is possible to get at the given distance, and in the given space. Required to show a vertical rock so near, that a castle, on the farthest edge of it, shall show its tiles and windows, – you cannot possibly make it look higher than Turner has. The way in which he has done this too is specially interesting, because it contains so point-blank a denial of the common idea that yellow is an approaching colour and blue a retiring one; the foreground being here wholly blue, and the farthest mass the strongest yellow.

In the early nineteenth century the Via Mala was celebrated as the 'most sublime and tremendous defile in Switzerland'. Murray's *Hand-book*, from which the quotation is taken, devotes three pages to a description of the pass, evoking vividly the exhilarating thrill of travelling through the close ravine (Murray 1838, pp.206–8). Another recommendation came from 'E.H.', the mysterious travelling companion, who accompanied Turner as far as Bregenz on his 1840 trip to Venice. In a letter to Turner, he professed that of 'all the passes I have yet seen, this is by far the best' (Gage 1980, p.178). In spite of such fulsome praise, Turner seems not to have visited the Via Mala until 1843 (see also cat.nos.71 and 80). The rocky forms of the soaring cliffs are recorded in a group of pencil sketches in the Turner Bequest (i.e. TB LXXXIV C, TB CCCXLIV 406 and possibly TB CCCXXXVI 8).

In devising this confrontational composition, Turner may have recalled the Alpine watercolours of J.R. Cozens, which he had copied as an adolescent at the home of Dr Thomas Monro, and which included views of the Via Mala (see K. Sloan, *Alexander and John Robert Cozens: The Poetry of Landscape*, London and New Haven 1986, figs.132–3, 135, 137–40).

75 The Valley of the Splugen

The Pass of the Splügen: Sample Study *c.*1841–2
Pencil and watercolour 243 × 304 (9⁹⁄₁₆ × 12)
Verso inscribed in red chalk: '10'
TB CCCLXIV 277 D36125
EXH: NG (75); Royal Academy 1974–5 (604); Cleveland 1977–8 (67, repr. p.86); The Hague 1978–9 (84, repr. p.113); Mexico City 1979 (82); Paris 1983–4 (242, repr. p.294); Tate Gallery 1987; Tate Gallery 1990; Tate Gallery 1993 (24, repr. p.44)
LIT: *Works*, XIII, pp.218, 372, ,611; *R on P*, p.116 as 'Approach to the Splugen Pass'; Dillon 1902, p.332; Serota 1970, p.110; Russell and Wilton 1976, p.109; Wilton 1979, p.483; Wilton 1982, p.64, pl.96

We descend to Coire [Chur], *and look back from near Ragatz to the higher hills.*

Very remarkable as an example of Turner's occasional delight in a perfectly straight road, seen for four or five miles of its length at once. He realised this sketch at his own choice with great care; the drawing is now in the possession of Mr. Munro [fig.37].

Ruskin locates this view a considerable distance north of Splügen, on the stretch of road between Chur and Bad Ragaz. Support for this identification comes from the title given to the finished drawing of the subject when it was sold as part of Munro of Novar's collection in 1878. The Christie's catalogue for the sale listed the work as 'Baths of Pfeffers: Ragaz, Pass of Splügen'; the baths at Pfeffers were an established tourist attraction which Murray recommended 'no one should omit to visit from Ragatz' (Murray 1838, p.170). These two independent pieces of similar information concerning the topography suggest a common source, presumably Turner himself at the time this sample study was first presented in 1842. Certainly, the completed watercolour, with the inscription 'BAINS' in the foreground, indicates that the location is near a spar of some kind. An alternative location has been suggested by Andrew Wilton, who believes the church on the left to be that at Andeer, with the view up towards the Via Mala. Of all the sample studies and specimen drawings shown in 1842, the 'Splügen' was the subject that Ruskin most coveted. He considered it both 'the noblest Alpine drawing Turner had ever till then made' (*Works*, XIII, p.480) and 'the best Swiss landscape yet painted by man' (*Works*, XXXV, p.309). However, while waiting for permission from his father to buy it, the drawing was purchased by Munro of Novar. Ruskin pined for it continually over the years (see cat.no.22), so that his father desperately sought a means of acquiring it, apparently resigning himself finally to its loss when Munro raised its value from 80 to 400 guineas. It was only after the Christie's sale in 1878 that Ruskin's admirers were able to present him with the watercolour he had desired for so long. The contrast established in this sample study between the distant golden peaks and the blue and mauves of the darker valley was also used in a watercolour of the Rhine at Rhäzüns, a little further up the valley, near Reichenau (TB CCCLXIV 217).

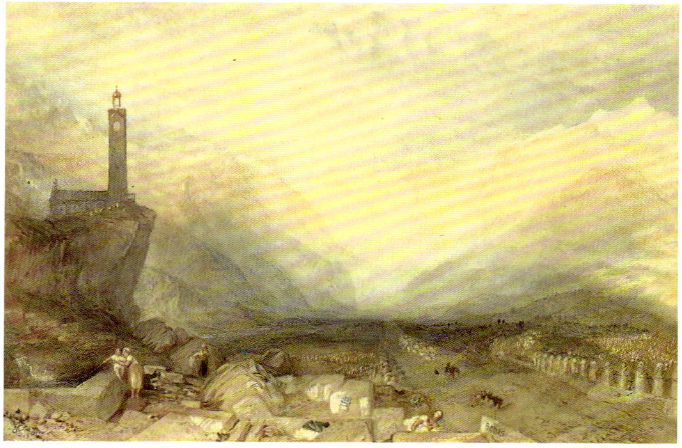

fig.37 'The Pass of the Splügen' 1842, watercolour (W 1523).
Private Collection

75

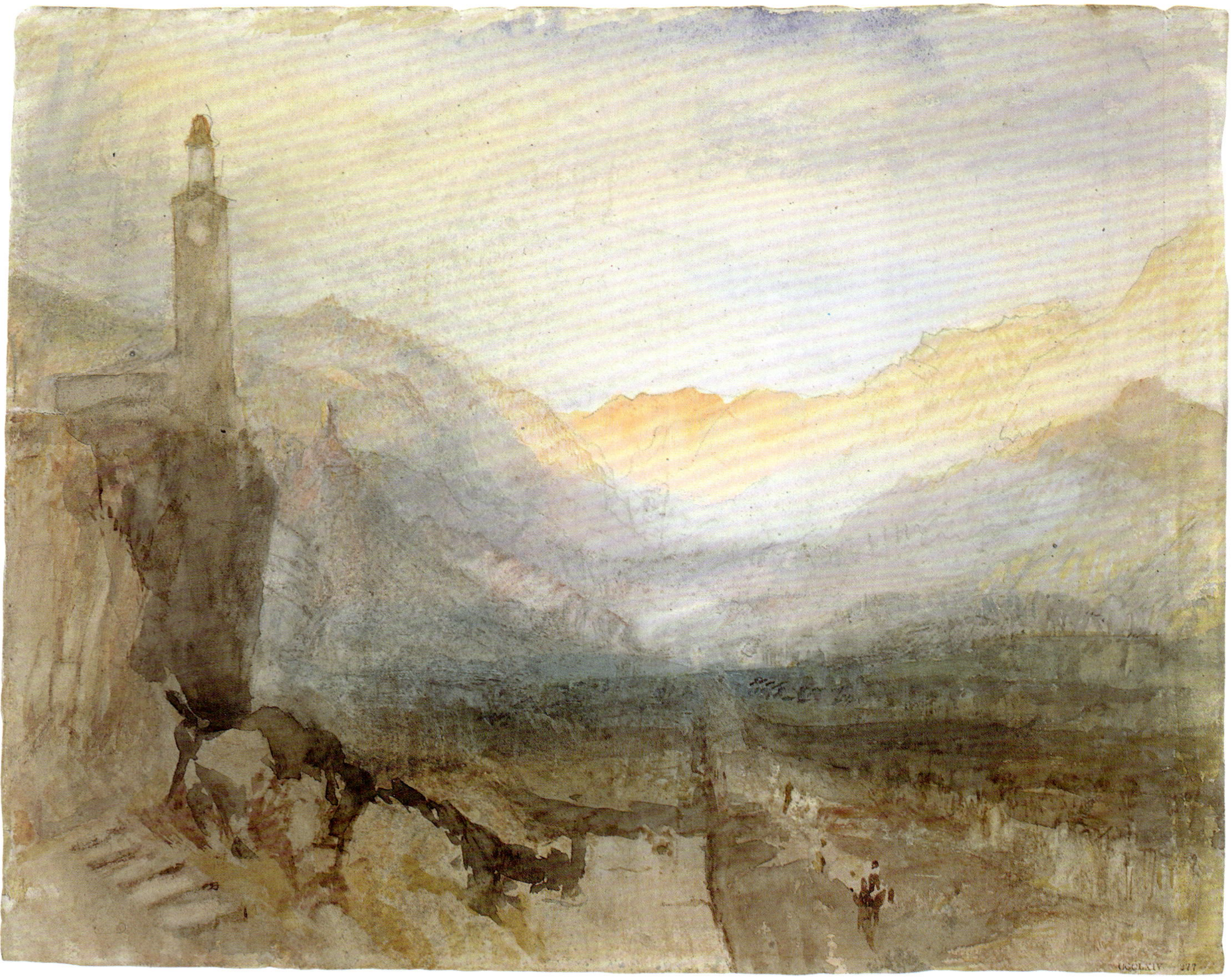

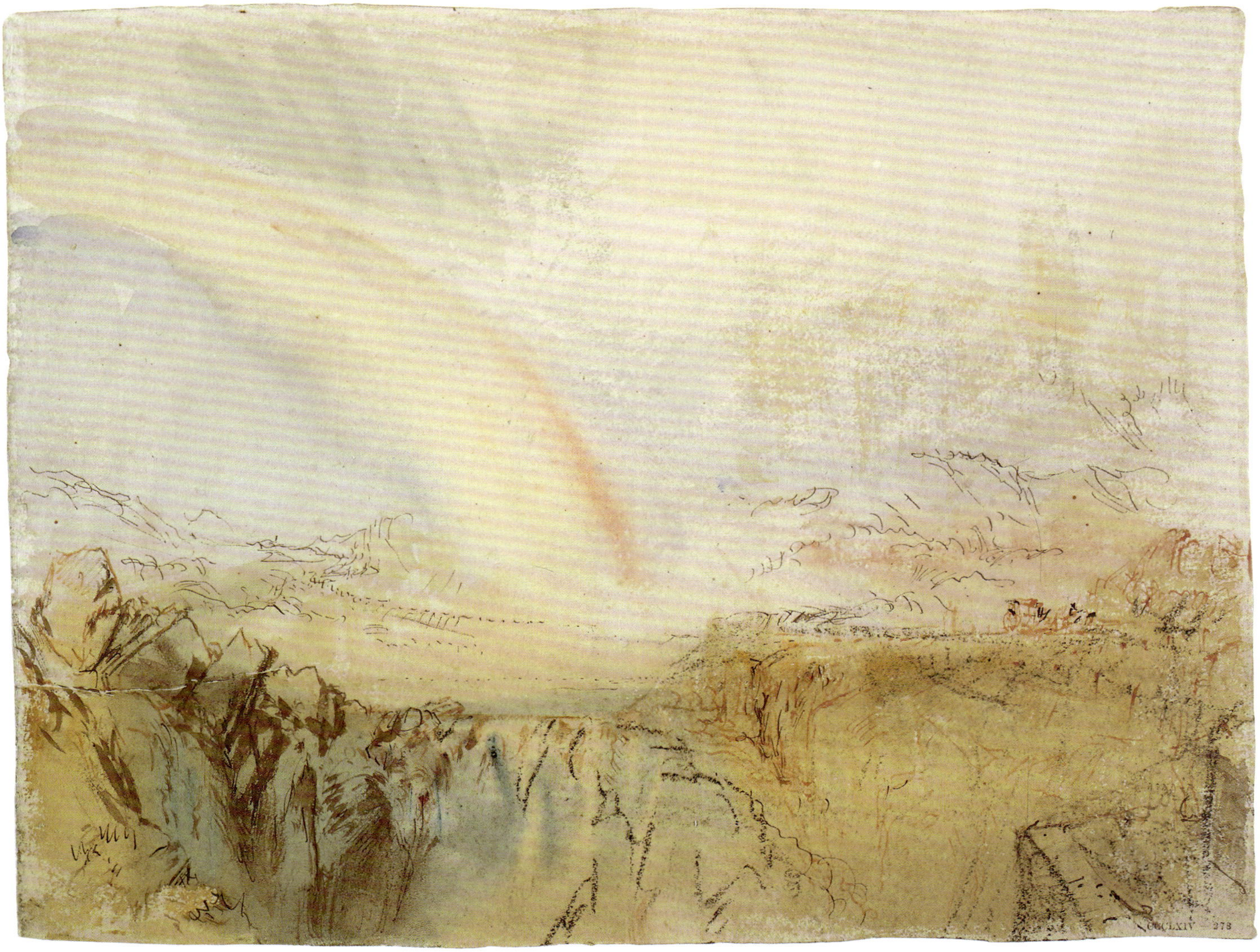

76 Descent from the Alps

An Alpine Pass, with a Rainbow *c.*1842–3
Watercolour, with pen 221 × 288 ($8\frac{3}{4} \times 11\frac{3}{8}$)
TB CCCLXIV 278 D36126
EXH: NG (76); New York 1966 (91, repr. p.56); Athens, Georgia 1982 (87)
LIT: *Works*, XIII, pp.218–9, 611, as 'Alpine Pass, with Cascade and Rainbow'; *R on P*, p.116

I am not sure where we are; but certainly on a good road, and in a comfortable chaise. The pen-drawing under the rainbow, where the road comes down the hill, is very free and beautiful; and the heap of stones at the top of the waterfall, on the left, one of the best bits of sketching in this series.

The pile of rocks in the foreground of this watercolour recalls the massive blocks Turner developed in his view of the Pass of Faido (cat.no.40). While the finished view included a carriage turning the bend in the road, Turner omitted this human incident in his study. Here, the coach on the right-hand side serves both to heighten the drama of the natural effect and is a reminder of the network of coaching-roads that linked the principal towns of Switzerland. By the 1840s there was an assortment of different types of transport, ranging from the regular routes of the public *diligences,* through to smaller vehicles for private hire, such as the *voiturier* or the *char-à-banc*. Another watercolour showing the progress of a carriage through a mountain pass is TB CCCLXIV 129. See also the coach poised to cross the bridge in cat.no.72.

77 River Scene, with Fortress

Fribourg: The Convent de la Maigrauge, in the Valley of the River Sarine, from the South 1841
Pencil and watercolour, with pen
235 × 335 (9¼ × 13¼)
TB CCCXXXV 25 D33565
EXH: NG (77)
LIT: *Works*, XIII, pp.219, 373, p.611; *R on P*, p.116 as 'Alpine Fortress and Torrent'

Another subject which temporarily embarasses me; but it is clearly a recognisable one, and of considerable interest; the fortress walls on the right being grand, and the city, or opposite citadel, of great extent. As a drawing, it is a valuable lesson in composition; if you hide the block timbers above the river with your hand, the fortress immediately becomes thin and flimsy; but when the lines of the timber are put in, as you can see through them everywhere, the fortress walls become instantly firm and solid by the contrast.

One of the sketchbooks from Turner's 1841 journey to Switzerland contains about twenty studies of Fribourg, mostly recorded in pencil, with the details heightened in red colour (TB CCCXXXV). This previously unidentified view is taken from the bottom of the valley of the River Sarine (or Saane in German), which runs through Fribourg. The dark form with towers at the centre is the Convent de la Maigrauge, which is also seen from a higher vantage-point in another watercolour from this book (TB CCCXXXV 16; Tate Gallery 1993, no.17, repr.). At the top of the escarpment on the right are the walls of the Convent de Montorge. The low viewpoint, which inevitably draws the eye to the distant buildings on the heights above, was a format Turner had adopted for the group of views of Luxembourg he had made two years before (see Tate Gallery 1991–2, pp.173–83). Another view of Fribourg from this angle, but closer to the convent, is TB CCCXXXV 6. In both works Turner's fanciful use of slightly acidic oranges and pinks is balanced by more sober tones of grey and blue. Fribourg was one of the four Swiss towns which Ruskin set out to record 'elaborately' as a means of illustrating Turner's watercolours (see Hayman 1990, pp.64–77). Although he had himself

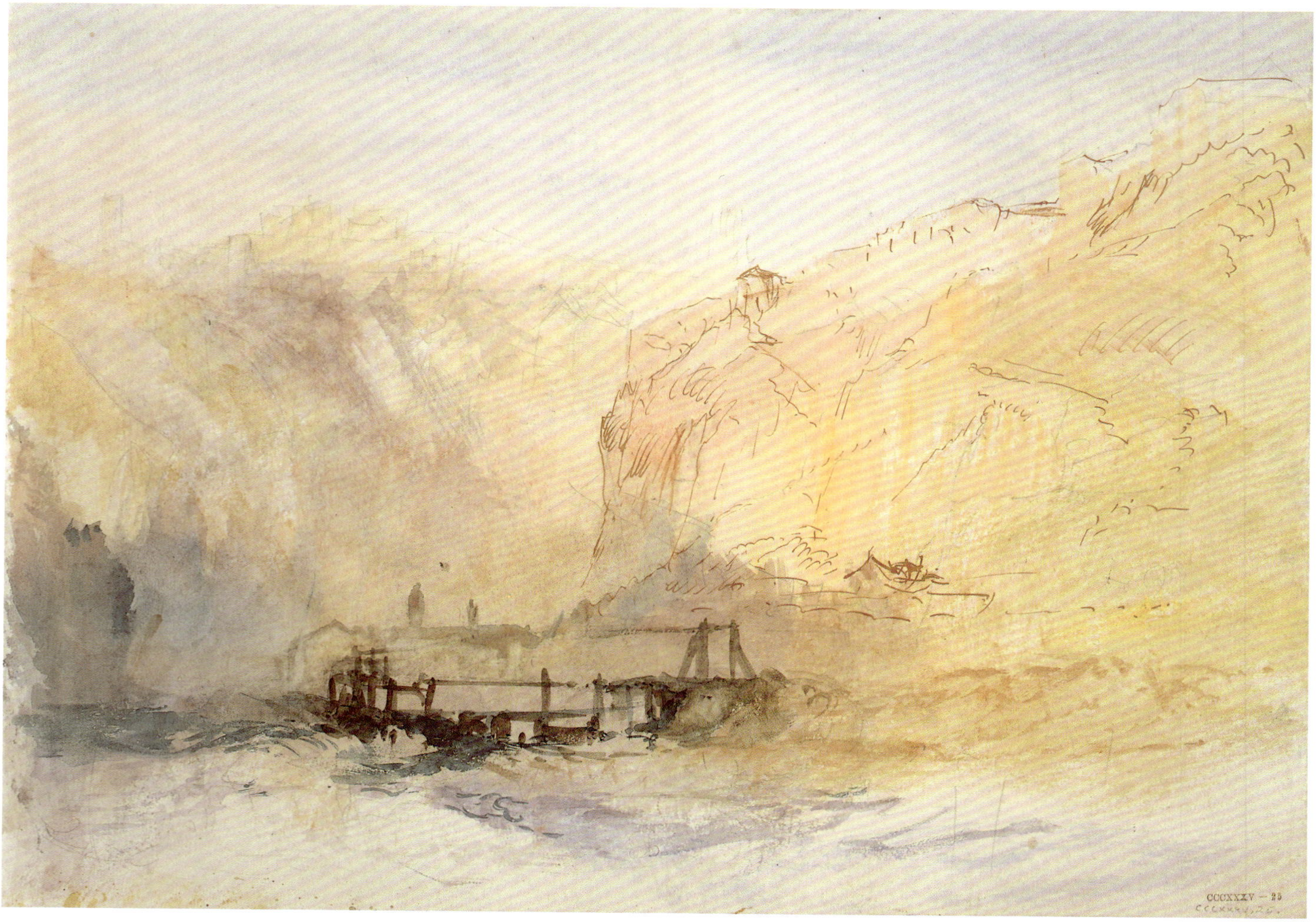

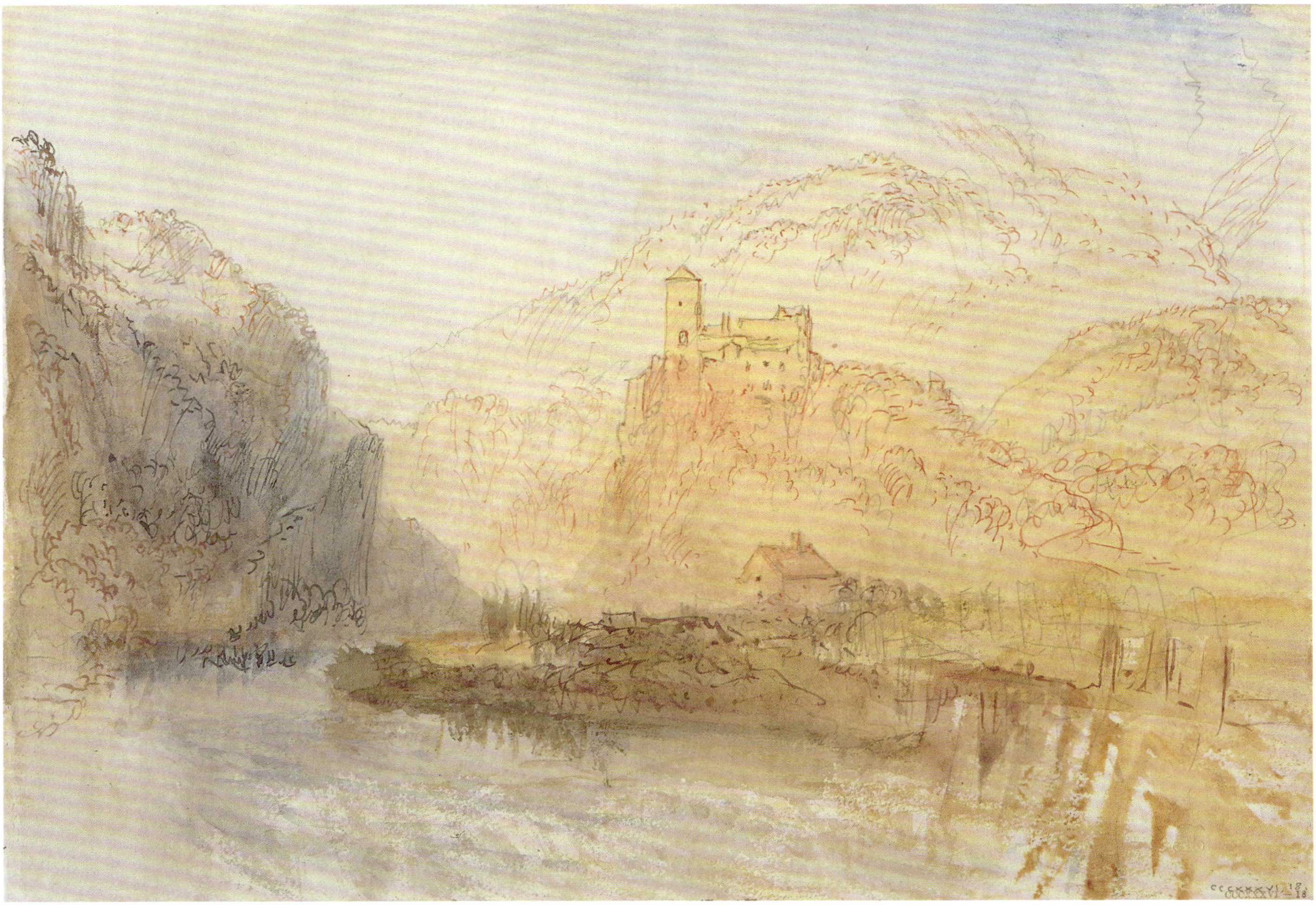

sketched at Fribourg as early as 1835 (Bembridge 1283; Walton 1972, p.27, fig.15), Ruskin had only a vague idea that Turner had made such a thorough study of its buildings and its spectacular setting. This is clear from his recollection at the time of Turner's death that Griffith had mentioned a 'very fine' group of Fribourg, which at that stage he had not seen (Bradley 1955, p.113).

78 River Scene

River Scene, with a Church, near Bellinzona ?1843
Pencil and watercolour, with pen 227 × 327 (8 15/16 × 12 7/8)
Watermarked: J WHATMAN | TURKEY MILL | 1839
Verso: pencil sketch of a valley with a church tower
TB CCCXXXVI 18 D33597
EXH: NG (78); Cape Town 1936–7 (Frame 21); Tate Gallery 1959–65
LIT: *Works*, XIII, pp.219, 372, 611; *R on P*, pp.116–7, as 'River Scene, with Château'; Serota 1970, p.134

An example of Turner's slightest work in his grandest temper. There is no laziness, and no failure; but intense haste and concentration of power; every line and blot being of value. Note, for instance, the use of the thin white touches through the grey of the river, and of the touches out in the distance, which actually create the stream out of nothing. The truth of the radiating lines in the dark rock on the left, and the noble curves of the fortress on the right from its vertical wall, would need an essay of several pages, and the help of many diagrams, to illustrate properly.

The last comments suggest that Ruskin was thinking of analysing this watercolour in the same way he had already dissected the view of 'Coblenz' in *The Elements of Drawing* (see cat.no.8). The watercolour comes from the *Bellinzona* sketchbook (TB CCCXXXVI), which was almost certainly used by Turner in 1843. The chapel depicted must be in one of the smaller villages close to Bellinzona, but has so far not been possible to identify. A pencil sketch on the verso of f.7 of this sketchbook is also of the same building. Two of the other pages from the sketchbook depict a different, larger, church perched loftily above a group of houses (TB CCCXXXVI ff.2, 3); Ruskin inscribed the verso of f.2 with the comment, 'Chapel just | below Bellinzona | on road to Locarno'. Both watercolours are in fact views of Monte Carasso at Sementina, to the south-west of Bellinzona.

79 River Scene. Evening

Rheingrafenstein and Ebernburg on the River Naar 1844
Pencil and watercolour, with pen
229 × 327 (9 × 12⅞)
TB CCCXLIX 21 D35145
EXH: NG (79); British Museum 1937–8; Düsseldorf 1950–1 (33); Adelaide 1961 (36, repr. p.26). This subject will be discussed by Cecilia Powell in the catalogue for the forthcoming exhibition *Turner in Germany*, Tate Gallery 1995
LIT: *Works*, XIII, pp.219–20, 372, 611; *R on P*, p.117; Serota 1970, p.134

I have arranged these unknown subjects together, merely because they belong to one class of scenery, and are all studies in Turner's best method of work. I fear that the localities of some may be hardly ascertainable: but the reader may be assured that they are all studies from real places, and I shall be grateful for any hint and help which travellers may be able to give me, leading to their identification.

Turner discovered Rheingrafenstein and Ebernburg on his 1844 tour, while exploring the Neckar and its tributaries. Another view of Ebernburg is cat.no.81. A.J. Finberg catalogued this watercolour as a sheet from the *Rheinfelden* sketchbook (TB CCCXLIX; see cat.nos.81, 83, 85–90). As in cat.no.77, Turner did not confine himself to naturalistic colours, and instead produced an effect that is extraordinarily original.

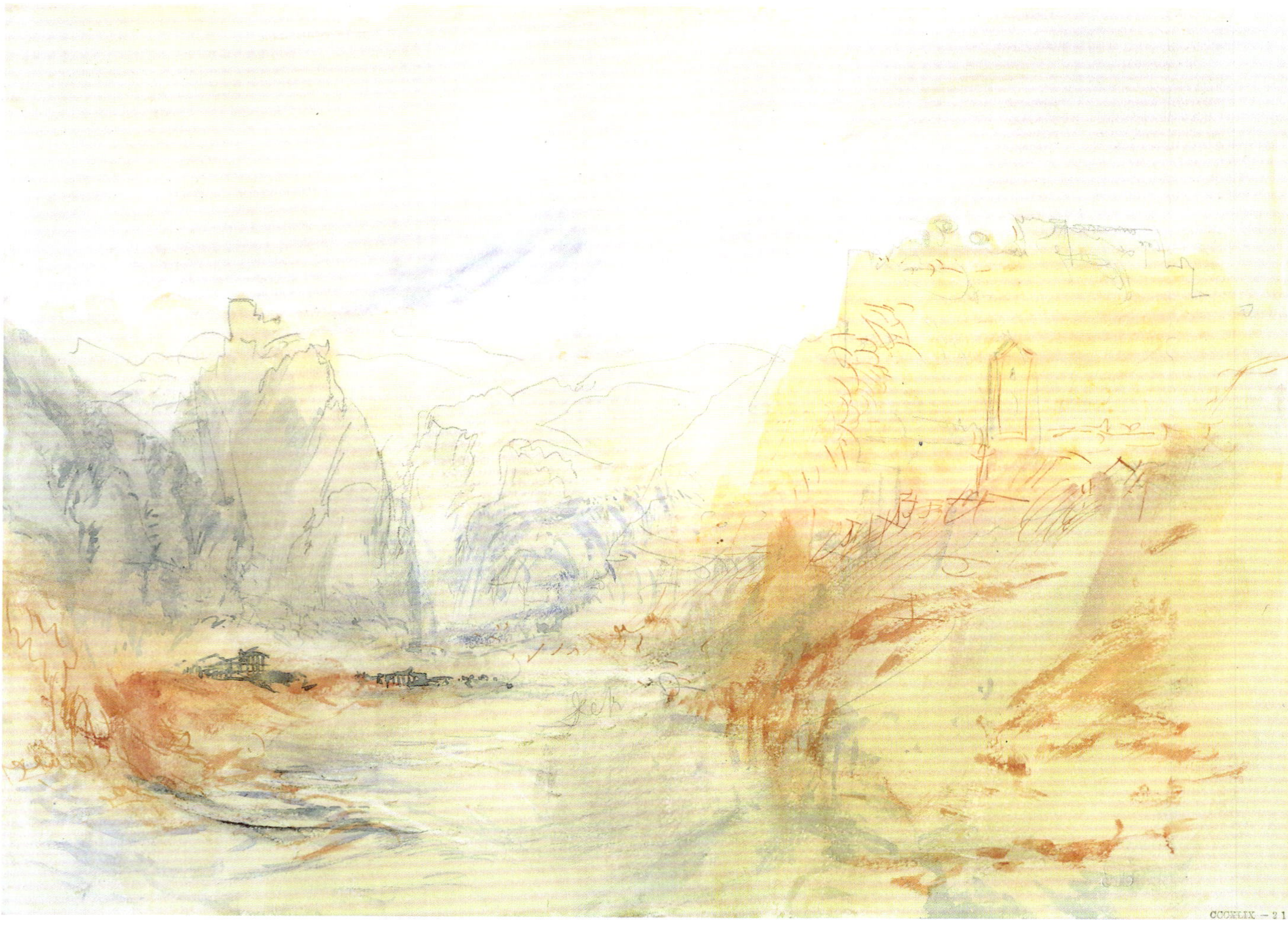

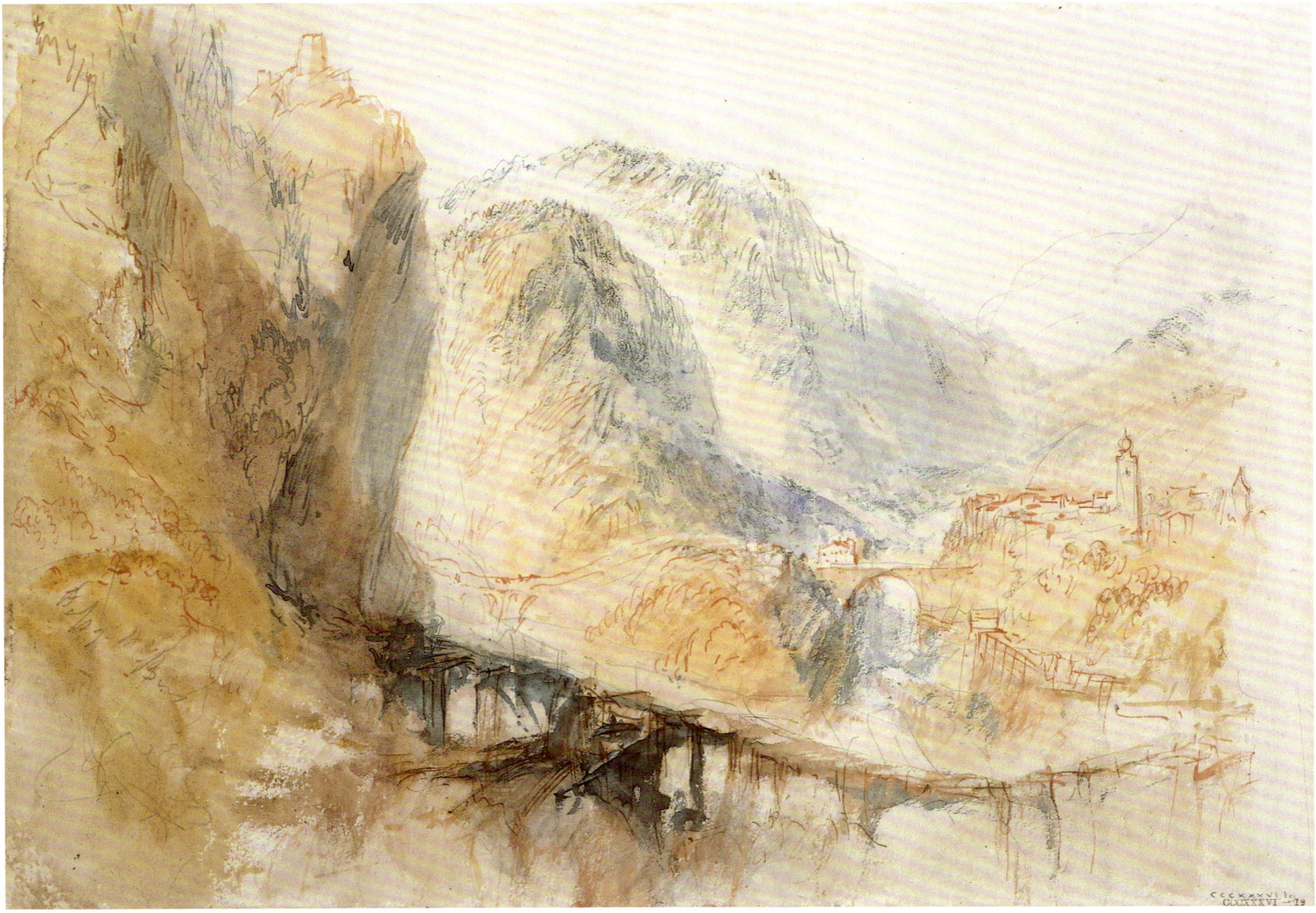

80 Scene in the Tyrol

Thusis, with the Entrance to the Via Mala *c.*1843
Pencil and watercolour, with pen 226 × 327 ($8\frac{15}{16}$ × $12\frac{7}{8}$)
Watermarked: J WHATMAN | TURKEY MILL | 1839
Verso: pencil sketch of castle above a valley
TB CCCXXXVI 19 D33599
EXH: NG (80); National Gallery 1936–9; Tate Gallery 1953–9; Washington 1963–4 (69, repr.); Folkestone 1971–2 (17); Munich 1972–3 (155, as 'Tiefencastel'); Madrid 1983 (92, repr. p.99)
LIT: *Works*, XIII, pp.220, 372 as 'Miner's Bridge', 611 as 'Alpine Scene, Village and Bridge'; *R on P*, p.117; Russell and Wilton 1976, p.104, repr.

The grandest subject, if we include quantity and picturesqueness as elements of grandeur, in all the series. I wish I knew where it is, and who the baron was who first perched himself on that overhanging rock on the left. I hope to illustrate this drawing at length, as well as Nos.72 and 78.

In this subject, Turner's handling of watercolour comes together with his deft penwork to achieve a subtly harmonious effect. The suggestion of diffused light at the mouth of the ravine on the left is particularly successful. This is the entrance to the Via Mala, which lies close to the village of Thusis. In Turner's depiction, the tower with the onion dome is that of the Reformed church. Above, on the brim of the ravine, sit the ruins of Hohenrätien. According to Murray, these are 'traditionally reported to owe their origin to Rhoetus, chief of the Etruscans, who, driven out of Italy by an invasion of the Gauls, established his stronghold on this spot B.C. 287, and transplanted into the Alps the people and language of Etruria' (Murray 1838, p.206). Sadly, none of the works listed by Ruskin in this entry was ever treated more extensively in his writings.

81 Scene with Torrent and Fortress

Ebernburg from the Valley of the Alsenz 1844
Pencil and watercolour, with pen
229 × 326 (9 × 12⅞)
TB CCCXLIX 24 D35148
EXH: NG (48). This subject will be discussed more fully by Cecilia Powell in the catalogue for the forthcoming exhibition *Turner in Germany*, Tate Gallery 1995
LIT: *Works*, XIII, pp.220, 372 as 'Fortress', 610 as 'Castle near Meran'; *R on P*, p.107; Wilton 1982, p.73, pl.123

These next two subjects may also probably be in the Tyrol. I have no doubt of ultimately discovering them. This one is singularly grand and simple in conception; its colour exquisitely pure, and its execution at once delicate and vigorous; – it is not possible to do more with the given number of touches. Note especially how the main promontory of rock is thrust forward merely by the gleam of white paper left at its foot in the rosy dash of colour.

Nothing can be more magnificent than the standing of the buildings on the rock, the firm irregularity of their battlements, and the indications of sloping cleavage in the cliff itself.

The grey mass in the foreground is the dark side of a piece of rock hanging over the torrent, which is indicated in its descent under the bridge by a few touches of blue. This sketch cannot be too long or patiently studied.

This and the following watercolour were catalogued by A.J. Finberg as part of the *Rheinfelden* sketchbook (TB CCCXLIX), which Turner used chiefly on the Rivers Limmat and Rhine in 1844. Another watercolour study, which appears to show the same fortress, but which lacks the defining penwork found on this sheet, is on a page of the 1844 *Heidelberg* sketchbook (TB CCCLII 4). Towards the end of the nineteenth century, the title of the work was revised at the National Gallery to suggest that it depicted a castle near Merano, in the Tyrol. However, even before the correct identity of the castle was established by Cecilia Powell, it seemed unlikely that this could be a view made in the Tyrol, since Turner is not known to have visited that area in 1844. See also cat.no.79.

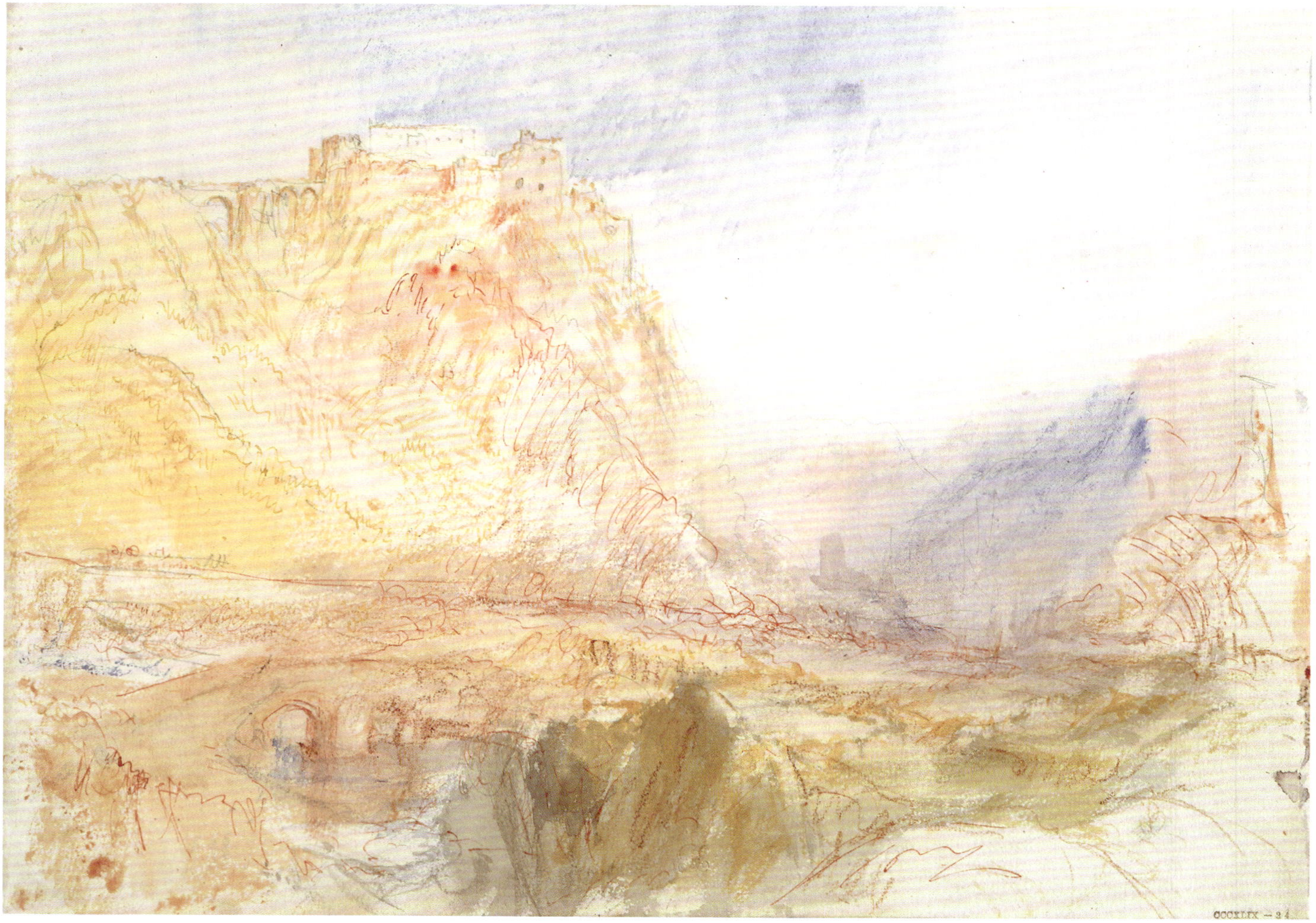

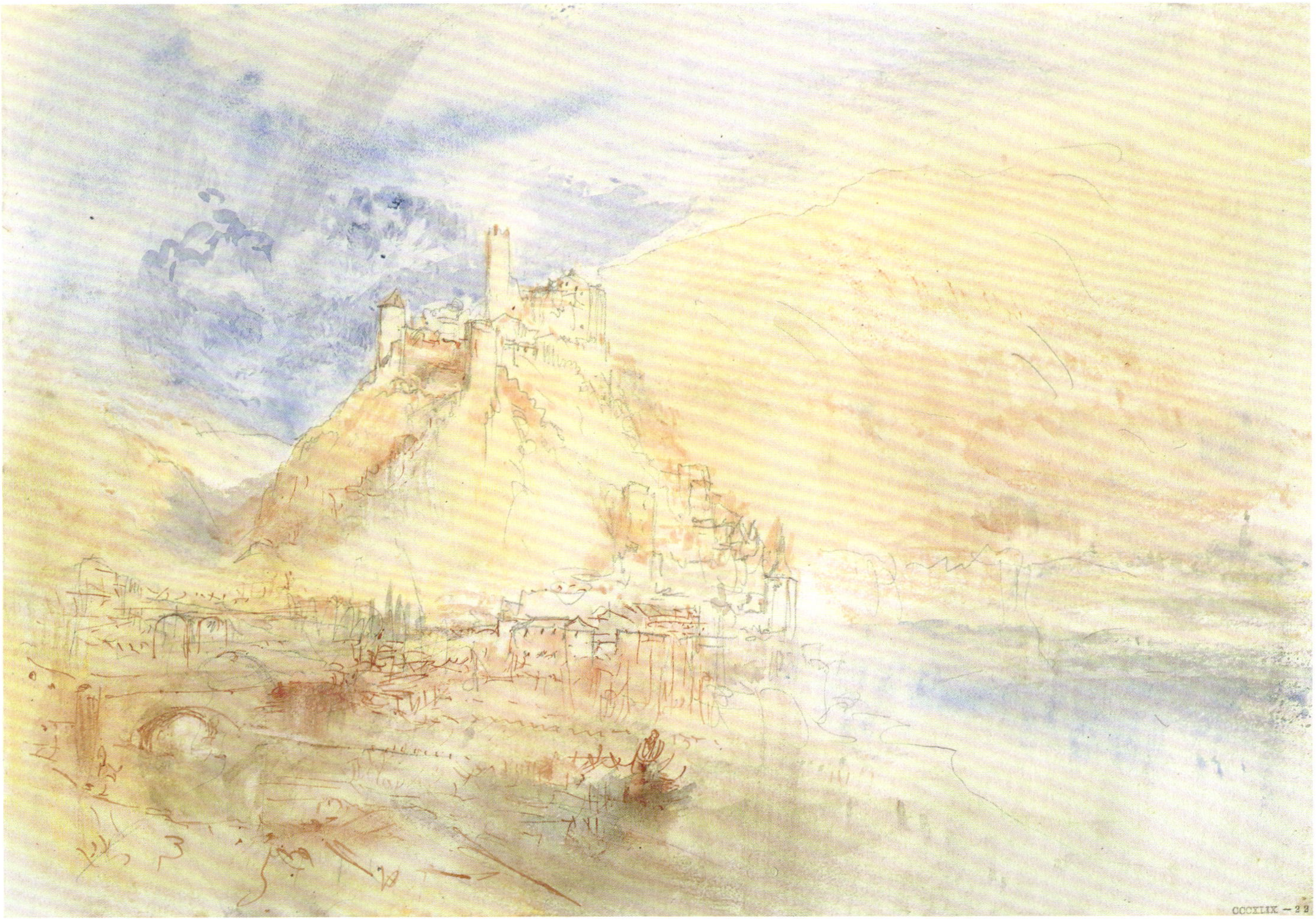

82 Scene with City and Fortress

Hirschhorn, on the Neckar 1844
Pencil and watercolour, with pen and scraping-out
229 × 326 (9 × 12⅞)
Verso: small sketch of ?a valley
TB CCCXLIX 22 D35146
EXH: NG (82). This watercolour has been identified by Cecilia Powell and will be discussed in her forthcoming study of Turner's travels in Germany (Tate Gallery 1995)
LIT: *Works*, XIII, pp.221, 372 as 'Fortress', 611 as 'Village and Castle on the Rhine'; *R on P*, p.118; Finberg 1910, repr. pl.LXXXIII, opp. p.140

Far inferior to the last, this is still of great beauty and interest, remarkable chiefly for the extent of space in the calm water on the right, attained with hardly any labour. Turner has got into some scrape which provoked him excessively as he drew the nearest wall of the fortress, the paper being there deeply dented with his knife as he effaced the work; these indentations produce a slight shadow, which gives part of the effect to the drawing: if the paper were smoothed by being mounted, the intention of the painter would be lost in that part of the drawing.

See cat.no.11.

83 [Untitled]

Baden, from the North 1844
Pencil and watercolour, with pen 229 × 326 (9 × 12⅞)
TB CCCXLIX 13 D35137
EXH: NG (83); Folkestone 1966; Folkestone 1971–2 (18)
LIT: *Works*, XIII, pp.221, 372, 611 as 'Baden (Switzerland), looking South'; *R on P*, p.118

The next eight subjects are from two towns, I believe in eastern Switzerland, but they will be quite easily identified.

This is a very interesting composition, owing to the way in which the yellow foreground turns the river, while it carries down its principal lines. Hide the two figures and scratched lines at the bottom, and see how the space and length of road or terrace in the further hill, leading the eye to the grey bridge which was to be the point of the whole.

Ruskin discovered the subjects of cat.nos.83–90 during a tour of Switzerland in 1858, shortly after he had completed his work cataloguing the Turner Bequest. Two years later, in his Preface to the final volume of *Modern Painters*, he recounted how he had identified this 'magnificent series' largely on the strength of his suspicion that they 'appeared to be of some towns along the course of the Rhine on the north of Switzerland' (*Works*, VII, p.5). The group of three watercolours of Baden on the River Limmat, north of Zurich, were among his discoveries that summer. The spa town had been popular with tourists since ancient times and was first visited by Turner in 1802 (*Lake Thun* sketchbook, TB LXXVI ff.15 verso, 59, 63). The three watercolours selected by Ruskin date from a tour of forty-two years later and were taken from the *Rheinfelden* roll sketchbook (other watercolours of Baden from this book are TB CCCXLIX ff.12, 23, 25). Two of the smaller sketchbooks in the Turner Bequest contain pencil memoranda of Baden, which could date from either 1841 or 1844, but are most probably from the later year (*Rhine and Switzerland* sketchbook, TB CCCXXV ff.27 verso, 34 verso; and the *Berne, Heidelberg and Rhine* sketchbook, TB CCCXXVI ff.3 verso, 4).

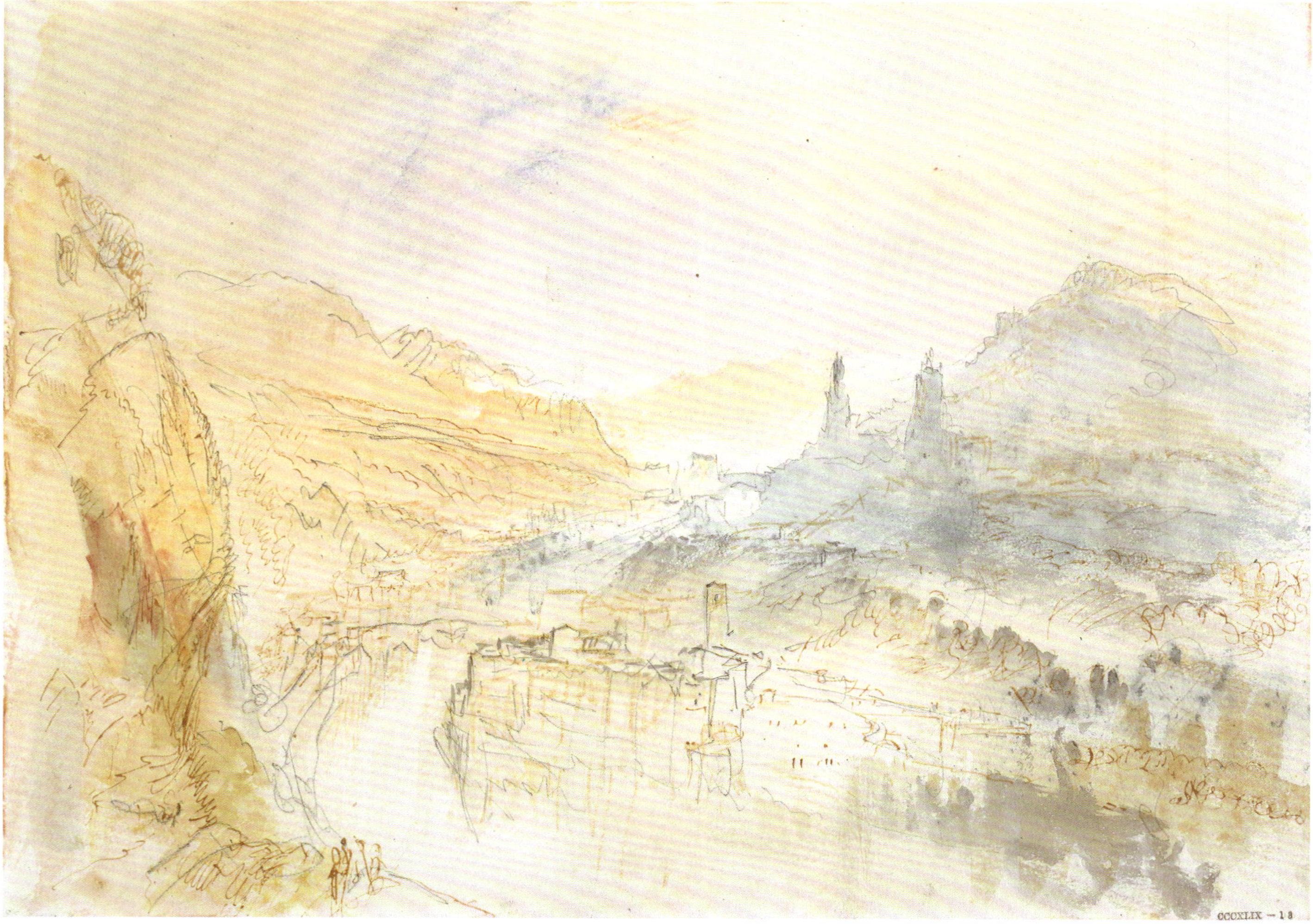

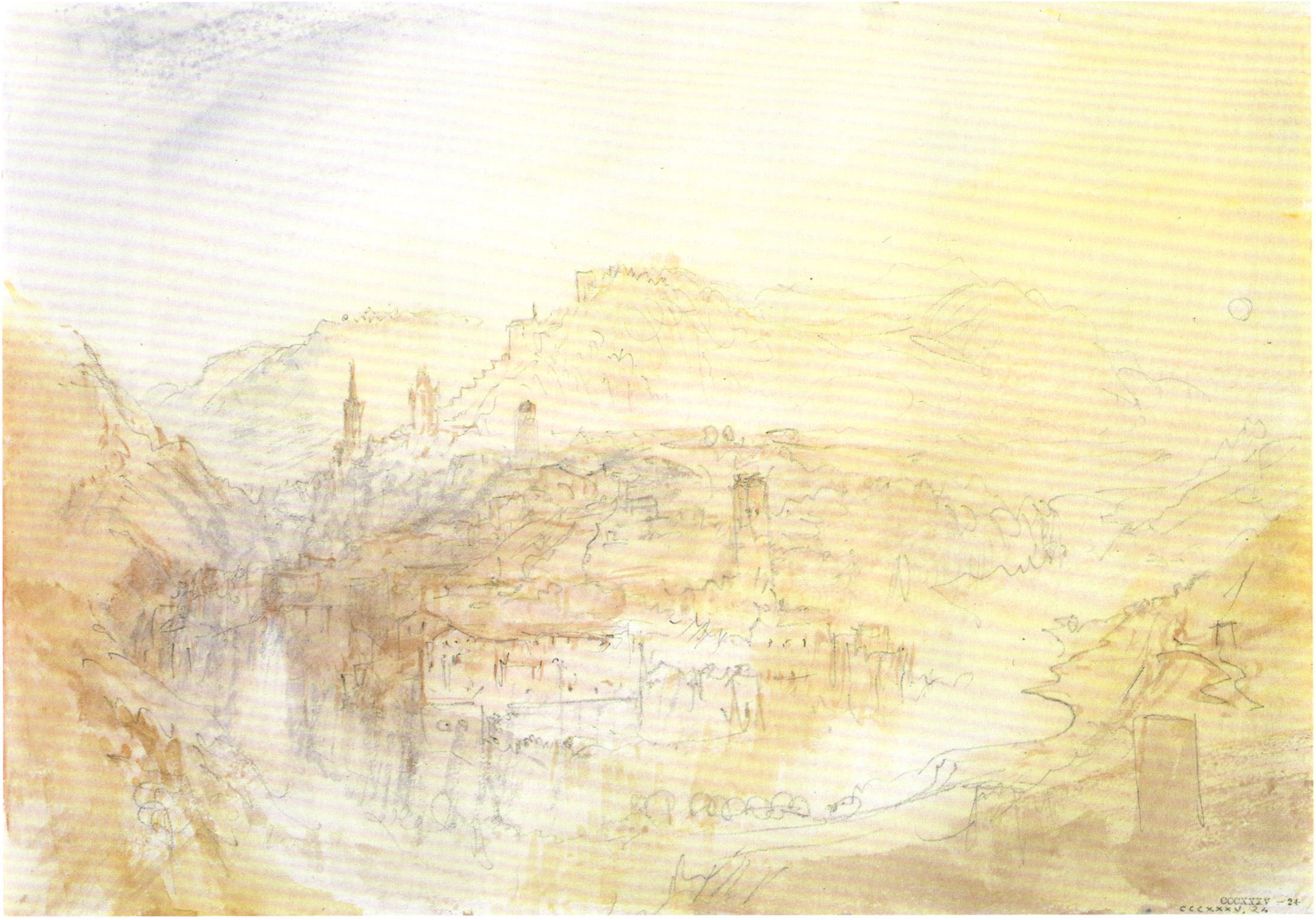

84 [Untitled]

Baden, from the North 1844
Pencil and watercolour 229 × 325 (9 × 12 13/16)
TB CCCXXXV 24 D33564
EXH: NG (49) [NB: Finberg 1909, p.1161, also lists TB CCCLII 17 as NG (49)]
LIT: *Works*, XIII, pp.221, 372, 610, as 'Fribourg'; *R on P*, p.118; Butlin 1962, pp.76–7, where the work reproduced to accompany the comments republished here was TB CCCLII 17 (see above for an explanation of this confusion); A.Wilton, *Turner Watercolours in the Clore Gallery*, 2nd ed., 1988, pp.140–1, pl.63 as 'Baden, Switzerland, 1841'; Hayman 1990, p.44, repr.

Walking a little nearer the town towards those terraces, we turn back, and looking down the river, see the sunset. The ease, power, and value of the pencil lines which trace the river shore, and the quantity of sunlight which is got through the golden colour almost at a dash, by the gradation to the white at the lower shore, renders this one of the most curious drawings in the series.

Turner's pencil record of the panoramic view over Baden

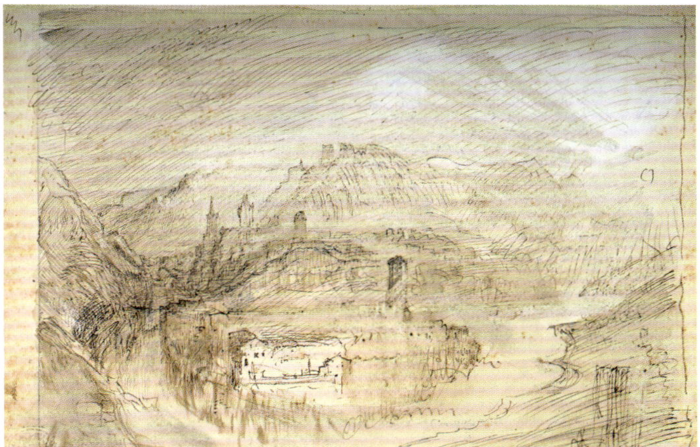

fig.38 John Ruskin, 'Baden, from the North' after J.M.W. Turner *c*.1857–8, ink and wash. *The Education Trust Ltd, Ruskin Galleries, Bembridge School, Isle of Wight*

from the opposite side of the river is given greater substance by the wash of warm yellow watercolour which unifies his design, a characteristic device in many of his late works. The raised viewpoint adopted here, and in the other views of Baden (cat.no.83 and TB CCCXLIX 25), is another feature common to many of the final watercolours, and is only distantly reminiscent of the fact-finding views of earlier topographers. Ruskin made a copy of this composition in pen and ink, most probably as an *aide memoire* to assist his identification of the town during his travels in 1858 (Bembridge 1573; fig.38). Alternatively, he may have depended on the copies of the Baden subjects by William Ward (1829–1908), now in the collection of the Fogg Art Museum at Harvard (1970.66 and 1970.67; the latter derives from this watercolour). Ward was a talented copyist, who worked as an assistant to Ruskin at the National Gallery during the years that the Bequest was being prepared for public display.

85 [Untitled]

Baden, from the South-east 1844
Pencil and watercolour, with pen 228 × 325 ($9 \times 12\frac{13}{16}$)
TB CCCXLIX 14 D35138

EXH: NG (85); Berne 1947–8 (100); Tate Gallery 1959–65; Zurich 1976–7 (90); Tate Gallery 1993 (35, repr. p.50)
LIT: *Works*, XIII, pp.222, 372, 611; *R on P*, p.119 as 'Baden (Switzerland), looking North'; Finberg 1910, repr. pl.LXXVI, opp. p.149; M. Kitson, *J.M.W. Turner*, 1964, repr. p.70; R. Upstone, 'Some Identified Views of Baden, Switzerland Dating from 1802, and 1843 or 1844', *Turner Studies*, vol.9, no.2, 1989, pp.57–60, repr. p.60; Hayman 1990, p.43, repr.

We arrive at the town, but, before entering it, walk a little way to the other side of the bridge gate, in order to sketch its towers in their gathered group under the fortress.

I do not know a more careful outline drawing of Turner than this.

In this view Turner delineates the chief architectural features of Baden. Nearest the viewer, to the right of the covered bridge, is the Landvogteischloss, formerly the governor's residence. A little way above the bridge is the spire of the church of Mariä Himmelfahrt und St Damian, with the decorated tower of the town gate, the Bruggerturm, to its right. Perched above the town are the ruins of Castle Stein, now largely destroyed. Before beginning this watercolour Turner had absorbed its indi-

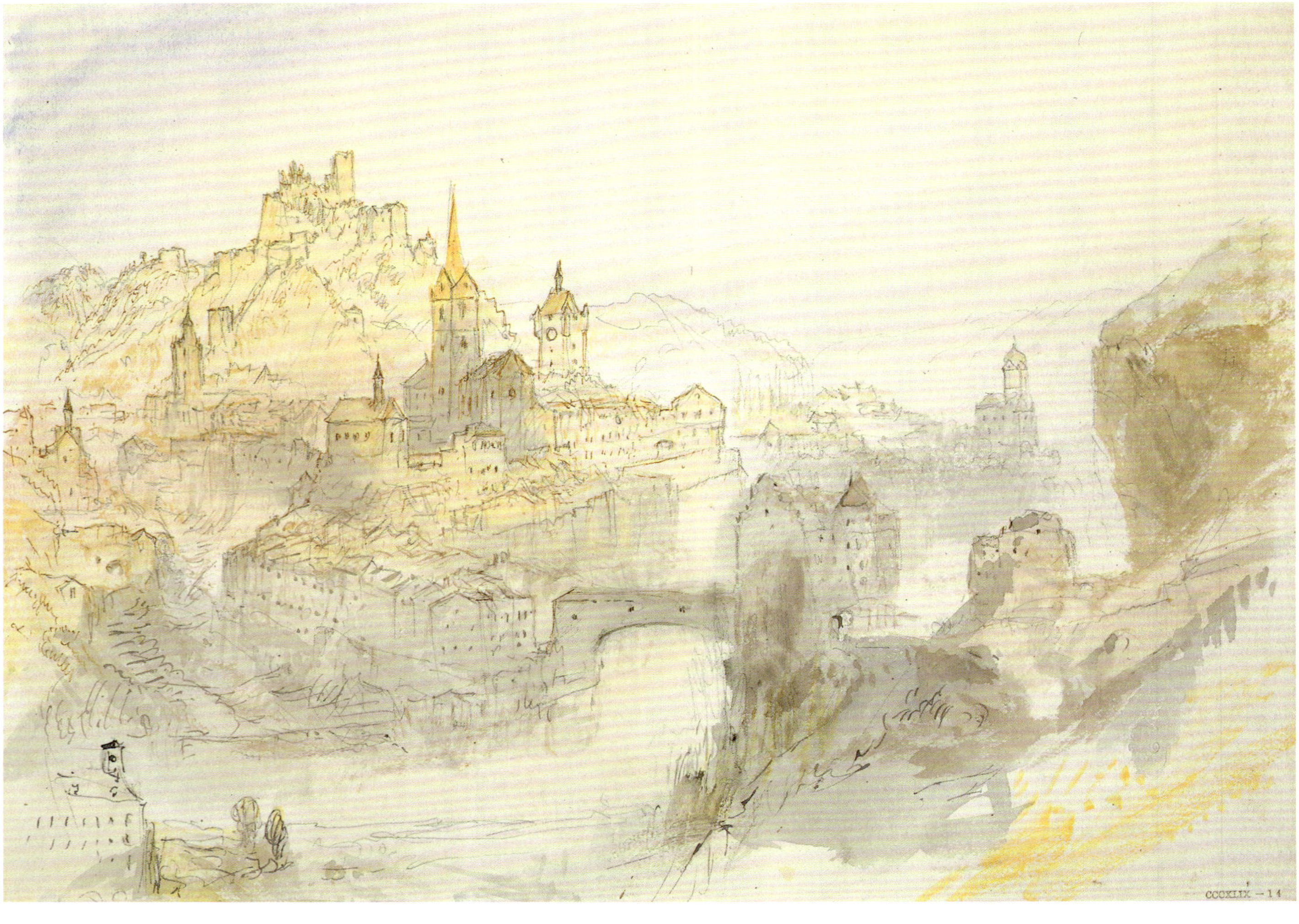

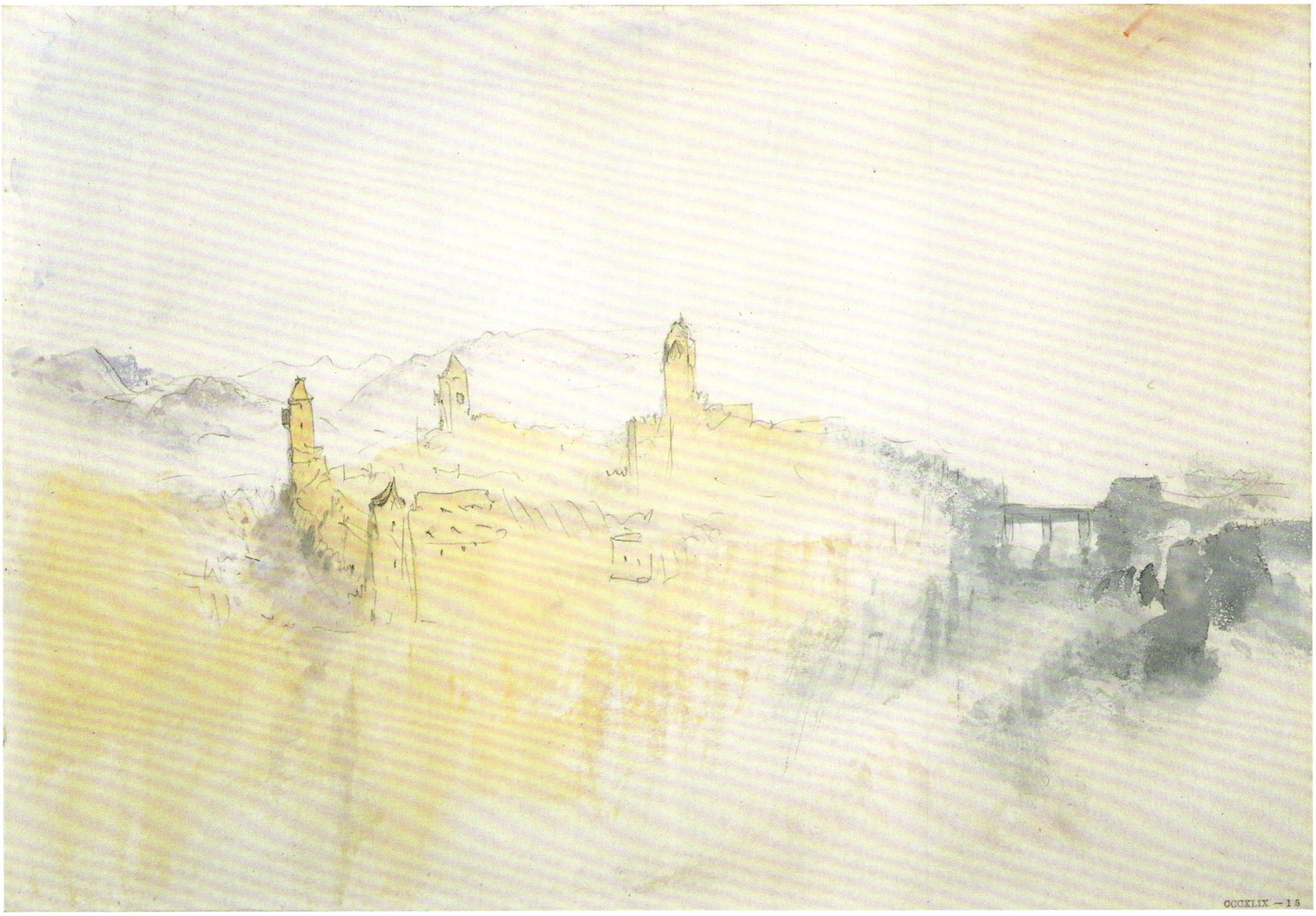

86

vidual details by making a group of thumbnail sketches, both in his sketchbooks and on loose sheets of paper (see the *Rhine and Switzerland* sketchbook, TB CCCXXV ff.27 verso, 34 verso; and TB CCCXLI 405–407). He also set out the composition on a slightly smaller piece of paper (TB CCCXLIV 432, Upstone 1989, fig.7). This thorough preparation helps to explain his ability to render here the essential structure of his chosen view so precisely.

86 [Untitled]

Rheinfelden, from the North-east 1844
Pencil and watercolour 229 × 328 (9 × 12 15/16)
Watermarked: J WHATMAN | 1844
Verso: Pencil sketch of ?Rheinfelden (2 bridges, 2 spires)
TB CCCXLIX 15 D35139
EXH: NG (86)
LIT: *Works*, XIII, pp.222, 372, 611; *R on P*, p.119 as 'Rheinfelden: Looking across the Rhine'

General view of the second of the two towns. The united breadth and tenderness of this slight suggestion of a noble subject, render it to my mind very interesting. The clear look of the distant mountain range is rare in Turner's work at this period; but the same clearness of effect occurs in the following series of studies, 87–89.

Turner visited Rheinfelden at the end of the summer of 1844. It was then little more than a small town, girt by medieval walls, with a fortress bridge by which travellers could cross the Rhine from Germany to Switzerland. The hot waters that have since turned it into a spa town were only discovered the year after Turner's visit. The following five views were among those which Ruskin could not identify at the time he was writing this catalogue. However, in May 1858 he spent a week at Rheinfelden sketching and making daguerreotypes of the buildings featured in Turner's watercolours. He wrote to his father on 22 May:

> If you want to see where I am, just call at the National Gallery as soon as you go back to town; I fancy you will be back before I leave; and ask

Wornum to let you look at the frames Nos. 86, 87, 88, 89, 90; they are all very like except only that the town, which Turner has made about the size of Strasburg, consists of one street and a few lanes, and what he has drawn as mountains are only the wooded Jura, but pretty in shape ... the grey walls above covered with ivy, and with all their towers yet unfallen. You will see them in Turner's sketches. [*Works*, VII, p.xxix; see also his subsequent letter to Mrs Hewitt, 22 May 1858, Hayman 1982, p.176]

Ruskin placed this evanescent watercolour of the town as the first of the group, but it is more probable that Turner did not embark on this kind of study until after he had become familiar with the architectural motifs in the view. The three towers at the left here are part of the old walls surrounding the town: the nearest is the Messerturm, above which is the Storchennestturm, and in the distance is the Obertortum.

87 [Untitled]

Rheinfelden, from the North-west 1844
Pencil and watercolour, with pen 229 × 329 (9 × 13)
Inscribed, lower left: '[?Lough]'
Watermarked: J WHATMAN | 1844
TB CCCXLIX 16 D35140
EXH: NG (87)
LIT: *Works*, VII, pp.436–7, repr. from an engraving by J.H. Le Keux, pl.82 as 'The Nets in the Rapids' (top); XIII, pp.222, 372, 611; *R on P*, p.119 as 'Rheinfelden, looking up the Rhine'; Hayman 1990, p.114, repr.

The same town, from the other side of its bridge gate. Nobly composed. Note the use of the distant grey mountain range in binding the white houses together into a mass.

As well as this group of watercolours, Turner recorded his impressions of Rheinfelden in the *Rhine and Switzerland* sketchbook (TB CCCXXV f.39 verso). It is apparent that he was attracted by the irregular forms of the covered bridge, which had tremendous appeal as a picturesque sketching subject. At the southern end of the bridge are the ruins of the castle of Stein, which were razed by the

87

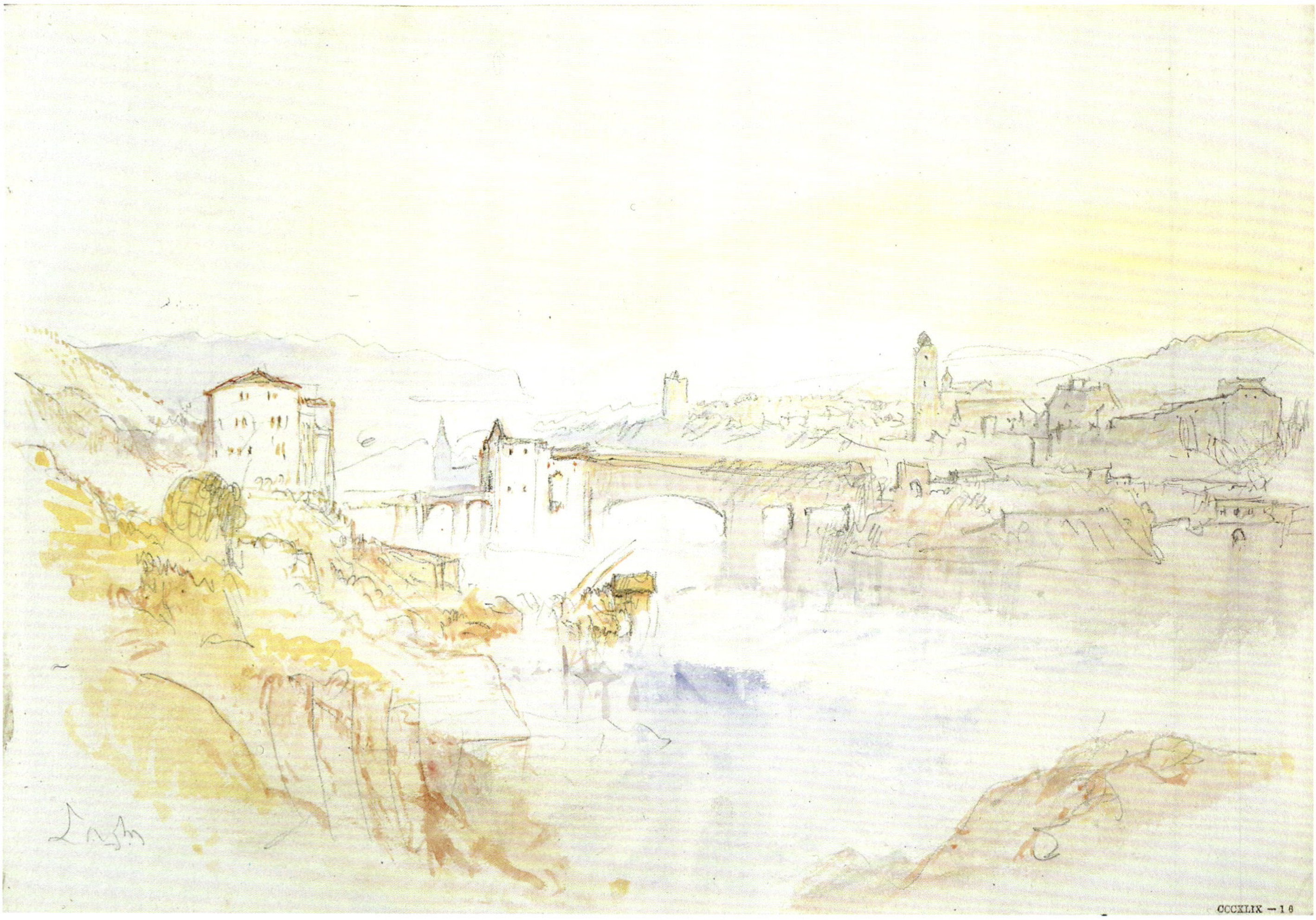

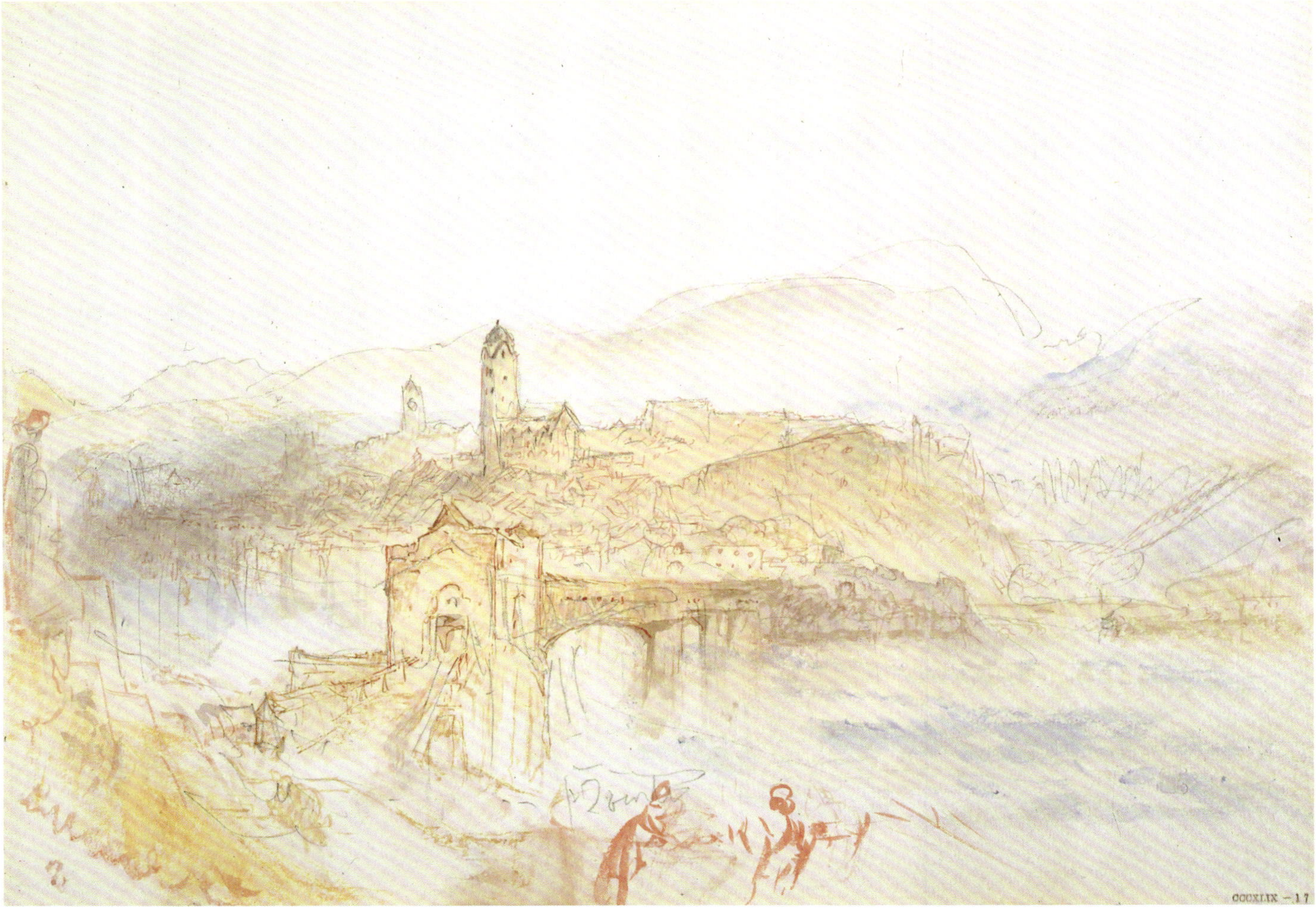

army of the Swiss Confederacy in the fifteenth century. The other architectural feature in all the views of Rheinfelden is the tower of the late Gothic church of St Martin. As part of his research into Turner's sketching habits, Ruskin made his own drawings from 'every side which Turner had drawn it, giving every detail with servile accuracy, so as to show the exact modifications he made as he composed his subjects' (p.20, fig.11). Two of these appeared in volume five of *Modern Painters* (pls. 83 and 84), where he also used engravings by J. Le Keux of this watercolour and cat.no.89 to 'give an idea of the way [Turner] used to walk round a place, taking sketch after sketch of its aspects, from every point or half-point of the compass' (*Works*, VII, p.436).

88 [Untitled]

Rheinfelden, from the North 1844
Pencil and watercolour, with pen 229 × 330 (9 × 13)
Inscribed, beside figures, '[?2 Gents]'
Watermarked: J WHATMAN | 1844
Verso: two pencil sketches of Rheinfelden
TB CCCXLIX 17 D35141
EXH: NG (88); Berne 1947–8 (101); Tate Gallery 1990
LIT: *Works*, XIII, pp.222, 372, 611; *R on P*, p.119 as 'Rheinfelden, from the end of the Bridge'

The same town from the approach to the bridge. A beautiful instance of serpentine continuity in composition; beginning with the red figures, the line of it winds over the bridge, back to the left in the town, up to the right by the first wall – then away to the left down into the dark shadow of the river, and returns up to the right along the mountain range, to their utmost summit. Hide the red figures, which are added to the serpent to form its head, and see how the composition loses.

89 [Untitled]

Rheinfelden, from the North-west 1844
Pencil and watercolour, with pen 228 × 330 (9 × 13)
Watermarked: J WHATMAN | 1844
TB CCCXLIX 18 D35142
EXH: NG (89)
LIT: *Works*, VII, pp.436–7, repr. from an engraving by J.H. Le Keux, pl.82 as 'The Nets in the Rapids' (bottom); XIII, pp.222–3, 372, 611; *R on P*, pp.119–20 as 'Rheinfelden, the covered bridge'; Hayman 1990, p.114, repr.

Exquisitely beautiful. A separate study of the little fishing house which occurs in the great view, No.87.

The piece of building on the left, between the bridges, is peculiarly massive and grand.

From his fieldwork Ruskin discovered that in this watercolour Turner had exaggerated the size of the fishing hut to suggest something of the force of the rapids on either side of the bridge; the real scale of the little structure is evident in Ruskin's own drawing of the scene (*Works*, VII, pl.83) and in one of the daguerreotypes made for him by Frederick Crawley (Hayman 1990, p.117). Ruskin considered that Turner often undertook this kind of distortion to throw emphasis on a particular part of his composition, in this case the garrison on the bridge. His footnote on this watercolour in *Modern Painters* noted that 'the modifications of form in the tower itself are all skilful and majestic in the highest degree. The throwing the whole of it higher than the bridge, taking the peak from its gable on the left, and adding the little roof-window in the centre, make it a perfectly noble mass instead of a broken and common one' (*Works*, VII, pp.436–7).

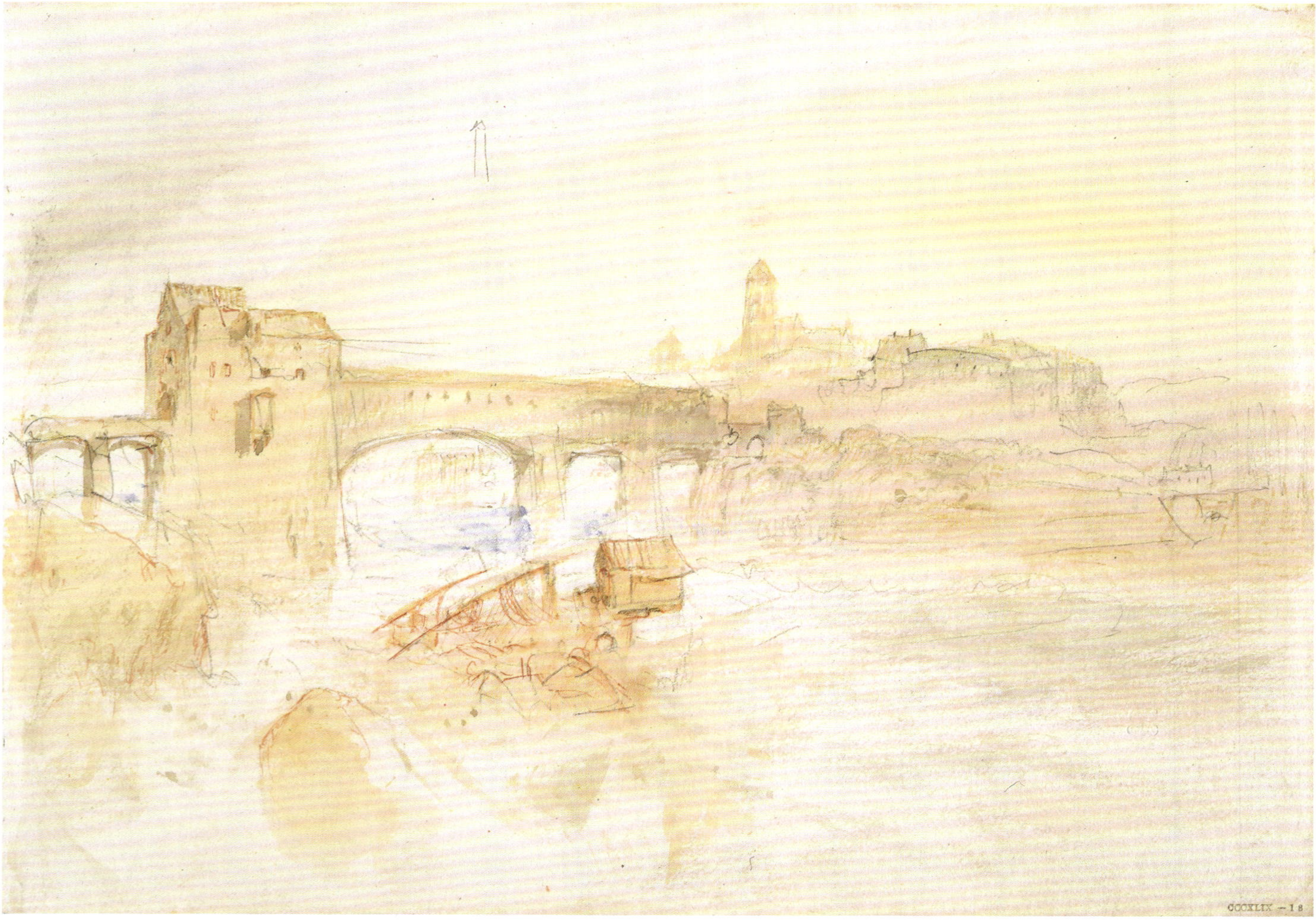

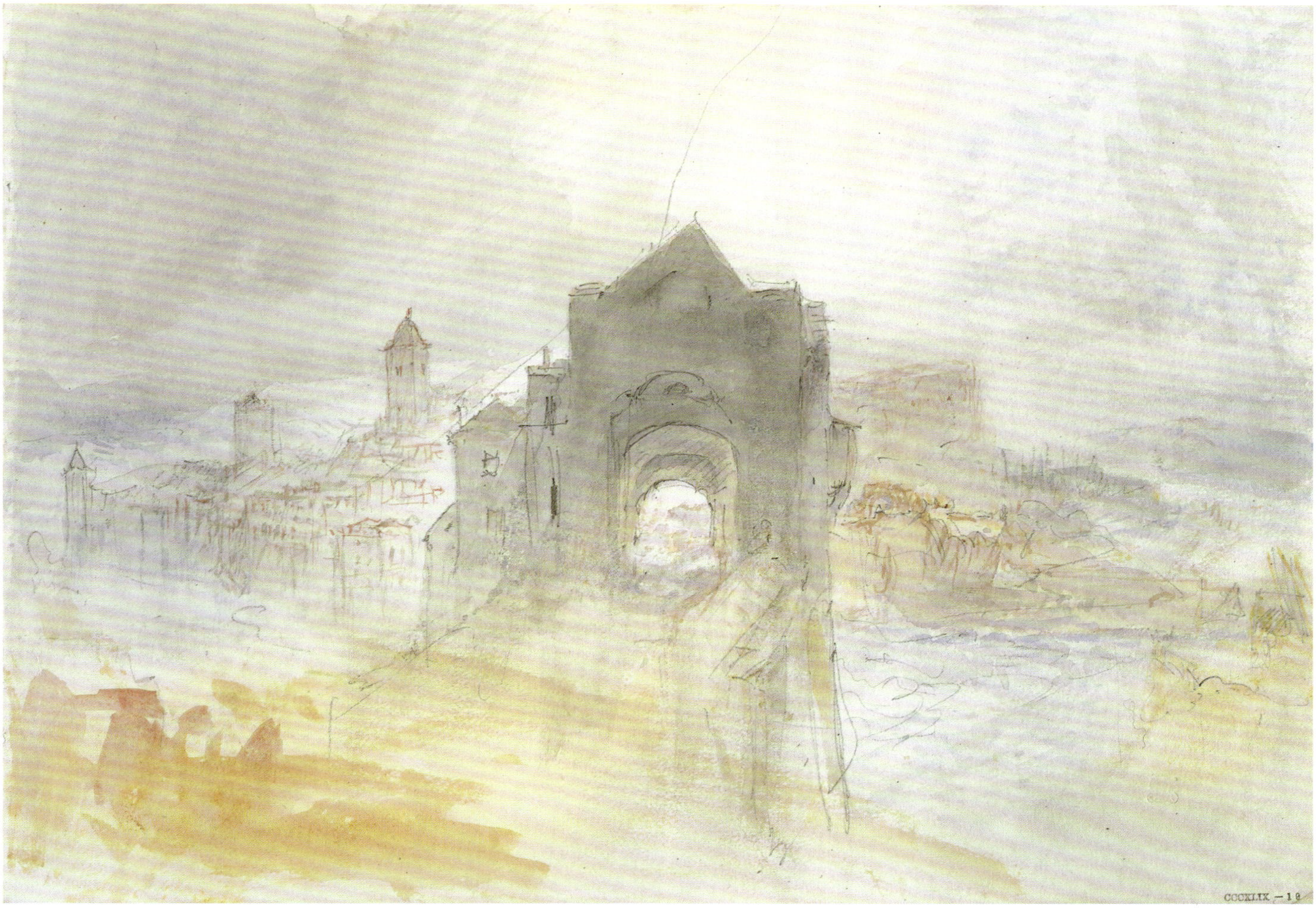

90 [Untitled]

Rheinfelden, the Covered Bridge, from the North 1844
Pencil and watercolour 229 × 330 (9 × 13)
Watermarked: J WHATMAN | 1844
TB CCCXLIX 19 D35143
EXH: NG (90); Berne 1947–8 (102)
LIT: *Works*, XIII, pp.223, 372, 611; *R on P*, p.120, as 'Rheinfelden: Entrance to the Covered Bridge'

Entrance to the town over the bridge. I have only framed it as a completion of the series of views of this city. It is a thoroughly bad sketch (for Turner); every way slovenly and substanceless.

Although Ruskin was dismissive of this subject, he was nevertheless sufficiently fascinated by Turner's work at Rheinfelden to commission two daguerreotypes of this part of the bridge (Bembridge, Daguerreotypes nos.120, 121; see p.20, fig.10).

91 Lausanne. The valley between the lower and higher towns

Lausanne: From the West 1841
Pencil and watercolour, with pen 235 × 331 ($9\frac{1}{4} \times 13\frac{1}{16}$)
Verso: watercolour sketch of the view across Lake Geneva towards the Dent d'Oche (see also cat.nos.92 verso, 93 verso, 94 verso, 95, 100)
TB CCCXXXIV 3 D33527
EXH: NG (91); Zurich 1976–7 (46); Tate Gallery 1983; Melbourne 1985; Tate Gallery 1992–3 (107, repr. p.81)
LIT: *Works*, XIII, pp.223, 372, 612; *R on P*, p.120 as 'Lausanne, looking East'; Wedmore 1900, p.359; Wilton 1982, p.63, pl.90

Careful and beautiful; and very characteristic of Turner's way of getting views of things which nobody else would have thought of. The foreground appears to be one of the narrow paths through the vineyards, – steps on the right going down to other terraces. The green hill beyond is the ridge which the Geneva road descends, between two rows of trees which Turner has carefully indicated. Beyond this, again, is the blue outline of the Dent d'Oches on the other side of the lake. The character of the quaint Swiss roof of the cathedral tower is admirably rendered on the left.

Turner made a substantial group of watercolours while at Lausanne in 1841. He had also paused there five years before during a tour of the Alps with his friend H.A.J. Munro of Novar. On that visit he had largely confined his observations to pencil sketches of the Cathedral of Notre-Dame and the Château St-Maire, as seen from the north and east (TB CCXCIII ff.45 verso–49, 52–53). In the intervening years work had begun on the Grand-Pont, the viaduct that spans the valley between the church of St-François (on the right in this watercolour) and that of St-Laurent. It may have been this new feature that encouraged Turner to make more distant views from the western side of the town in 1841, and especially from the valley itself (see also cat.nos.93 and 94).

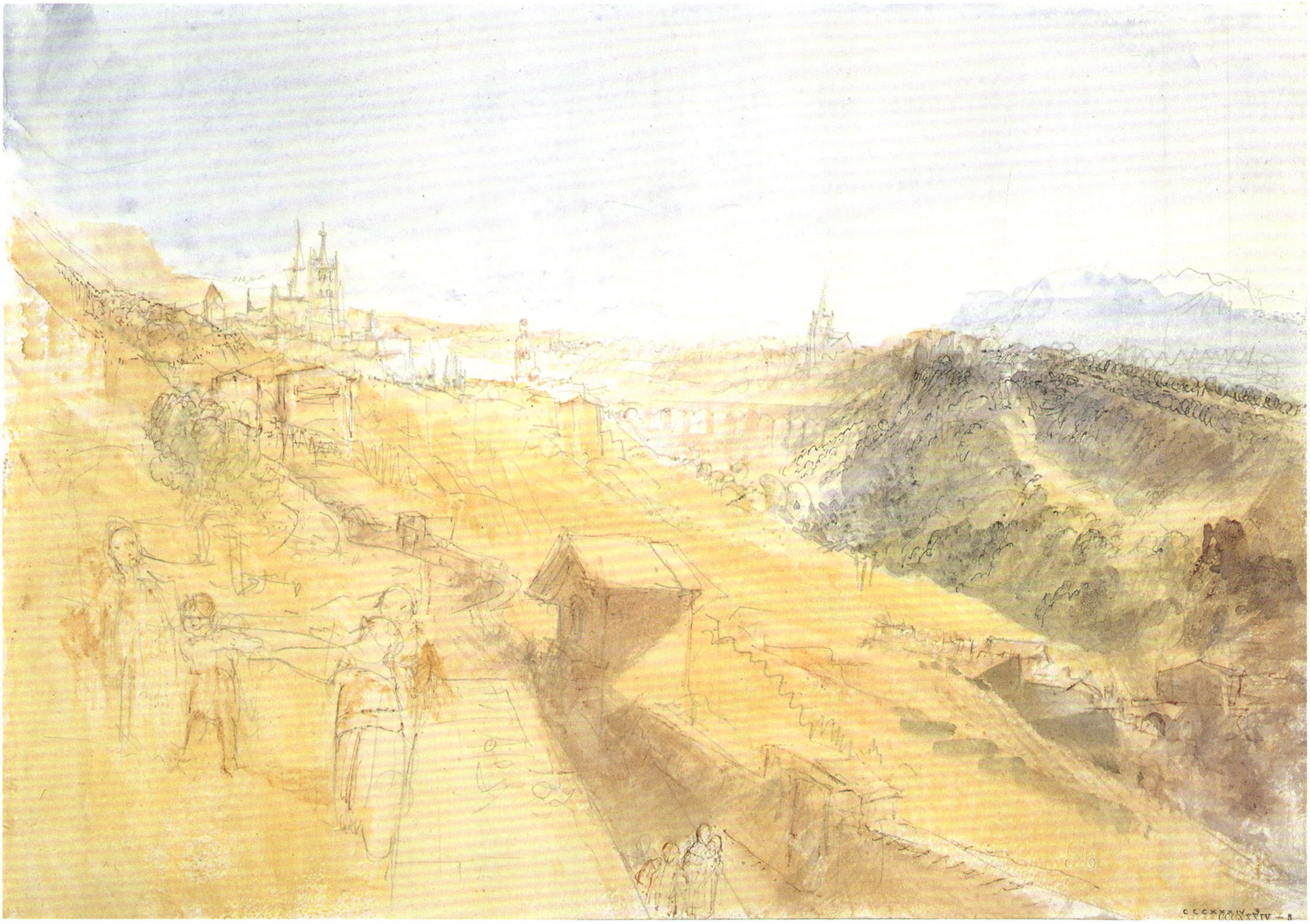

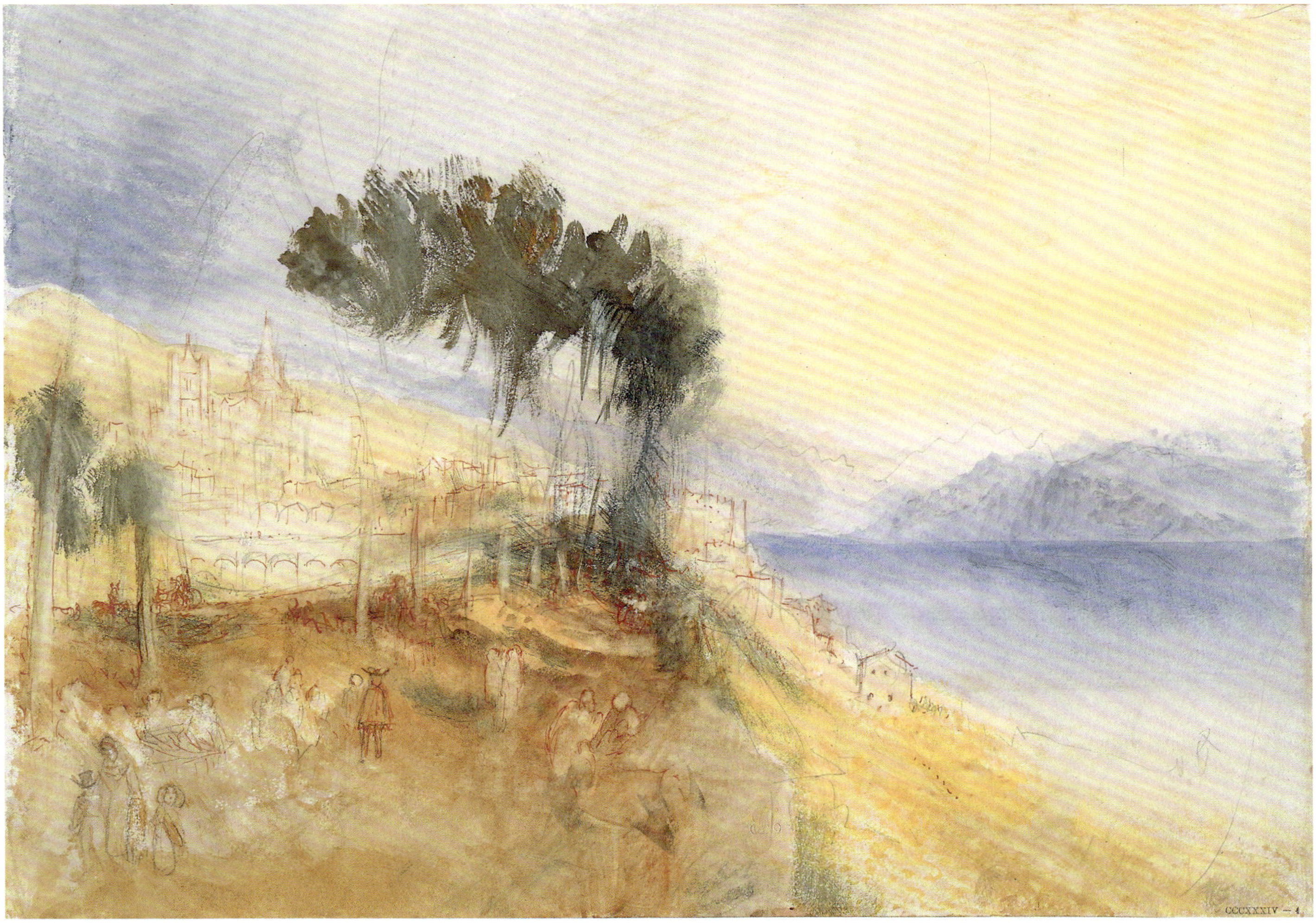

92 The Promenade of Lausanne

Lausanne and Lake Geneva, from the West 1841
Pencil and watercolour, with pen 236 × 334 (9 5/16 × 13 3/16)
Watermarked: J WHATMAN | TURKEY MILL
Verso: watercolour sketch of the view from above Lausanne, looking across to the Dent d'Oche (see also cat.no.91)
TB CCCXXXIV 4 D33528
EXH: NG (92); National Gallery 1936–9; Tate Gallery 1959–65; Cleveland 1977–8 (64, repr. p.83); Athens, Georgia 1982 (83); Tate Gallery 1983; Melbourne 1985; Tate Gallery 1987; Tate Gallery 1992b (92, repr. pp.70, 123)
LIT: *Works*, XIII, pp.223, 372, 612; *R on P*, p.120 as 'Lausanne, looking East from the Terrace'; Russell and Wilton 1976, p.85; Wilton 1982, p.63, pl.91

We have here the avenue itself which was in the distance of the last subject, – a carriage and four driving down on the left, one postillion only, in the foreign fashion; the cathedral is seen through the trees, and the outline line of the Mont Combin in the distance beyond the lake. The walk in front of us is one of the favourite resorts of the townspeople; a nurse with two children is sketched on the left.

A number of Turner's watercolours of Lausanne are enlivened by the ghostly forms of figures promenading along the various terraces. The tree-lined avenue in this view is one that John Murray praised in his guidebook: 'Partial and pleasing glimpses of the lake are obtained from the terraces within the town, and from that of Montbenon, just outside the walls, on the way to Geneva' (Murray 1838, p.145). Turner adopted a golden colouring in this work, suggesting the watery light of late afternoon. After he had indicated the attenuated forms of the trees, he rapidly wiped his almost dry brush across the centre of the design to produce a blurred cloud representing the leafy tree-tops.

93 The Valley of Lausanne

Lausanne, from the West 1841
Pencil and watercolour, with pen 233 × 332 ($9^{3}/_{16} \times 13^{1}/_{16}$)
Inscribed, top right, 'Road'
Verso: watercolour sketch from above Lausanne, looking across to the Dent d'Oche (see also cat.no.91)
TB CCCXXXV 22 D33562
EXH: NG (50); San Marino 1951–2 (Frame 30); Athens, Georgia 1982 (84)
LIT: *Works*, XIII, pp.224, 372 as 'Lausanne', 610 as 'Fribourg'; *R on P*, p.108; Russell and Wilton 1976, pp.82–3 as 'Fribourg'

Included in the series chiefly to show the different views which Turner would take of the same subject at different times; it is far inferior, as a study, to the Nos.91 and 94. The foreground, especially the white object in it, is wholly unintelligible.

Both this and cat.no.94 are views from the valley below Montbenon looking back towards Lausanne; another, slighter impression of this view is TB CCCXXXIV 8. A.J. Finberg catalogued this sheet as a page of the *Freiburg* sketchbook (TB CCCXXXV), but it almost certainly came originally from the same book as cat.nos.91–2, 94.

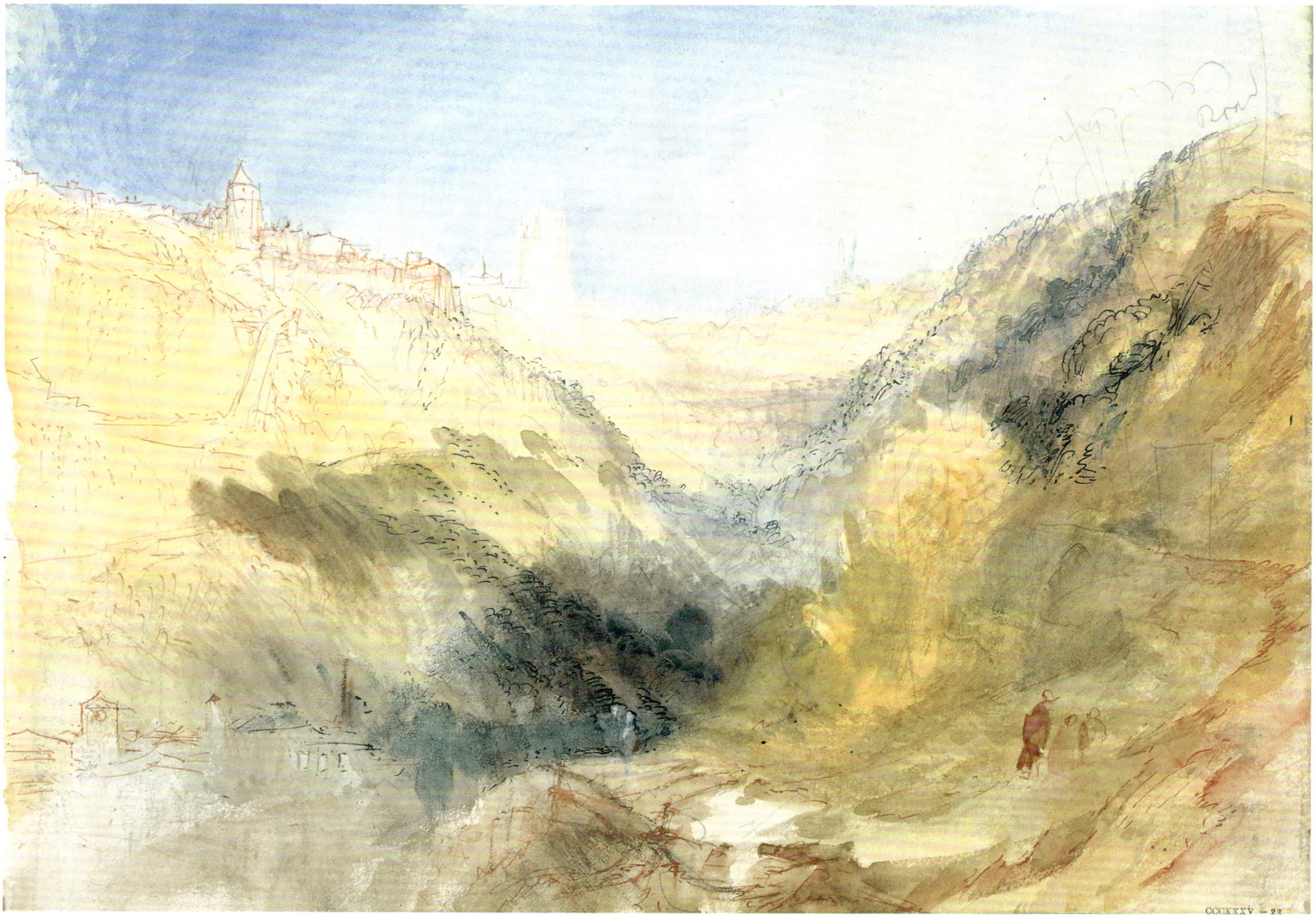

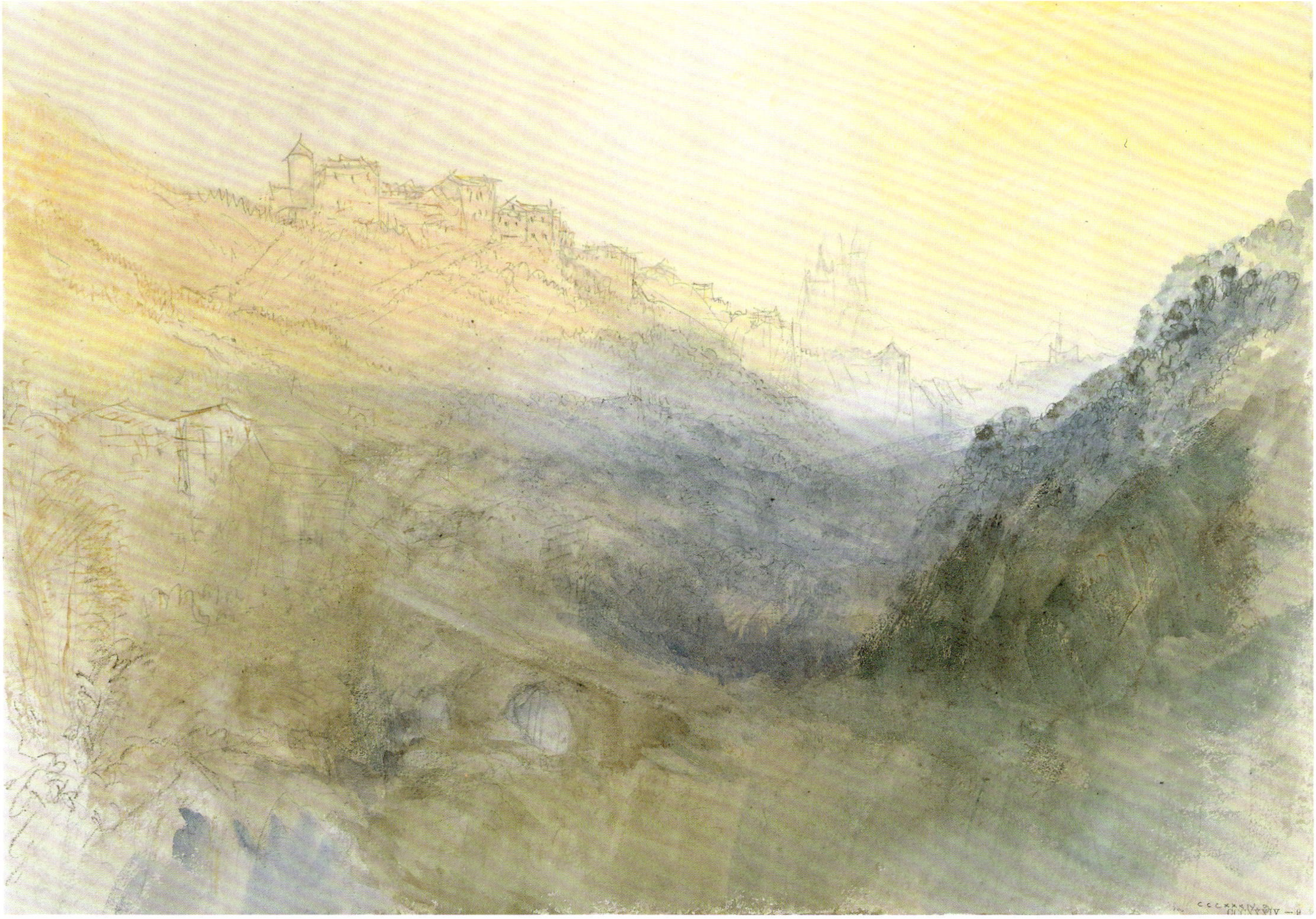

94 Lausanne

Lausanne, from the West: Sample Study 1841
Pencil and watercolour, with pen 235 × 332 (9¼ × 13$^{1}/_{16}$)
Verso: watercolour sketch of the view from above Lausanne (see also cat.no.91)
TB CCCXXXIV 9 D33533
EXH: NG (44)
LIT: *Works*, XIII, pp.224, 372, 610; Wedmore 1900, p.360

It draws towards evening as we wander about the ravine, and the cathedral towers fade in the tender light. We prepare to cross the bridge and to the higher town. Very beautiful; almost unique, in this series of sketches, for quietness of colour; its bank of purple and plumy trees, against the golden light, is drawn with great care and completion.

Like cat.no.93, this watercolour includes a group of buildings on the hill above which may include the Tour de l'Ale, part of the fourteenth-century fortifications. This sketch was one of those that Ruskin urged his father to acquire, should the possibility arise, shortly after Turner's death (see p.16, fig.6). Without the benefit of any form of reproduction, he was able to recall very precisely the sketch he had last seen ten years before. As well as making his own thumbnail outline of the buildings, he vividly remembered the sombre mood of 'purple and blue sunset – very misty' (Bradley 1955, p.112). It seems probable that Turner intended to make a finished drawing of this Lausanne subject in 1842. But in fact none of the sets of Swiss watercolours recorded by Ruskin included a view of the town. There are, however, four watercolours of Lausanne that are similar to the style of Turner's sample studies, and which may have been shown to his prospective clients (TB CCCLXIV 350 and W 1455, Whitworth Art Gallery, Manchester; W 1458, private collection (c/o Agnew's) and W 1459, private collection).

95 The Lake of Geneva and Dent d'Oche. By sunset: from above the town

Lake Geneva, with the Dent d'Oche, from above Lausanne
1841
Pencil and watercolour 235 × 338 ($9\frac{1}{4} \times 13\frac{5}{16}$)
Verso inscribed with lines of partly illegible poetry
TB CCCXXXIV 10 D33534
EXH: NG (95); Amsterdam 1936 (243); Paris 1937 (112); Tate Gallery 1959–65; Dresden 1972 (107); Lisbon 1973 (51, repr. p.131); Zurich 1976–7 (52); Cleveland 1977–8 (65, repr. p.84); Toronto 1980–1 (119, repr. p.95, pl.31); Tate Gallery 1987; Tate Gallery 1990; Tate Gallery 1993 (23, repr. p.28 and p.44)
LIT: *Works*, XIII, pp.224, 372, 612; *R on P*, p.121: Shanes 1990, pp.81–2 n.14

Out and out the worst sketch in the whole series; disgracefully careless and clumsy, but too beautiful in subject to be left out. Interesting also in its noticing of the long cypress-like lines of reflection, cast down so unaccountably from the crags. I am nearly certain Turner made the sketch on account of the curious echo which these reflections give to the cypresses.

Turner depicted the glassy surface of Lake Geneva, as seen from above Lausanne, on a number of the sheets which once formed the *Lausanne* sketchbook (see under cat.no.91 verso). Another watercolour sharing this viewpoint includes a slow procession towards the cypress-lined graveyard depicted here, and has long been referred to as 'Funeral at Lausanne' (TB CCCXXXIV 2). It has recently been suggested by Eric Shanes that all these views 'seem to show the view from the same spot and the artist has in each case therefore invented his foreground topography and activity' (Shanes 1990). Although Shanes is perhaps right to suspect that Turner 'saw a parallel between the final movements of daylight across a mountain-top and the ultimate progression of man', it is quite likely that Turner did actually make at least some of these views from a real cemetery. This was the cemetery of Pierre de Plain, which lay '2 miles out of Lausanne, beyond the Calvaire, on the Berne road' (Murray 1838, p.146). If we recall that Turner spent some of his adolescent years painting scenery for the theatre, it becomes clear that this particular graveyard would have been of interest, since it contained the tomb of John Philip Kemble (1757–1823), the great actor, whom he may have

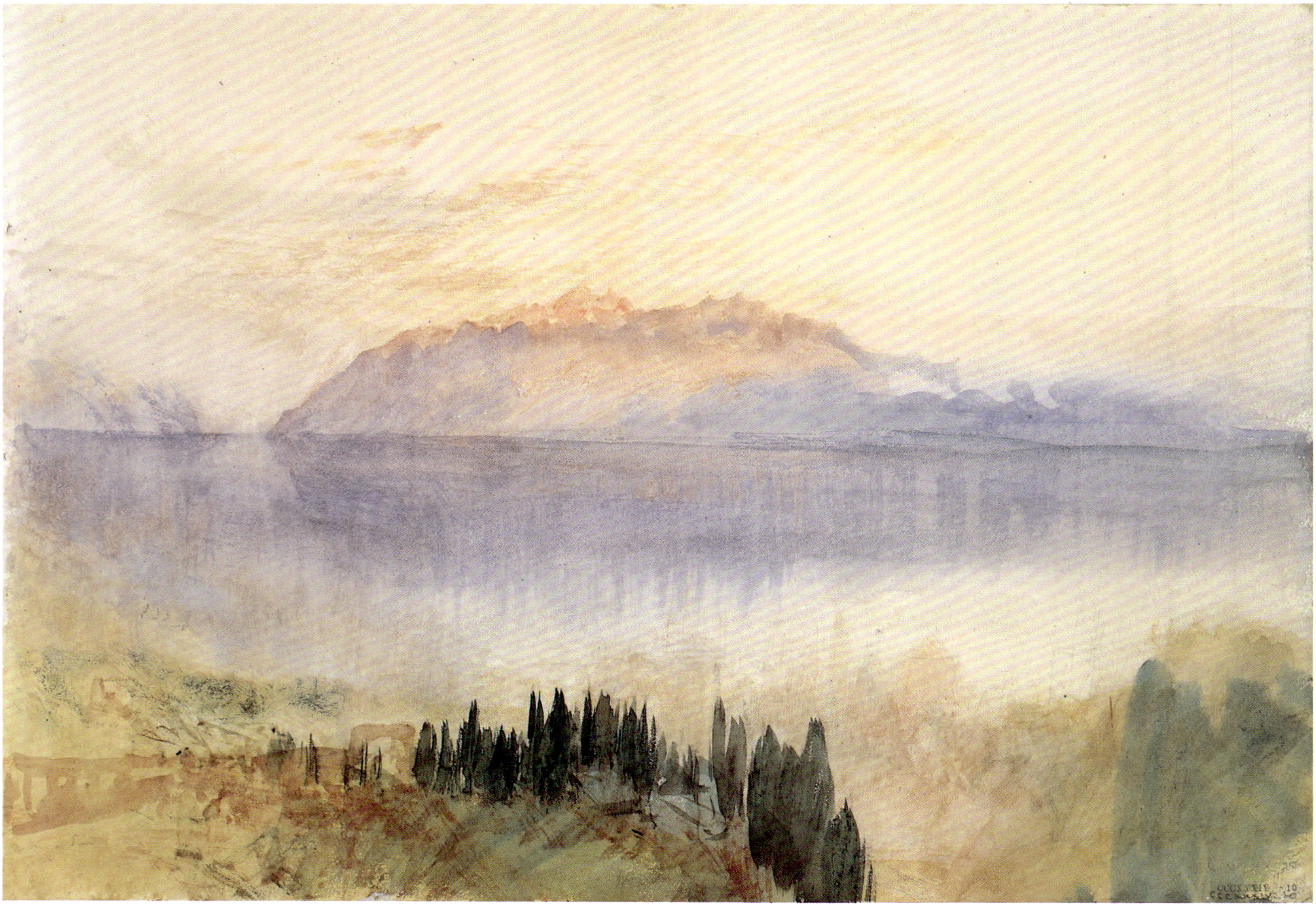

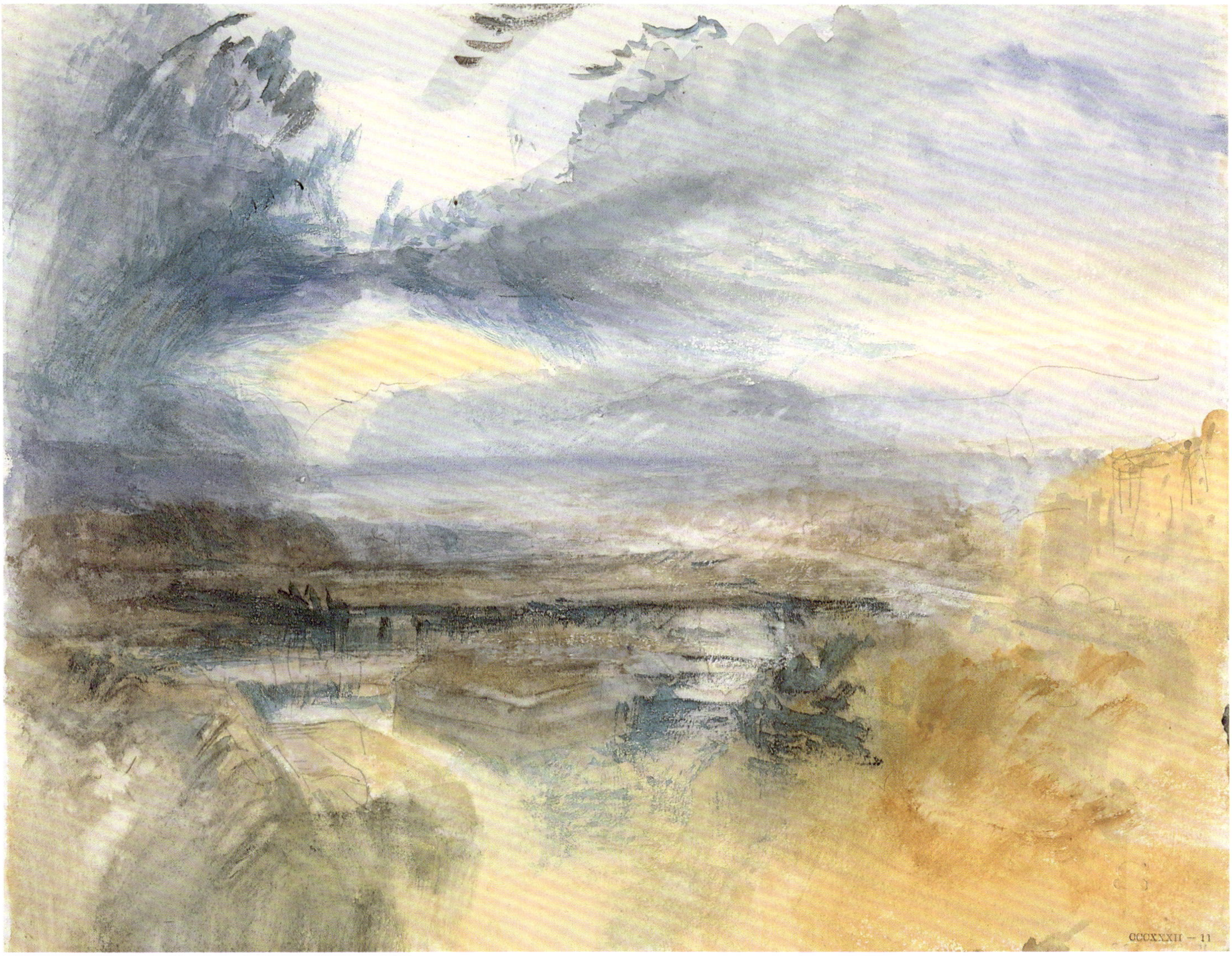

known through his friend Sir Francis Bourgeois (1756–1811). Turner was perhaps referring to Kemble in the lines he inscribed on the verso of this sheet, which contain the phrase 'For how I mark thy tomb'.

96 The Ramparts of Geneva. From the upper town

Geneva: Fort l'Ecluse Seen in the Distance from the Old Walls 1841
Pencil, watercolour and gouache 229 × 292 (9 × 11½)
Watermarked: J WHATMAN | TURKEY MILL | 1841
TB CCCXXXII 11 D33481
EXH: NG (42); New York 1966 (89, repr. p.48); Dresden 1972 (104); Lisbon 1973 (48, repr. p.125); British Museum 1975 (269, repr. p.152); Zurich 1976–7 (51, repr. p.21); Tate Gallery 1977–8
LIT: *Works*, XIII, pp.224–5, pp.372, 610; *R on P*, p.105; Wedmore 1900, p.361; Serota 1970, p.133; Russell and Wilton 1976, p.120

These fortifications are now destroyed, and this sketch is valuable as a record of the lovely effect which the clear, green, and living water of the Rhone gave to the old moats; its strong current being carried through all of them on this side of the city. The mountain opening in the distance is that through the Jura, at Fort l'Ecluse, where the Rhone escapes from the valley of Geneva.

Entirely majestic and beautiful in conception. The shadow of the clouds on the Jura, and the rosy light on the hills behind their darkness, to the right, are peculiarly true and lovely. Observe how the bastion in the centre is drawn, owing its whole material existence to little more than the one gleam of light on its angle, obtained by a touch of the brush, through the wet colour, running a little of the tint to its edge, in a dark line which rounds the top of the wall.

Even though there are several watercolours and drawings by Turner of Geneva and Berne, Ruskin's dislike of the recent developments in both cities led him to exclude them from his 1857 catalogue (with this exception). He also chose not to include them in his attempt to document Swiss history. He wrote to Lady Trevelyan that he hoped 'that Berne and Geneva will be properly humiliated at being left out of the list, as too much spoiled to be worth notice' (*Works*, XXXVI, p.244). Ruskin identified this extravagantly coloured impression as the view to the west from Geneva; even before the destruction of the eighteenth-century ramparts and bastions it must have been difficult to recognise the precise topography of Turner's watercolour. Another view over the fortifications, towards the lake, is TB CCCXXXII 15).

97 The Allée Blanche. From the foot of the Glacier de Miage

A Mountain Valley ?1843
Pencil and watercolour 243 × 300 (9⁹⁄₁₆ × 11⁷⁄₈)
TB CCCLXIV 276 D36124
EXH: NG (47); Toronto 1980–1 (98 as 'A Mountain Valley, ?1836', repr. p.175)
LIT: *Works*, XIII, pp.225, 372, 610; *R on P*, p.107 as 'The Allée Blanche, looking to the Col de la Seigne'

A noble drawing, though not much like the place, which I only recognise by the peculiar outlines on the right hand. But its exquisite gradations of colour, and the perfect expression of the retiring ridge which leads up to the left-hand peak, make this one of the best mountain drawings in the series.

Hide the touch of dark blue in the distance, and see what becomes of it all.

97

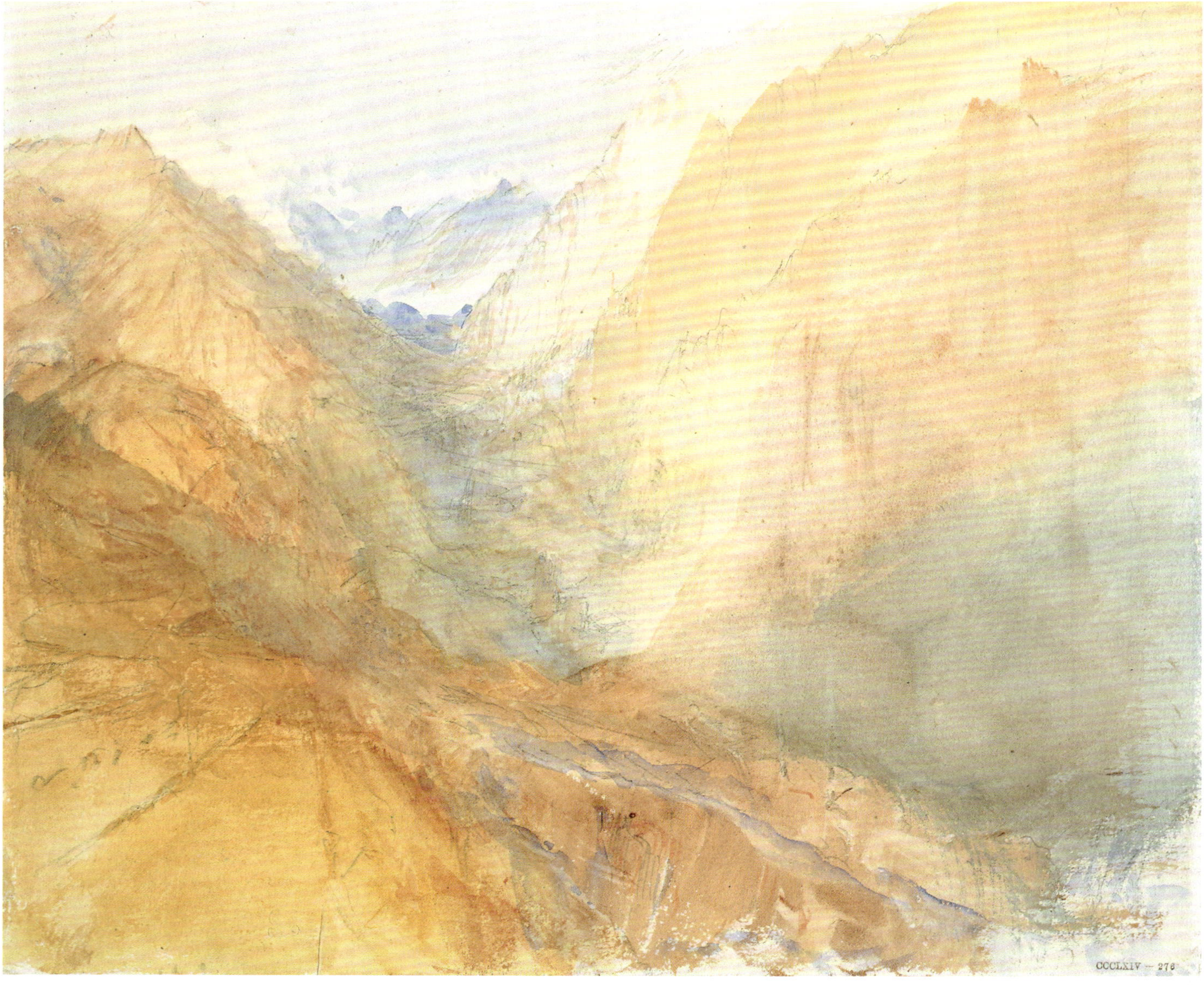

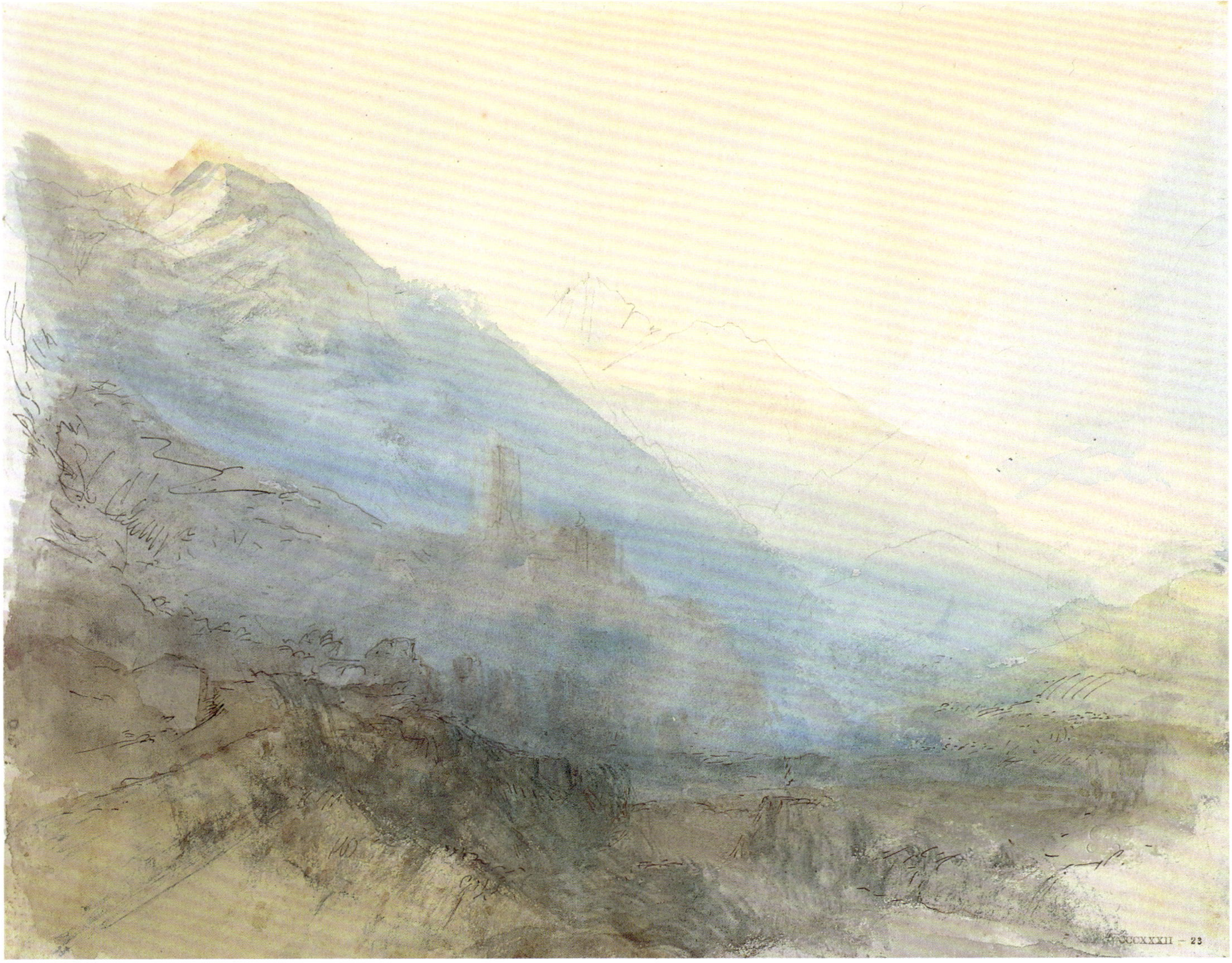

Ruskin considered this sketch to have been made on the same journey as cat.no.73. However, so far, neither subject has been satisfactorily identified. For Ruskin, this work must have seemed an unique and impressive composition. He noted in volume four of *Modern Painters* that generally 'Turner felt that, among these, highest hills, no serious or perfect work could be done; and although in one or two of his vignettes ... he showed his knowledge of them, his practice, in larger works, was always to treat the snowy mountains merely as a far-away white cloud, concentrating the interest of his pictures on nearer and more tractable objects' (*Works*, VI, pp.293–4).

98 Martigny

Martigny: The Castle of La Bâtiaz, from the South
c.1841–2
Pencil and watercolour, with pen 229 × 291 (9 × 11½)
TB CCCXXXII 23 D33493
EXH: NG (81); British Museum 1975–6 (274, repr. p.154); Copenhagen 1976 (ex cat.); Hamburg 1976 (112, repr. p.155); Zurich 1976–7 (54); Tate Gallery 1983; Melbourne 1985; Tate Gallery 1988; Tate Gallery 1990
LIT: *Works*, XIII, pp.225, 372, 611; *R on P*, p.117, as 'Martigny and Château'; Serota 1970, p.130; Wilton 1982, p.64, pl.95

So I believe, at least: but the pencil marks in the ruin are not so conclusive as I should like to have them.

The excessive haste with which the colour has been thrown on the sketch, not in the least coinciding with the pencil outlines, and yet the subtlety of the effects wrought as the wash was laid on, render this memorandum very interesting.

Turner is not known to have visited Martigny in either 1841 or 1842, the years in which he is most likely to have made this study. He first sketched the town, dominated by the castle of La Bâtiaz on his tour in 1802 (TB LXXIV 16, 87, V). Many years later he made a vignette of the castle for the 1830 edition of Samuel Rogers's poem *Italy*; this was, of course, the volume Ruskin received as an impressionable thirteen-year-old.

99 Vevay

Vevay: Looking South-east along the Shore of Lake Geneva
1841
Pencil and watercolour, with pen 229 × 293 (9 × 11 9/16)
Watermarked: J WHATMAN | TURKEY MILL | 1841
TB CCCXXXII 21 D33491

EXH: NG (46); Zurich 1976–7 (53); Tate Gallery 1977–8; Tate Gallery 1988; Tate Gallery 1990
LIT: *Works*, XIII, pp.226, 372, 610; *R on P*, pp.106–7; Wedmore 1900, p.362; Serota 1970, p.133

One is really provoked with Turner for not having completed the foreground of this lovely drawing, which most travellers in Switzerland will recognise with delight.

It is interesting to see how in putting in the red outlines, Turner always avoids his first pencilled ones. Thus he uses his outline of the roof, when he adds the crimson. The poplars in the distances are 'Old Vevay.'

In much the same way that Turner indicated the presence of large crowds as an organic lifeforce in his views of Zurich (cat.nos.21–2), he has here sketched a group of figures busy at the edge of the lake. By presenting human activity in such an indistinct way, Turner is able to unify his composition much more satisfactorily, while at the

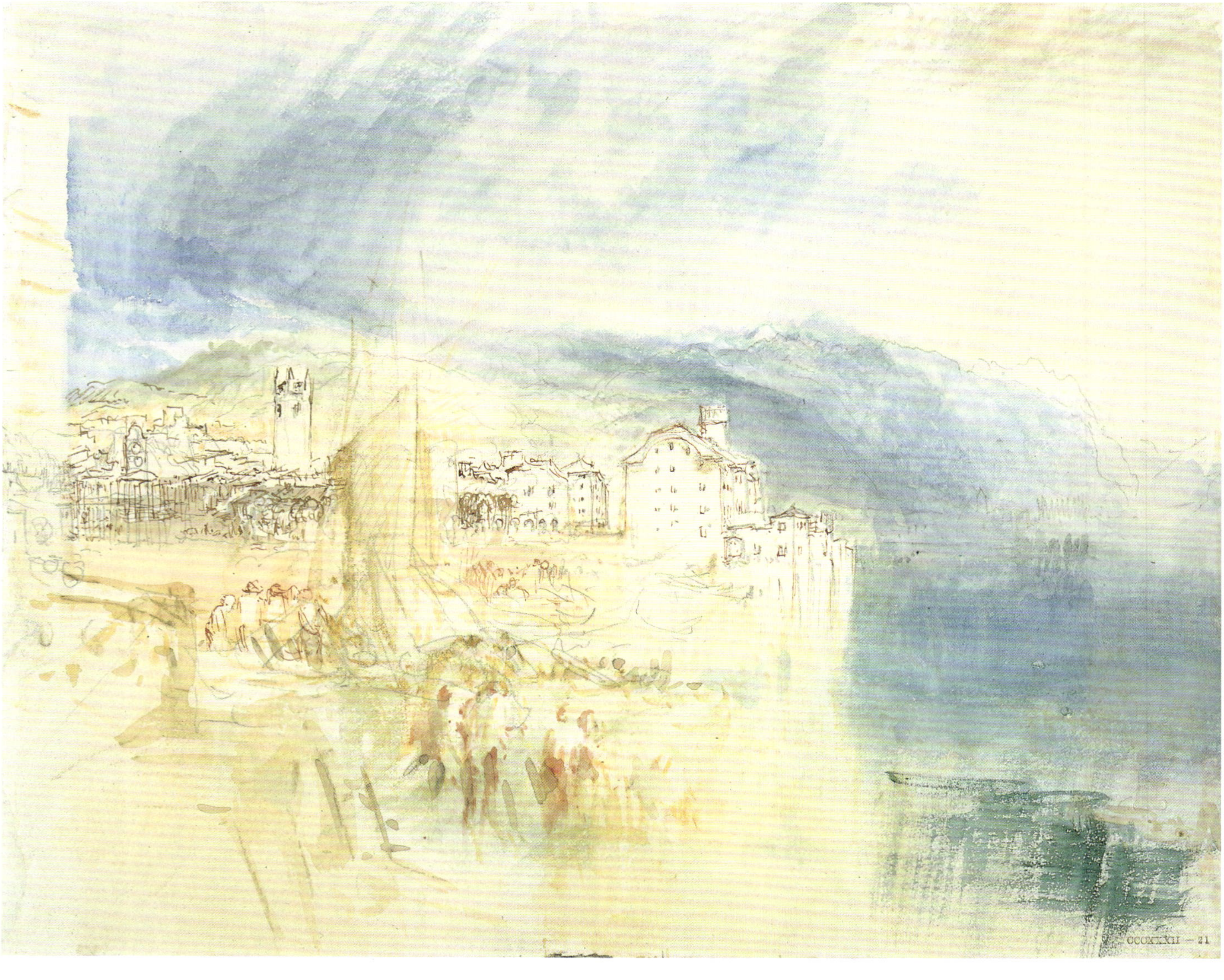

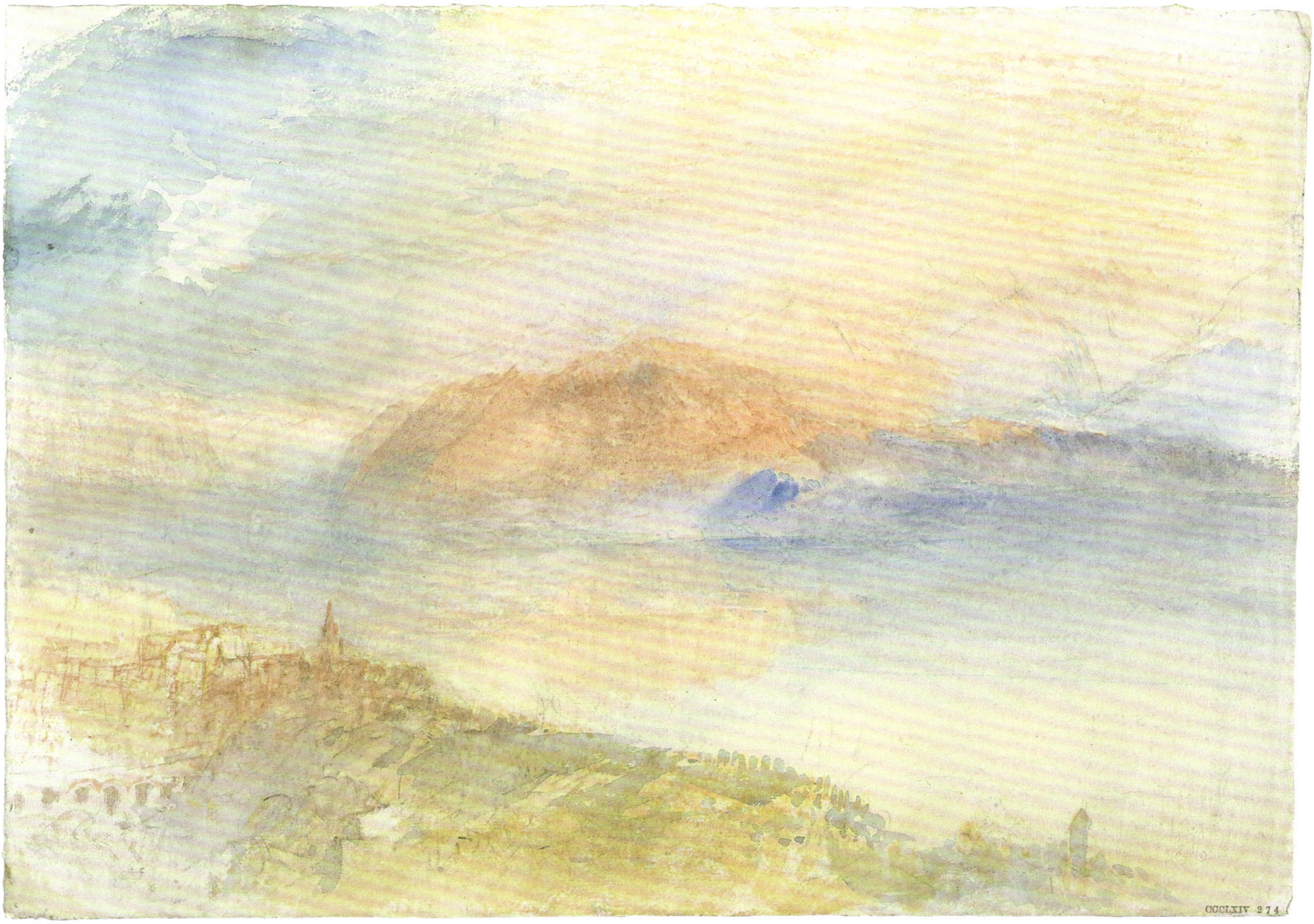

same time suggesting the connection between his figures and their surroundings. Many of the buildings depicted in this view can still be identified: the tower beside the sail is that of church of St-Martin, and to its left is the old Corn Exchange in the market place. Turner also made another view of Vevay from a slightly more distant spot (TB CCCXXXII 7).

100 The Lake of Geneva

The Lake of Geneva with the Dent d'Oche, from above Lausanne 1841
Pencil and watercolour 230 × 328 ($9^{1}/_{16}$ × $12^{15}/_{16}$)
TB CCCLXIV 274 D36122
EXH: NG (41); British Museum 1933b; Berne 1947–8 (82); Toronto 1980–1 (121, repr. p.187)
LIT: *Works*, XIII, pp.226, 372, 610; *R on P*, pp.104–5

We return to Lausanne, and take our places by the night diligence for France. The sun goes down as we ascend the hill above the town. We look back to the mountains of Savoy, under the last glow; and bid farewell to them.

As noted under cat.no.95, Turner repeatedly attempted to capture the view over Lake Geneva from above Lausanne. His watercolours mostly depict the Dent d'Oche, on the other side of the lake, by rosy sunset light. This was a view enjoyed by many other visitors to Lausanne in the nineteenth century, including James Fenimore Cooper (1789–1851), who remarked that it offered 'one of the grandest landscapes of this the noblest of all earthly regions' (Murray 1838, p.145).

Appendix I

The First Selection of Watercolours from the Turner Bequest, 1856

Ruskin was not the first to select and exhibit watercolours from the huge collection of works found in Turner's studio. A committee met at the National Gallery on 5 December 1856 in order to choose which works would be shown on screens between the windows of the Turner Gallery at Marlborough House. The members of the committee were Charles Lock Eastlake (Director), William Russell (one of the Trustees), Ralph Wornum (Keeper), and three of Turner's executors: H.A.J. Munro of Novar, Clarkson Stanfield and David Roberts. A report of the meeting was drawn up and presented at the Meeting of the Trustees on 15 December 1856 (National Gallery Archives).

The following works were selected and put on display at the end of January 1857. The group of 102 works remained on display until Ruskin's own arrangement of watercolours and sketches was made available to the public later that year.

Included in the list below are any comments recorded in the committee's report as to the means of mounting and framing the drawings.

1 Battle of Fort Bard, Val d'Aosta
TB LXXX G; W 399

2 Edinburgh from Carlton Hill
TB LX H; W 348

3 Funeral of Sir Thomas Lawrence
TB CCLXIII 344; W 521

As nos.1–3 were known to have been exhibited at the Royal Academy during Turner's lifetime, the committee recommended that they should be framed in the traditional manner, so that the drawing actually came into contact with the frame, without any form of mount.

4 Folkestone from the Sea
TB CCVIII Y; W 512

Described by the committee as a 'somewhat smaller drawing of a Seaport with boats and figures'. It was proposed that this watercolour should be treated in a similiar manner, but that it should first be mounted.

5–28 Twenty-four Subjects from Turner's *Liber Studiorum*

All but a few of this group had already been mounted before Turner's death, and it was decided to follow the style of mount already adopted. The sepia studies were shown in gilt rather than oak frames.

29–44 Sixteen Rogers's *Italy*

The subjects of these works are not specified, but since the committee hoped to frame four of the vignettes to a frame, it is possible to conclude that the selection omitted the larger designs. Ruskin noted that 'St Maurice' (TB CCLXXX 147; W 1154) was part of this group (*Works*, XIII, p.97).

45–9 Ivy Bridge
TB CCCVIII X; W 442

'and four others – which have been kept together'.

With reference to the Schedule of works brought to the National Gallery from Turner's studio, it seems that the works which most neatly fit this description are a group of four vignettes showing different types of fish on the beach (TB CCLXIII 342, 343, and TB CCLXXX 3, 4; see Gage 1987, p.231, repr.). This is confirmed by Ruskin's comment on one of these subjects in the 1856 *Notes on the Turner Gallery at Marlborough House* (*Works*, XIII, p.97). These vignettes were given 'French mounts' (i.e. they were protected by a sheet of card with a space in the centre corresponding to the size of the drawing) and displayed in gilt frames.

50–66 Seventeen English River Scenery
TB CCVIII A–H, K–P, R, V and W; W 732–49

This group had already been mounted and was given gilt frames.

67–83 Seventeen Views on the River Seine
TB CCLIX 102–11, 128, 130, 131, 133–136; W 951–970

84–101 Eighteen Views on the River Seine
TB CCLIX 112–27, 129, 132; W 971–90

Nos.67–101 were found as 'two packets'. They were attached by one hinge at the centre of the top edge and displayed in French mounts, three to a frame. It was noted that other drawings from the Seine series had been mounted 'under the direction of the artist', and it was hoped that the new mounts would correspond with the style of those already treated.

102 Venice: The Arsenal
TB CCCXVI 27 (Stainton 1985, no.75)

Although it is not mentioned as one of the drawings selected in December 1856, Ruskin referred to this subject in his *Notes on the Turner Gallery at Marlborough House* as one of the drawings 'at present exhibited' (*Works*, XIII, p.97).

Appendix II

Turner's Late Finished Watercolours, 1841–51

The information presented here is based on Ruskin's recollections, which were compiled over thirty years after the events he described. His autobiography, *Praeterita*, includes a brief history of the group of watercolours Turner produced in 1842. But Ruskin gave a more detailed survey in the Epilogue he appended to the later editions of his *Notes ... on his Drawings* by Turner, for the 1878 exhibition at the Fine Art Society (*Works*, XIII, pp.475–85). The latter commentary was written at the time of one of Ruskin's bouts of mental illness and contains a number of inconsistencies, which suggest it is not altogether reliable. Nevertheless, it provides a useful outline of Turner's intentions and achievements, and is valuable as the first-hand account of one of Turner's principal clients.

There are, however, a number of other sources which offer a more accurate reflection of events as they actually happened. These include the various volumes of Ruskin's Diary, his extensive correspondence with his father during this period, and the family account books, which record the payments made for nearly all of the watercolours in their collection. The letters, in particular, contain many references to Turner's work, from which it is possible to glean much information about the relationship between the artist and his clients.

Altogether, Ruskin thought that Turner had completed a total of twenty-seven watercolours during his last ten years. He recorded this piece of information in the 1857 catalogue (republished here), where he also set out the number of drawings produced in each year: 'ten in 1842, five in 1843, ten in 1845, and two in 1850' (see cat.no.8). However, as is suggested in the following notes, the number Turner actually completed may have easily exceeded thirty.

I have also referred to Nicholas Serota's groundbreaking MA Report on Turner's Alpine tours (Courtauld 1970), and to Andrew Wilton's 1979 catalogue of finished drawings and watercolours outside the Turner Bequest. Some important, previously unpublished, correspondence from Turner, which sheds light on the evolution of these watercolours, has recently been unearthed by Selby Whittingham (see the Bibliography for full details of each of these works).

1842

According to Ruskin, the first group of Swiss watercolours was produced because Turner 'wanted to make some drawings to please himself; but also to be paid for making them' (*Works*, XXXV, p.309). Consequently, in the spring of 1842, Turner offered to make a set of twenty finished drawings, later revised to ten, based on sketches from his Swiss tour of the previous summer. In a recently discovered letter, he admitted to the collector Benjamin Godfrey Windus that one of the reasons he had adopted this procedure was to produce a series of uniform size, thereby keeping each of the original sketches in its 'primitive state' (Whittingham 1993, p.97).

Thomas Griffith sought commissions for the finished works from B.G. Windus, the Ruskins, Elhanan Bicknell, Hugh Andrew Munro of Novar and possibly other loyal collectors, to whom he proposed a price of eighty guineas for each watercolour. Ruskin remembered being shown fifteen sketches, together with four already developed 'specimens' of what the finished works would look like (*Works*, XIII, p.477).

The account in the Epilogue states that Windus was the first to be shown the new works. Ruskin later claimed that in subsequent years he and his father had always been given first choice of Turner's new sketches (see Bradley 1955, p.124).

In recalling his intense desire to own the view of the Splügen Pass (see cat.no.75), Ruskin revealed that he was shown the sketches at a time when his father was not at home (*Works*, XIII, pp.480–1; XXXV, pp.309–10). This is most likely to have been in February or March 1842, when it is clear from the family correspondence that John James Ruskin was away, travelling on business (Van Akin Burd 1973, II, pp.706–17). In any case, Ruskin must have seen the sketches before April, when he returned to Oxford to sit his final exams. His father wrote to him there on 20 April to tell him that Windus was not prepared to buy any of the 'specimen' drawings, nor to commission others (Van Akin Burd 1973, II, p.734).

John James Ruskin's account books in the collection at Bembridge record that he paid for the watercolours of 'Ehrenbreitstein' and 'Lucerne' in August, and it is perhaps reasonable to assume that the drawings were waiting for the Ruskins on their return from their summer tour.

Sketches of 1841–2

1 The Pass of the Splügen: Sample Study
TB CCCLXIV 277; cat.no.75
Verso inscribed in red chalk: '10'

2 The Blue Rigi: Sample Study
TB CCCLXIV 330; repr. p.150, fig.39
Verso inscribed in red chalk: '17'

3 The Red Rigi: Sample Study
TB CCCLXIV 275; cat.no.35
Verso inscribed in pencil, 'E', and in red chalk, '15'

4 Lake Lucerne: The Bay of Uri from above Brunnen: Sample Study
TB CCCLXIV 354; cat.no.33
Verso inscribed in pencil, 'Lucerne', and in red chalk, '37'

5 The Dark Rigi: Sample Study
TB CCCLXIV 279; cat.no.31
Verso inscribed in pencil, 'H.A.Munro Esqr', 'K', and in red chalk, '11'

6 Zurich: Sample Study
TB CCCLXIV 291; cat.no.22
Verso inscribed in pencil, 'J.A.Munro Esqr', '4', and in red chalk, '10'

7 Brunnen on the Lake of Lucerne: Sample Study
W 1528; repr. p.150, fig.40
Private Collection

8 Lucerne from the Walls: Sample Study
TB CCCLXIV 290; cat.no.23
Verso inscribed in pencil, 'J Ruskin Jn^{r} Esqr', and in red chalk, '17'

9 Coblenz ('Ehrenbreitstein'): Sample Study
TB CCCLXIV 286; cat.no.8
Verso inscribed in pencil, 'J.Ruskin Jn^{r} Esqr' and '9'

10 Constance: Sample Study
TB CCCLXIV 288; cat.no.20
Verso inscribed in pencil, '8', and in red chalk, '12'

?11 Lausanne, from the West: Sample Study
TB CCCXXXIV 9; cat.no.94
Writing to his father in 1851, Ruskin noted that the packet of 1841 sketches had included a view of Lausanne 'in purple and blue sunset – very misty', which from Ruskin's thumbnail outline appears to be this watercolour. See p.16, fig.6, and Bradley 1955, p.112.

?12 Lausanne: Sunset
TB CCCLXIV 350
The possibility that this watercolour was one of Turner's sample studies was first noted by Nicholas Serota (Serota 1970, p.103 n.6; repr. in *Turner and the Sublime*, Toronto 1980, no.90).

?13 Lausanne: The Cathedral from the South-west
TB CCCXXXIV 6
Verso inscribed in pencil: 'x o | 2'

?14 Lausanne from the Signal
W 1458
Private Collection

?15 Lake Lucerne
W 1470
Manchester City Art Galleries

?16 Lake Lucerne, the Rigi in the Distance – Moonlight
W 1478
Whitworth Art Gallery, University of Manchester
See Serota 1970, p.103 n.6.

fig.39 'The Blue Rigi: Sample Study' 1841–2 (TB CCCLXIV 330)

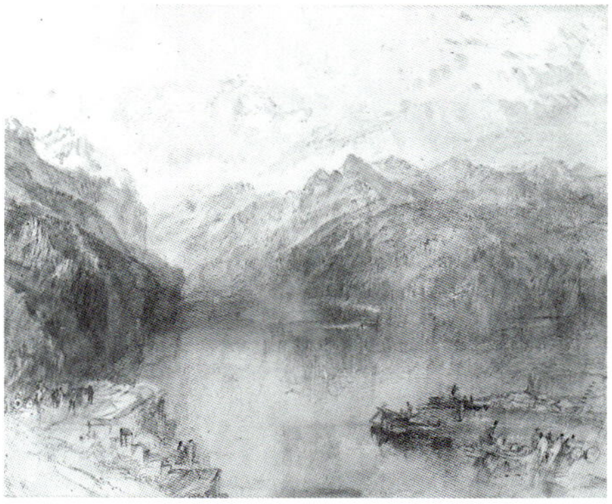

fig.40 'Brunnen on the Lake of Lucerne, with a Steamer: Sample Study' 1841–2 (W 1528)

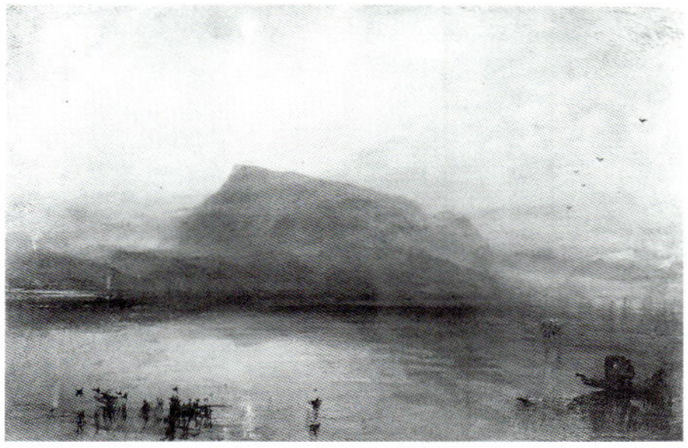

fig.41 'The Blue Rigi' 1842 (W 1524)

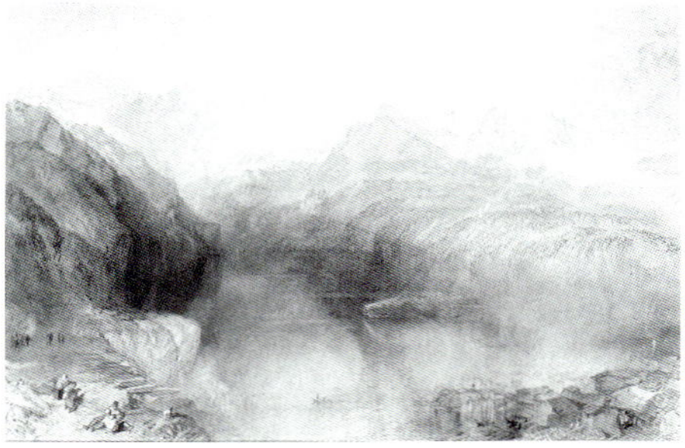

fig.42 'Brunnen on the Lake of Lucerne' 1842 (W 1527)

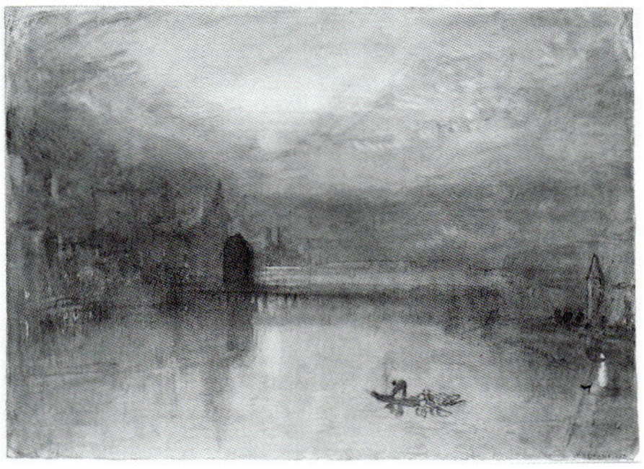

fig.43 'Lucerne by Moonlight: Sample Study' 1842–3 (TB CCCLXIV 324)

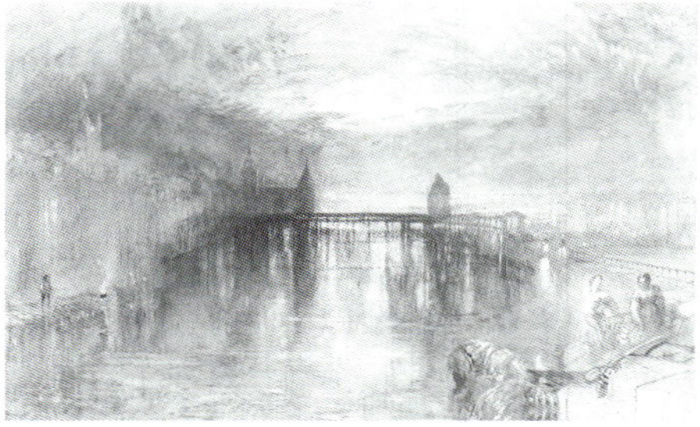

fig.44 'Lucerne by Moonlight' 1843 (W 1536)

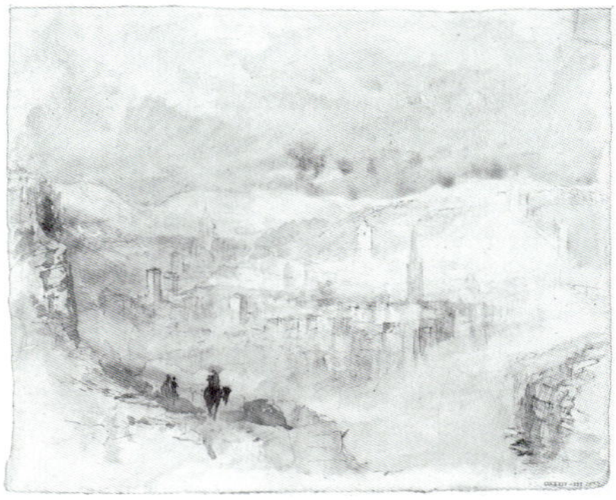

fig.45 'Schaffhausen: Sample Study' 1844–5 (TB CCCLXIV 337)

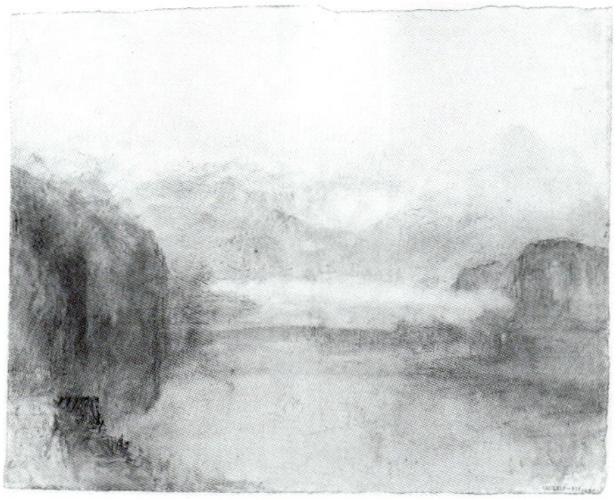

fig.46 'The Lake of Lucerne, from above Brunnen. Sunset: Sample Study' 1844–5 (TB CCCLXIV 338)

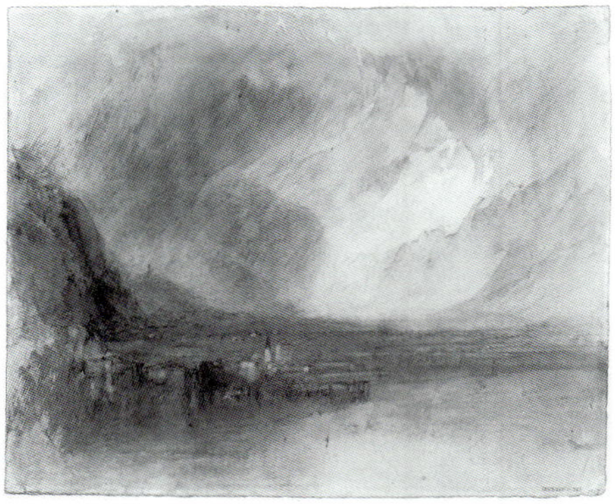

fig.47 'Fluelen, from the Lake of Lucerne: Sample Study' 1844–5 (TB CCCLXIV 385)

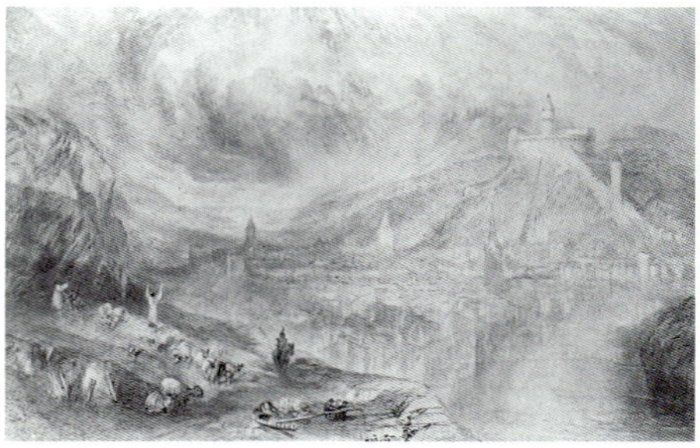

fig.48 'Schaffhausen' 1845 (W 1540)

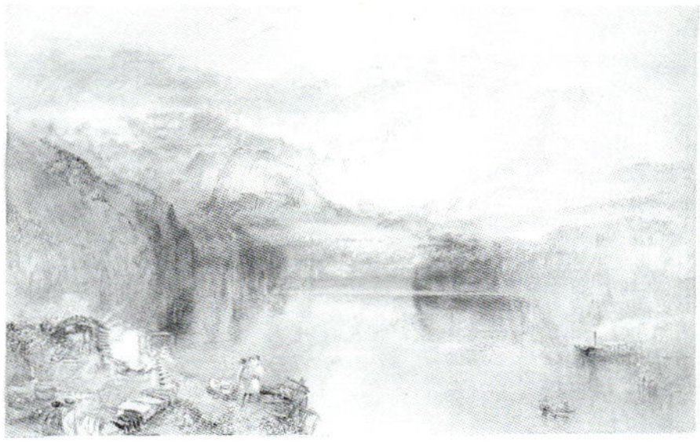

fig.49 'The Lake of Lucerne, from above Brunnen. Sunset' 1845 (W 1543)

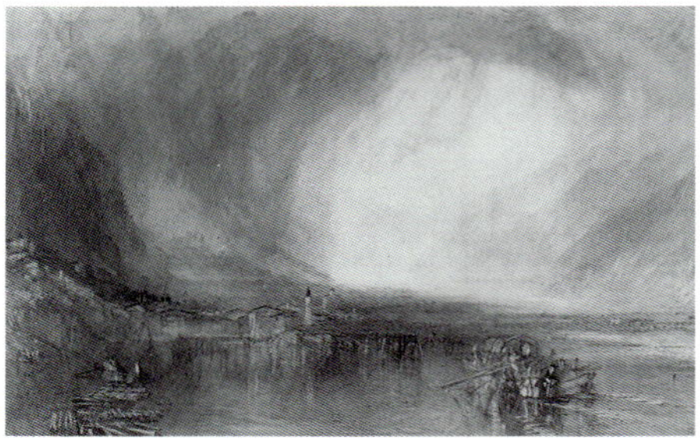

fig.50 'Fluelen, from the Lake of Lucerne' 1845 (W 1549)

?17 The Rigi, Last Rays
TB CCCLXIV 219

?18 Zurich
TB CCCLXIV 311
See Serota 1970, p.103, n.6.

19–20
Although Ruskin recalled being offered a total of fifteen sample sketches to choose from, a recently discovered letter from Turner to Windus reveals that the group may have originally been as large as twenty (Whittingham 1993, p.97). One or two of the large group of studies depicting the Falls at Schaffhausen could have been among this first batch of working designs (see W 1460–7). There are also two watercolours of Heidelberg, which resemble the handling of some of the other studies of 1841–2 (TB CCCLXIV 325 and W 1326, Fitzwilliam Museum, Cambridge). Like no.12 above, both works are topographically vague, and may have been based on sketches from the 1830s, rather than from the more immediate experiences of Turner's 1841 tour.

The Ten Finished Watercolours of 1842

The First Four Finished Specimens

Ruskin described these as 'specimens, or signs, as it were, for his re-opened shop' (*Works*, XIII, pp.477).

1 The Pass of the Splügen
W 1523; p.122, fig.37
Private Collection
Bought by H.A.J. Munro of Novar.

2 The Blue Rigi
W 1524; repr. p.150, fig.41; repr. in colour in Russell and Wilton 1976, pp.86–7
Private Collection
Bought by E. Bicknell.

3 The Red Rigi
W 1525; p.76, fig.31
National Gallery of Victoria, Melbourne, Felton Bequest 1947
Bought by H.A.J. Munro of Novar.

In the 1878 Epilogue, Ruskin at first claimed he could not remember who had bought this watercolour (*Works*, XIII, p.480). But a few pages later he stated that it had been acquired by Munro (*Works*, XIII, p.483). His vagueness here is probably in part a reflection of his bitterness towards Munro, whom he resented as a rival for the best Turner drawings. Subconsciously, he may have wanted to efface Munro's connection with the watercolour, since within four years of its execution it had become part of his own collection. This is clear from John James Ruskin's account books, which show that it was paid for in February 1846. It was not bought outright, but was part of a deal that required the Ruskins to part with a watercolour of Oxford they had bought in August 1840 (?W 853).

4 Lake Lucerne: The Bay of Uri from above Brunnen
W 1526; p.73, fig.29
Private Collection, New York
Bought by H.A.J. Munro of Novar.

Watercolours Commissioned in 1842

5 The Dark Rigi
W 1532; p.71, fig.27
On loan from the Nivison Collection to the Laing Art Gallery, Newcastle upon Tyne
Commissioned by H.A.J. Munro of Novar.

6 Zurich
W 1533; p.59, fig.21
British Museum
Commissioned by H.A.J. Munro of Novar.

7 Brunnen on the Lake of Lucerne
W 1527; repr. p.150, fig.42
Private Collection, courtesy of Agnew's
Commissioned by E. Bicknell.

This watercolour was recently exhibited at Agnew's, London (*Turner Watercolours*, 1994, no.9, repr. in col.).

8 Lucerne from the Walls
W 1529; p.60, fig.22
Board of Trustees of the National Museums and Galleries on Merseyside (Lady Lever Art Gallery)
Commissioned by J. Ruskin and paid for in August 1842.

9 Coblenz ('Ehrenbreitstein')
W 1530; see p.43, fig.18
Untraced (see cat.no.8)
Commissioned by J. Ruskin and paid for in August 1842.

10 Constance
W 1531; p.57, fig.19
York City Art Gallery
First owned by T. Griffith, who sold it to the Ruskins in June 1843 (see cat.no.20 and John James Ruskin's account book). Ruskin later sought to alter the facts when he told Charles Eliot Norton in 1872 that 'Turner drew Constance and Coblentz for me' (Bradley and Ouse 1987, p.269).

1843

The entry in Ruskin's Diary for 16 January 1843 confirms his later recollection that Turner again offered to make a group of finished watercolours this year. He wrote with some excitement that 'Turner is going to do ten more drawings and I am in a fever till I see the subjects' (*Diaries*, I, p.239). Of the ten watercolours proposed, Ruskin stated that only five were commissioned (*Works*, XIII, p.484). However, in the 1857 Catalogue, he indicates that the view of Bellinzona was also one of the sketches completed this year, which brings the total to six (see under cat.no.48). It seems that the group of studies he was shown included several views of Bellinzona, for in 1845, when planning his visit to the Swiss town, Ruskin told his father that he expected to discover three of Turner's subjects there (Shapiro 1972, p.177).

The Sketches of 1842–3

1 Küssnacht, Lake of Lucerne: Sample Study
TB CCCLXIV 208; cat.no.29
Verso inscribed in pencil: 'Kusnacht and Tells Church and Gesler Castle | Lake of Lucern | No.2', '(?) X 99' '* 6' and 'Mr Munro'

2 Arth, on the Lake of Zug: Sample Study
TB CCCLXIV 280; cat.no.28
Verso inscribed in pencil: 'Art. Lake of Zug | No.9', 'X S10', and Mr Munro'

3 Lucerne by Moonlight: Sample Study
TB CCCLXIV 324; repr. p.150, fig.43
Verso inscribed in pencil, 'Munro | Lucerne' and in ?Munro's hand 'HAJM', and in red chalk '46'

4 Goldau, with the Lake of Zug in the Distance: Sample Study
TB CCCLXIV 281; cat.no.27
Verso inscribed in pencil, 'Goldau – Rigi – and Lake of Zug | No.7' and 'X 05'

5 The Pass of St Gotthard, near Faido: Sample Study
TB CCCLXIV 209; cat.no.40
Verso inscribed in pencil, 'Pass Piolano | Tessin | No.14', and 'X 0 12 | 29'

6 Bellinzona from the Road to Locarno: Sample Study
TB CCCXXXII 25; cat.no.48
Verso inscribed in pencil, 'Bellinzona | No.12 | 13 | X 014 | Mr Munro'

?7 Bellinzona from the South-west: Sample Study
W 1489
Verso inscribed in pencil: 'Bellinzona | No.11'
Manchester City Art Galleries
Another watercolour of Bellinzona bears the inscription 'Bellinzona No.10' on its verso (W 1457, Indianapolis Museum of Art; this subject is currently catalogued as a view of Chamonix).

?8 Bellinzona from the West
W 1491
National Gallery of Ireland, Dublin

?9 Dazio Grande: Sample Study
W 1492; repr. pp.16, 18, figs.6, 7
Museum of Art, Rhode Island School of Design, Gift of Richard Brown Baker in memory of Harvey and Marion Baker
In 1851 Ruskin reminded his father that they had seen this sketch as 'part of the Goldau batch' (Bradley 1955, p.113). However, in his 1878 Epilogue, he associated it with the 'sample' sketches of 1841–2 (*Works*, XIII, p.477). Since Ruskin's first, clearer, thoughts are more likely to be accurate, it seems more appropriate to list the work with the other sketches he made in the St Gotthard Pass (see also W 1497).

?10 Lake Lucerne from Brunnen
TB CCCLXIV 313
An inscription in red colour on the verso is only partly visible, although the date '1842' is clearly legible.

Finished Watercolours of 1843

1 Küssnacht, Lake of Lucerne
W 1534; p.68, fig.26
Manchester City Art Galleries
Commissioned by H.A.J. Munro of Novar.

2 The Lake of Zug: Early Morning
W 1535; p.67, fig.25
Metropolitan Museum of Art, New York, Marquand Fund. 1959
Commissioned by H.A.J. Munro of Novar.

3 Lucerne by Moonlight
W 1536; repr. p.150, fig.44; repr. in colour in Russell and Wilton 1976, pp.98–9
British Museum

Commissioned by H.A.J. Munro of Novar.

In 1852 Ruskin listed this drawing as one of those he was especially keen to acquire, although it did not rank as highly as either the 'Splügen' (W 1523) or the 1842 view of 'Lake Lucerne from Brunnen' (W 1526); all three works were at that date in Munro's collection (see Bradley 1955, pp.144–8). Perhaps because he failed to acquire this moonlight subject for himself, Ruskin later became vague as to the subject of Munro's third commission in 1843. A checklist of the watercolours in Munro's possession, which was compiled (?by Ruskin) for the first edition of Thornbury's biography of Turner, refers to the drawing as 'Lucerne (or Zurich) – Moonlight' (Thornbury 1862, II, p.396). Although it was subsequently sold as a view of Lucerne at Christie's in 1877, Ruskin persisted in his uncertainty as to the topography depicted in the Epilogue to his catalogue of the 1878 Fine Art Society exhibition, where he described it as a view of 'Zurich by moonlight, level over the rippling Limmat' (*Works*, XIII, p.484).

There is another reference to a view of Lucerne in one of Ruskin's letters to his father in January 1852. It comes as part of a protracted attempt to induce guilt in his father for the various lost opportunities of acquiring the best of Turner's pictures, and seems to refer to the year 1843:

> When you offered me the beautiful little oil Venice in the Academy [?'The Sun of Venice Going to Sea', B&J 402, Tate Gallery] you know I would not have it – because I wanted to make Turner work. Then he remained two years without working – and did me at last the three bad pictures [see below under 1845] – Then when Griffith had the beautiful Lake Lucerne, now Munro's – at 80 guineas – still I would not have it because I wanted to make Turner do more – which he never did. (Bradley 1955, p.127)

It is not clear from this account whether these events all occurred in the same year, but other information suggests that they must have taken place over a relatively short period of time. For example, other than the views of the Rigi, Munro is only known to have acquired two watercolours of Lake Lucerne before 1845: the specimen of 1842 and the subject listed here.

Although the sample study for this drawing bears an annotation that implies that it was commissioned by Munro, it is possible that he did not acquire it immediately after its completion. This possibility would help to clarify two entries in Ruskin's Diary for 1844. On both 25 January and 11 April, he recorded going to Griffith's showroom to study a view of Lucerne, which he seems to have admired (*Diaries*, I, pp.261, 272). If this work is the subject of these references, it would mean that Munro did not actually buy this view of Lucerne until at least the later part of the spring in 1844. Alternatively, it is possible that Turner made another watercolour of Lake Lucerne at the end of 1843, which is now untraced (see also under 1844).

4 Goldau
W 1537; p.66, fig.24
Private Collection

Commissioned by J. Ruskin.

The family account books do not record the date on which J.J. Ruskin paid for this and the view on the St Gotthard (generally referred to by the family as 'Tessin'). However, frames for the watercolours were acquired on 31 August 1843.

5 The Pass of St Gotthard, near Faido ('Tessin')
W 1538; p.83, fig.34
Mr and Mrs Eugene Victor Thaw, USA

Commissioned by J. Ruskin.

See also under 'Goldau'.

6 Bellinzona from the Road to Locarno
W 1539; p.92, fig.35
City of Aberdeen Art Gallery and Museums Collections

Commissioned by H.A.J. Munro of Novar.

1844

Towards the end of 1843 Ruskin discussed with Turner the possibility of more Swiss watercolours being ready early in 1844. It would have been reasonable to assume that Turner might want to attempt another group of drawings at this point, especially as he had gathered an abundance of new material on his tour during the summer of 1843. When the two men met on 12 December 1843, Ruskin found the artist evasive, and recorded in his Diary that Turner 'Says he fears there will be no sketches this spring: I shall be sadly disappointed' (*Diaries*, I, p.254). However, on 10 May the following year (before Turner set off again for Switzerland) Ruskin noted, 'I have seen fifteen new sketches of Turner to-day and I believe I shall get him to do some which makes me happy' (*Diaries*, I, p.275). At an unknown later date, Ruskin appended the comment 'These never done'. There seem to be no other references to these sketches, although it is possible to suggest a handful of subjects that could have been presented as 'sample studies' after the 1843 tour.

Sketches of 1843–4

1 Near the Pass of S. Bernardino: A Bridge over a River in a Gorge
TB CCCXXXVI 17; cat.no.72

2 The Via Mala, Looking towards Thusis
TB CCCLXIV 362; cat.no.74

3 The Devil's Bridge, St Gotthard
W 1499
Verso inscribed in pencil, 'Devil's Bridge No.8 | 04 X' and '20'
Syndics of the Fitzwilliam Museum, Cambridge

4 Hospenthal, Fall of St Gotthard, Morning
W 1500
Syndics of the Fitzwilliam Museum, Cambridge

5 Hospenthal, Fall of St Gotthard, Sunset
W 1501
Verso inscribed in pencil, 'Hospital N., St Gothard | No.5. X 014'
Syndics of the Fitzwilliam Museum, Cambridge

6 Brunnen, Lake Lucerne
W 1485
Verso inscribed in red chalk, '20'
Courtauld Institute of Art, University of London

7 Brunnen, Lake of Lucerne in the Distance
W 1486
Verso inscribed, in pencil, 'Brennern | Lake of Lucerne | 15 | 18' and 'x 8'
Syndics of the Fitzwilliam Museum, Cambridge (584)

8 The Lowerzersee, with Schwytz and the Mythen
W 1488
Private Collection

Turner developed this subject on a larger scale a few years later (W 1562, Victoria and Albert Museum, 980–1900).

9 Sion, near the Simplon Pass
W 1494
Victoria and Albert Museum

This subject was also repeated as one of the last set of large finished watercolours (W 1553, Manchester City Art Galleries).

10–15 Ruskin recorded seeing fifteen sketches. See above.

1845

Although B.G. Windus had one of the most representative collections of Turner's work in watercolour, it was not until 1845 that he acquired any of the late Swiss watercolours. New evidence suggests that one reason for this delay may have been a disagreement between Windus and Turner, stemming from the artist's fear that Windus was buying and selling his works for large profits (Whittingham 1993, p.104 n.2, letter from Mrs Mary de Putron).

In the autumn of 1844 Ruskin and Griffith attempted to heal the rift between artist and patron by inviting Windus to order new Swiss subjects from Turner. A rapprochement was effected at a dinner at Windus's home in October, and shortly afterwards Ruskin informed him that Turner was about to embark on a set of ten drawings. In seeking to encourage Windus to give commissions for two works Ruskin admitted that he had his own reasons for hoping that a group of ten commissions could be secured:

> That the selfish desire of seeing these lovely thoughts realized, weighs with me – and makes me thus impudent – I cannot deny – but from my heart – the stronger and principal motive is my desire to see those kindly relations already resumed between Turner and you – sealed by an act of condescension on the side of the injured party – and to see your noble collection completed by examples of these peculiar & vigorous conceptions. (Letter of 21 October 1844, Whittingham 1993, p.103)

Turner was already busy with other work at the end of 1844. In a letter to Francis McCracken at the end of November, he mentions a commission for a view of the top of the Rigi and a 'lake of Lucerne sunrise', although it cannot be assumed that these works (as well as a Venetian subject) were to be made in watercolour (see Gage 1980, pp.201–2, no.273, letter of 29 November 1844).

Ruskin's letter of 21 October 1844 stated that six subjects had been ordered and that Griffith had already ordered a pair, but was prepared to allow Windus to consider them for himself once the group was completed (Whittingham 1993, p.103). That Windus may have changed his mind on seeing the finished watercolours is suggested by the fact that the verso of the view of Fluelen is inscribed with his name, but is known to have been first owned by Munro of Novar (see Finished Watercolours of 1845, no.9, below).

Sadly, Ruskin made his list of these subjects for the Epilogue of his 1878 *Catalogue* at a time when his sanity was deserting him. His recollection of the titles of the works has proved confusing, not least because he lists only eight subjects, while actually mentioning nine (the view of Zurich, bought by Windus, is not included in his itemised list, but is discussed in the comments that follow (see *Works*, XIII, p.476); and he ignores completely the second view of Fluelen, owned by Munro of Novar).

Ruskin's rather imprecise descriptions of the views of Lake Lucerne especially have led scholars to infer that he bought three views of this lake in 1845 (see *Works*, XIII, p.476, and Wilton, nos.1542–4). However, the entries for this year in John James Ruskin's account book prove that this was not the case.

The only view of Lake Lucerne that Ruskin definitely acquired in 1845 was described by him as 'a faint Lucerne with floating vapours, they and the mountains passing away' (*Works*, XIII, p.476). This clearly refers to the hazy view of the lake from above Brunnen (see no.4 below; W 1543). Elsewhere he wrote of this watercolour as a view 'by Sunset, with the chain of the Alps'. This second description appears in a letter to his father, dated 30 May 1845, written while he was travelling in Italy and Switzerland (Shapiro 1972, pp.90–1). His father had apparently asked him to state the titles of the watercolours they had ordered that year. In return Ruskin made a list, in which the view of Lake Lucerne appears as the second item. As well as this subject, Ruskin mentioned three other drawings: 'Schwytz from Brunnen, Mythen in distance (Lake Lucerne)' (see no.6), 'Gorge of St Gothard above Altorf in storm' (see no.7), and 'Rapperschwyl over lake of Zurich'. The last subject is not listed in any of the catalogues of Ruskin's collection of Turner watercolours, and does not seem to be referred to by him again, at least in any of his published correspondence. Furthermore, the entry in the family account book for August 1845 records only a payment for three works. The reason for this is apparent in one of a handful of unpublished letters from John James Ruskin to his son dating from the summer of 1845. After a meeting with Turner on 30 July, the elder Ruskin reported that, 'He was in great good humour; said he feared he could not do the last ordered picture. only three as he must relax & he had been kept by the Royal Academy occupied for weeks with their Business – In a month or so we should have three – I said we must wait his time but it could never come wrong & that we were much obliged by the Liber S. He apologised for delay' (Letter dated 30/31 July and 1 August 1845, Bembridge, MS.; see also below no.10, under Sketches of 1844–5).

The view of Lucerne itself from the lake, which Turner also completed in 1845, was not actually acquired by Ruskin until March the following year (no.3 below). It was then obtained for £126 from Griffith, who allowed the Ruskins to return the *England and Wales* watercolour of 'Kenilworth' to cover part of the cost. A few years later John James Ruskin drew up a list in his account book of the Turner watercolours in their collection. The view of Lucerne is there referred to as the 'Grand Lucerne'. As he explained in 1878, Ruskin parted with the drawing in the mid-1860s, when he became disillusioned with the gradual destruction of the town's architectural heritage. It is important to notice that Ruskin does not claim to have commissioned this drawing. He simply lists it as 'My Town Lucerne. Griffiths' (*Works*, XIII, p.476), and his note on the preparatory study in the 1857 catalogue indicates that Turner chose to complete it himself (see cat.no.24). Confusion has perhaps arisen because the provenance for the finished work suggests that it was purchased from Ruskin by Mrs Newall. In the list made over thirty years after Turner completed his drawings, Ruskin included Mrs Newall as the client for another view of Lucerne. Apart from this note by Ruskin, there are no other records of that watercolour (*Works*, XIII, p.476, No.3). Since it is unlikely that such an important late work could entirely disappear without trace, one is forced to consider the possibility that Ruskin's confused mind introduced Mrs Newall by error. On the other hand, at a time when he was capable of more considered judgements, Ruskin had been quite clear that the 1845 set had been made up of ten works (*Works*, XIII, p.194, no.8). At the moment it is impossible to clarify this issue, as very little is known of Mrs Newall and her collection of Turner watercolours.

A further factor to be considered is the length of time it took Turner to complete his commissions this year. When Ruskin sent his father the list of their Swiss subjects at the end of May, Turner was clearly still at work on the watercolours. His slow progress throughout the summer was the source of much anxious anticipation by both Ruskins (see Ruskin's letters to his father, dated 29 June, 29 July, and 15 August (Shapiro 1972, pp.133, 165, 172); the drawings are also mentioned in several of the unpublished letters from John James Ruskin in the collection at Bembridge – see 25 July, 30 July, 7/8 August, 20 August).

The Ruskin family account book logs a payment for their three watercolours in August. But this must have been right at the end of the month, for when John James Ruskin visited Griffith on the 19th he could get 'no information of Turner', other than the reassurance that 'the pictures will start out someday' (letter dated 20 August 1845, Bembridge MS.). The precise date that Turner delivered the watercolours is not known, but must have occurred only a few days before he set out for his short excursion to Normandy (see cat.nos.1–5).

By the second week of September the watercolours were hanging in the drawing-room at Denmark Hill and John James Ruskin had written to his son, praising two of the new subjects, while admitting he could find 'beauty' in the third (see Ruskin's letters to his father, 15 and 18 September 1845; Shapiro 1972, pp.202–3, 206–7). When he saw the group for himself, Ruskin was not entirely happy with the view of 'Altorf' (no.7) and later exchanged it for the watercolour of 'Fluelen' that Munro had commissioned (no.2). It was this year that Ruskin had in mind when he grumbled to his father that, 'Munro and I engage Turner to do us three drawings each – his are all good – mine all bad' (17 April 1852; Bradley 1955, p.251). In August 1846, Ruskin told the portrait artist William Boxall of his perception of Turner's declining abilities: 'I don't know what I shall do when he fails altogether. I have been in the habit of feeding on him ever since I was fourteen, and already from what I saw of last year's work there seems to me a great blank in the world which nothing can ever supply' (M.J.H. Liversidge, 'John Ruskin and William Boxall: Unpublished Correspondence', *Apollo*, vol.85, 1967, p.42).

Although Turner's working period in 1845 had seemed unduly protracted to the Ruskins, Elhanan Bicknell felt that the results looked 'raw' and showed signs of being too 'hurried'. His visit to the Ruskin's house to see the new works is recorded in a letter from John James Ruskin dated 19 September (Shapiro 1972, p.247–8). Bicknell was already deeply involved in a row with Turner on two points: the number of proofs Turner was entitled to of an engraving of the 'Fighting Téméraire'; and the discovery of watercolour in the whaling subject that Bicknell had recently acquired, which Turner was then made to finish in oil (B&J 415, Metropolitan Museum of Art, New York). Consequently, Bicknell's dissatisfaction with the Ruskin watercolours gave him the opportunity to snub the artist by cancelling three drawings he had ordered. If completed, the Bicknell commission would have taken the total number of watercolours executed in 1845 to twelve or thirteen.

Apart from the disagreement with Bicknell, Turner angered the Ruskins by getting Griffith to attempt to raise the price of the watercolours from eighty guineas to £100 when it was time to pay for the completed works (see Shapiro 1972, p.247, and p.230). As a result, the friendship between Turner and Ruskin may have become a little strained over the ensuing months, although not sufficiently awkward to prevent Turner from sharing in the Ruskins' celebrations at New Year in 1846. An entry in Ruskin's Diary for 1854 refers to a break in their association, but that seems to apply to another incident towards the end of Turner's life, most probably in 1848 (see *Diaries*, II, p.489, and Gage 1980, p.221, no.312, and p.281).

Sketches of 1844–5

1 Schaffhausen: Sample Study
TB CCCLXIV 337; repr. p.150, fig.45; repr. in col. in Wilton 1982, pl.116
Verso inscribed in pencil, '17' | 'Munro | 'Schaffhausen' and in ?Munro's hand, 'HAJM', and in red chalk, '30'

Although the inscription on the verso indicates that Munro ordered his watercolour on the strength of this design, Turner seems also to have referred to another sketch of Schaffhausen when preparing the finished work (TB CCCLXIV 218).

2 Fluelen: Morning (Looking towards the Lake of Lucerne): Sample Study
TB CCCLXIV 282; cat.no.37
Verso inscribed in pencil, 'Lucerne | Munro' and in ?Munro's hand 'HAJM', and in red chalk, '39'

3 Lucerne from the Lake: Sample Study
TB CCCLXIV 386; cat.no.24
Verso inscribed in pencil: 'Lucerne | 8 | 10' and in another hand 'J.R.'

4 The Lake of Lucerne, from above Brunnen. Sunset: Sample Study
TB CCCLXIV 338; repr. p.150, fig.46; repr. in col. in Wilton 1982, pl.122
Verso inscribed in pencil: 'Ruskin | Lucerne'

5 A Fête Day in Zurich: Early Morning: Sample Study
TB CCCLXIV 289; cat.no.21
Verso inscribed in pencil, 'Windus | Zurich | 7', and in ?Windus's hand 'BGW', with an illegible number in red chalk

6 Brunnen, from the Lake of Lucerne: Sample Study
TB CCCLXIV 375; cat.no.32
Verso inscribed in pencil, 'Ruskin | Lucerne looking towards | Schwitz', and in red chalk, '36'

7 Storm in the St Gotthard Pass. The First Bridge above the Altdorf: Sample Study
TB CCCLXIV 283; cat.no.39
Verso inscribed in pencil, 'JR', 'Altorf', and in red chalk, '35'

8 Lake Lucerne, from Brunnen: Sample Study
TB CCCLXIV 385; cat.no.34
Verso inscribed, in pencil, 'Lucerne', and in another hand 'J.R.', with '29' in red chalk

9 Fluelen, from the Lake of Lucerne: Sample Study
TB CCCLXIV 381; repr. p.150, fig.47; repr. in col. in Wilton 1982, pl.119.
Verso inscribed in pencil, 'Windus | Altorf'

?10 Rapperswil on Lake Zurich
Ruskin mentions a view of 'Rapperschwyl over lake of Zurich' as one of the four works he had commissioned from Turner in 1845 (see Shapiro 1972, p.90). It is possible that the sample study for this subject is the watercolour in the Art Institute of Chicago, currently listed as a view of Lucerne (W 1471). When he was recovering from his period of madness, Ruskin annotated the sketch with the comment, 'I don't know the place | J Ruskin 1880 | J M W T Late Time | and very bad | for him'.

Finished Watercolours of 1845

1 Schaffhausen
W 1540; repr. p.150, fig.48
Toledo Museum of Art, Ohio
Commissioned by H.A.J. Munro; acquired by John James Ruskin (on behalf of his son) in May 1851 for £200 (see John James Ruskin's account book in the collection at Bembridge, and Bradley 1955, p.168).

In 1878 Ruskin considered this 'the best' of the 1845 batch, although he later parted with it, 'because the Rhine was falsely calm instead of rapid' (*Works*, XIII, p.476).

2 Fluelen: Morning (Looking towards the Lake of Lucerne)
W 1541; p.78, fig.32
Yale Center for British Art, New Haven
Commissioned by H.A.J. Munro of Novar; this work was exchanged before the end of 1848 for the view of 'Altdorf', first owned by Ruskin (no.7 below). Ruskin also claimed that he parted with the watercolour of 'Brunnen' as part of the deal (see no.6 below). Once 'Fluelen' was in his collection, Ruskin had nightmares which convey his fear of losing the watercolour (*Diaries*, II, pp.743–4).

3 Lucerne from the Lake
W 1544; p.61, fig.23
Mr and Mrs Eugene Victor Thaw, USA
'Realised for his own choice'; sold to J. Ruskin on 31 March 1846 by T. Griffith. The family account book lists the watercolour as the 'Grand Lucerne'.

4 The Lake of Lucerne, from above Brunnen. Sunset
W 1543; repr. p.150, fig.49
Private Collection, courtesy of Agnew's
Commissioned by J. Ruskin and paid for in August 1845.

5 A Fête Day in Zurich: Early Morning
W 1548; p.58, fig.20
Kunsthaus, Zurich
Commissioned by B.J. Windus.

6 Brunnen from the Lake of Lucerne
W 1545; p.71, fig.28
Sterling and Francine Clark Art Institute, Williamstown, Massachusetts (1865)
Commissioned by J. Ruskin and paid for in August 1845. In a letter to his father at the end of 1851, Ruskin refers to this subject as 'your Schwytz', perhaps indicating his father's special affection for this work (Bradley 1955, p.112). More importantly, this reveals that the watercolour was then still in their collection, thereby contradicting Ruskin's recollection in 1878 that he had parted with both 'Altorf' and 'Brunnen' in exchange for the view of 'Fluelen' commissioned by Munro (no.2; see *Works*, XIII, p.476).

7 Storm in the St Gotthard Pass. The First Bridge above Altdorf
W 1546; p.81, fig.33
Whitworth Art Gallery, University of Manchester
Commissioned by J. Ruskin and paid for in August 1845. Ruskin exchanged this work for Munro's 'Fluelen' (no.2); this is confirmed by an annotation in John James Ruskin's account book beside the entry for 'Altorf', which reads '(new picture | Munro)'.

8 Lake of Lucerne, from Brunnen
W 1547; p.75, fig.30
Indianapolis Museum of Art
Commissioned by B.J. Windus.

9 Fluelen, from the Lake of Lucerne
W 1549; repr. p.150, fig.50; repr. in col in Yale Center for British Art 1992–3, p.72, no.8
The Cleveland Museum of Art, Ohio, Mr and Mrs William H. Marlatt Fund
Possibly commissioned by B.G. Windus (see sample study), but apparently first owned by H.A.J. Munro of Novar.

The verso of the sample study is inscribed 'Windus', but it is not known if he ever owned the finished version. Munro may have acquired this subject either as a pair to the view of Fluelen now at Yale (no.2 above; W 1541), or as a replacement after he had passed that drawing to Ruskin.

?10 Lake Lucerne
When he was working on his first catalogue of the Turner Bequest in 1857 Ruskin thought that Turner had completed a set of ten watercolours in 1845 (*Works*, XIII, p.194, no.8). As explained above, this number may have been arrived at by deriving two works from one provenance, or because Ruskin overlooked the fact that Turner only completed three of the four works he had commissioned. In 1878 Ruskin believed that Mrs Newall ordered a view of Lake Lucerne. Nothing further is known of that drawing (see *Works*, XIII, p.476).

1848–50

In the 1857 *Catalogue of the Turner Sketches in the National Gallery*, Ruskin implies that there was a break in Turner's production of Swiss watercolours between a set of ten in 1845 and a final pair produced in 1850 (see p.42, no.8). This overview, however, fails to include the watercolours of the 'Brunig Pass' and the 'Descent from St Gothard to Airolo', which are mentioned by Turner at the beginning of 1848 (Gage 1980, p.308) and which Ruskin's father paid for on 12 August (nos.1, 2 below; see Gage 1980, pp.219–20, nos.308, 310; it is possible that the works referred to by Turner in January were preliminary sketches rather than the fully developed watercolours). Ruskin's omission of this group may, in part, reflect the disappointment he felt over Turner's later works.

The finished drawings arrived at Denmark Hill while Ruskin was travelling in Normandy, but his father made his own thumbnail sketches of them to send him. In reply, a letter from Ruskin, dated 24 August 1848, conveys a slightly nonchalant attitude towards Turner's latest productions, while also revealing that other drawings were expected:

> As for the Turners, pray do not annoy yourself; I daresay Turner will give me the sketches, but I do not care; at any rate do not let us offend him, but get the rest of our drawings, if possible, as we have got the two, perhaps least agreeable – for the price we are partly indebted to ourselves – my book must have done it, or it must have had no effect at all; let us only think whether the drawings still are not well worth the money. To compare any new one with Coblentz is vain; I expect nothing like it, but I would not give that drawing for £500 unless I were starving. All the others have water in them except two, and by your account of the colour, I cannot help hoping much even from Brunig. All Turner's green and blue drawings that I ever saw were magnificent. How does it compare with our bad Altdorf, with the crutches? – the dark colour in the middle of that, the trees, I think *really* bad. (*Works*, XXXVI, p.92)

As we have seen, Ruskin claimed Turner produced a set of two watercolours in 1850. The subjects of these works can be surmised from various sources, but, once again, the evidence is rather more complicated than Ruskin would have us believe. At the time of Turner's death, John James Ruskin referred to a very late drawing in their collection. He told his son, 'I would not part with the Grindelwald Drawing, however bad – it is perhaps the last touch of the hand of the old man & thus extremely interesting. The Fox Munro has one I think' (25 December 1851, Bembridge MS.; see also the letter of 1 January 1852, where Ruskin replied, 'Keep red last picture as you say: it is now valuable', Bradley 1955, p.121).

The reference to Munro is significant, for Thornbury lists two watercolours in Munro's collection which are most probably from this last group: 'St Gothard' and 'Ditto, Airolo in the distance' (Thornbury 1862, II, p.396). When Munro's collection was broken up after his death, Christie's sold two watercolours, which seem to relate to these views of the St Gothard (11 May 1867, lot 171, 'Pass of St Gothard', £399 to Agnew; and 6 April 1878, lot 84, 'Descent of St Gothard', £525 to Agnew).

Although this seems to provide a clearer outline of the final groups of watercolours, the question of how many works Turner produced during these final years is complicated further by Ruskin's comment in a letter of 1 January 1852. As well as advising his father not to part with the watercolour of Grindelwald mentioned above, Ruskin wondered if Turner had 'destroyed the other eight – which he began for me' (Bradley 1955, p.121). The eight watercolours can perhaps be accounted for by a handful of late watercolours, mostly of Swiss subjects, which have been grouped together by Andrew Wilton (see W 1553–69). At the moment, the early history of these works has not been fully documented; however, none appears to have been owned by Ruskin.

Finished Watercolours of 1847–8

1 Brunig Pass
W 1550
Private Collection, USA
Commissioned by J. Ruskin and paid for on 12 August 1848.

This subject is based on a colour sketch that Turner may have executed during his 1844 tour (W 1551, private collection, USA). At the beginning of 1852 Ruskin had agreed with his father's assessment that the view of Grindelwald (Finished Drawings of *c.*1845–51, no.1, below) was probably Turner's last drawing. However, by June he seems to have changed his mind. He wrote from Verona on 1 June: 'The Brunig must not be sold at anything less than 150, it is valuable as Turner's last watercolour drawing, and done for me. I would rather for the present keep it' (Bradley 1955, p.292).

2 The Descent of the St Gothard
W 1552
Private Collection
Commissioned by J. Ruskin and paid for on 12 August 1848.

Turner apparently developed this study from two related studies: W 1516, Rhode Island School of Design, Providence, Rhode Island; and W 1566, Fogg Art Museum, Cambridge, Massachusetts.

Finished Watercolours of *c.*1845–51

1 The Grindelwald Pass
Untraced
Commissioned by J. Ruskin. See the comments above.

2 St Gotthard
Untraced
Commissioned by H.A.J. Munro of Novar. See above.

3 St Gotthard. Airolo in the Distance
Untraced
Commissioned by H.A.J. Munro of Novar. See above.

4 Sion, near the Simplon Pass
W 1553
Manchester City Art Galleries

5 Pallanza, Lake Maggiore
W 1556
Shizuoka Prefectural Museum, Japan

6 Oberhofen, on Lake Thun
W 1557
Indianapolis Museum of Art

7 ?Lake Nemi
W 1560
Private Collection, Switzerland

8 The Lauerzersee, with Schwytz and the Mythen
W 1562
Victoria and Albert Museum

9 Lake with Hills (?Brienz)
W 1563
Victoria and Albert Museum

10 A Swiss Pass
W 1565
Victoria and Albert Museum

11 ?Lake of Thun
W 1567
Taft Museum, Cincinnati, Ohio

12 Heidelberg
W 1554
National Galleries of Scotland, Edinburgh

13 Florence
W 1568
Private Collection, Japan (c/o Agnew's)

14 Genoa
W 1569
Manchester City Art Galleries

Bibliography

All books published in London unless otherwise stated.

Van Akin Burd (ed.), *The Ruskin Family Letters: The Correspondence of John James Ruskin, His Wife, and Their Son, John, 1801–1843*, 2 vols., 1973

John Lewis Bradley (ed.), *Ruskin's Letters from Venice 1851–1852*, New Haven and London 1955, 2nd ed. 1978

John Lewis Bradley and Ian Ousby (eds.), *The Correspondence of John Ruskin and Charles Eliot Norton*, Cambridge 1987

Martin Butlin, *Turner Watercolours*, 1962

Martin Butlin, *Watercolours from the Turner Bequest, 1819–1845*, 1968

Martin Butlin and Evelyn Joll, *The Paintings of J.M.W. Turner*, revised edition, London and New Haven 1984

Mungo Campbell, *Turner in the National Gallery of Scotland*, Edinburgh 1993

Kenneth Clark, *Ruskin Today*, 1964

W.G. Collingwood, *The Life and Works of John Ruskin*, 2 vols., 1893

E.T. Cook, *Ruskin on Pictures: A Collection of Criticisms by John Ruskin not heretofore Re-printed and now Re-edited and Re-arranged. Vol.1, Turner at the National Gallery and in Mr Ruskin's Collection*, 1902

E.T. Cook, *Hidden Treasures at the National Gallery*, 1905

E.T. Cook and A.Wedderburn (eds.), *The Works of John Ruskin* (Library Edition), 39 vols., 1903–12

Barbara Dawson, *Turner in the National Gallery of Ireland*, Dublin 1988

James S. Dearden, 'The Ruskins as Collectors of Turner: A Review of Luke Herrmann, *Ruskin and Turner*', *Connoisseur*, vol.172, no.691, Sept. 1969, p.40

James S. Dearden, *Ruskin, Bembridge and Brantwood: The Growth of the Whitehouse Collection*, Keele University Press 1994

E. Dillon, 'Turner's Last Swiss Drawings', *Art Journal*, 1902, pp.329, 362

J. Evans and J. Howard Whitehouse (eds.), *The Diaries of John Ruskin*, 3 vols., Oxford 1956–9

E.M. Fawkes, 'Mr Ruskin at Farnley', *Nineteenth Century*, vol.27, April 1990, pp.617–23

A.J. Finberg, *A Complete Inventory of the Drawings of the Turner Bequest: with which are Included the Twenty-three Drawings Bequeathed by Mr Henry Vaughan. Arranged Chronologically*, 2 vols., 1909

A.J. Finberg, *Turner's Sketches and Drawings*, 1910

A.J. Finberg, 'With Turner at Geneva', *Apollo*, Jan. 1925, pp.38–42

A.J. Finberg, *In Venice with Turner*, 1930

A.J. Finberg, *The Life of J.M.W. Turner, R.A.*, revised, 2nd ed., Oxford 1961

John Gage, 'The Distinctness of Turner', *Journal of the Royal Society of Arts*, vol.123, July 1975, pp.448–58

John Gage (ed.), *Collected Correspondence of J.M.W.Turner ... with a Memoir by George Jones*, Oxford 1980

John Gage, *J.M.W. Turner: 'A Wonderful Range of Mind'*, New Haven and London 1987

V. Gilardoni, *Luci e Figure di Bellinzona: Negli Acquerelli di William Turner e Nelle Pagine di Giorgio Orelli*, Bellinzona 1978

John Hayman (ed.), *John Ruskin: Letters from the Continent, 1858*, Toronto 1982

John Hayman, *John Ruskin and Switzerland*, Waterloo, Ontario 1990

Luke Herrmann, *Ruskin and Turner: A Study of Ruskin as a Collector of Turner, Based on his Gifts to the University of Oxford; Incorporating a Catalogue Raisonné of the Turner Drawings in the Ashmolean Museum*, 1968

R. Hewison, *John Ruskin: The Argument of the Eye*, 1976

David Hill, *Turner in the Alps: The Journey through France and Switzerland in 1802*, 1992

Tim Hilton, *John Ruskin: The Early Years, 1819–1859*, New Haven and London 1985

C. Lewis Hind, *Turner's Golden Visions*, 1925

Charles Holme (ed.), *The Genius of J.M.W.Turner, R.A.*, Special Winter no., *Studio*, 1903

John Dixon Hunt, *The Wider Sea: A Life of John Ruskin*, London 1982

Michael Kitson, 'Ruskin and Turner', *Turner en France*, exh. cat., Centre Culturel du Marais, Paris 1981, pp.619–24

J.G. Links, *The Ruskins in Normandy: A Tour in 1848 with Murray's Hand-book*, 1968

Mary Lutyens, *Effie in Venice*, 1965

John Murray, *Hand-book for Travellers in Switzerland*, 1838

M. Pianzola, 'William Turner et Genève', in *Pour une histoire qualitative: Etudes offertes à Sven Stelling-Michaud*, 1976

W.G. Rawlinson, A.J. Finberg and Sir Charles Holroyd, 'The Watercolours of J.M.W.Turner', *Studio*, Special number, Spring 1909

David Robertson, *Sir Charles Eastlake and the Victorian Art World*, Princeton 1978

Ruskin, see under Cook and Wedderburn

John Russell and Andrew Wilton, *Turner in Switzerland*, Zurich, 1976

M. Schefold, 'William Turner in Heidelberg und am Neckar', *Jahrbuch der Staatlichen Kunstsammlungen in Baden-Württemberg*, V, 1968, pp.131–50

Nicholas Serota, 'J.M.W. Turner's Alpine Tours', unpublished M.A. Report at the Courtauld Institute of Art 1970

Eric Shanes, *Turner's Human Landscape*, 1990

Harold I. Shapiro (ed.), *Ruskin in Italy: Letters to his Parents 1845*, Oxford 1972

Lindsay Stainton, *Turner's Venice*, 1985

W. Thornbury, *The Life of J.M.W. Turner, R.A. Founded on Letters and Papers Furnished by His Friends and Fellow Academicians*, 2 vols., 1862 revised, 2nd ed., 1877

Paul Walton, *The Drawings of John Ruskin*, Oxford 1972

W.C. Ward and A.M. Brooks (eds.), *John Ruskin's Letters to William Ward*, Boston, Massachusetts 1922

Sir F. Wedmore, *Turner and Ruskin: An Exposition of the Work of Turner from the Writings of Ruskin*, 2 vols., 1900

William White, *Notes on a Biographical Series of Fifty Drawings and Sketches by J.M.W. Turner, R.A., Belonging to the National Gallery Collection* [Catalogue of the '4th Loan Collection'] 1896

Selby Whittingham, 'Windus, Turner & Ruskin: New Documents', *J.M.W. Turner, R.A.*, no.2, 19 Dec. 1993, pp.69–116

Andrew Wilton, *The Life and Work of J.M.W. Turner*, Fribourg 1979

Andrew Wilton, *Turner Abroad: France, Italy, Germany, Switzerland*, 1982

Andrew Wilton, *Turner in his Time*, 1987

F. Zink, 'Turner in Heilbronn am Neckar', *Zeitschrift für Kunstwissenschaft*, VIII, 1954, pp.225–8

Exhibitions

NG Each drawing or watercolour catalogued by Ruskin was allocated a number, a list which expanded over the years as the number of watercolours exhibited increased. References to these numbers are made in the various catalogues of the Turner Bequest by Ruskin. The simplest way of identifying a particular drawing is to consult the concordance published by Cook and Wedderburn in the Library Edition of Ruskin's *Works* (XXXVIII, pp.385–90)

1878 *Catalogue of Sketches by Turner Lent by the Trustees of the National Gallery to the Ruskin Drawing School, Oxford*. Catalogue notes by John Ruskin; see *Works*, XIII, pp.560–8 (1878–1916)

1891 *4th Loan Collection: Watercolours from the Turner Bequest Selected for Display at Regional Galleries*. For details of catalogue see Bibliography, under William White. Shown at more than twelve venues between 1891 and 1915

1924 *Catalogue of the Special Loan Collection of Paintings in Oil, Watercolours, etc., by J.M.W. Turner, R.A.* Catalogue by C. Bernard Stevenson. Laing Art Gallery and Museum, Newcastle

1931–4 *Display of Watercolours from the Turner Bequest, Lent from the British Museum*. No catalogue. Tate Gallery (until March 1934)

1933a *English Art*. No catalogue. British Museum

1933b *Copies by Sir Herbert Jekyll*. No catalogue. British Museum (Feb.–June 1933)

1934 *Display of Watercolours from the Turner Bequest*. No catalogue. Victoria and Albert Museum (from 1934)

1934–5 *Watercolours from the Turner Bequest [Loan Series B]*. No catalogue. Public Gallery and Museum, Hove (Dec. 1934 – March 1935)

1934–5 *Four Screens*. No catalogue. British Museum

1934–7 *Display of Watercolours from the Turner Bequest*. No catalogue. Tate Gallery

1936 *Twee Eeuwen Engelsche Kunst*. Catalogue by D.C. Röell and Kenneth Clark. Stedelijk Museum, Amsterdam (July–Oct. 1936)

1936–7 *Watercolours from the Turner Bequest [Loan Series G]*. No catalogue. Exhibition organised by the Empire Loan Collections Society. National Gallery, Cape Town, South Africa (May 1936 – June 1937)

1936–9 Display of Watercolours at the National Gallery (Staircase). No catalogue

1937 *Watercolours from the Turner Bequest [Loan Series C]*. No catalogue. Towner Art Gallery, Eastbourne (Jan.–March 1937)

Aquarelles de Turner: Oeuvres de Blake. Catalogue by Laurence Binyon and Campbell Dodgson. Bibliothèque Nationale, Paris (Jan.–Feb. 1937); *Ausstellung von englische Gemälden und Aquarellen, W. Blake und J.M.W. Turner*. Verein der Museumfreunde, Vienna (March–May 1937)

The Treatment of Water. No catalogue. British Museum (Feb. 1937)

1937–8 *Four Screens*. No catalogue. British Museum

1937–52 *Display of Watercolours from the Turner Bequest*. No catalogue. Tate Gallery (Dec. 1937 – Sept. 1938; continuing after the war until Dec. 1952)

1938 *La Peintre anglais, XVIII et XIX siècles*. Musée de Louvre, Paris (Feb.–Aug. 1938)

1938–9 Display of Watercolours at the National Gallery (Staircase). No catalogue

1946–7 *Loan of Turner Watercolours from the British Museum [Loan Series C]*. Graves Art Gallery, Sheffield (Sept. 1946 – Feb. 1947)

1947–8 *Turner 1775–1851*. Catalogue by John Rothenstein and Humphrey Brooke. An exhibition circulated by the British Council: Stedelijk Museum, Amsterdam (?Nov. 1947); Berner Kunstmuseum, Berne (Dec. 1947 – Feb. 1948); Orangerie, Paris (?March 1948); Palais voor Schone Kunst, Brussels (March–April 1948); Museum vor Schone Kunsten, Liege (?May–June 1948); British Pavilion, XXIV Venice Biennale (?July–Aug. 1948); Palazza Venezia, Rome (?Sept. 1948)

1948–9 *Watercolours from the Turner Bequest [Loan Series B]*. No catalogue. Ferens Art Gallery, Hull (Nov. 1948 – Jan. 1949)

1950–1 *Aquarelle aus dem Turner Nachlass im Britischen Museum veranstaltet vom British Council*. Exhibition arranged by the British Council: Düsseldorf (Oct. 1950); Wiesbaden; Mannheim; Haus der Kunst, Munich (Jan.–Feb. 1951); Germanisches National Museum, Nuremberg (Feb.–March 1951)

1951 *Celebration of the Centenary of Turner's Death [Loan Series B]*. No catalogue. National Museum of Wales, Cardiff (Feb.–March 1951)

1951–2 *Turner Watercolours*. No catalogue. Organised by the British Council. Henry H. Huntington Library and Art Gallery, San Marino, California (Oct. 1951 – May 1952)

1953 *J.M.W. Turner, R.A. 1775–1851. An Exhibition of Pictures from Public and Private Collections in Great Britain*. Catalogue by Sir John Rothenstein. Whitechapel Art Gallery, London (Feb.–March 1953)

1953–9 *Display of Watercolours from the Turner Bequest*. No catalogue. Tate Gallery, London (Jan. 1953 – April 1959)

1955–6 *L'Acquarelle anglaise 1750–1850*. Catalogue by Paul Oppé. Musée Rath, Geneva (Oct. 1955 – Jan. 1956); Le Cabinet des Estampes de L'Ecole Polytechnique Fédérale, Zurich (Jan.–March 1956)

1958 *Eight Centuries of Landscape and Natural History in European Watercolour, 1180–1920*. British Museum (April 1958)

1959 *The Romantic Movement*. Handlist and introductory essay by Sir Kenneth Clark. Tate Gallery, London

1959–65 *Display of Watercolours from the Turner Bequest*. No catalogue. Tate Gallery, London (July 1959 – Jan. 1965)

1960 *Loan Exhibition of Turner Watercolours from the British Museum [Loan Series C]*. No catalogue. Wakefield Art Gallery (Feb.–April 1960)

1961 *Paintings by J.M.W. Turner, R.A. 1775–1851. Lent by the Tate Gallery, London*: National Gallery of South Australia, Adelaide (March–April 1961); Art Gallery of New South Wales, Sydney (April–May); National Gallery of Victoria, Melbourne (June–July 1961); Queensland National Art Gallery, Brisbane (July–Aug. 1961); Art Gallery of Western Australia, Perth (Aug.–Sept. 1961)

1963–4 *Turner 1775–1851: An Exhibition of Watercolours from the British Museum, London, Presented in Association with the British Council*. Catalogue essay by Edward Croft-Murray. Bridgestone Gallery, Tokyo (Sept.–Oct. 1963); Fine Arts Museum, Osaka (Nov. 1963); City Hall Art Gallery, Hong Kong (Jan. 1964)

Turner Watercolours from the British Museum. A Loan Exhibition Circulated by the Smithsonian Institute: National Gallery of Art, Washington (Sept.–Oct. 1963); Museum of Fine Arts, Houston (Nov. 1963); M.H. de Young Memorial Museum, San Francisco (Dec. 1963 – Jan. 1964); Cleveland Museum of Art (Jan.–March 1964); William Rockhill Nelson Gallery of Art, Kansas City

(March–April 1964); Brooklyn Museum, New York (May 1964); National Gallery of Canada, Ottawa (June–July 1964)

Ruskin and his Circle. Catalogue by Sir Kenneth Clark. Organised by the Arts Council, Arts Council Gallery, London (Jan.–Feb. 1964)

1964–5 *Loan of Turner Watercolours from the British Museum*. No catalogue. Graves Art Gallery, Sheffield (Dec. 1964 – Jan. 1965); University of Nottingham Art Gallery (Jan.–March 1965)

1966 *Turner Watercolours*. No catalogue. New Metropole Art Centre, Folkestone (Jan.–Feb. 1966)

Turner: Imagination and Reality. Catalogue by Lawrence Gowing. Museum of Modern Art, New York (March–June 1966)

Exhibition of Watercolours by J.M.W. Turner. Catalogue by Francis Hawcroft. Whitworth Art Gallery, Manchester (May–June 1966)

1968–9 *Bicentenary Exhibition 1768–1968*. Royal Academy (Dec. 1968 – March 1969)

1969 *Dué Stoleté Britského matérstui: od Hogartha k Turneroui*. Catalogue by Peter Cannon-Brooks. Národní Galerie, Prague (May–June 1969); Galerie nationale de Slovaquie, Bratislava (July–Aug. 1969); Volkerkunde Museum, Vienna (?Sept.–Oct. 1969)

1970–1 *Turner Watercolours Lent by the British Museum*. Introduction by Luke Herrmann. Musées Royaux des Beaux-Arts de Belgique, Brussels (Nov. 1970 – Jan. 1971)

English Landscape Painting in the 18th and 19th Centuries. National Museum of Western Art, Tokyo (Oct.–Nov. 1970); National Museum of Modern Art, Kyoto (Dec. 1970 – Jan. 1971)

1971–2 *Turner: Major Loan Exhibition. Theme – Water, Lakes, Streams, Rivers and Seas. Late Watercolours by Courtesy of the Trustees of the British Museum*. Catalogue by John Eveleigh. Folkestone Art Centre (Dec. 1971 – Jan. 1972)

1972 *La Peintre romantique anglaise et les Préraphaelites*. Entries on Turner by John Gage. Petit Palais, Paris (Jan.–April 1972)

J.M.W. Turner – Gemälde. Aquarelle. Catalogue by Werner Hoftman, Andrew Wilton, Henning Bock, Ursula Prinz, William Vaughan and Andreas Haus. Gemäldegalerie Neuer Meister, Dresden (July–Aug. 1972); Nationalgalerie Staatliche Museen Preussischer Kulturbesitz, Berlin (Sept.–Nov. 1972)

1972–3 *Das Aquarell, 1400–1950*. Catalogue by Walter Koschatzky. Haus der Kunst, Munich (Oct. 1972 – Jan. 1973)

1973 *Turner (1775–1851): Desenhos, Aguarelos e Oléos*. Catalogue by Andrew Wilton and Luke Herrmann. Fundação Calouste Gulbenkian, Lisbon (June–July 1973)

1974 *Turner and Watercolour: An Exhibition of Watercolours Lent from the Turner Bequest at the British Museum*. Catalogue by John Gage. Circulated by the Arts Council: Herbert Art Gallery, Coventry (April 1974); Graves Art Gallery, Sheffield (May 1974); Castle Museum, Norwich (June 1974); Leeds City Art Gallery (June–July 1974); Bristol City Art Gallery (July–Aug. 1974); Towner Art Gallery, Eastbourne (Aug.–Sept. 1974)

1974–5 *Turner 1775–1851: Bicentenary Exhibition Celebrating the Artist's Birth*. Catalogue by Martin Butlin, John Gage, Evelyn Joll and Andrew Wilton. Royal Academy (Nov. 1974 – March 1975)

1975–6 *Turner in the British Museum: Drawings and Watercolours*. Catalogue by Andrew Wilton. British Museum (May 1975 – Feb. 1976)

1975–6 *Turner 1775–1851: Oils and Watercolours*. Catalogue by Graham Reynolds. Hermitage Museum, Leningrad (Oct.–Nov. 1975); Pushkin Museum, Moscow (Dec. 1975 – Jan. 1976)

1976 *J.M.W. Turner: Akvareller og tegninger fra British Museum*. Catalogue by David Loshak. Statens Museum for Kunst, Copenhagen (Feb.–May 1976)

William Turner und die Landschaft seiner Zeit (Kunst um 1800). Catalogue by Werner Hofman, Andrew Wilton and Siegmar Hosten. Kunsthalle, Hamburg (May–July 1976)

Turner and Ruskin. Brantwood, Coniston (Aug.–Sept. 1976)

1976–7 *Turner und die Schweiz*. Catalogue by Andrew Wilton. Kunsthaus, Zurich (Oct. 1976 – Jan. 1977)

1977–8 *Display of Watercolours from the Turner Bequest*. No catalogue. Tate Gallery (Jan. 1977 – June 1978)

Turner Watercolours: An Exhibition of Works Loaned by the Trustees of the British Museum. Catalogue by Andrew Wilton. Circulated by the International Exhibitions Foundation: Cleveland Museum of Art (Sept.–Nov. 1977); Detroit Institute of Arts (Dec. 1977 – Feb. 1978); Philadelphia Museum of Art (March–April 1978)

1978 *Turner Watercolours from the Turner Bequest at the British Museum*. Catalogue by Timothy Clifford. Shipka Gallery, Sofia (April 1978); Belgrade (May 1978); Muzeul de Arte al R.S. Romania, Bucharest (June–July 1978); National Gallery of South Africa, Cape Town (Sept.–Oct. 1978); Pretoria Art Museum (Nov.–Dec. 1978)

1978–9 *Turner 1775–1851: Oil Paintings on Loan from the Tate Gallery, and Other English Collections, and Ninety Watercolours from the British Museum*. Catalogue by John Silleris. Haags Gemeentemuseum, The Hague (Dec. 1978 – Feb. 1979)

1979 *Exposicion del Gran Pintor Ingles, William Turner. Oleos y Acurelas*. Catalogue by John Gage. Museo de Arte Moderno, Bosque de Chapultepec, Mexico City (Aug.–Sept. 1979); Museo de Bellas Artes, Caracas (Oct.–Nov. 1979)

1980 *William Turner: Köln und der Rhein. Aquarelle, Zeichaungen, Skizzenbüchen, Stiche*. Catalogue by Agnes von der Borch. Wallraf–Richartz Museum, Cologne (Oct.–Nov. 1980)

1980–1 *Turner and the Sublime*. Catalogue by Andrew Wilton. Art Gallery of Ontario, Toronto (Nov. 1980 – Jan. 1981); Yale Center for British Art, New Haven (Feb.–April 1981); British Museum (May–Sept. 1981)

1981 *J.M.W. Turner 1775–1851*. Catalogue by Lindsay Stainton, Dimitrios Papastamos and John Gage. National Pinakothiki, Alexander Soutzas Museum, Athens (Jan.–March 1981)

1981–2 *Turner en France: Aquarelles, Peintures, Dessins, Gravures, Carnets de Croquis*. Catalogue by Jacqueline and Maurice Guillaud, Andrew Wilton, David Hill, Nicholas Alfrey, John Gage, Lindsay Stainton, Michael Kitson and Robin Hamlyn. Centre Culturel du Marais, Paris (Oct. 1981 – Jan. 1982)

1982 *J.M.W. Turner: Watercolours from the British Museum*. Catalogue by Lindsay Stainton. Georgia Museum of Art, University of Georgia (March–May 1982); Houston Museum of Fine Arts (May–July 1982)

1983 *J.M.W. Turner: Dibujos y acurelas del Museo Brit·nico*. Catalogue by Lindsay Stainton. Museo del Prado, Madrid (Feb.–March 1983)

John Ruskin. Catalogue by Jeanne Clegg and Tim Hilton. An Arts Council Exhibition: Mappin Art Gallery, Sheffield (May–June 1983); Walker Art Gallery, Liverpool (July–Aug. 1983); Abbot Hall Art Gallery, Kendal (Aug.–Sept. 1983); Museum of Modern Art, Oxford (Sept.–Nov. 1983)

Turner Abroad: France, Italy, Germany, Switzerland. No catalogue. Display to celebrate the publication of Andrew Wilton's book of the same title. Tate Gallery (June–Dec. 1983)

1983–4 *J.M.W. Turner*. Catalogue by John Gage, Jerold Ziff, Nicholas Alfrey, Evelyn Joll and Andrew Wilton. Grand Palais, Paris (Oct. 1983 – Jan. 1984)

1984 *J.M.W. Turner. Akvarelle, Mälningar, Grafik*. Catalogue by Torsten Gunnarsson. National Museum, Stockholm (Feb.–May 1984)

1985 *Turner Abroad: France, Italy, Germany, Switzerland*. No catalogue other than the book by Andrew Wilton (see also under 1983). National Gallery of Victoria, Melbourne (May–June 1985); Queensland Art Gallery, Brisbane (July– Aug. 1985); Art Gallery of New South Wales, Sydney (Sept.–Oct. 1985)

1986 *Turner*. Catalogue by Martin Butlin, Evelyn Joll, Ian Warrell and Andrew Wilton. National Museum of Western Art, Tokyo (Aug.–Oct. 1986); Kyoto Municipal Museum of Art (Oct.–Nov.) 1986.

1987 *Watercolours from the Turner Bequest*. No catalogue. Display to mark the opening of the Clore Gallery. Tate Gallery (April–Oct. 1987)

Turner and the Channel. Catalogue by David Blayney Brown. Tate Gallery (Oct.–Dec. 1987)

1988 *Turner and Architecture*. Catalogue by Ian Warrell and Diane Perkins. Tate Gallery (March–July 1988)

Miscellany of Watercolours from the Turner Bequest. No catalogue. Tate Gallery (July–Sept. 1988)

1989 *Turner and the Human Figure: Studies of Contemporary Life*. Catalogue by Ann Chumbley and Ian Warrell. Tate Gallery (April–July 1989)

Ruskin and the English Watercolour: From Turner to the Pre-Raphaelites. Catalogue by Ann Sumner. Whitworth Art Gallery, Manchester (April–May 1989); Holburne Museum and Craft Centre, University of Bath (May–July 1989); Bankside Gallery (Aug.–Sept. 1989)

1990 *From Venice to the Alps: Watercolours from the Turner Bequest*. No catalogue. Tate Gallery (April–June 1990)

Visions of Venice: Watercolours and Drawings from Turner to Procktor. Catalogue by Timothy Wilcox, John Christian and J.G. Links. Bankside Gallery (Oct.–Dec. 1990)

1991–2 *Magnificent Switzerland: Views by Foreign Artists 1770–1914*. Catalogue by William Hauptman. Fondazione Thyssen-Bornemisza, Villa Favorita, Lugano (Aug.–Oct. 1991); Musée d'art et d'histoire, Geneva (Nov. 1991 – Feb. 1992)

Turner's Rivers of Europe: The Rhine, Meuse and Mosel. Catalogue by Cecilia Powell. Tate Gallery (Sept. 1991 – Jan. 1992); Musée d'Ixelles, Brussels (Feb.–April 1992); Rheinisches Landesmuseum, Bonn (May–July 1992)

1992a *Turner: The Fifth Decade. Watercolours 1830–1840*. Catalogue by Anne Lyles. Tate Gallery (Feb.–May 1992)

1992b *Turner and Byron*. Catalogue by David Blayney Brown. Tate Gallery (June–Sept. 1992)

1992–3 *Victorian Landscape Watercolours*. Catalogue by Scott Wilcox and Christopher Newall. Yale Center for British Art, New Haven (Sept.–Nov.); Cleveland Museum of Art (Nov. 1992 – Jan. 1993); Birmingham Museum and Art Gallery (Feb.–April 1993)

Turner as Professor: The Artist and Linear Perspective. Catalogue by Maurice Davies. Tate Gallery (Oct. 1992 – Jan. 1993)

1993 *The Great Age of British Watercolours 1750–1880*. Catalogue by Anne Lyles and Andrew Wilton. Royal Academy (Jan.–April 1993); National Gallery of Art, Washington (May–July 1993)

Turner: The Final Years. Watercolours 1840–1851. Catalogue by Robert Upstone. Tate Gallery (Feb.–May 1993)

John Ruskin and Victorian Art. Catalogue by James Dearden, Joichiro Kawamura and Masami Kimura. Isetan Museum of Art, Tokyo (Feb.–March 1993); Ishibashi Museum of Art, Kurume (April–May 1993); Nara Sogo Museum of Art (May–June 1993); Tochigi Prefectural Museum of Fine Arts, Utsunomiya (June–Aug. 1993)

John Ruskin and the Victorian Eye. Catalogue by Susan P. Casteras, Susan Phelps Gordon, Anthony Lacy Gully, Robert Hewison, George P. Landow and Christopher Newall. Phoenix Art Museum (March–May 1993); Indianapolis Museum of Art (June–Aug. 1993)

Romanticismo: Il nuovo sentimento della natura. Catalogue entries on British works by David Blayney Brown and John Gage. Palazzo delle Albere, Trento (May–Aug. 1993)

Index of Places Depicted

Numbers refer to catalogue entries

Concordance of Works Included in the Catalogue

D No.	TB No.	Cat.No.	D No.	TB No.	Cat.No.	D No.	TB No.	Cat.No.	D No.	TB No.	Cat.No.
D32120	CCCXV 4	60	D33497	CCCXXXII 27	41	D35148	CCCXLIX 24	81	D36133	CCCLXIV 282	37
D32121	CCCXV 5	61	D33527	CCCXXXIV 3	91	D35150	CCCXLIX 26	9	D36135	CCCLXIV 283	39
D32122	CCCXV 6	62	D33528	CCCXXXIV 4	92	D35151	CCCXLIX 27	10	D36137	CCCLXIV 284	6
D32123	CCCXV 7	63	D33533	CCCXXXIV 9	94	D35228	CCCLII 8	14	D36138	CCCLXIV 285	7
D32124	CCCXV 8	64	D33534	CCCXXXIV 10	95	D35229	CCCLII 9	15	D36139	CCCLXIV 286	8
D32125	CCCXV 9	65	D33562	CCCXXXV 22	93	D35230	CCCLII 10	17	D36141	CCCLXIV 287	19
D32126	CCCXV 10	66	D33564	CCCXXXV 24	84	D35231	CCCLII 11	11A	D36142	CCCLXIV 288	20
D32127	CCCXV 11	67	D33565	CCCXXXV 25	77	D35233	CCCLII 13	12	D36143	CCCLXIV 289	21
D32128	CCCXV 12	68	D33592	CCCXXXVI 14	46	D35234	CCCLII 14	18	D36145	CCCLXIV 290	23
D32129	CCCXV 13	69	D33594	CCCXXXVI 15	44	D35235	CCCLII 15	13	D36147	CCCLXIV 291	22
D32153	CCCXVI 16	51	D33595	CCCXXXVI 16	42	D35236	CCCLII 16	16	D36201	CCCLXIV 341	36
D32154	CCCXVI 17	52	D33596	CCCXXXVI 17	72	D35447	CCCLIX 12	2	D36202	CCCLXIV 342	26
D32155	CCCXVI 18	53	D33597	CCCXXXVI 18	78	D35448	CCCLIX 13	4	D36203	CCCLXIV 343	45
D32156	CCCXVI 19	54	D33599	CCCXXXVI 19	80	D35449	CCCLIX 14	3	D36204	CCCLXIV 344	38
D32157	CCCXVI 20	55	D33631	CCCXXXVII 28	49	D35451	CCCLIX 16	5	D36216	CCCLXIV 354	33
D32158	CCCXVI 21	56	D33632	CCCXXXVII 29	50	D35452	CCCLIX 17	1	D36223	CCCLXIV 361	71
D32159	CCCXVI 22	57	D35137	CCCXLIX 13	83	D36053	CCCLXIV 208	29	D36224	CCCLXIV 362	74
D32160	CCCXVI 23	58	D35138	CCCXLIX 14	85	D36055	CCCLXIV 209	40	D36225	CCCLXIV 363	73
D32161	CCCXVI 24	59	D35139	CCCXLIX 15	86	D36122	CCCLXIV 274	100	D36237	CCCLXIV 375	32
D32162	CCCXVI 25	70	D35140	CCCXLIX 16	87	D36123	CCCLXIV 275	35	D36249	CCCLXIV 384	43
D33481	CCCXXXII 11	96	D35141	CCCXLIX 17	88	D36124	CCCLXIV 276	97	D36250	CCCLXIV 385	34
D33491	CCCXXXII 21	99	D35142	CCCXLIX 18	89	D36125	CCCLXIV 277	75	D36252	CCCLXIV 386	24
D33493	CCCXXXII 23	98	D35143	CCCXLIX 19	90	D36126	CCCLXIV 278	76	D40516	no TB No.	47
D33494	CCCXXXII 24	30	D35144	CCCXLIX 20	11	D36127	CCCLXIV 279	31			
D33495	CCCXXXII 25	48	D35145	CCCXLIX 21	79	D36129	CCCLXIV 280	28			
D33496	CCCXXXII 26	25	D35146	CCCXLIX 22	82	D36131	CCCLXIV 281	27			

Photographic Credits

Aberdeen Art Gallery
Agnew's
Beinecke Rare Book and Manuscript Library, Yale University Library
British Museum
Richard Caspole
Christie's Images
Cincinnati Art Museum
The Cleveland Museum of Art
The Education Trust Ltd, Ruskin Galleries, Bembridge School, Isle of Wight
The Fogg Art Museum, Harvard University
The Houghton Library, Harvard University
Indianapolis Museum of Art
Kunsthaus Zurich
Laing Art Gallery
Schecter Lee
David A. Loggie
Manchester City Art Galleries
Metropolitan Museum of Art, New York
Andrew Morris
Museum of Art, Rhode Island School of Design
National Gallery, London
National Gallery of Victoria, Melbourne
National Museums and Galleries on Merseyside
The Pierpont Morgan Library, New York
Prudence Cuming Associates Ltd
Royal Academy of Arts
Sterling and Francine Clark Art Institute, Massachusetts
Tate Gallery
Toledo Museum of Art
The Whitworth Art Gallery
Yale Center for British Art